Endtimes?

Also by DANIEL R. SCHWARZ

BOOKS (Author)

Disraeli's Fiction
Conrad: "Almayer's Folly" to "Under Western Eyes"
Conrad: The Later Fiction
The Humanistic Heritage: Critical Theories of the English Novel from James to Hillis Miller
Reading Joyce's "Ulysses"
The Transformation of the English Novel, 1890–1930: Studies in Hardy, Conrad, Joyce, Lawrence, Forster, and Woolf
The Case for a Humanistic Poetics
Narrative and Representation in the Poetry of Wallace Stevens: "A Tune Beyond Us, Yet Ourselves"
Reconfiguring Modernism: Explorations In the Relationship Between Modern Art and Modern Literature
Imagining the Holocaust
Rereading Conrad
Broadway Boogie Woogie: Damon Runyon and the Making of New York City Culture
Reading the Modern British and Irish Novel 1890–1930
In Defense of Reading: Teaching Literature in the Twenty-First Century

BOOKS (Editor)

James Joyce's "The Dead": A Case Study of Contemporary Criticism
Narrative and Culture (co-edited with Janice Carlisle)
Joseph Conrad's "The Secret Sharer": A Case Study in Contemporary Criticism
General Editor, Series entitled *Reading the Novel* and nine volumes including my *Reading the Modern British and Irish Novel 1890–1930*
Consulting Editor, *The Early Novels of Benjamin Disraeli*
Editor, *Damon Runyon: Guys and Dolls and Other Writings*

Endtimes?

Crises and Turmoil at the *New York Times*
1999–2009

Daniel R. Schwarz

excelsior editions

State University of New York Press
Albany, New York

Cover photo courtesy of Gabriel Argudo Jr.

Published by State University of New York Press, Albany

For information, contact State University of New York Press, Albany, NY
www.sunypress.edu

Excelsior Editions is an imprint of State University of New York Press

Production by Diane Ganeles
Marketing by Fran Keneston

Library of Congress Cataloging-in-Publication Data

Schwarz, Daniel R.
    Endtimes? : crises and turmoil at the New York Times, 1999–2009 / Daniel R.
Schwarz.
        p. cm.
    Includes bibliographical references and index.
    ISBN 978-1-4384-3897-9 (hardcover : alk. paper)
    1. New York Times.   I. Title.

PN4899.N42T5675 2001
071.747—dc22   2011004175

10 9 8 7 6 5 4 3 2 1

For My Wife, Marcia Jacobson—
With Love, Appreciation, and Gratitude

Contents

Acknowledgments

Many past and present *New York Times* editors, reporters, and executives have been extraordinarily generous with their time in allowing me to interview them one on one and in almost all cases tape the interview. I am indebted to them for their cooperation and insights. These interviews have been supplemented by telephone and e-mails. Jonathan Landman has been particularly helpful in answering my questions. My wife, Marcia Jacobson, has not only read the entire manuscript more than once but at every stage has made editorial corrections and conceptual suggestions. I can only express my profound gratitude to her contribution. James Peltz, co-director of SUNY Press, has encouraged me to write the inclusive book I wanted to write. Diane Ganeles ably orchestrated the entire editorial and production process. Fran Keneston helped with publicity.

I am grateful and appreciative to a number of students who have done independent study projects with me and who have contributed to the final manuscript in one way or another. Most notable have been Jennifer Schlesinger, Joseph Mansky, and Nessia Sloane. Others who have participated in research for this book include Carolyn Byrne, Meaghan Corbett, Rebecca S. Counter, Michael Gelinas, Felicia Kennedy, Miri Listokin, Michelle Pascussi, Christine Ryu, Elliot Singer, Alexandra Springer, and Leena Suthar. I also am pleased to acknowledge the continued support I have gotten from the Cornell English Department staff, especially Vicky Brevetti, Darlene Flint, and the late Robin Doxtater. I cannot thank my students and colleagues enough for providing me intellectual stimulation and a supportive working environment.

A Note on the Text

As my title indicates, my focus is on the 1999–2009 period when the newspaper industry and particularly the *Times* underwent a major transformation in the face of business challenges and when the *Times* was beset by a series of crises and challenges to its reputation, including the Jayson Blair scandal and its misreporting on Saddam Hussein's weapons of mass destruction. I looked back at the *Times* from a 2010 vantage point and did some further updating in March 2011.

Since my book was finished before the September 2011 change in editorship was announced, I am not putting Keller's editorship in the past tense or taking account of other 2011 developments such as the most recent New York Times Company's quarterly reports. Nor do I discuss events like the 2011 *Times*'s running stories garnered from Wikileaks, although that source and the *Times*'s use of it change the way news is gathered in comparison to the revelations of the Pentagon Papers.

Unless otherwise noted, quotations not attributed to an article, book, or other source are drawn from my personal interviews with the speakers themselves, on the date indicated.

Daniel R. Schwarz
November 1, 2011

Introduction

No one really thinks about it as just something to make the money. Its mission is not to make the money, it's a quasi-public institution. . . . The op-ed page [public discourse] is and remains the bulletin board of the world.

—Gerry Marzorati, April 10, 2005

Everyone is entitled to his own opinion, but not his own facts.

—attributed to Daniel Patrick Moynihan

I. My March 1, 2011, Open Letter to the *Times*'s Current Publisher and Its Executive Editor

Dear Arthur Sulzberger Jr. and Bill Keller:

Without neglecting the continuing triumphs of what I still regard as the world's finest newspaper, what follows is my discussion of the problems facing the *New York Times* and my suggestions for how to solve some of them. I have two stories to tell. The first is the story of a great newspaper reinventing itself for the twenty-first century and seeing its mission in the most idealistic terms by viewing itself as what Gerry Marzorati, the former *Sunday Magazine* editor, calls a "quasi-public institution." Representing a decisive and perhaps final turn in the way newspapers operate and the American audience receives information, full commitment to digital media in the form of the paper's website, nytimes.com, has been the centerpiece of that reinvention.

But I also have a second, sadder story to tell, namely, the story of a newspaper flailing around as it tries to find its place in a world where digital news has rapidly been replacing print news, where the concepts of truth and verification are up for grabs, and where changing business conditions undermine print circulation and advertising revenue, replacements for which have not been found.

I have been a *New York Times* reader—some would say, addict— since I learned to read. I am not only a product of my times but of the *Times*. I have had a lifelong love affair with the *New York Times*. As a Cornell University English professor, I have recommended the op-ed pages and the editorial pages to my students as examples of well-argued, literate prose that presents ideas in a lucid format and, in the case of op-ed pieces, reveals unique voices.

Proust has his madeleine, I my *Times*. For me it implies satisfying private moments when I recused myself from worries and lost myself in a world beyond my own concerns. Even though it doesn't leave its mark—its ink—on my hands as it used to, it leaves its mark indelibly on my brain and heart.

Reading the *Times* is a catalyst for intellectual energy, and, yes, part of the fun of being alive. I have learned more in my life from the *Times* than from any single written source. My father and grandfather read the *Times* every day unless strikes prevented publication. Much of what they knew about not only national and world events but also cultural developments they learned from the *Times*.

Mr. Sulzberger and Mr. Keller, I admire your courage in protecting the independence of the press and calling the government to account. In many ways, this is an improvement over the complicity between government and press in prior eras. Perhaps once we all were more trusting of our government and, like the *Times* and other media, not only wanted to believe in the ethics of our leaders, but had somewhat greater evidence for our trust than we do now. In the areas of foreign and cultural news the *Times* still outdistances its competitors. In its belated revelations about the Bush administration's domestic wiretapping and, later, the government's overseeing bank transactions—both in the name of national security—the *Times* was in the forefront of national coverage.

The *Times* provides me with a vast store of information, challenges me every day with its columns and investigative journalism, and plays an integral role in keeping me informed. But the *Times* also presents a product that is at times frivolous, panders to every possible audience, buys into reductive identity politics, and puts the interests of the institution ahead of those of its readers. When I am angry or frustrated with these and other failings, I feel as if I am disappointed in a close friend or family member.

The *Times*, I believe, has drifted from its moorings as it searches desperately to replace and replenish its audience and be all things to all people. Although I applaud your reaching out to younger people, the eclecticism with which you have adjusted to a changing time, and your catholic tastes in culture, I do think on occasion you miss the chance to discuss from a larger perspective what should be included in cultural coverage and why. While appreciating the sheer volume of what you publish each day, I think better editing might provide more examples of great writing. Perhaps too much emphasis is put on the magazine component of the contemporary *Times* and not enough on hard news.

Cordially,
Dan Schwarz

II. The *Times*'s Historical Position

For more than one hundred years, the *New York Times* has been a repository of America's historical memories and cultural contexts as well as a record of how we saw ourselves and how the world saw us. Current and back issues of the *Times* are a diary of how our history has unfolded from day to day. People who need or want to be informed still read the *Times* to learn what is going on in the geopolitical world and to be sure they know what other informed people know.

The *Times* once had an identity as the authoritative and accurate newspaper—the paper of record—that readers could depend on to know what was going on in the nation and the world. Now it is searching for an identity, trying to figure out what it will be in the twenty-first century. In the 1970s, Punch Sulzberger and Abe Rosenthal pulled the *Times* through a crisis by making the paper more interesting and readable, in part by introducing the multisection paper with a magazine component. It may well be that the *Times* is in even more of a crisis today, and the question is not only can the paper be saved as we know it, but were Bill Keller and Arthur Sulzberger Jr. the people to do it?

To paraphrase Winston Churchill, the *Times* remains the worst newspaper in the world except for all the others. Certainly in many ways the *Times* is much better than it was fifty years ago or even twenty years ago. Although the *Times*'s influence has been somewhat reduced, it still has considerable social, political, and economic influence on America and the world. Yet, in its desperate effort to find new readers and prosper economically in an environment where circulation and advertising revenue are not keeping pace with costs, the *Times,* I believe, has somewhat compromised its standards and is delivering a diluted product that is less an authoritative newspaper than a potpourri of information, some of it cutting-edge material in terms of news and investigative journalism but some merely prolix, soft, magazine-type articles. In part because its readers are aware of major news stories from other sources, the *Times* has become as much a daily magazine as a newspaper, and the magazine articles at their best provide far more useful life advice than they once did on relationships, health, beauty, fashion, dining, money, travel, and alternatives for spending discretionary dollars.

The *Times*'s audience also has changed. The Internet and cable TV have challenged the *Times*'s relevance as a main source of news. Many more people consult the paper's own website than read the paper itself, and many of those readers access the website for specific information rather than for the full experience of reading the major stories and opinions. It is possible that younger readers have become somewhat anaesthetized to the news and place less priority on being informed about national and international news than prior generations. No doubt the increasingly cynical attitude toward government of most Americans has been fostered by events dating from the Vietnam War and the Pentagon Papers to the bogus claims of weapons of mass destruction (WMDs) as an excuse to launch the invasion of Iraq. It is quite possible that our belief that we can know truth and our respect for journalistic authority have changed. Although we should not exonerate recent administrations from both parties from bending the truth, our skepticism if not cynicism also has been exacerbated by an elected national government—namely, the George W. Bush administration—between January 2001 and January 2009 that had little respect either for truth or for the other two major branches of government, the judicial and the congressional.

The Internet is the essential underpinning of the globalization of information and brings conflicting constituencies to the same site. But, mirroring major TV news channels, the Internet blogosphere also creates balkanization, when every subgroup retreats into its own sites and blogs and reads only what it wants to believe. Thus, conservatives watch Fox and listen to Rush Limbaugh and Glenn Beck and read pundits who agree with them, and liberals do much the same with MSNBC and Keith Olbermann and Rachel Maddow. A significant downside, therefore, to the Internet blogosphere and discussion sites is what Andrew Keen has called, in his book of the same name, "The Cult of the Amateur," where gatekeeping is undermined and what we think of as knowledge is subjective because the "lines between fact and nonsense, between expertise and rant, become blurred."

III. Specific Challenges to the *Times*

In part, the *Times* is under siege for reasons it cannot fully control. We are living in a divided country—divided between red and blue states, whites and racial minorities, liberals and conservatives, pro-choice and pro-life activists, the well-to-do and those struggling to make ends meet, the educational and professional meritocracy that increasingly replicates itself and those trying to make some steps up the class ladder. We also are in a country increasingly polarized between those who believe that we are part of God's plan and that there are fixed immutable truths and those who believe that we are shaped by our experiences, psyches, values, and capacities to understand—and that much of what we call "reality" is provisional, and much that we call "truth" depends on cultural and historical expectations.

But in the 1999–2009 period, the *Times* brought the siege on itself by often disappointing its readers and stockholders; the causes are multiple and one part of the subject of this book. Questionable leadership was an issue. The current publisher, Arthur Sulzberger Jr., has enormous faith in his own opinions, to the point of arrogance. Former executive editor Howell Raines was forced to resign after failing to control some reporters and offending many senior staff members. On important occasions, the *Times* has been manipulated or misled by its sources, who often do not want to speak for attribution, and sometimes speak for their own purposes. Although the retiring executive editor, Bill Keller, has brought stability to the newsroom, his judgment in complying with the Bush administration's request to withhold a vital story affecting the 2004 election is suspect. Moreover, he has at times allowed his section editors the latitude to write prolix and vapid stories—and on occasion, erroneous ones—to fill enormous space. This dumbing-down of its daily product to include vacuous features produces what I call *Timeslite*; when *Timeslite* focuses in detail on celebrity gossip and misbehavior as well as grim accounts of murders, we have what I call *Timestrash*. On occasion, the focus on sexual promiscuity and experimentation seems as much for shock value as to inform.

In the face of declining circulation as a percentage of the population and declining advertising as a percentage of gross national product, along with stockholder alarm at challenges to its revenue stream and falling stock prices, the *Times* also has diluted the quality of its product, in part by attempting to be all things to all people. Thus, it has invented sections with thin content, such as *ThursdayStyles, SundayStyles,* and *Escape,* and the various *"T"* magazines, with the purpose of attracting specialized advertising.

My book is hardly a history of America, but it does touch on how we have come to be where we are in the relationship between the media and the government, and questions whether the necessary and even desirable gulf between the national government and the press need be as acrimonious as it is. To some extent, I believe that the acrimony during the Bush administration was due to the belief of major political figures that the press—and in particular the *Times*—was dominated by those who wished to bring it down and embarrass it at a time when the country should have, in its view, been united behind its war efforts. Such a belief allowed the Bush administration to believe it had the right, perhaps even the duty, to manipulate the news.

To study the *Times* is to study American culture. Before the cultural revolution in America that began in the late 1960s—and, with some exceptions, for the entire twentieth century—the *Times* presumed that its readers shared a somewhat stable and homogenous culture. The assumptions and values of that culture were for the most part expressed and sustained on its news pages (if not its columns, too), and deviations from those cultural norms were considered oddities.

The contemporary *New York Times* opens a window on who we are and who we expect to be. Covering virtually every aspect of our culture, from books, theater, and dining to health, fashion, and money, it shows us our desires, needs, demands, disappointments, fixations, and obsessions. It teaches us about our culture's illusions, delusions, accomplishments, and vanities. Indeed, the *Times* enacts some of our own cultural conflicts. Many of us want a world of ethnic diversity and choices, yet we don't want to abandon certain Norman Rockwell myths of what America is. We cling to a democratic vision and belief in meritocracy, while we enjoy reading about the lives of the rich and famous—the restaurants they eat at, their galas, and the gossip about their love lives.

In this book, I shall be thinking about the historical role of the *Times* in American culture, the way that the *Times* both reflects *and* creates social history, and even more about what the *Times* is now. By means of its selection, arrangement, and presentation of subjects, the *Times* influences cultural changes even as it purportedly reports on them. The *Times* rarely takes the lead in cultural innovation, but once it fully commits to a change in direction, it becomes a leader in shaping who we are. To cite the obvious: the *Times*'s recent sexual openness has partly been forced by the AIDS epidemic, just as greater emphasis on women was forced by feminism's resistance to male dominance.

In discussing crucial issues that pertain to the *Times*, I often discuss issues that pertain to America, for the internal life of the *Times* represents cultural issues reflected in the world far beyond the paper itself. On its editorial side the *Times* has become more liberal socially than it has ever been. Setting itself at odds with the Bush administration, the *Times* took a leadership position in many aspects of the cultural wars, including discussion of changing sexual mores, gay marriage, stem cell research, and women's choice on abortion. For example, in the face of creationism advocated by the religious right, it devoted the entire June 26, 2007, *Science Times* section to updating how anthropologists and biologists now understand evolution and what issues remain to be explored.

IV. My Interviews

As an English professor who has written about American and New York City culture, I have relied on my mantra: "Always the text; always historicize." Thus, my methodology for discussing the *Times* comes from close reading of the texts of the articles within the paper and on its website and from an effort to establish a historic context and narrative for the 1999–2009 decade, rooted to an extent in the *Times*'s larger history from 1896, when Adolph Ochs purchased it. I supplemented my research with taped interviews—often discussions, really—with the *Times*'s past and present senior editors; only one subject objected to my taping, and in that case my student assistant and I took notes. On occasion, the subject of my interview would ask that a few comments be off the record, but I was surprised at how much most of my subjects opened up.

Although sometimes persistence was required, I found the senior editors and journalists willing to speak to me to be frank, congenial, and informative. I sometimes met dead ends and stonewalls, but often even the most reluctant, protective, and wary interviewees opened up once they agreed to be interviewed, often seemingly forgetting they were being taped, and I am grateful and appreciative for the access given to me. To be sure, some senior editors and journalists responded perfunctorily or not at all to my first request for interviews, whereas others could not have been more gracious. Some of the interviewees, seeing that I was prepared and had a track record of book writing, generously served as intermediaries to secure further interviews.

Once the interviews began, usually in the Times building, I found a great range of responses, ranging from helpfulness and good will in the vast majority of cases, to a few cases where I encountered discourtesy, suspicion, and an arrogant sense of presumptive privilege, as if the world of the *New York Times* were the only world. On a very few occasions, I felt that as an academic I was regarded by the interviewees as an outsider who was hopelessly unfamiliar with what seemed the Rosicrucian-like mysteries, practices, and terminology of the newsroom.

Rather ironically, a handful of senior *Times* people are disdainful of those seeking information about their world, even though they are committed to the process of seeking information simply by working for a newspaper, and the preeminent one at that. Rather than answer questions, some *Times* editors and journalists on occasion tooted their own horns or tried to proselytize the interlocutor to get him to see the importance of their own work in the news media world and even their importance in reference to their own colleagues at the *Times*.

I was well aware of the irony that a handful of *Times* editors required questions in advance, when they would have resented that stipulation from American political figures or foreign dictators. When I moved outside the approved agenda, I would hear, on occasion, a good deal of impatience, if not whining.

What I discovered is that each day's edition of the *Times*—both in the published version and online—is like a new mini-chapter. Unlike when I wrote books on literary figures who were dead, the primary texts for this study changed every day. It is as if I returned to Joyce's *Ulysses* or Melville's *Moby Dick* and found new characters that were not there the last time I looked. I hope the pages that follow show that I have found both the material and the experience of writing this book both fascinating and exhilarating.

1

Crises and Turmoil at the
New York Times, 1999–2009

We are experiencing a period of feeling under siege, though it is not the first time.

—Bill Keller, October 10, 2004

This is a place right now that's going through trauma. . . . The predictions that were supposed to make Wall Street happy turned out to be unreachable. . . . [W]e're still sort of wondering about Judith Miller, and we've pretty much gotten over Jayson [Blair] and Howell [Raines]. . . . There's serious stuff going on here now that's unprecedented, and people are tired and stressed-out, a long run of tough news. From the World Trade Center on it's been the stuff that's emotionally draining, people have been emotionally on edge. Depressed. . . . People will tell you more because they feel it. You're walking right in and half of it is falling into your tape recorder [and] you [are here to] pick it all up.

—Soma Golden Behr, former assistant managing editor,
October 11, 2005

It's absolutely true that [*Times*] people are concerned about the future of the paper. How could they not be? People are worried personally, are they going to have jobs? Are they going to have careers? They're worried about the civic mission and whether we're going to keep performing it. . . . People want to know what they should do. Should they adapt to the new world? And they want help [because] it's hard. We're very open-minded about it, but it isn't easy.

—Jonathan Landman, former deputy managing editor
and now cultural editor, October 9, 2006

A general comment on the newspaper business: It's bad business. For hundreds of newspapers to send out their own reporters and have separate bureaus, all for the same news to be reported with only minor variation, and then go through the huge cost of printing and home delivery, there must be so much wasted ink and paper too—it just seems unsustainable! . . . Nobody gives a [damn] about yesterday's news, they want it now, in real time, from twenty-four-hour news channels and Internet feeds. . . . There are only so many people like you or me who like the ritual of sitting down with a coffee and the *Times,* doing the crossword, taking pleasure in folding the pages back, and keeping up on Frank Rich. I'm sure you've thought about it, but it was something that just occurred to me—the newspaper business is horrendously inefficient and increasingly irrelevant to our generation's "I need it now" mentality.

—Elliot Singer, Cornell Class of 2008;
in a note to the author dated September 2005

I. Defining Crisis and Turmoil: Issues and Responses

May 20, 2010: I am sitting in executive editor Bill Keller's Manhattan office in the elegant new building on Eighth Avenue that now houses the *New York Times*. It is six years after I first interviewed Keller when I began to think about writing a book about the *Times*. It was a time when not only its economic viability was already showing serious cracks, but its integrity and stature were also, in his words, "under siege." In the wake of the Jayson Blair scandal and the tumultuous change in editors, he saw a major part of his mission in 2004 as "stabilizing the newsroom."

Because the world of the *Times* had changed a great deal since 2004, and our last conversation had focused on his months as editor since 2003, when he took over from Howell Raines after the Jayson Blair scandal, my questions to him now focused on whether he was presiding over a voyage without a destination and to inquire whether the cargo was still "truth." As Keller put it to me that day:

[It]'s not entirely clear to me where the ship is headed, but there is a precious cargo that we carry on that ship. That is, a particular kind of journalism that isn't everybody's kind of journalism but is of great value when you do it right. Sometimes we screw it up, but when you do it right it's a really special thing. As long as we're still sailing and we're still afloat and as long as the cargo is still on board . . . it's a whole lot better than the actual destination. . . . [As to the cargo], "truth" is more of a grand philosophical concept, but [the cargo is] honest, fair-minded, well-crafted journalism.

Keller has presided over a major transition to digital media; although nytimes.com continues to evolve, it has a much larger audience than the published paper. Yet, in part because of the 2008–2009 recession and in part because the *Times* has only recently put in place a circulation model in which subscribers pay for the Internet edition and has yet to find an advertising model that replaces lost print revenue, the economic challenge has become increasingly severe. Indeed, as former deputy managing editor and now cultural editor Jonathan Landman remarked to me on June 9, 2010:

Print paper is still the economic foundation of the news organization. Without it there wouldn't be this fantastic newsgathering machine. . . . [T]here isn't yet revenue from the web alone to support a *New York Times* newsgathering operation. Whether there will be [a newsgathering operation] in the foreseeable future is a good question. I don't know the answer to it. And how long print will give us? Print has given us a safety cushion, a brief edge, a period of time for the economics to readjust. Is it enough? I don't know.

Although Keller's face had more lines in 2010 than in 2004 and his hair was greyer, as befits a man approaching sixty-two, the athletic-looking and trim Keller gives the impression of an extraordinarily competent, even-tempered man who is comfortable in his own skin and able to withstand the continuous scrutiny by the blogosphere that now comes with his position. He knows he works in what he calls a "fishbowl": "Sometimes [the continuous scrutiny] gets a little microscopic and small minded . . . but on the other hand it's probably a useful reminder to us of how it feels to be at the other end of our microscope."

Speaking to me on May 10, 2010, Keller balances optimism with a strong component of living in and understanding the moment:

The problem is not so much the transition to creating journalism online—we're pretty good at doing that—but finding a business model that will kick in when the print business model runs out of useful life, and I think that we can kind of see how that's going to work out now. We've got a pay model, at least the broad outlines of one set up for next year, and it's one that is flexible enough that we can adapt to certain things, and we still have a healthy, still healthy print newspaper that buys us enough time to make sure that the digital business model functions. So I'm a lot less anxious about the survival of the *New York Times* than I guess I was when we first talked.

The title of my book speaks for itself. Under the leadership of the current publisher, Arthur Sulzberger Jr., and the executive editors Keller, Howell Raines, and Joseph Lelyveld, the *New York Times* has ricocheted from crisis to crisis for the past decade. Crisis implies a decisive turn in a sequence of events or the history of an institution, usually threatening stability. My book discusses a series of these turns from the ascendance of digital media and the change in the economics of the newspaper industry. But it also discusses the *Times*'s misreporting of the claims that Iraq had weapons of mass destruction (WMDs) in the lead-up to the invasion of Iraq in 2003.

Poor decision making on the part of Sulzberger and Raines gave support to those who wanted to begin the second Iraq War. Despite all its news resources and with the knowledge that it had been duped by the government during the Vietnam War and on many other occasions, the *Times* believed in the existence of WMDs and, indeed, one of its reporters, namely Judith Miller, a supposed expert in this area, gave credence to the government's position that the discovery of such weapons was imminent. Miller played a large role—along with Thomas Friedman's columns—in giving cover to Democrats (and even moderate Republicans) who were ambivalent about supporting the invasion of Iraq.

My book also pays considerable attention to the *Times*'s questionable judgments in its presentation of a number of other stories, including accusations about sexual misconduct on the part of the Duke lacrosse team, the Wen Ho Lee spy accusations, the *Times*'s handling of Judith Miller's jailing for First Amendment issues, and the unproven innuendoes that John McCain had an inappropriate relationship with a lobbyist. My book also considers the implications of Jayson Blair's plagiarism and fabricated stories, and other articles that should have been better vetted, including the late 2008 and early 2009 coverage of why Caroline Kennedy wasn't selected as Hillary Clinton's replacement as New York State's senator after Clinton was appointed secretary of state. All these misjudgments not only undermined the *Times*'s own claims to be presenting strongly researched facts but also contributed to the current skepticism and cynicism about the news.

"Turmoil" suggests agitation and confusion, sometimes in response to the aforementioned misreporting and misjudgments, but often in the face of uncontrollable events. To be sure, the *Times* leadership continually has made its best efforts to bring events under control, but often, as this book recounts, they failed or only partially succeeded.

Although some of the crises and turmoil have been of the *Times*'s own doing, including bad economic decisions and errors in reporting and editing, much if not most of it has been due to conditions beyond the *Times*'s control. These include the 2008–2009 recession, a shift from print to digital media, and a change in what audiences want away from objective reporting to the kind of interpretive and partisan presentation that is found on cable news—notably Fox News and MSNBC—and in the blogosphere.

One of the *Times*'s major problems is that people not only read newspapers less than they used to but also spend less total time consuming news from all sources than they once did. With both readers and advertisers in mind, the *Times* is continuously trying to create a product that meets an audience that has less time and inclination to read, as well as more outlets for information from which to choose. It still needs to find a way to make its website economically viable in terms of attracting enough advertising revenue and finding a model to charge for its use. The *Times* launched a new experiment in charging for online access in March 2011, but as of this writing it is not clear whether that will vastly increase revenue.

What each of the recent *Times* executive editors have in common is (a) a commendable sense of mission and responsibility; (b) a belief that he, the executive editor—heroically and in the face of occasional opposition from staid colleagues, the publisher, and readers—spear-headed major social changes while holding the position; and (c) a conviction that he brought the *Times* as an institution into the contemporary world during the period of his editorship. What each executive editor also has or had is what might be called a pedagogical mission to bring some of the *Times*'s backward-looking readers into the contemporary world. Sometimes this sense of a teaching mission teeters on the edge of self-importance or, in the case of Raines, of arrogance, but on the whole it is impressive and even touching.

Although the *Times*'s influence has been somewhat reduced, it still has tremendous social, political, and economic influence on America and the world. Indeed, what infuriates some of the *Times*'s critics is its powerful reach; most major metropolitan newspapers in America subscribe to the Times News Service, which takes already published *Times* articles and puts them in a format for other print and digital publications to use.

II. The *Times*'s Place in American Culture

Before speaking in detail of the crises and turmoil facing the *New York Times*, we need to acknowledge what the *Times* institutionally and historically does and what it stands for:

1. The *Times* has a passion to inform the public and commitment to do it as well as possible.

2. The *Times* has traditionally had respect for its readers as representatives of the most educated and informed segment of the public.

3. The *Times* has an idealistic view of its mission, expressed in the credo of Adolph Ochs when he took control of the *Times* in 1896, namely, "to give the news impartially, without fear or favor."

4. In its insistence on a free press and a willingness to defend that principle even at financial risk, the *Times* has a strong commitment to the First Amendment's guarantees.

5. The *Times*—with all its shortcomings, to be discussed in detail in the following pages—turns out a daily printed and digital product of extraordinary quality.

I believe the *Times* is still the best and most influential newspaper in the world. When it musters its resources to cover cataclysmic events like the terrorist attacks of September 11, 2001, the 2005 Hurricane Katrina, the disputed 2009 Iranian elections, the 2010 oil spill in the Gulf of Mexico, or the 2010–2011 Mideast revolutions, the *Times* leaves in its wake not only print media but all media. Every day wonderful articles appear in the current *Times*, notwithstanding my view that it often loses focus on the actual news and, in some feature stories, is no better than a quite ordinary daily magazine.

I could cite thousands of examples of its quality, but let me single out for praise Linda Greenhouse's and now Adam Liptak's current coverage and analysis of the Supreme Court, Thomas Friedman's trenchant discussions of globalization, Nicholas Kristof's columns on child prostitution in Cambodia or genocide in Darfur, Jane Brody's Tuesday "Personal Health" column, the informative and lucid articles in the rest of the *Science Times,* Michiko Kakutani's book reviews, the Friday visual arts reviews, as well as, on a daily basis, fine news and analytic articles on international, national, scientific, cultural, and metropolitan events. Nor should we forget wonderful investigative stories such as the ones in July 2005 that revealed widespread Medicaid fraud in New York; the three-part September 2006 series about the untrained and arbitrary behavior of New York State justices of the peace; and the coverage in November 2007 about the effects and implications of China's huge Three Gorges Dam. More recent major investigatory stories include Natasha Singer's August 4, 2009, piece about how pharmaceutical companies pay for ghost-written medical papers ("Medical Papers by Ghostwriters Pushed Therapy") and the August 11–12, 2009, stories about those responsible for harsh tactics in the wake of 9/11 (Scott Shane, "2 U.S. Architects of Harsh Tactics in 9/11's Wake" and David Johnston and Mark Mazzetti, "A Window Into C.I.A.'s Embrace of Secret Jails"). As part of an increased focus on New York's ineffective and corrupt state government, in 2010 the *Times* shined a light on Governor David Paterson's ineptitude and cronyism, especially his intervention in a domestic abuse charge against one of his top aides.

Another plaudit: On September 25, 2007, the *Times* published a magnificent issue of Tuesday's *Science Times* entitled "The Space Age" with a subtitle "On Oct. 4, 1957, a Tiny Satellite Stunned the World. 50 Years Later, *Science Times* Looks Back and Ahead." The featured article by John Wilford, "With Fear and Wonder in its Wake, Sputnik

Lifted Us into the Future," discussed how Sputnik changed the way we saw the world. The issue also contained Dennis Overbye's rueful piece, "One Giant Leap, Followed by Decades of Baby Steps," about the lack of progress in space since Apollo 11 landed on the Moon in 1969.

6. The *Times* has made a valiant effort to understand and write about contemporary America's economic, ethnic, religious, and sexual diversity. The *Times* has defined not only what is important in international affairs, American politics, and cultural trends, but also in travel, dining, dress, and social behavior.

7. The *Times* is a vast source of information unrivalled by any newspaper or other single website. Certainly no newspaper or website approaches the depth and erudition of its coverage of foreign news, culture, or substantive metropolitan news.

As Andrew Rice remarked in his Sunday, September 9, 2007, cover article for *Slate* that compared major stories about Iraq in that day's issues of the *New York Times* and *Washington Post:*

> The NYT's and WP's lead stories on Iraq are both all-hands-on-deck affairs—six reporters share a byline on the Post's story, while a whopping 18 contributed to the *Times*'s [story]—and the differences between the pieces say a lot about the respective papers' personalities. The *Times* story is Baghdad-centered and reads like an authoritative assessment, while the *Post* story is Washington-centered and reads like a very momentous gossip column. The differing approaches underscore an old argument in journalism (and elsewhere) over whether history is made in the trenches or at the highest reaches of government. (Rice, "Murmurs of a Reckoning")

Of course, the *Times* has the reporter staff and budget to do such a hands-on story and the *Post* does not, so this—as Rice does not emphasize or even notice—was a budgetary decision disguised as a policy one.

8. The *Times* remains the most important barometer of culture in the United States. In its daily and weekly arts sections, the *Times* is a leader in defining cultural excellence.

To cite two examples, the *Times* in large part established the reputations of Wendy Wasserstein and Woody Allen as national figures rather than as artists whose work was often limited by their focus on the doings of the elite class of Manhattan. The *Times* has also created and sustained much of the image the rest of the country and even the world has of New York City as a cultural mecca.

9. The *Times* provides, at its best, eloquent short essays that put readers in the epicenter of a complex situation and enable them to experience vicariously and empathetically a world beyond their own.

Such an essay was Kirk Semple's July 30, 2006, *Week in Review* piece, "City of Dread: Where the Collateral Damage Is in the Mind," about the effects of living with the threat of constant violence in Iraq. Not only is the piece well written and succinct, but by focusing on the life of a female Iraqi journalist who works as reporter and translator—while necessarily keeping her position a secret—Semple shows the difference between living in Saddam Hussein's dictatorship, when all one had to do was not criticize the president, and living in Iraq now. Everything becomes, in the Iraqi journalist's words, "an accessory" to staying alive. Semple concludes with a spare one-sentence conclusion: "What matters to Iraqis now is whether they are planning to get through the day alive and how they plan to try."

10. The *Times* inspires pride and loyalty in its senior editors and journalists.

Although sometimes bordering on hubris if not hagiography, such pride and loyalty provides valuable continuity. As Suzanne Daley, the national editor, mused to me: "One of the things about this room that may be peculiar to the *New York Times* is I've worked here twenty-eight years, but I can look out that door and see people who were here before I got here. People work here forever and whatever you do follows you around" (February 17, 2006). The *Times* as an institution reminds me of the academic world in which I have lived my life, a world with conservative reflexes no matter how innovative its initiatives.

11. Meeting the needs of its readers, the *Times* has expanded its range of cultural, business, and investigative stories and value-added journalism—that is, information and advice on how to live successfully in terms of preserving one's health, investing wisely, and spending one's money with good judgment, as well as what to eat, where to dine, and how to dress.

This expanding range is related to the need to find new audiences by touching on a wide diversity of interests. An example is "The Choice" blog—edited by Jacques Steinberg and begun March 30, 2009—which provides information on college admissions and financial aid as well as information for prospective and entering college students.

12. The *Times* has greatly expanded its use of photography—introducing color in 1995—and graphics, as well as employed a greater variety in subject matter and writing styles.

13. The *Times* has, for the most part, probing editorials, provocative columnists, and informed op-ed articles.

14. The *Times* is willing to pull an ad if a late-breaking story requires it; when Chief Justice William Rehnquist died, late on a Saturday night in September 2005, the *Times* stopped the presses, pulled an ad out, and included a two-page obituary.

III. Major Problems Besetting the *Times*

1. Business Problems: The Hegemony of the Marketplace and the Emphasis on Bottom Line

I begin by quoting from my October 11, 2005, interview with Arthur Sulzberger Jr.: "Welcome to what you have to do: you grow and you expand or you begin to contract and die, and there's no such thing as stability in life and there's no such thing as stability in business. You're either growing or you're dying. We're growing."

Although the *Times* has a long history of insulating the editorial side from the business side—and by that I mean the entire process of producing the newspaper each day—increasingly more of the newspaper's policies are disguised versions of economic decisions. Or as Arthur Gelb told me in June 2005, echoing the words of Deep Throat to Robert Woodward in the film version of *All the President's Men*, to understand the contemporary New York Times Company, I should "follow the money." Most past *Times* luminaries view with dismay the proliferation of the Sunday *"T"* magazines—devoted to fashion, design, travel, real estate—because they regard them as little more than advertising vehicles with barely any content. Nor are most of the retired senior editors whom I interviewed fans of such fluff sections as *Escape*, *ThursdayStyles*, and *SundayStyles*, which they regard as being without much substance.

The *New York Times* is a public corporation beholden to stockholders, even though the Sulzberger family has a controlling interest. Because the family controls the voting stock, the *Times* has been somewhat insulated from market considerations such as falling profits or the commotion caused by mistakes and embarrassing decisions made by the publisher or senior editors. But that is far less the case today than it was in 1999. It should be mentioned that other newspaper companies are also controlled by families, including the Washington Post Company (the Grahams), and thus the *Times*'s situation is not an anomaly. Dow Jones (controlled by the Bancrofts), Knight Ridder (dominated by the Ridders), and the Tribune company (controlled by the Chandlers) all have changed hands within the past two years.

But the *Times* is much less vulnerable than the *Wall Street Journal*, which was sold to Rupert Murdoch in 2007. New York Times Class A shareholders elect only about 30 percent of the board, the size of which varies a little; the Sulzberger family, which controls almost 90 percent of the Class B shares, elects the remaining 70 percent or so. Moreover, since 1995 these B shares are in a single trust, in which all family members share equally. The single trust means the family speaks with one voice.

Yet more and more, the *Times* operates and thinks as a business, or at least its ever more important business side does. The *Times* is concerned with the rising costs of newsprint and employee compensation, as well as with stagnant revenues in advertising. One major economic problem is how to replace newspaper advertising with Internet advertising. Not only have many corporations abandoned newspaper advertising, but the *Times* has been hurt over the years by the mergers and closings of New York City department stores—including Gimbels, B. Altman's, Bonwit Teller, and Abraham and Strauss—which at one time were a major source of daily advertising revenue. The *Times* also has an expensive new building at 620 Eighth Ave., into which it moved on November 19, 2007.

2. The Challenge of the Internet

The *Times* has been transformed from the Old Gray Lady speaking to—and often for—the New York and Washington establishment as well as influential political and business leaders throughout the country to a more complex voice in our digital and skeptical era. As its editors openly acknowledge in interviews, the *Times* is unsure of the long-term effects of the Internet and is not sure how it should respond to or plan for the future, although in 2011 it began charging nonsubscribers to the printed paper for its digital site. The *Times* knows that the role of print media has changed and that its potential audience gets rapid and visual information from TV and the Internet. To be sure, it took some time for the *Times* to become fully aware that it publishes in a world in which the Internet plays an important role for many readers, but the contemporary *Times* has now put enormous resources into its digital site, nytimes.com, and knows that is where much if not all of its future lies.

Internet reporting does not require a specific deadline, but even more pressure is put on major media reporters, whose deadline becomes "as soon as possible" lest a rival website beat him or her to the story. *Now* replaces the artificial deadline of previous years, that is, the stipulated time when the paper (or network news) went to press. Thus, nytimes.com publishes the time when a story is posted as if to stress the immediacy of the newsgathering activity and as if to boast that the *Times* is cognizant of a race with rivals. The *Times* adds and revises details as soon as they become available; corrections can be made instantly. By posting news on the web as stories break, read-ers—including interested parties, and past and potential sources—can intervene before the story reaches the paper, correcting and amending and perhaps, on occasion, even manipulating the story as it evolves toward the printed version.

Nytimes.com is continually updated by its news desk under Jim Roberts. As Arthur Jr. said to me: "We are now the world's largest newspaper-owned website. . . . In truth the expansion of the *New York Times* when you include print, the web, and now, of course, [video has] been a remarkable success story. We are no longer bound by the word 'paper' and 'newspaper.' We are bound by the word 'news' " (October 11, 2005).

The *Times* Internet audience is far more national and international than that of the print edition and that influences what is emphasized on nytimes.com, particularly in the case of the online "Global Edition."

The *Times*'s Opinionater site no longer lists and gives access to major blogs. Perhaps that is because the *Times* had no control over the editorial content of external blogs other than the capacity to drop the blog from the Opinionater site. Simply put, one could access from the *Times* site opinions and information that the *Times* had not approved or vetted. One cannot stress enough that this was a radical shift in authoritative coverage and a radical democratization, for now the reader as much as the newspaper decided what its readers needed to know.

The *Times*'s longtime credo—"All the news that's fit to print"—has become, in actuality, "What every reader wants to read." There was a time when the very fact that the *Times* printed something was reason enough for most of its readership to read and think about it. In a time of rising costs and declining circulation and advertising, the *Times* often follows the quite plausible theory that if it can find any way online or in the newspaper to catch a reader's interest and perhaps get him or her to read further, it will create a future reader.

Just as many Fox News viewers turn to a channel that fulfills their own conservative views if not their prejudices, there is a danger in this new hypertext/hypermedia word city that readers will not pursue news or analyses outside the box of their own interests and preconceived views. And reading and listening simply to confirm one's own prejudices is, I argue, dangerous for democracy.

3. Instances of Inept Leadership

There have been serious questions about the competence of the current publisher, Arthur Sulzberger Jr., who has enormous faith in the rectitude of his own opinions. In managing a multimedia company, Sulzberger seems—not unlike former President George W. Bush—to be competing with and working out issues with a living father who seems more comfortable in his skin than his son. Janet Robinson, since 2004 the CEO of the New York Times Company, has Arthur Jr.'s confidence, but may not be the best conduit for newsroom input.

Arthur Jr.'s first choice for executive editor created doubts. He wanted to make a choice for editor that had the impact that his father's choice of Abe Rosenthal did, and he wanted to make transforming decisions like his father's move to a four-section paper in the 1970s and his father's publication of the Pentagon Papers. Sulzberger chose Howell Raines as executive editor rather than Bill Keller because Raines convinced Sulzberger that he shared his energy and politics. (The choice of the then-executive editor, Joe Lelyveld, was his managing editor, Keller.) Raines, a charismatic figure who projects immense self-confidence, convinced Sulzberger that he could raise the energy level and productivity in the newsroom as well as fulfill Sulzberger's desire for greater diversity by the appointment of Gerald Boyd as its first black managing editor.

But Raines failed to control his reporters and offended most of his senior employees to the point that they mutinied, and Sulzberger seems to have been out of touch with the level of animosity generated by Raines as well as by Judith Miller. Miller was the one-time star reporter whose First Amendment rights the *Times* defended despite her questionable reporting techniques and skewed judgment. Her 2005 resignation was due in part to her having misled senior editors and in part to her faulty recollection. I discuss Miller in detail in chapter 9.

Raines's successor, Bill Keller, the executive editor until September 2011, was much more cautious, politic, and well liked by his staff than Raines, and under him the *Times* made efforts to increase transparency and accessibility. But Keller withheld a vital story about government wiretapping of its citizens, a story that might have affected the 2004 election.

The *Times* had considered the reader's interest by appointing, after the Jayson Blair fiasco, a public editor as the readers' representative and ombudsman. Keller at first allowed his section editors more leverage to do what they pleased to fill enormous space; as space requirements became more stringent and the number of sections decreased, he had to exercise more control, although there is, to my mind, still plenty of prolix fluff.

Whispers about whether Arthur Jr.—sometimes pejoratively called "Pinch" in contrast to his father's nickname "Punch," and regarded by his critics as arrogant and self-important—will survive have been heard within the *Times* community for years, beginning with the Blair–Raines debacle, but these whispers also lead to another question: "Who might succeed him?" Although the Sulzberger family controls the majority of the Class B voting stock, nothing feeds insecurity among the business community—which judges even an august company like the *New York Times* on profit and loss—more than a declining stock price.

When there are problems, Sulzberger consults the family and the now thirteen-member board of directors, and to date he seems to have their support. The most likely and perhaps only possible heir seems to be his cousin, Michael Golden, publisher from 1997 to 2003 of the *International Herald Tribune,* which has been owned since 2003 by the New York Times Company. Golden is vice chairman of the New York Times Company and, since March 2009, president and chief operating officer of the Times Regional Media Group. But his name is not Sulzberger and he turned sixty-two in 2011. It is not as if the *Times* scoured the world to find the most able and qualified successor to Sulzberger's father. After all, although Sulzberger was trained to succeed his father, he achieved his position—or at least his opportunity—by nature of his position in a family hierarchy. Now he is training his own son, Arthur Gregg Sulzberger, who has been writing for the *Times* since 2009.

Some *Times* people with whom I spoke thought that in his successive choices of Raines and Keller, Sulzberger erred, first choosing Raines, who some senior staff members considered arrogant and power hungry, and then in response returning to Keller, a man who at first didn't seem to be a forceful leader and who, in contrast to Raines, went out of his way to avoid conflicts.

In the period surrounding the forced resignation of Judith Miller in fall 2006, Keller was criticized for continuing a tour of Asian bureaus rather than returning to handle the crisis. The Miller controversy did no good to the *Times*'s morale or to Keller's stature. Although reporters worked feverishly to uncover her source, Keller knew the source but declined to tell his own reporters. By keeping his own counsel, Keller was responsible for an enormous waste of time and talent.

Put another way, he deflected the *Times* from the work it should have been doing. Keeping his own counsel also had the effect of undermining the confidence that the editors and reporters had in the executive editor and the publisher, confidence that is essential for the *Times* to function effectively. The result was the increasing balkanization of the *Times*, creating a situation where each major editor was looking out for his or her own territory and had an eye on the next power shuffle. To some extent I think that this balkanization has abated as the years move further from the Iraq debacle and the Miller controversy. Keller's eight-year editorship ended in September 2011, but the present and former senior staff at the *Times* are not without internal critics—and their criticism does not compare in intensity with that of outside critics.

Furthermore, under Sulzberger's auspices, Keller waited more than a year to apologize for the WMD reporting fiasco. Finally, he was extremely vague about why the *Times* withheld—supposedly in the interest of national security—information for a year about the government's illegal wiretapping, when releasing it prior to the 2004 election might have affected the results of the presidential race. Nor has he adequately explained why it was appropriate to publish the story in late 2005.

4. Manipulation of the *Times* by Its Sources

The *Times*'s institutional mythology and Sulzberger's personal mythology both are heavily influenced by the 1971 publication of the secret Vietnam War history known as the Pentagon Papers under the courageous auspices of his father, Punch Sulzberger, and then-managing editor Abe Rosenthal. The *Times*'s benchmark for revealing secrets, the Pentagon Papers represent the historical fault line between a press that stands with the government in mutual trust and one that has an adversarial relationship based on standing up to the government. The Pentagon Papers showed that the government could lie to the public and manipulate the press, and the *Times*—notwithstanding often being duped afterward—became from then on a more skeptical observer of government.

Of course, the press depends for information on cozying up to potential sources, and the administration and congressional members depend on using reporters to get out information that they want in circulation. Put another way, those sources who do not want to speak for attribution often speak for their own purposes and/or deliberately mislead the media.

Did the *Times* best serve its readership in the way it handled Miller's reporting of WMDs? Shouldn't Miller have been challenged to produce more evidence to support her (and other reporters') WMD reports and to reveal her sources to senior editors? Furthermore, when, during the investigation into the leaking of the identity of covert CIA agent Valerie Plame, Miller refused to testify to a grand jury about an interview with a senior administration official who turned out to be the vice president's chief of staff, Lewis Libby, shouldn't the *Times* have insisted that she reveal her sources and what she knew to her editors, so that its publisher and senior editors could weigh the legal issues of her case against its readers' right to know?

In theory, but not always in practice, the *Times* has become more skeptical, in the wake of Miller's case, of talkative government sources that give them privileged information. But more often than not, newspapers—including the *Times*—provide space and broadcast media provide airtime for officials to press their agendas and make their points; often the media unwittingly allow disinformation to pose as information because they don't take the time to examine what is being said. Although this is far more prevalent in broadcast journalism, especially with live interviews, it does happen in the press far more than it should. As Clark Hoyt said in my May 19, 2010, interview, as he was completing his third and final year as public editor of the *Times*, "I think that there have been . . . notable occasions where the *Times* has been less than properly skeptical of official government information, and the most famous, relatively recent example is the war in Iraq."

Two factors contribute to this gullibility and tacit complicity in providing less than accurate information. First and most importantly, reporters and government officials rely on one another to do their respective jobs, in some cases trading information back and forth like baseball cards. Second, reporters and government officials, especially in Washington, D.C., often send their children to the same private schools, eat at the same restaurants, live in the same neighborhoods and buildings, and go to the same dinner parties. Washington journalists at times become complicit in spreading speculation, gossip, and predictions that support one or another political position.

In a June 30, 2010, online dialogue with Gail Collins, David Brooks wrote, "It is true that when you interview people you do develop relationships, and there is some pressure not to burn the people you admire and rely on." Or, as Hoyt said to me: "[Y]ou always have to worry that there is a degree of self-correction that goes on out of fear of compromising that access in some way" (May 19, 2010).

Quoting "senior government officials" may not be in the interests of the readers. Even using such officials for background information should be consigned to rare usage except in a dire national emergency. As it is practiced today, these unidentified officials often engage in disinformation and manipulation of the press, as well as gossip and innuendo.

To be sure, at times whistle-blowers need to be protected, and the newspaper has to keep national security in mind. But, having said that, we might ask: Does the *Times* provide too large an umbrella for these categories? And on the business pages and even on the sports pages—for example, in reporting on the use of steroids by baseball players—is the *Times* as scrupulous as it should be? Now that more than six years have passed since Keller's June 23, 2005, staff memo about using sources more judiciously, can we say that—to quote from his memo—the use of anonymous sources "is not a routine, but an exception"? What may have changed is that editors now know "the identity of any unnamed sources" and that, unlike the past, there are, I am told, no exemptions, but is a reporter's sharing anonymous sources with an editor really sufficient to prevent their overuse? Surely, in 2011, isn't it time to insist that sources identify themselves in all but the most extraordinary circumstances?

Are editors pressing reporters for adequate disclosure—that is, what Keller in the aforementioned memo summarized as "how the sources know what they know, what motivated them to share information, and why they are entitled to anonymity"? What assurances do readers have that this policy is practiced when the journalists and editors are driven by the desire for scoops? The ruling passion of a good journalist is curiosity, but what happens when competitiveness for recognition, stature, and prizes takes priority over or competes with serious, probing journalism?

Despite written ground rules, the problem of using anonymous sources when it is not necessary persists, as Hoyt makes clear in his April 17, 2010, public editor's column entitled "Squandered Trust," in which he discusses recent examples of how the "*Times* continues to hurt itself with readers by misusing anonymous sources." Although Hoyt allows for their use in important stories like Governor David Paterson's intervention in an aide's domestic dispute involving violence, I concur with his view that, as he put it to me in our May 19, 2010, discussion, it is usually undesirable: "It's just not fully appreciated [by the *Times*] how rarely anonymous sources should be used for the credibility of the newspaper. There are stories like the story for which the *Times* won a Pulitzer prize about the Bush administration's extra-legal eavesdropping operation in the name of deflating terror. But when an anonymous source appears in a fashion review or an article about the décor of an apartment building, we have frivolous, foolish cases that devalue the currency of anonymous sourcing."

5. Poor Judgment in Deciding What to Publish

The editors of a newspaper and even its journalists are gatekeepers or crossing guards who decide what information we should get and what we shouldn't, and between 1999 and 2009 the *Times* made some major misjudgments.

Gatekeeping—which includes decisions on how to handle material gleaned from sources—is the concept of deciding what appears in the paper or on the website. It includes the journalist's decision on which facts to include and how to shape the presentation of those facts; it includes how the editors ask the journalist to rewrite—or how they themselves rewrite—and edit; it includes how the headline editors cast the story; and it includes where the editors place the story. As the newspaper of record, the *Times*'s gatekeeping in the past shaped our historical perspective. As I show in chapter 10, gatekeeping decisions shaped the way the Holocaust was presented by the *Times*, how the creation of Israel was addressed, and how the conflicts between Israel and its neighbors have been presented.

Once the most authoritative newspaper in the United States, if not the world, and now aspiring to maintain that position, the *Times*'s greatest asset is reader confidence. Recent radical misjudgments in its gatekeeping function have affected confidence and ultimately the *Times*'s influence as the leading institution of the Fourth Estate. Put another way, when its gatekeeping function fails and the information on important matters proves false, the *Times* itself becomes the story, to the detriment and embarrassment of the *Times*, and the *Times* loses some of its hard-earned credibility.

The *Times* was bullied by the administration into supporting the invasion of Iraq and even into withholding evidence before the 2004 election of an assault on civil liberties. Deference to power makes the press—and in particularly the Washington press—lax about making the appropriate gatekeeping decisions. At its worst, as former columnist Russell Baker points out in "Goodbye to Newspapers," gate-keeping failure "means a readiness to tell the narrative of government as the powerful tell it" (*New York Review of Books,* August 16, 2007).

Between 1999 and 2009, the *Times* made some major gatekeeping misjudgments. One such failure was the misidentification on the March 11, 2006, front page of the man who claimed he was the hooded Abu Ghraib prisoner who was photographed with wires attached to his extended hands. To its credit, the *Times* did print a front-page story correcting the mistake, but, as public editor Byron Calame pointed out in "The Wrong Man: Deception, Mistaken Identity, and Journalistic Lapses," the *Times* had published an article that correctly identified the man less than two years earlier (March 26, 2006). In this case the *Times*, rather than doing its own research as it should have, seems to have been influenced by incorrect assertions in other news sources— *Vanity Fair* and PBS, both of which have far fewer resources than the *Times* does—and to have relied on a misunderstanding of assertions from human rights organizations.

Sometimes gatekeeping issues are complex, and one can make a case for a decision to print as well as a decision not to print. I have already mentioned what I regard as another gatekeeping failure, that is, Keller's handling of the wiretap story, where withholding information may have affected the 2004 election, and I discuss gatekeeping issues in detail in the chapters on the twenty-first-century *Times*.

6. Challenges to the Freedom of the Press

The issues of when to rely on confidential sources and how much con-stitutional protection reporters who use those sources should receive are central to journalism in a democracy. In part because it often breaks the most important stories that challenge the secrecy of especially the federal government—but also that of states and cities—the *Times* is the No. 1 target of those who wish to limit the First Amendment.

The Bush administration and many congressional Republicans frequently reminded the press that their self-defined role of Fourth Estate does not make them a branch of government. As Adam Liptak, formerly the *Times* reporter specializing in legal affairs and now the Supreme Court correspondent, noted on June 3, 2006: "Federal courts have been increasingly hostile in recent years to assertions by journalists that they are legally entitled to protect their confidential sources. . . . The Supreme Court has ruled that the First Amendment offers reporters no protection, at least in the context of grand jury subpoenas. Though most states have so-called shield laws that protect journalists' confidential sources, those laws are usually irrelevant in cases brought in federal court" ("News Media Pay in Scientist Suit"). Among many others, Hoyt has written convincingly of the need for federal shield laws (see, e.g., "Squeezed by the Courts," April 20, 2008). Although I think anonymous sources have been overused, the *Times*—and other media—do need to protect sources in cases of what Hoyt calls "vital public interest," but such occasions need to be severely limited.

The *Times* is basically a conservative institution deeply committed to holding its place in society and seeing itself as a preserver of crucial values, most notably those encompassed by the First Amendment. When defending these values, it is uncompromising in its defense of what it believes are the prerogatives of a free press and unwilling to bend to other views of the Constitution. Thus, for the *Times* there seemed to be little if any distinction between defending its right to publish the Pentagon Papers and protecting Judith Miller's defiant refusal to report what she knew about the revelation that Valerie Plame was a CIA agent. To the *Times,* both cases represented incursions on the freedom of the press.

The courts have held against the *Times* in crucial cases where they tried to protect their sources. A notable libel case brought by a government scientist, Stephen Hatfill, cited columnist Nicholas Kristof's contention that Hatfill should be a suspect in the anthrax inquiry. A federal magistrate ruled against the *Times* for failing to identify all of Kristof's sources, notably two FBI agents. In another case, the Supreme Court refused to block a U.S. prosecutor's access to reporters' phone records. In 2004, it looked as if a proposed federal shield law that would help reporters protect their sources would be passed by Congress; the proposed law has not only been watered down since then but remains unpassed.

7. Space Management and the Diminished Place of News

At its best, the *Times* is a symphony where each section complements the others. At its worst, it is a cacophony where too much is included.

As sections have proliferated and the number of pages expanded, the percentage of the paper devoted to what by any stretch of the imagination can be called news has diminished. John Geddes, managing editor in charge of space management, asserts: "With the cost of newsprint, we have tried to be constrained" (quoted in Byron Calame, "All the News that Fits the Allocated Space," January 29, 2006). But we need to ask why international stories of importance are postponed and neglected, while insipid and prolix stories get seemingly endless space. The real issue is the plethora of non-news stories and the expansion of soft stories to fill the back of the book.

What I call *Timeslite* (and could call *Timesfluff*) not only undermines gravitas and often shows an alarming lack of proportion and judgment on the part of the *Times* staff, but it also takes space from important foreign and national news. Virtually every day a story appears on the front page that has no business there. A paradigmatic example from Sunday, May 29, 2006, is Andrew Newman's story "Unto the City the Wildlife Did Journey," an account—beginning with a humorous parody of biblical prose—of animals entering the New York metropolitan region. The problem is that the story is no story because the sightings of bears in New Jersey or a coyote in Central Park have been reported before in the *Times* and are no surprise to even the most confirmed city dweller. Possibly one could justify a feature story about wildlife in New York in the metropolitan section, but it is hardly a front-page story on a day when consigned to the inside pages were stories about East Timor's descent into chaos, a German Pope waffling about the Nazis, an earthquake in Java that killed 4,500 people, and the debate over whether the federal government under the president's auspices could seize papers from Congressman William J. Jefferson's office. (To be fair, on rare occasion these page 1 stories about New York life are replaced in the national edition of the paper, but not necessarily by weightier stories.) Indeed, notwithstanding the coverage of the seizure of Congressman Jefferson's papers on Sunday in the *Week in Review*, would not a front-page news analysis of the implications of what is really a major constitutional issue have been appropriate?

If *Timeslite* is the dumbing down of the *Times*'s daily product to include vacuous articles and features, including the kind of economic voyeurism represented by the intermittent series of articles on the superrich—such as those that began on page 1 of the *Sunday Magazine* section on October 14, 2007—then *Timestrash* includes coverage of such things as sensational murders, celebrity gossip, Mafia tidbits, and the porn industry. *ThursdayStyles* and *SundayStyles* are the major sites for such pieces.

Timeslite and *Timestrash* are both part of the *Times*'s response to its circulation and advertising crises. The *Times* is flailing about in terms of who its audience will be beyond its core—and that means finding new readers in terms of location, age, income, and education. Much of *Timelite* and *Timestrash* are stories aimed at specific audience segments. At times, the *Times*'s desire to address audience segments interested in special topics puts it in a position of an all-you-can-eat buffet: lots of choices, but many of them mediocre.

Along with soft stories often go slack writing and careless editing. As former national editor Soma Golden Behr observed in my October 11, 2005, interview, which took place in the midst of the evolution of the *Times* from a newspaper to more of a daily magazine: "Sometimes, we are not editing hard as we should be, especially page 1 stuff. I hate to read a story on page 1 that confuses me; that [kind of presentation] really pisses me off. I don't think we should give readers that problem, I think we do that with too much regularity. . . . The writing can be very, very good, but mostly I think it's very mediocre. . . . I don't think there's enough editing, some stories are just too hard, and stories shouldn't be hard. . . . You find you have to read a story twice, and you shouldn't have to do that."

8. *Times* Editors Often Are Out of Touch with Its Core Readers

The *Times*'s editors sometimes seem to forget or misunderstand why its dedicated readers value the *Times*. Thus, the current masthead editors as well as other senior editors boast about the *Times* no longer being the "paper of record" as if that were a badge of honor. What they mean is that it doesn't reprint entire speeches or the transcript of news conferences or daily stock and bond prices. Yet most of the *Times*'s readership values the *Times* because for them "paper of record" means accurate and informed reporting. Although a strong component of why we read the *Times* is the pleasure of reading—for amusement and recreation—do we not read newspapers primarily to be sufficiently and efficiently informed and to satisfy our curiosity about how our government functions and how other countries function as distinct nations and in the world community?

If the factual story has been told—often in a few sentences—on the Internet and on radio—and if that story has been given a spin on cable news, and at first glance "is not that important anymore," as former managing editor Arthur Gelb remarked during my June 11, 2005, interview, what do readers want from the *Times*? When the newspaper's news story is anticipated by other sources and the story has already been told, what the *Times* can provide is context and analysis.

Readers do not want to read a newspaper that at times patronizes them and sometimes arrogantly looks down at them from a steep and icy peak. Yet sometimes the *Times* seems unaware that its audience does not live entirely in the high-income areas of Manhattan and other upscale metropolitan areas. Recently, under the rubric "The Critical Shopper," Cintra Wilson wrote a nasty article about J. C. Penney and the people who shopped there: "J. C. Penney has always trafficked in knockoffs that aren't quite up to Canal Street's illegal standards. . . . To this end, it has the most obese mannequins I have ever seen. They probably need special insulin-based epoxy injections just to make their limbs stay on" ("Playing to the Middle," August 11, 2009). This tasteless piece generated so many negative comments that Hoyt took it up in his August 22, 2009, public editor column, "The Insult Was Extra Large."

In his memoir, *The Times of My Life and My Life at the Times*, a book showing a reasonable amount of self-knowledge but hardly self-effacing humility, Max Frankel hyperbolically writes:

> It must be impossible for anyone not suckled on the *Times* to comprehend the emotion that its lifelong readers invest in the paper's triumphs and failures, real and imagined. To its faithful readers . . . the *Times* represents the only meaningful reality because it bonds Americans of thought and power. Our ink assumes the force of blood and joins us to our readers in a perpetually loving, feuding family. (Frankel, 477)

(Although I appreciate Frankel's hyperbole and enthusiasm, I would only half-jokingly say that those readers who think the *Times* represents "the only meaningful reality" must be devoid of human relationships and not only need to get a life, but may need medication if not hospitalization.)

Nevertheless, readers of the *Times* turn to it for an accurate and judicious selection and arrangement of the facts as well as insightful news analyses, and they still think of the *Times* as a daily newspaper rather than a magazine. Many of these same people are disappointed when the front page features *Timeslite* articles such as a piece on a Wesleyan baseball player who in 1996 reached out and caught a baseball for a controversial home run that helped the Yankees win an important game (April 12, 2006). They do not want to be required to watch TV news, which increasingly provides little factual information about complex national and international issues. Some older readers do not want to access the Internet—including nytimes.com—for news, and others who do access the digital site daily still prefer the print newspaper. Yet with each passing year, the number of people who do not use the Internet is decreasing and more and more *Times* readers have turned away from the print version.

9. Decreasing Emphasis on Foreign News, Especially
Outside War Areas

Although foreign news is expensive and the extent of the *Times*'s coverage is necessarily in part a function of budgetary considerations, it is at the heart of the *Times*'s reputation as one of the world's great newspapers. Foreign reporters are expensive because they require long-term housing, office space, secretarial support, security, and often translators, preferably native speakers who know the local culture.

With two hundred nations to cover and with the Internet as a means of conveying that information, the amount of available information has drastically increased over the years. As Susan Chira, foreign news editor from 2004 to September 2011, said to me: "The amount of foreign space in terms of average column inches between 1996 and 2004 or 2005 increased by [almost] half" (February 17, 2006). Yet, given the proliferation of the "*T*" magazine sections and the enlargement of other back-of-the-book sections, notably *Home, Style,* and *Dining,* and, compared to prior decades, *Business* and *Sports,* it is factually correct—and a serious issue—to notice that a much smaller percentage of the *Times* is now devoted to foreign coverage and, indeed, to national news. Also, with so many countries to cover, we often find foreign reporting interruptus—that is, the *Times* fails to provide a full evolving narrative of major international stories and lets them often drop from focus for weeks and months at a time. In the 1999–2009 period, I could cite examples from Haiti, Cyprus, Zimbabwe, Nigeria, Cambodia, and even Lebanon and Syria.

At times, the 2009 *Times* Iranian coverage needed an evolving narrative with more background and context rather than assuming that readers had a broad knowledge of Iranian history and had read every previous story. For example—and this is only one of many—Neil MacFarquhar's June 17, 2009, "Clerics May Be Key to Outcome of Unrest" mentioned the mullahs without perhaps giving enough information about the Iranian revolution and the theocracy that replaced the Shah.

Compared with the time in the latter part of the twentieth century, when Europe and our Cold War enmity with the USSR were the main concerns—joined by China after the Nixon trip in February 1972—foreign news, other than war news, is less likely to dominate the front page. As Ted Koppel wrote in his January 29, 2006, op-ed, "And Now a Word for Our Demographic," "The age of the foreign correspondent, who knew a country or region intimately, is long over." Thus Michael Wines, the correspondent based in the Republic of South Africa, seemed to be behind the curve and reported the essential story of President Robert Mugabe's supporters burning down shops and shacks in Harare, the capital of neighboring Zimbabwe, a few weeks after it occurred in late spring 2005. The reason I know this is that my wife and I were in Zimbabwe at that time and knew from listening to and observing what was going on.

Although Mugabe has not been generous with access, the *Times* should have had a well-placed Zimbabwean journalist on the ground, especially because the country had—at that time—a relatively free press and the *Times* had plenty of warning that Zimbabwe was descending into chaos. To be fair, Chira reminded me that Wines told her that he had "risked his life to get in anonymously and not as a reporter. . . . He got in surreptitiously" (February 17, 2006). Although it did not seem to me difficult to enter and depart from Zimbabwe, perhaps Wines was known by Zimbabwean authorities to be a *Times* reporter.

Certainly, the percent of major areas that the *Times* covers with its own correspondents has diminished as the number of sites to which it needs to pay attention has increased. The *Times* has replaced an ongoing narrative about major nations with episodic coverage, and an overview of the next level of nations with intermittent and disjointed reports. Thus, readers have no overview of what issues challenge Sweden or Belgium and only a kind of anecdotal overview of even Italy and Germany. Perhaps some of the best analytic articles are about the mysterious politics of China. The United Kingdom is covered most adequately, but often without sufficient depth. Although reasonable attention is given to the United States' oscillating and often-tense relationship with France and our fascination with its culture, the kind of trenchant, succinct analysis I find in the *Economist* often is missing. At times, much of so-called foreign news consists of digressive features rather than essential information about political relationships or economic situations and their social implications.

I also want to differentiate between foreign news and news of the wars in Iraq and Afghanistan and their often domestic implications. These wars have understandably been a major focus, but allotting staff and print and Internet space to them tends to deflect the focus on news from the other two-hundred-plus nations. The Iraqi war absorbed a disproportionate number of column inches between 2003 and 2009, and, especially since President Barack Obama announced an escalation on December 1, 2009, the Afghanistan war—begun in 2001—has been receiving a great deal of attention as well. Indeed, according to Chira, as a response to the neglect of other areas, for the first time at the *Times*, editors on the foreign desk in New York were assigned to specific geographic areas so that Iraq and the War on Terror did not completely dominate foreign news.

With the resources of on-site observation, photography, the Internet (where local observers can post almost instant reports), and jet travel supplemented by internal air and chartered planes, the news media can now do far more to provide a thick reading of events than they could in the past. Now that other major American news media—except the Associated Press, whose on-site reporters tend to succinctly report basic facts—have either drastically cut their foreign coverage or virtually abandoned foreign reporting, except for Iraq and Afghanistan, a great deal of weight falls on the *Times*. Whereas history once lacked the eyes and ears of journalism, it now relies more and more on journalism to get it as right as possible. In a partisan world in which Fox News and the blogosphere shape opinions, the *Times*'s role should be to report ongoing history in a less reductionist manner than the one-dimensional polemical media and to provide when necessary multiple explanations for complex political, economic, sociological, and cultural events and issues.

The Israeli–Palestinian conflict is a paradigm of a story that needs to be placed within the framework of historical context and that needs to be revisited for in-depth news analyses. For example, we need relevant historical context to understand ongoing reports of rocket fire from Gaza or Israeli incursions into Gaza or Israel's political assassinations of Hamas leaders. Although eventually the *Times* stitched together some of the story, we might have hoped for more probing reporting and follow-up as well as more immediate contextual explanation for Israel's September 6, 2007, destruction of Syria's nuclear site. To be fair, the *Times* has covered in-depth Israel's anxiety about Iran's nuclear development.

When the *Times* is reporting on the Israeli–Palestinian conflict, those readers who don't follow the narrative closely and those who respond with passion on one side or the other need to be reminded of the complexities of that conflict. And this need for an overarching framework is true for stories from other recurring hot spots, such as Iran, Lebanon, Haiti, Cyprus, or Northern Ireland. Readers might find it helpful if Susan Chira could occasionally write a piece for the *Week in Review*—as of summer 2011 the *Sunday Review*—about the difficulty of covering complex issues. In the case of the Israeli–Palestinian conflict, she might discuss the particular sensitivity needed to present the continuing events in a conflict that has lasted for sixty years and more.

I discuss coverage of the war in Iraq in depth in subsequent chapters. An important issue, with implications beyond this particular story, is whether the *Times*, particularly in the early months of the invasion of Iraq—which began March 19, 2003—provided accurate information or whether the *Times* was deceived by generals and administrative propaganda. A second issue is whether restricting journalists' movements, either by the military or by the newspaper itself, has had the effect of suppressing the news. And a third is whether from the outset the *Times* should have or even could have stepped back and given more of an overview of the situation there. Chira remarked to me, with characteristic frankness, "We have extremely good journalists there, we have the crème de la crème and they are experienced war correspondents. . . . [Yet] I think we have struggled mightily. I don't think we give as full a picture as they would like. They're stuck, you know, because if they venture out too far they're going to get killed. However, we've worked extremely hard to give a range of perspectives using every tool we've got, using Iraqi reporters who risk their lives to be [our] eyes and ears. I think that we do the best we can under very limited constraints or circumstances" (February 17, 2006).

A recent example of the difficulty of covering news stories in chaotic situations where access is limited was Iran after *Times* reporters had been expelled. Thus, an August 16, 2009, article, "Clerics' Call for Removal Challenges Iran Leader," gave the following attribution: "Robert F. Worth reported from Dubai, United Arab Emirates, and Nazila Fathi from Toronto." Clearly, the *Times* relied on—and with considerable success—a network of secret sources, some probably highly placed within Iran, as well as Iranians in exile, scholars who specialize in Iran, and those who have emigrated, along with such "New Media" tools as cell phones (especially photographs taken with cell phones), text messaging (including Twitter), and YouTube.

10. The Urban and Cosmopolitan Bias of the *Times*

As long as the *Times,* mirroring the famous Saul Steinberg cartoon, thinks of Manhattan and select parts of Brooklyn, Connecticut, Westchester, and Long Island as the center of the universe, its status as a national newspaper is open to question. When writing about the Amish, Zoroastrians, Hasidic Jews, or even those living in rural New York State, not to mention Middle America or the Deep South, *Times* reporters seem to have difficulty imaginatively and empathetically entering into the consciousness of those on whom they report. They often write as if they were anthropologists discovering some bizarre tribe in the Amazon, although over the decade I have seen some progress in understanding the humanity of those who have chosen different paths. But even as the *Times* has become more of a national newspaper, it has, ironically, taken on more of a certain kind of New York coloration, seeing Manhattan and, more recently, sections of Brooklyn as centers of sophisticated life and showing the hipness of both in an effort to speak to a younger audience.

11. Transformation of News Presentation

Although not ignoring the often-splendid prose that appears in the *Times*, I want to consider the ways that *Times* writing has changed over the past decade, because it relates to the *Times*'s changed sense of its mission.

The *Times* has changed the idea of a news story from the inverted pyramid, in which the lede conveys the most important information, to more complicated structures that tend to revolve around a micro-cosmic focus on a telling anecdote. Some of this change in writing is the result of a movement known as the New Journalism, which developed in the late 1960s and early 1970s. Rather than giving historical background and facts, New Journalism focused on dramatizing scenes, finding specific details to show how individuals present themselves, and selecting dialogue to reveal how a particular person thinks. An effective example of how this kind of focus on the lives of specific people can supplement hard data is Jennifer Steinhauer's three-part series on how the 2008–2009 financial crisis affected Beth Court, "a block of eight homes in Moreno Valley, Calif., about 60 miles from Los Angeles" (August 23–24, 2009).

So-called New Journalists understood that reporting is not stenog-raphy and that reporters necessarily do more than just report facts but also select and arrange them into coherent constructs. New Journalists were convinced that simple factual reporting was not adequate to either the cultural or political turmoil of the late 1960s and the following decades, and that news should not be only the history of the politi-cally and culturally powerful. They sought innovative and imaginative ways to reconfigure nonfiction narratives, including journalistic stories. Examples would be Truman Capote's discussion of an obscure murderer in *In Cold Blood* (1965) and Gay Talese's *The Kingdom and the Power* (1969), still one of the best studies of the *Times*.

But the downside of New Journalism is that too much leeway leads to the newspaper's missing the essential ingredients of a story and allowing imaginative writing to replace factual reporting. Particularly when not covering hard news, the *Times*'s prose has become more subjective and more attitudinal. At times, we saw this in the coverage of the 2008 election, particularly in the early primary season with spot interviews of prospective voters and with reporters' responses to secondary candidates.

Because it is impossible to convey the entirety of an event and the way every participant is affected by it and to imagine its implications and aftershocks, it follows that at times focusing on the implications of an event for an individual or family helps center a story. But measur-ing events in terms of the reporter's perceptions—often reinforced by the particular experience of one or more of those affected—also can deflect attention from the essentials. When individual vignettes are present in virtually every bylined news story, including major stories affecting large numbers of people, these vignettes can interfere with the reader's understanding of larger implications. If a nuclear disaster were to hit New York, I fear that the opening paragraph would concern a homeless man or woman sitting in Times Square amidst his or her garbage bags. In other words, the focus on the human drama can be a detriment to providing the essential story.

More broadly, the focus on the human dimension parallels—and may be both influenced by and influencing—the changing emphasis in the university world from seeing history not so much as the story of political leaders but as the story of ordinary people living in a given place and time. Thus, rather than emphasize the stories of presidents, prime ministers, popes, and kings, New Journalism—taking its cue from New Historicism and vice versa—emphasizes the effects of events on the less powerful, whether it be women, less-advantaged social classes, or victims of natural and political events over which individuals have little control. The danger is that the reporter loses focus on major political and economic trends.

New Journalism spawned some offspring that took journalists far away from reporting and often lost account of the facts. At its most idiosyncratic, New Journalism opened the door for feature writing that allows the author a great deal of leeway in presentation and allows him or her to follow individual personal interests and move into self-immersed writing with allusions that few beside the author understand. As John Darnton, former cultural editor, remarked to me on June 21, 2005, "Insider references . . . some of them extremely obscure . . . [make] readers who don't catch the allusions feel excluded. And you never want to exclude readers, I think."

12. Errors in Reporting and Editing

The most serious errors in reporting and editing are factual errors, with the most notable being allegations of WMDs in Iraq, but there are many other notable ones. Although the *Times* does print corrections, it needs to make fewer errors. To be sure, extraordinary errors and misjudgments may bring editorial apologies in the form of a "From the Editors" piece, such as the May 26, 2004, "The *Times* and Iraq," or the September 26, 2000, piece under the heading, "The *Times* and Wen Ho Lee." In recent years, sometimes significant retractions of stories that had more short-term implications have been embedded in the public editor's column; thus Clark Hoyt reported in his column about the aforementioned J. C. Penney article by Cintra Wilson: "Bill Keller, the executive editor of the *Times*, was unhappy, too. The column, he said, 'would make a fine exhibit for someone making the case that The Times has an arrogant streak.' Keller said his mother was a Penney's shopper for much of her life, and she would have found the review 'snotty.' He told me that he wished it had not been published" ("The Insult Was Extra Large," August 22, 2009).

The exacerbated race to get scoops about government incompetence, to discover the most sensational facts of a "discovery" or investigative story even if the facts later need be corrected (such as overwrought stories of rape and pillage in New Orleans in the aftermath of Hurricane Katrina, or the alleged rape by Duke's lacrosse players), and to provide instant analysis and background on unfolding stories contribute to factual errors and distorted perceptions. So, too, as I have mentioned when discussing gatekeeping, does the desire to please and even manipulate officials as a means of getting further inside information, even as officials are manipulating reporters to control the outflow of news in their favor. Nor should we ignore the desire of competitive and ambitious reporters to outperform their colleagues at the *Times* and elsewhere as well as to please demanding editors and thus get promotions and better assignments. Furthermore, not only do senior editors want to outdo other news sources, but also the *Times*'s journalists, editors, and publisher always cast a competitive eye on possible Pulitzers and other major awards.

Major errors can result from failure to check facts, whether due to sloppy editing, overconfidence in star reporters, or failure to examine the motives of sources. The *Times*'s editors need to be certain that its reporters know what they are talking about and that they are not zealously over-reading data or being manipulated by sources. Even if 95 percent of their investigative stories are valid, their credibility is tarnished by the remaining 5 percent. In the current period, where for many truth takes a back seat to ideology, errors give the *Times*'s political enemies—especially those whose judgment or integrity the *Times* has questioned—an opportunity to discredit the *Times*. Although much of the media jumps with glee on the *Times*'s mistakes, the conservative media are always the shrillest.

The *Times* is self-regulating and wants to do the right thing when it errs, but it is often slow to recognize when it goes off track, perhaps because of its very size and perhaps because of an institutional self-importance that at times pervades the building and is especially inherent in its senior editors and journalists.

13. Transparency: *Times* Paranoia

Given its importance as the world's leading newspaper, and given some of its recent failures, which I have been discussing, the *Times* should be a model of transparency. Although one would hope for open doors and windows at an institution devoted to shining light on dark spots and informing readers about what is actually happening, that transparency, although vastly improved during the Keller years, could still be greater, especially in discussing its financial circumstances.

Prior to Keller's editorship, which began in July 2003, the *Times's* first defense when criticized was often to recoil to an iconoclastic perspective and look at its critics with some bemusement if not disdain. To be sure, under Keller, this gradually has changed for the better. In the past several years, following an initiative of Keller's—who has articulated and practiced a policy of greater openness—numerous editors have done an online "Talk to the Newsroom" Q&A with readers on the web, but it should be noted that the editors decide which questions are answered and that the readers have no chance for follow-up questions.

The public editor has been another strong step in the direction of transparency. Yet even now, as I know from my interviews, the *Times* needs to be aware of the dangers of thinking the worst of its critics and skeptics—some of whom are not ideologues—and being fearful of those who want to shine a bright light on how the paper works. Because of the Jayson Blair and Judith Miller episodes and the barrage of criticism in the blogosphere, the senior editors may feel they need to be more on guard than in the past.

Not surprisingly, the *Times* likes to control what is written about it. In that sense, it on occasion mimes the paranoia that it despises in government, and it practices some of the same spin techniques— notably when discussing finances and staff changes—as those practiced in Washington. To be sure, senior staff members are busy and have a paper to produce. Perhaps, too, they are overwhelmed with interview requests and feel the need to protect their time.

But, this does not completely explain why some senior staff are reluctant to let outsiders be informed about what they are doing and either refuse virtually all interviews or want to control the questions or get defensive when asked about stories written under their supervision. Because the *Times* is the central player in the nation's Fourth Estate, it is essential that the public understand what they are doing and why. Explaining that—the what and the why—is the purpose of this book.

2

The Way We Were

A Brief History of the *Times*
with a Focus on Major Events

The *Times* has not figured out which way the future is going. . . . It's too big and clumsy a product for these days.

—Max Frankel, April 16, 2005

[I want to] persuade you not to write a better-in-the-old-days nostalgia book. If you do, it won't be true.

—Jonathan Landman, October 11, 2006

The best editor was Abe [Rosenthal]. Brilliant man of journalism. . . . In my day, reporters were hard drinkers and smokers. There was bravado, a macho man figure. . . . Journalism is not a perfect craft. It never has the full story. Many editors twist the story. If so, retribution and eventually the truth will come out. . . . There are scoundrels in journalism. Even on the *New York Times*.

—Arthur Gelb, June 21, 2005

Effective leadership is not about making speeches or being liked; leadership is defined by results not attributes.

—Peter Drucker, *Managing the Future: The 1990s and Beyond*

I. Introduction

Like most complex and successful institutions, the *Times* lives by its own historical narrative, and that historical narrative can be reductive.

It has its own creation myths and its own brushes with danger. Once there were giants of the earth: Adolph S. Ochs (1896–1935), his son-in-law Arthur Hays Sulzberger (1935–1961) and his son Arthur Ochs "Punch" Sulzberger (1963–1992). Arthur Hays Sulzberger's son-in-law Orvil E. Dryfoos (1961–1963) had a relatively brief term before dying at age fifty, and did not have time to make a significant mark. The aforementioned patriarchs are the bedrock on which the *Times* was founded and a tradition that is never far from the mind of the current publisher, Punch's son, Arthur Ochs Sulzberger (1992–), who is also known as Arthur Jr. Until 2007, the fourteenth floor of the old New York Times building on West Forty-Third Street is where the *Times's* publisher and the corporate executives had their offices. (For a splendid historical account of the Ochs-Sulzberger family and their relationship to the *Times*, see *The Trust: The Private and Powerful Family Behind the New York Times*, by Susan E. Tifft and Alex Jones.)

The simplified mythic narrative: Ochs created the modern *Times* virtually *ex nihilo*. Arthur Hays kept it going through the Depression, wartime, and the postwar era as the paper of record and the preeminent U.S. newspaper in terms of foreign and Washington news, the latter with a big assist from Arthur Krock and James Reston, who often were in a position to break significant stories because of their privileged relationship with the government. The *Times* also became the arbitrator of cultural excellence and played a role in establishing New York culture as the centerpiece of American culture, even if the film industry was in California, and it still plays a role in defining excellence in cultural activities in America.

Of course there is another more complex narrative, too. For much of the twentieth century, the *Times* saw itself as the voice of the socially and politically dominant culture, even while its Jewish ownership was part of a minority culture. I discuss how the ownership family—the Ochs and Sulzbergers—resolved this by assimilationist stances, including a tradition of non-Jewish senior editors, and a strong desire not to display overtly their Jewish heritage. As Jews, they spoke for and reflected the values of German Jews who emigrated in the mid-nineteenth century, founded and joined Reform and Conservative temples, and tended to adopt American values. In the 1940s and 1950s, the *Times* aligned itself with the paradigmatic American values: nuclear family, heterosexuality, male privilege, well-educated Ivy Leaguers, and people of means. To be sure, James "Scotty" Reston's optimistic belief in the redeemed American soul and his belief that it was his task to fine-tune our morality played an important role in shaping the American temperament of the *Times*'s readers in the years stretching from the 1940s, when he wrote a hortatory book entitled *Prelude to Victory* (1942), well into the later years of the twentieth century. As Gay Talese put it in *The Kingdom and the Power*, "His writing expressed faith in the nation's future [and] was gentle with the Establishment . . ." (19).

Before the cultural revolution in America that began in the late 1960s—and with some exceptions for a long time after that—the *Times* presumed a somewhat stable and homogeneous culture shared by its readers; on its news pages (if not its columns, too) the *Times* minimized cultural differences and responses. In the 1940s and 1950s, the *Times* consigned the place of women, the life of gays, and the tribulations of minorities to the outer fringes when mentioned at all. Sexuality was an unspoken subject and little attention was given to class differences.

II. Coverage of the Normandy Invasion in 1944 and Comparison with the 2004 *Times* Sixty Years Later

A major focus of this book is the transformation of the *Times*, and one way to understand that transformation is to look at a time when the interests of the government and the *Times* were closely allied. I begin with coverage of the Normandy invasion, when the *Times* conceived itself as the newspaper of record and published full documents like the 130,000-word Pearl Harbor investigative report the day after its August 1945 release—and yet it agreed not to quote President Roosevelt without his permission (Gelb, *City Room*, 34, 39).

Notwithstanding the limit on newsprint, during World War II the *Times* covered the war (with some notable exceptions) from the perspective of American cheerleaders and presented its readers with official war communiqués and speeches, most published in full. Page 1 included maps showing the latest battlefront and troop maneuvers; beneath them was a summary of war news, often in the form of official reports to pool reporters from the various press agencies.

Let us compare the first pages of issue No. 31,545 (June 6, 1944) and No. 52,867 (June 1, 2004). Both are Tuesdays, both carry the same *Times* imprint above the date. The 2004 page carries four colored photos, whereas the only graphic on the 1944 page is a basic but effective black-and-white map of southern England, the North Sea, the English Channel, Normandy, and the parts of Belgium and Netherlands close to the North Sea—a map marking what was known about the Normandy invasion from Allied communiqués, German news reports, and reporters who accompanied the invasion. Each story in 2004 carries a byline, whereas in 1944 only the two lead stories have bylines. The two 1944 bylines were male reporters; in 2004 there were far more female reporters and reporters of color. Much of the 1944 paper contains the exact wording of official documents, whereas in the 2004 version there is none of that, unless one counts the short quotation by an American general to the effect that the new Iraqi government needs to be helped by further American support.

Looking at page 1 of the June 6, 1944, *Times,* one sees straight news without analysis. Even for secondary news that is hardly urgent, the 1944 *Times* is dedicated to being the newspaper of record. One of the articles—"Conferees Accept Cabaret Tax Cut," referring to the results of a House-Senate conference committee—would probably not have made the first page in 2004. Another, "Federal Law Held Ruling Insurance," would have led with a clearer headline that stressed that the article was about a Supreme Court ruling that stipulated that large insurance companies were part of interstate commerce and thus subject to the Sherman Anti-Trust Law. Although the war headlines are vigorous, urgent, and exciting—particularly the large lettered lead over the entire page: "ALLIED ARMIES LAND IN FRANCE IN THE HAVRE-CHERBOURG AREA: GREAT INVASION IS UNDER WAY"—the domestic ones are drab and often uninformative.

To understand how fully the *Times* was committed to being the paper of record, we need to recall how it printed speeches, listed members of the cabinets of relatively obscure countries, and that as late as 1954 the Saturday *Times* had a regular list of incoming ships. We notice in 1944 the staid unexciting layout on the first page, the dearth of pictures, and the neglect of popular culture.

Yet the 1944 edition effectively captures the historic moment. Even the smaller war headings are quite compelling, capturing the full kinetic drama of war with powerful verbs mapping the relentless progress of the Allied army: "Pursuit on in Italy/Allies Pass Rome, Cross Tiber as Foe Quits Bank Below City/Planes Join in Chase/1200 Vehicles Wrecked—Eighth Army Battles Into More Towns." Note how the headline for the article (which appeared in the third column from the right) drops the relatively weak "is" in the first headline, giving way to the more active and kinetic verbs: "pass," "quits," "join in," "wrecked," "battles." Beginning with the first paragraph, the aforementioned article is brilliantly theatrical war reporting: "The Allies' armor and motorized infantry roared through Rome today without pause, crossed the Tiber River and proceeded with the grim task of destroying two battered German armies fleeing to the north."

But in contrast to the contemporary *Times*'s current emphasis on a specific "who"—often to the detriment of answering "what," "where," "when," and "how"—no attention on June 6, 1944, is given to lives lost, limbs maimed, individual suffering, or exaltation. Or take the smaller headline in the eighth column from the right: "Eisenhower Acts/U.S., British, Canadian Troops Backed by Sea, Air Forces/Montgomery Leads/Nazis Say Their Shock Units Are Battling Our Parachutists." Essential information is conveyed succinctly to the reader; at a glance the reader knows that the Allies in tandem have launched a major invasion directed by their top military leaders. The "are" construction of "to be" is suppressed in the second headline.

On Sunday, June 6, 2004, the eloquent lead editorial, entitled "June 6, 1944," contemplates the enormous stakes "when civilians as surely as soldiers felt the whole of their lives concentrated on the outcome of a few hours" and, with an implied glance at the war in Iraq and President George W. Bush's prevarications, concludes: "This is a day to respect the memory of 60 years ago and perhaps, to wonder what we might rise to if only we asked it of ourselves."

In 2004, the *Times* relied more on its own reporters rather than on United Press (UP) and Associated Press (AP) reporters. In 1944, perhaps because the war demanded shared reporting, one often finds eight of ten front-page articles taken from the AP and only two by the *Times*'s own reporters. These articles shared with other newspapers subscribing to AP and UP services presented facts (or at least the facts as the sources wanted to present them) without notable opinion. In 1944, the *Times* did not question the war effort. Reporters clearly had more latitude in the 2004 *Times*, and there was much more stress on long feature stories, often stories derived from investigatory work.

The two-section *Times* of 1944 has been replaced by a multisection newspaper, divided into five or six lettered sections with their own page numbers. As the June 2004 table of contents indicates, "A" was *International and National News*, "B" was *Metro* (i.e., news of the metropolitan area), "C" was *Business Day*, "D" was *Sports*—called *SportsMonday* on Monday and sometimes a tad longer than the sports on days other than Sunday—"E" was *Arts*. By March 2005, Thursday had *ThursdayStyles*, a "G" section that replaced *Circuits*. For some years, there was a second business section, *World Business* designated by "W" every weekday, but that was merged in 2005 with the *Business* section. In 2011, the *Science Times* still appears on Tuesday, and *Dining* still appears on Wednesday. *Home* appears on Thursdays, and on Friday the *Times* contains two extra sections under the rubric *Weekend*, one on the performing arts, one mostly on the visual arts.

III. The *Times* in 1945

In 1945, the *New York Times*'s senior staff—publisher, managing editor (at the time there was no executive editor), assistant managing editor, a few star reporters—presented a series of lectures on how the newspaper was edited and published. The audience was a select group of public school teachers, and the introduction to the published collection of lectures was by Dr. John Wade, the then New York City superintendent of schools. In the contentious political and cultural climate of 2005, these lectures—published as a volume entitled *The Newspaper: Its Making and Its Meaning*—seem a tad naïve but they give us a window into the *Times*'s self-image at that time. Reading these lectures, I get a strong impression of the senior staff members' pride in their product, their passion for probity, and their patriotism for the United States. But I also see a collective sense of responsibility to the concept of freedom of the press and their commitment to the reader's best interests. Indeed, in their remarks, they on occasion allude to the constitutional debates of 1787 and 1789 about the role of the press.

To be sure, the audience were teachers and one goal undoubtedly was to create a new generation of *Times* readers among the teachers' students by discussing the value and necessity of the *Times*'s daily product. Nevertheless, I was impressed by the speakers' pride in their product—indeed their institution—and their focus on their readers. In the best sense, I see continuity between the values of the *Times* in 1945 and its values now.

In 1945, Arthur Hays Sulzberger speaks as disparagingly of reporting that is merely "a stenographic record" (*The Newspaper*, 175). As his grandson Arthur Jr., presiding over a large corporation, could not proudly say, but which his grandfather did say: "We have no investment except in our own business and in Government securities" (175). Notwithstanding the discomfort with paper rationing and censorship, one feels in Arthur Hays Sulzberger's words a strong and proud relationship with the government and pride in holding back information related to national security: "We have been in possession of much unpublished information, and secrets have been guarded because the security of the country was involved" (183). But he also understands that this cozy relationship must stop once the war ends, and he articulates this in terms of a shared experience to an audience of New York public school teachers that would have been heavily Jewish: "Wherever the press is controlled by government, the other fundamental freedoms go; just as human beings go behind barbed wire—go mysteriously, with only a rude knocking on the door at midnight" (181).

We smile when Reston speaks of the "girth" of the *Times* when it was two sections and perhaps forty pages or when longtime reporter Frank Adams spoke patronizingly but proudly of women's role at the *Times*, a role that increased due to the shortage of manpower during the war: "But women are persistent creatures, and have finally battered the doors against them" (122). We know that this issue came to a head later and resulted in lasting change. Knowing how complex and multifaceted truth is, we may even smile at the belief in facts and truth that permeates these talks. For example, even while acknowledging objective news is not easy to achieve, Adams believes: "[N]ews-facts have an existence of their own and in themselves. This ideal is what the philosophers might call absolute truth" (128). Yet Reston, among others, also stressed the need for reportorial analyses—what Leslie Markel calls "the deeper sense of the news"—and the need to be aware of past causes and future implications (104).

Much of what the editors and senior reporters said in 1945 is applicable today. As Reston wrote, "[T]he reporter has the duty to be on guard against the misuse of power on the part of public officials. It is only human for officials to prefer to conduct their business in secret, especially these days when they are overburdened with problems of the most perplexing nature" (96). Unfortunately some have been

saying that the *Times* itself has—in the wake of its 2003 coverage of
the run-up to the war in Iraq, its withholding of information about
government wiretapping, and its reasoning behind protecting Judith
Miller—been guilty of conducting its business in secret and has used
bad judgment and not lived up to its own responsibilities. Indeed,
what Reston says about the government might be applicable today
to the *Times* in its handling of the Miller case and the information
it withheld about wiretapping: "[T]he administration has the right to
work out its policies without undue interference from the press; I do
not think they have the right to hold up [a] decision until they can
create the right atmosphere for its acceptance" (103).

As if anticipating Miller's relationship with some of her sources,
Adams speaks to the possibility of the reporters having too cozy a
relationship with sources: "There are high public officials, and other
important personages who resort to flattery to gain undue influence
over reporters, or who throw their favorites an occasional exclusion-
ary story. But the reporter who falls for these devices always discovers
there is a quid pro quo" (115).

At the time of the lecture series the *Times* had 3,500 employees
and produced 500,000 printed copies containing 125,000 printed
words in eight columns. It had news bureaus in Washington, Albany,
Philadelphia, Chicago, San Francisco, and Boston, four hundred correspondents in all the important cities in the United States—although
they worked primarily for local papers—and had foreign correspondents in major cities but not then in Tokyo, Berlin, or Vienna because
of the war. The *Times* had the maximum number of permitted war
correspondents—about thirty—and printed about forty columns of
war news a day under the auspices of the military editor, Hanson
Baldwin. The city editor oversaw several departments, including the
Wall Street bureau; his counterpart was the night city editor. The
editorial page was made up of editorials, a few letters, and a column
by either Arthur Krock or Anne O'Hare McCormick.

Some of the lectures seem hopelessly idealistic by today's standards,
but we also can recognize the continuity with the idealism of today's
Times. Managing editor Edwin James spoke of the daily newspaper as
"the record of the dreams and hopes and accomplishments of untold
millions in many lands—and their disappointments" (3); if the newspaper is "current history. . . . And thus it goes every day, this story of
mankind," implicitly it is the *Times* that sets the standard of what the

history looks like and what it signifies (4). As managing editor, James decided how much space advertising got after advertising told him what it wanted. During the war, because of rationing, the news allotment was cut 30 percent to 155 columns; as James explained, "[T]he advertising department got what was left, subject to later adjustments if there was a big news break. In 1944 we omitted six million lines of advertising. We printed several million more lines of news than any other newspaper" (15).

What is striking is how many of the 1945 remarks anticipate today's media and news world. Citing Arthur Hays Sulzberger as "having often remarked that editors and publishers will find it increasingly necessary in the future to pay more and more attention to the 'inside of the newspaper,'" Turner Catledge anticipated the emphasis not only on analysis and context, but on value-added and enterprise journalism: "Newspapers will find it of mounting importance to develop and explain the underlying trends and influences inherent in the events that contribute to spot news [up-to-date immediately reported news]" (57). Catledge, formerly national correspondent and in 1945 appointed assistant managing editor, also made the point that the *Times* regarded itself as a national paper: "We try to forget, as far as possible, that we are publishing in New York. We do not look for, or emphasize, strictly New York angles at the expense of the national aspects of the story" (58).

I am struck by the idealism, passion, and sense of mission of the editors and reporters as the war winds down. Thus, Anne O'Hare McCormick, the *Times* Pulitzer-winning foreign correspondent, concludes: "Information is the shield [for young people] against mistakes, against dullness, against tyranny. The more they read and the more facts they absorb, the better able they are to detect falsehood and bias . . . the better able they are to protect themselves, and their country, from the perils and the punishment of mental isolation. I do not speak thoughtlessly when I say that it depends first on you and us—the schools and the press—to save our children from being lost in a world they do not know" (78). Not always in sympathy with how the government resorted to censorship and casting his own critical eye on what he and his fellow reporters were told, war correspondent Foster Hailey remarks: "Too often censorship has been used to cover up mistakes both of tactics and strategy and keep from the American public information as to the seriousness of general situations that, had it been known, might have headed off some of the strikes and general home front complacency" (84).

In the face of the wars in Iraq and Afghanistan, as well as the threat of terrorism, did we not see the Bush administration—and to a much lesser extent the Obama administration—obsessively trying to control the news when it would be better to allow information to circulate and informed debate to take place? Hailey issues a warning that is still timely; not only does the reader require a critical intelligence, but also "[T]he reader should consider the background of the controlling interests of the newspaper he reads in evaluating the news he finds there" (90).

IV. The *Times* in 1964

Let us briefly jump forward twenty years. In 1964, the *Times* still published documents and speeches that few people read through. In September 1964, the *Times* published sixty-four pages of the Warren Commission's report on the assassination of John F. Kennedy. But even by 1964 there was a much greater emphasis on interpretation than there had been twenty years earlier. By 1964, affected by the awareness that the Kennedy administration had been duplicitous in managing the news about the Cuban Missile Crisis, the *Times* expressed considerable skepticism about the administration's policies and published more articles from Communist countries that gave those countries' take on history and their view that America was the world's bully.

Before Watergate and the Vietnam War, the *Times*, as Gay Talese wrote in 1970, "was awed by what was official. It was easier, safer, to report accurate boring accounts of government activity than accurate interesting accounts" (*The Kingdom and the Power*, 355). During the Cold War, reporters and editors wanted to believe in their government and trusted the government in ways that would have left most 2004 readers incredulous. In recent decades, the *Times* has become less willing to accept the positions not only of city government but also national government.

The *Times*'s Washington correspondents—Arthur Krock and James Reston—were used by various administrations to give the stamp of authority and respectability to major policies. In exchange, these writers had scoops and privileged access to the upper reaches of the administration.

The appeal of Reston, who came to the *Times* in 1939, to the Sulzbergers, the publishers of the *Times*, derived from his idealism, his lack of cynicism, and his moralism. His reverence for America as a land of opportunity where ambition was rewarded echoed the sentiments and values of the Sulzberger family. His patriotic book, *Prelude to Victory* (1942), which saw the world war as a struggle between good and evil, winnable only if we made our personal goals subservient to "a national crusade for America and the American Dream," caught the imagination of America and England—and reflected Arthur Hays Sulzberger's own perspective. In the postwar era, Reston's column was mandatory reading for diplomats and academics, in part because he was a confidante of presidents, kings, and a series of secretaries of state. For two decades, he ruled over the Washington bureau and, when necessary, prevailed over the New York bureau. Of Reston, Harrison Salisbury writes he "was an essentially conservative man who grew steadily more conservative" (*Without Fear or Favor*, 91). He rarely criticized the Establishment, whose members often used his column to defend themselves; as Salisbury tartly writes, he became the "amanuensis" of the Establishment (9).

The *Times* evolves slowly, no matter how revolutionary one or another editor thinks his leadership is. By the 1960s, as Max Frankel writes, "Newspapers were ceasing to be mere expositors of government policy. . . . We were beginning to shun intimacy with people in power. We saw ourselves as more accountable to our readers than to our sources" (*The Times of My Life and My Life with the Times*, 227). Yet the *Times*, as Frankel acknowledges, missed Kennedy's sexual escapades and, more seriously, his illnesses such as Addison's disease, and was too trusting of what it was told during the Cuban Missile Crisis. Indeed, the *Times* gave President Kennedy a free pass in part because the senior editors and reporters were fascinated by his and Jackie's glamorous presences and captivated by his charisma. It is worth remembering that in those days, the *Times* prided itself on not prying into private lives and in being above gossip. Yet, it is a major oversimplification to write, as Frankel does, "Kennedy's ostentatious displays of coatless vigor and touch football agility kept us from the truth" (231).

V. Turner Catledge's Editorship, 1951–1968

In 1951, Turner Catledge, a Mississippi Democrat who had been a classmate of Senator John Stennis, became managing editor of the *Times*. When Catledge returned to the *Times* in 1943, after two years with the *Chicago Sun*, the *Times* was already evolving: Meyer Berger's lively New York columns had personality, more photographs appeared, and the paper had begun to discuss food and fashion.

Catledge's challenge was not only to create orderly management from what had become a system of enclaves and fiefdoms, but also to shape the *Times* in response to the rising power of television. He understood that the *Times* must do more interpretive reporting and more editing—which it did under Theodore Bernstein, assistant managing editor—to give the paper liveliness and its stories shape. Some of the reporters Catledge inherited had been paid according to the space occupied by their columns in the newspaper, and that encouraged padding. Catledge believed that the *Times* had hired "three men to do what one man could do" (*My Life and the Times*, 183).

Catledge could not have been easy to work for. His memoir gives a sense of the autocratic world of the *Times* where the editor-in-chief, whether he be called managing editor or executive editor, presided over the staff like an ancient king. As he put it, he assembled "a staff of people who were personally beholden to me." Or: "As a rule, if a man asked for a raise, I didn't think he deserved one" (183). One might add, to say nothing of a woman.

When Catledge took over, the *Times* was printing less news than in the 1920s and 1930s because printing costs had increased; moreover, since the end of World War II, in part because of the greater availability of newsprint, the space devoted to advertising had increased. The *Times* had a brilliant coterie of writers on foreign affairs, but a bloated and not always energetic New York office. Catledge tried to rein in the ostentatious lifestyle and independence of some of those foreign correspondents, who thought of themselves as a separate enclave that owed its allegiance to Cyrus Sulzberger. When Sulzberger took over Anne O'Hare McCormick's column in 1954, Catledge abolished the title held by Sulzberger of chief foreign correspondent. By 1968, before ceding the editorship to Abe Rosenthal, Catledge in his seventeen years as editor had for the most part gained control over what Frankel called "the separate fiefdoms of Scotty Reston in Washington, Cyrus Sulzberger in Paris, and Leslie Markel in the Sunday News Department" (428).

VI. The Sulzberger Family as Publishers

My impression after interviewing all the living executive editors as well as other senior editors—including some aspiring heirs apparent to executive editor—is that a highly competitive environment in the upper levels of management has been and is still part of the professional life of senior editors. This impression has been reinforced by my reading various memoirs, especially those of Max Frankel, Harrison Salisbury, and Arthur Gelb, as well as reading Tifft and Jones's historical survey of the *Times*, *The Trust*, and Talese's earlier *The Kingdom and the Power*. What also is clear is that in the final analyses all the editors-in-chief submitted to the will of the publishers.

Former executive editor Frankel believes that family leadership is essential to the *Times*, although of course the *Times* has never tested the alternative and, as I will discuss in chapter 5, some investors in 2008 would have liked to. Frankel credits Punch Sulzberger with resisting business models proposed by Lance Primis, who was Walter Mattson's successor as company president until Russ Lewis replaced Primis in 1996. According to Frankel, Primis "exaggerated the promise of his trivial ventures into electronic journalism and preened in front of staff about his pursuit of Wall Street's short-term, short-lived praises" (518). Frankel approvingly recalls A. J. Liebling's perception that "the only ones among us who . . . enjoyed freedom of the press" owned a newspaper (516).

Each head of the publishing family launched bold initiatives. Arthur Hays Sulzberger launched the European edition in 1949. In 1962, Dryfoos launched a Western edition under the leadership of Andrew Fischer. After the financial losses of the 1962–1963 newspaper strike, Punch closed the Western paper in 1964. Much of the planning for the Western edition was presided over by Amory Howe Bradford, vice-president and general manager. Soon after Punch Sulzberger took over as publisher in 1963, Bradford's place was taken by Harding F. Bancroft.

The 114-day newspaper strike of 1962–1963 played a major role in making Punch Sulzberger understand that the *Times* had to become more efficient, modernize its facilities and modes of operation, and have a tighter organizational structure in which bureau chiefs were supervised. In 1964, Punch gave Catledge the title of executive editor with authority over both Leslie Markel's Sunday edition—the circulation of which was approaching 1.5 million—and Reston's Washington bureau (see Talese 405). In fact, Daniel Schwarz (no relationship) was given the Sunday editorship and Markel was moved to the legendary fourteenth floor of the old Times building as associate editor. Tutored by his powerful predecessor Arthur Krock, Reston did not appreciate what he thought of as meddling from New York and considered quitting and taking a more lucrative offer from the *Washington Post* but knew that his influence depended on writing under the auspices of the *Times*. Reston had been bureau chief from 1952 to 1964 before giving way to his handpicked successor, Thomas Wicker, in 1964.

Catledge's successor as managing editor was Clifton Daniel, President Truman's son-in-law. Daniel was another Southerner who, like Catledge, was an Eisenhower supporter. After returning to the *Times* in 1955 as a strong candidate to succeed Catledge as managing editor, Daniel had managed to diminish assistant managing editor Theodore Bernstein's power. We need to recall that at the time being a Jew was a handicap to Bernstein's becoming managing editor. Talese writes of Clifton Daniel's elitist penchant in the 1960s and how when giving speeches he conveyed the *Times*'s "calm posture and pride in appearance, the respect for tradition and the certainty of its virtue" (488), while beneath the surface there were a variety of tensions.

In his valuable 1999 memoir, former executive editor Frankel makes the point that even after the May 1, 1960, U-2 episode, when the Russians shot down an American spy plane, the *Times* was "slow to shake the old habits of 'responsible reporting,' which often meant little more than deferring to officials in positions of responsibility" (Frankel, 208). In the early days of his presidency, President Johnson made three or four phone calls daily to the editor, Turner Catledge; according to Salisbury: "In President Johnson's early months no President in U.S. history had been as close to the *Times*, its publisher (these were Punch [Sulzberger]'s early months) and its editor, Catledge" (Salisbury, 89).

Beginning in 1961, the *Times*'s editorial page became more politically liberal, more strident, and more adversarial under the leadership of John Oakes. Oakes's father, who changed his name in 1917, was the brother of Adolph Ochs. The newly aggressive editorial page affected the *Times*'s reputation for impartiality; the *Times* "was increasingly perceived as politically liberal, anti-business, and shrill in tone" and still is by conservatives (see Tifft and Jones, 502). The *Times* became much more critical of two New York icons, Robert Moses, president of the 1964–1965 World's Fair and a controversial and arrogant master builder who uprooted neighborhoods in the name of highway development, and Francis Cardinal Spellman, who despite backing Joe McCarthy, previously had been given by the *Times*—and most media—an exemption from criticism but whose vigorous support of the Vietnam War was one reason for questioning his judgment.

Oakes led the *Times*'s opposition to the Vietnam War. He had the tacit support of his relative, Punch Sulzberger, whose own personal bent often was more conservative than the views of the editorial pages. But the *Times*'s senior staff was not without its hawks, most notably the military editor, Hanson Baldwin. The North Vietnam government's invitation to the *Times*'s Harrison Salisbury to visit Hanoi in December 1966 marked a turning point in American awareness of the damage that American bombing was doing to civilian targets. His stories contributed to the loss of confidence in the men who were conducting the war and to the Johnson administration's demise (Talese 335). In 1976, after choosing Abe Rosenthal as executive editor, Punch replaced Oakes with Frankel, whom he greatly valued and didn't want to lose, and whose editorial views were more moderate, more cosmopolitan, less shrill, and closer to his own views and those of Rosenthal than to the views of Oakes, whose editorial page was to the left of both Sulzberger and Rosenthal.

VII. The Rosenthal Era 1969–1986

The most important figure in the evolution of the *New York Times* was A. M. (Abe) Rosenthal. He was the dominant newsroom figure from 1969 as managing editor (although he didn't become the first Jewish executive editor until 1976). More than anyone else he was responsible for the development of the multisection modern *Times*.

As Robert McFadden put it in a front-page obituary, "He guided the *Times* through a remarkable transformation that brightened its sober pages, expanded news coverage, introduced new production technology, launched a national edition, won new advertisers and tens

of thousands of new readers, and raised the paper's sagging fortunes
to unparalleled profitability" (May 11, 2006). He oversaw the news
operation from 1969 to 1986, when he approached the mandatory
retirement age of sixty-five. He covered the Vietnam War, the publication of the Pentagon Papers, the Watergate scandals, the Cold War,
and the Middle East. While presiding over many changes, he was loyal
to the traditions and standards of the *Times*.

A Canadian immigrant, Rosenthal came from a modest back-
ground, had been a student at City College of New York (CCNY),
and was very much conscious of his Jewishness. His byline, "A. M.
Rosenthal," reflected the *Times*'s distaste for the very Jewish name
Abraham. Notwithstanding his strong Jewish identity, Rosenthal married
Mary Burke, an Irish Catholic. But he broke taboos when he assigned
Thomas Friedman to Lebanon and thought—mistakenly—that when
he assigned David Shipler to Israel, he had assigned a Jew.

Paradoxically, one area in which the *New York Times* lagged
until the 1960s was New York City news. Indeed, New York City was
ceded—along with sports—to the tabloids to the extent that many
literate New Yorkers bought two or more papers. In 1963, Rosenthal,
who made his reputation as a foreign reporter and won a Pulitzer—
specifically for his work in Poland in 1959—was made metropolitan
editor, a new title that replaced city editor. Arthur Gelb was named
his deputy. More than anyone else, Gelb was responsible for expanding
coverage of the arts in New York City.

Rosenthal and Gelb wanted to cover the tapestry of New York
City's diverse worlds with the same investigative attention that the paper
gave to national and international news. What Rosenthal wanted was
lively writing—vivid descriptions, metaphors, defining quotations, local
color—but lively writing without reporters' opinions. He favored more
personal writing with imagination, humor, and careful observation of
how people talked, acted, looked, and thought. He shook up his staff
by giving the best assignments to the best writers rather than to those
who had the most seniority, a practice he continued as he moved up
the editorial ranks.

In the years following World War II, the *Times* reflected and
sustained—by what it covered and what it didn't cover—a culture that
rarely acknowledged alcoholism, domestic abuse, senility, and sexual
behavior other than conventional heterosexuality. Even the subtle-
ties of class difference were minimized. By contrast, Rosenthal, as
John Darnton, a long-time *Times* writer and editor, told me, "totally

energized coverage of the city, so people began looking at things that almost never have been looked at before, police corruption, gangs" (June 22, 2005). Rosenthal's stress was on investigative reporting, not on sensationalism, albeit occasional stories had ingredients of the latter.

Under Rosenthal, the *Times* began to follow some of the tenets of the so-called New Journalism, which, as Nicholas Lemann has noted, changed "the conception of what journalism could be: at once powerful and devoted to the powerless, literary and intellectual, glamorous and dutiful, quasi-governmental in its status but in perpetual opposition to government" ("Fear and favor," *The New Yorker,* December 7, 2009, 92). As managing and executive editor, Rosenthal—and to some extent his successor, Frankel—presided over "the halcyon era of mainstream media" (92).

As Gelb put it in his somewhat self-congratulatory memoir, *City Room,* the aim of Rosenthal's innovative coverage as metropolitan editor was to give New Yorkers "the most comprehensive and imaginative city report ever produced" (344). He wanted to compete for readers with the major surviving tabloids, the *Daily News* and the *New York Post,* and this trend has continued and accelerated into 2011, with stories of gruesome crimes, at times in all their lurid detail, and celebrity gossip. For example, if there was a fire in Brooklyn, the audience got to hear about the human implications in terms of loss and the generosity or lack of it in the behavior of the neighbors. Under Rosenthal, the metropolitan desk flourished; notable accomplishments were:

1. A major article—six columns, beginning on the front page—on December 17, 1963, by Robert Doty on homosexual life in New York City. Although the story seems naïve from our contemporary point of view, it was groundbreaking then.

2. A January 4, 1965, story by Martin Arnold—beginning on the front page—on the drug culture in New York City, including the use of marijuana and hard drugs among the middle-class population.

3. A March 27, 1964, front-page piece by Marty Gansberg on the Catherine ("Kitty") Genovese murder, witnessed and ignored by thirty-eight of her Queens neighbors.

The latter was followed shortly thereafter by a *New York Times Sunday Magazine* piece by Rosenthal, "Apathy in New York," about how Kitty Genovese was stalked and attacked by a killer while thirty-eight Queens neighbors ignored her screams. These stories changed the culture of the *Times* and how readers regarded the paper. Expanding on his article, Rosenthal also wrote an eloquent short book on this episode entitled *Thirty-Eight Witnesses*.

Let us return to Rosenthal's place in our survey of the history of the *New York Times*. Rosenthal became assistant managing editor—one of four—and managing editor Clifton Daniel's deputy in January 1966. He became associate managing editor in 1968. A temporary detour to Rosenthal's rise was Sulzberger's decision in 1968 to ask then fifty-eight-year-old Reston to become executive editor, replacing Catledge. Reston's protégé, Tom Wicker, became associate editor. To some observers, it seemed as if the Washington bureau, which had prided itself on its independence and resisted efforts by New York to manage it, had triumphed by getting one of its own appointed as editor.

Reston and Rosenthal did not get along well. Reston, the Scotsman, and Rosenthal, the ambitious Jew from CCNY, had severe cultural and stylistic differences. Rosenthal resisted Reston's idea of having a handpicked staff of elite reporters with offices and secretaries and, at one point, threatened to resign. According to Salisbury, Reston's "tenure was marked neither by striking innovations nor great scoops" (410). By 1969, Reston returned to Washington, and Rosenthal was managing editor and imposing his leadership on every aspect of the *Times* except the editorial page and advertising. But Frankel, a Rosenthal rival, was now head of the Washington bureau, a bureau that had fiercely fought for its independence under Krock, Reston, and Wicker.

Once Reston's short and ill-fated term as executive editor ended, Rosenthal took control of the news operation, although no one succeeded Reston as executive editor. In 1976, Punch Sulzberger ran a competition between Frankel and Rosenthal to see who would become the next executive editor. The person who came up with the best plan for combining the Sunday edition and the daily edition was the winner, and that was Rosenthal. Seymour Topping became managing editor.

When Rosenthal was named managing editor in 1969 and later executive editor in 1976, he continued to focus on the goals that he brought to the *Metro* pages, namely to give verve to the paper's writing and to engage the reader's interest in the human side by means of personal anecdotes, well-placed quotations, and historical context. What Rosenthal succeeded in doing—with strong support from Punch Sulzberger—was to make the *Times* more than the "paper of record." He wanted the *Times* to discover and to explain the news as well as to show the importance of the news to its readers. His goal was to create a publication—indeed, to use a dreaded word, a *product*—that was more useful to its readers and advertisers and therefore more valuable in terms of return on cost. Thus, the *Times* could raise the price of its papers to subscribers and newsstand customers and the cost to advertisers.

To further these goals, the *Times*—under Punch Sulzberger and Rosenthal's leadership—made two major changes. At the end of April 1976, the *Times* began a two-year process of transforming itself—with the exception of the Saturday *Times*—into a four-section rather than a two-section paper, with a daily business section and a special section devoted to a single topic (sports on Monday, science on Tuesday, dining on Wednesday, home on Thursday, and arts—called *Weekend*—on Friday) and it developed an op-ed page that contained regular columnists expressing their opinions as well as occasional columns written by experts on particular subjects. These innovations have evolved, but they are the basis of today's *Times*. In recent years, the *Times* has added separate daily sports and arts sections each day, additional special sections (*Circuits* on Thursday, which a few years ago was replaced by *ThursdayStyles*; *Escapes* was added on Friday and then later subtracted), and the Saturday paper has expanded to four sections.

Introduced in 1978, these special sections were a dramatic and effective effort on the part of Rosenthal and Sulzberger to transform the Old Gray Lady into a far more flamboyant woman about town who wears many different guises, including that of a younger lady (or man) and perhaps that of a gay man (or woman). These trends accelerated beginning in 1992 after Arthur Jr. became publisher—the fifth publisher in the family line that began with Adolph Ochs and continued with Arthur Hays Sulzberger, Orvil Dryfoos, and Punch. Under Arthur Jr., the *Times* sought and continues to seek a younger audience and one that fulfills the *Times*'s demographic needs to sell itself to potential advertisers. The *Times* relies much more on market research than it used to, particularly on the business side. To be fair, in my interviews, I did not feel that Sunday section editors or the senior editors on the foreign or national or metro desk were overly interested in or even aware of such research—unless they were being disingenuous.

In addition to transforming the *Times* from a two-section to a four-section newspaper and adding the op-ed page, Rosenthal also reconfigured Sunday's sections; began suburban weeklies for New Jersey, Connecticut, Westchester, and Long Island; and introduced Sunday supplements focusing on travel, education, fashion, and health. These early versions of Sunday supplements are the basis for the various glossy Sunday supplements that currently accompany the *Sunday Magazine*. During Rosenthal's editorship, advertising lines increased and circulation increased moderately, but the important increase was in the higher-income readers that enabled the *Times* to raise its advertising rates.

Under Rosenthal's leadership, the *Times* news writing changed from simply reporting facts to more analytic and contextual reporting. He moved the *Times* to a more lively style at a time when some of the writing was thorough and detailed, but also repetitious, colorless, and ponderous. For example, before Rosenthal, a story on the Paraguay dictator Stroessner might include the names and positions of the newly installed cabinet members. A follow-up story the next day might repeat most of the same information. What Rosenthal wanted to do—and what he articulated to his staff—was to transform the *Times*'s stodgy image, while maintaining its commitment to objectivity, seriousness, and truth.

From all accounts, Rosenthal was imaginative, innovative, and passionate. Yes, his leadership often was stormy, and, yes, toward the end of his editorship, he confused his position as executive editor with the institution of the *Times* itself—which is another way of saying that he thought of himself as indispensable. Yet he always believed that the newspaper was the star to which the entire staff should be devoted. He believed that the *Times* was not only central to the Fourth Estate but to democracy and to informing the world. As Thomas Friedman put it, for Rosenthal the power of the *Times* "comes from the quality and fairness of its reporting" ("Shoe Leather and Tears," May 12, 2006).

In 1971, Daniel Ellsberg approached *Times* reporter Neil Sheehan with what came to be called the Pentagon Papers, which was essentially a suppressed government history of the Vietnam War. While Rosenthal was managing editor and with the full support of the publisher Punch Sulzberger, the *Times* published the Pentagon Papers—McNamara's study of the origins and conduct of the Vietnam War, a study dating back to Eisenhower and even Truman and continuing through Kennedy and Johnson—an event that, according to Salisbury, established that

"The *Times* no longer was handmaiden, supporter, crony, adherent, bondsman, counselor or confident to the 'government' but was itself an independent power with independent rights, independent judgment and independent responsibility" (14). Basically the papers revealed what Salisbury laconically called "the contrast between what the Presidents did and what they say" (392).

In the September 28, 2004, issue of the *Times*, on the op-ed page, Ellsberg urged someone to do the same with papers on the historical context and preparation for the war in Iraq. It was as if the *Times* now felt guilty for its role in promoting the war in Iraq and wanted to compensate by printing a piece that encouraged a reprise of its role in exposing government deceit.

Rosenthal, according to Salisbury, was a conservative at heart. He was deeply troubled by the turbulence of the late 1960s and 1970s, especially by events such as the 1968 Democratic national convention. As Clyde Haberman told me in an interview while Rosenthal was still alive, "Abe was the editor who pushed probably against all his personal instincts for the publication of the Pentagon Papers. I'm sure that this would be incomprehensible now to people who live in a world that the only thing that matters is your politics and all journalism and all actions depend on whether you are left or right or purple. I'm sure Abe's every instinct was that this was a terrible thing to do, to expose the government of a country he loved very deeply. On the other hand journalistically there was no alternative" (June 21, 2004).

The *Times* editorially questioned the government during the Cuban Missile Crisis (but not—in part due to Kennedy hagiography and in part due to accepting the logic of the Cold War—as aggressively as it should have), the Vietnam War, and other major policy decisions, but it was the publication of the Pentagon Papers under Punch Sulzberger and Rosenthal that created the substantive and continuing skeptical distance between the government and the *Times*. By the end of the Nixon administration, which considered the *Times* to be run by the radical left and considered Watergate a press cabal originating with the *Washington Post* but cultivated by the *Times*, the gulf between the administration and much of the Eastern media—including the networks, especially CBS—had become an unbridgeable distance. Although in subsequent years that distance has oscillated, with some administrations more tolerant than others of the Fourth Estate, it has never returned to what it once was.

The *Times* has been much faulted for missing Watergate, which was exposed by the investigative reporting of the *Washington Post*'s Carl Bernstein and Bob Woodward with their access to Deep Throat, and which led to Nixon's 1974 resignation. Some outside observers and some within the *Times* blamed then Washington bureau chief Frankel for missing the story. But the *Times*'s investigative reporters, including John Crewdson, Bill Kovach, and Seymour Hirsch, did do some good work to further the story, although it is fair to say that early on Frankel did not realize the significance of the event. Even now many of those who were in leadership positions at the *Times*—and some who still are—argue defensively that, as Salisbury puts it, "Watergate was decided not by the press, not by Bob Woodward and Carl Bernstein . . . [but that] the make-or-break factors" were James McCord's letter to John Sirica that was released March 23, 1973, and John Dean's decision to go to the prosecutors (443).

Salisbury, who is both fascinated and repelled by Rosenthal, writes about how prior editors were "reined-in, outwardly composed," whereas Rosenthal was turbulent, "restless, uneasy" (400). He was an irascible, passionate, and abrasive man who elicited strong loyalties and strong dislikes from those with whom he worked. Rather than delegate responsibility, he himself hired reporters and editors. He amply rewarded those whom he liked, and sidetracked those whom he felt did not meet his standards for the *Times*. He built some careers, and occasionally dismantled others, but he often gave reporters who didn't meet his standards a second chance. As Thomas Friedman wrote in "Shoe Leather and Tears," "Abe was a truly unique jumble of integrity, mercy, tyranny, and compassion."

Veteran reporter Clyde Haberman described Rosenthal's impact to me:

> To his credit Abe Rosenthal saved the paper because the paper cannot exist without money, plain and simple. I love it when people say you only want to make money. This paper was moribund, as I understand it; its survival was not sure by any means. Working with the business division, breaking down the firewall we're never supposed to breach, he and Gelb created a bunch of sections that soon became imitated by every paper in the country. The first was called *Weekend* which was things to do in and around town, followed by

what critics would sneer at as the grabbing sections, starting with *Dining* on Wednesday and *Home* . . . then came
sports. Abe came under a lot of heat.

That you're dumbing down the paper, [that] you're
going far from the *Times*'s roots is a theme that will occur
with every editor, even with Keller and the 13-year-olds'
blow job story [Haberman is referring to the May 30,
2004, *Sunday Magazine* by Benoit Denizet-Lewis entitled,
"Whatever Happened to Teen Romance (And What is a
Friend with Benefits)"]. Every change produced cries from
every corner that it was the end of western civilization as
we know it. Abe realized how far he wanted to go. One
day without a special section was Tuesday. The business
department wanted to make it an advertising magnet, like
fashions, and that's where Abe put his foot down to have
something truer to the *Times*'s traditions, and that's where
Science Times came about. It was a science section and this
newspaper has been for a century the daily newspaper that
reports on developments and theories in the world of science as time went on. (June 21, 2005)

Science Times has been a great success and has evolved into a value-
added section that has a strong focus on health news.

Rosenthal bridled at dumbing down the *Times*'s feature sections.
Because Rosenthal was in declining health, I didn't interview him
before he died, but his surviving contemporaries—Frankel, former
executive editor Joe Lelyveld, Gelb, former assistant managing editor
Soma Golden Behr—had grave doubts about such frothy sections as
ThursdayStyles and *SundayStyles*.

In his May 12, 2006, column under the rubric "NYC," Haberman
tells the story he told me about how Rosenthal fired him in June 1966
for fabricating a CCNY graduation award—the Brett Award "to the
student who has worked hardest under a great handicap—Jake Barnes
[of *The Sun Also Rises*]"—when Haberman was the campus correspondent for the *Times*. Although grateful that he returned to the *Times*
years later, Haberman believes that Rosenthal was completely right for
firing him: "The correctness of his decision becomes ever more clear
with the grievous wrongdoings of the Blairs and Kelleys [Jack Kelley
of *USA Today* who, like the *Times*'s Jayson Blair, was revealed to have

fabricated stories] and the other journalist-fabulists who bizarrely keep popping up. . . . Readers, he said to me, should be able to believe what they read in news columns."

Rosenthal's great column on Auschwitz shows his eloquent and succinct legacy—and perhaps his humanistic values of sympathy, empathy, and moral righteousness—as well as how far today's paper with its prolixity and anecdotes without focus at times departs from his writing values. In his beautifully constructed short piece "There Is No News from Auschwitz," which appeared in the *Sunday Times Magazine* (August 31, 1958), not a word is wasted, not an adjective superfluous. Repetition of understatement—"there is no news to report," "there is nothing new to report"—and description of the pedestrian and ordinary events of the day of his visit contrast with the horrors that took place in Auschwitz. In some ways, this is traditional *occupatio*, where the writer claims he will not do something and in fact does it; in this case while saying he will not mourn the lost victims, Rosenthal in fact does mourn them and does so eloquently: "Brzezinka and Oswiecim are very quiet places now; the screams can no longer be heard" (reprinted May 14, 2006).

The piece begins by evoking a warm sunny day and moves quickly to an explanation of why nature's beauties and life's pleasantries are inappropriate for Brzezinka, the site from which the article is written. Few readers would recognize that place name or the next cited place Oswiecim, until Rosenthal tells them that both places "formed part of that minutely organized factory of torture and death that the Nazis called Konzentrationslager Auschwitz." By the time Rosenthal returns to that sunny day, the reader realizes for a brief moment he has relived the horrors, relived the reporter's visit, and understood that evil is not only in the atrocities but also, the absence of good.

Rosenthal's emphasis on the absence of those who once were here is underlined by deft use of negatives: "The guide does not say much either, because there is nothing much for him to say after he has pointed"; "There is no place to pray at Auschwitz." His article should be required reading for today's *Times* writers. Not a word is wasted as he describes the setting for what Hannah Arendt calls "the banality of evil." To not write, he asserts, "would somehow be a most grievous act of discourtesy to those who died here." Rosenthal's response represents our response. He does not distract from his story with long vignettes about other visitors. Rosenthal uses everyday words we can all understand; he writes elegant parallel sentences, and he takes an understated tone that has the effect of accentuating the outrages he describes. But he also can use effective fragments: "Thousands of pictures, the photographs of prisoners. They are all dead now, the men and women who stood before cameras, and they all knew they were to die."

The magnificent understatement of Rosenthal's column ironically becomes a scathing comment on the failure of the *Times* to report the events when it would have mattered. But we return to that subject.

Rosenthal did not want to leave the editorship and resented being pushed out of his position. After his editorship years, he wrote an op-ed page column entitled "On My Mind" from January 6, 1987, to November 5, 1999. In the column, he urged political and religious freedom around the world and took a strong pro-Israel position. Rosenthal showed his somewhat conservative bent as a columnist, but according to Thomas Friedman, his politics never entered into his editing. After having his *Times* column terminated against his wishes, he wrote a weekly column for the *Daily News* from 2000 to 2004.

Rosenthal believed a journalist could ferret out the truth and could define the moral meaning of an event for his readers. In other words, he could mediate the original event and not only tell what happened but shape the story so that the meaning of what happened would emerge. He understood that the writing of a story was different from gathering data and interviewing sources, and was an action of its own. As he put it, "If you don't have a sensation of apprehension when you set out to find a story and a swagger when you sit down to write it, you are in the wrong business" ("Abe Rosenthal of the Times," Editorial, May 12, 2006).

Rosenthal is quoted in that same May 12, 2006, editorial as once saying, "When something important is going on, silence is a lie." This could refer to the *Times's* failure to report the Holocaust, the necessity of publishing the Pentagon Papers, and the need to penetrate the shroud of secrecy that the Bush administration cast over events. Although Rosenthal invented the four-part newspaper and the feature sections, he would have been chagrined, I think, at the direction they on occasion have been taking, the prolixity and pointlessness of some stories, the presence of triviality on the front page, and the movement away from factuality implied in the failure to be the paper of record on roll-call votes or stock quotes. Rosenthal was a morally serious man for whom terms like truth, accuracy, objectivity, right, and courage were values. He would have thought that too many of today's editors and reporters—including some at the *Times*—believe that truth is relative and meaning up for grabs.

By 1984—to make another jump of twenty years from the starting point in 1944—virtually all the articles were written by *Times* reporters, and the *Times*, now in four sections, had changed its format to six columns rather than eight. It was midway between the daily magazine it would become and the straitlaced newspaper of record it had been.

VIII. Arthur Sulzberger Jr.

In 1992, Arthur Sulzberger Jr. became publisher, succeeding his father Arthur Ochs "Punch" Sulzberger, and took over a paper of great stature but with some financial concerns and, notwithstanding its share of Pulitzers, with a reputation of being somewhat staid and lacking innovation in the immediate years prior. He is and has been at the eye of the storm and is a pivotal figure in this story. Since 1992, and especially in the past decade, the *Times* has careened from crisis to crisis. It is worth noting that Arthur Jr. did not succeed his father to the powerful position of chairman of the Times Company until 1997 (with Russell Lewis as CEO in charge of the company's operations reporting to Arthur Jr. as the chairman).

The current Sulzberger—called "Arthur" by his senior staff—spent a lot of time in his early years as publisher defining his leadership as different from his father's, while at the same time seeking to replicate his stature. His father was conflict-adverse; a bright if not slightly arrogant man, Arthur Jr. seems to like at least some conflict and tension. He gives the impression of believing in presumptive privilege due the heir to the *New York Times*.

Born in 1951, Arthur Jr. is a youngish looking man who turned 60 in September 2011. He presents himself as a man of great confidence and takes the initiative in conversation as a way of controlling the agenda. He believes in his own physicality and cites his Outward Bound experience while in high school as important to his development in terms of learning about himself and about the necessity of working as a team. He prides himself on his boldness and ability to survive difficult situations.

He has a liberal ideology expressed in terms of commitment to diversity, and he wants to be loved even though he is hardly loveable. He is proactive, sarcastic at times, loquacious, and has a defensive edge. He conveys the impression that he feels unappreciated for his principled stand on behalf of Judith Miller and for the financial acumen that enables him to produce the most influential newspaper in the world. He prides himself on understanding the business model necessary for the paper to survive.

In an interview, Arthur Jr. challenges the questioner as often as he answers the question. Put another way, he draws the line or puts up a wall between himself and the interviewer. He is wary of dropping his guard. He expects his listeners to understand that he is presiding over an American, if not a world, institution, and that he is not the publisher of a mere newspaper practicing mere journalism. It is as if he regards himself as the secretary general of the Fourth Estate.

Notwithstanding the current financial crisis in the newspaper industry and in particular at the *Times*, Arthur Jr. is presiding over the most important newspaper in the world—one that has notable columnists, experts in a wide range of fields, and produces a remarkable if sometimes flawed product every day. He is in a position where, like a major elected official or university president, his every move is weighed and watched by smart and wary people within the *Times* community and within the investment community. But I would argue that for the paper to survive, it is most important for Arthur Jr. to be in touch with his readers. It is that constituency that has been let down by his often problematic if not wrongheaded decisions, from how the *Times* handled the Wen Ho Lee story and the WMD stories to his appointment of Howell Raines in 2001 and his making the Miller interview with Lewis Libby into a First Amendment issue.

What Arthur Jr. was trying to do in 2005, and, indeed, every day of every year, is imagine what a newspaper should be in 2011—and 2018 and 2029—and how he can deliver a product that will maintain his reader base while attracting future readers. When I asked him how the paper had changed, he responded by citing a front-page article the previous day on the melting of Arctic ice caps, noting that it had been complemented both by a web page and a story on the Discovery channel (then owned in part by the *Times*):

> Ten years ago we would have put it in the paper. Story would have been just as good, graphics would have been just as good, but you wouldn't have had the web element, and we certainly did not have the television element. We would not have been able to offer our customers . . . the depth of

the experience they received via other media, and that's the critical change I think has taken place in *New York Times* journalism in the last decade and speaks as much to our future as does anything. (October 11, 2005; the *Times* sold its stake in the Discovery channel in April 2006)

IX. From Max Frankel to Bill Keller

Frankel, cosmopolitan, genial, and—when I interviewed him in 2005 in his elegant triplex on West 67th Street—forthcoming, proud, yet disarmingly modest, became executive editor at age fifty-six and held the position from 1986 to 1994. His more subdued and democratic style was the antithesis of the dictatorial and irascible Rosenthal's. By abandoning some of Rosenthal's authoritarian ways but not his essential vision of the contemporary *Times*, Frankel democratized decision making but, according to current *Times* historiography, could have been more open to the place that women needed to play in the *Times* of the later twentieth century.

Rosenthal, who had run the *Times* from 1969 to 1986, first as managing editor and then as executive editor—and had beaten Frankel out for the executive editorship in 1976—was something of a bête noire for Frankel. Frankel entitled one chapter of his 1999 memoir, *The Times of My Life and My Life with the Times,* "Not-Abe" to underline his view that his own role was to bring a more collegial style to the *Times.* Their public feud included an article in *Vanity Fair* in 1999 in which Rosenthal castigated Frankel, singling out his memoir for disdain.

Frankel wanted to extend the range of popular culture in both the daily and *Sunday Times*—a goal to which Howell Raines also aspired during his tenure. Under Frankel, the *Times* was transformed into a national paper. The aforementioned special sections that transformed the *Times* more and more into a daily magazine continued, although it wasn't until 1997 that the transformation—with separate sections for arts and sports and the Saturday paper having four sections with an *Arts* section within the *Metro* section—was complete. Under Frankel's leadership, circulation rose but advertising revenues declined.

Notwithstanding some notable successes, Frankel made a major gaffe when he named a woman who claimed she was raped by William Kennedy Smith, a Kennedy relative, in an article that implied that the woman was promiscuous and unstable (April 17, 2001). A few days earlier, in a front-page story, Maureen Dowd previewed *Nancy Reagan: The Unauthorized Biography*, a sensational book by an author with dubious credentials claiming that Mrs. Reagan fooled around with Frank Sinatra while the president was away. Also running in spring 1991 were articles on do-it-yourself sex videos and polygamy in Utah. It seemed as if the *Times* was making an effort—but a tasteless one—to catch up to the sexual revolution; to many readers, the *Times* was embarrassing itself and foregrounding if not inventing a category I call *Timestrash* (see Diamond, *Behind the Times*, 3–8).

Joe Lelyveld was executive editor from 1996 to 2001 before being succeeded for two tumultuous years by Raines, and then again for a few months following Raines's resignation. Unpretentious, straightforward, and modest in person, Lelyveld explained to me that executive editors, even while putting their own stamp on the newspaper, carry out the publisher's policies:

> Whoever was editor during my time was going to bring color into the paper, was going to have a six section paper, it was going to go national and in an aggressive way. Those decisions had been made, and [the paper] was just waiting for the plants to be completed, the Flushing plant mainly. And the Internet happened and somebody had to react to that. It would be crazy for any individual to claim responsibility for corporate decisions. You manage how they're implemented editorially day to day, but the framework was the result of interminable discussion. (June 22, 2005)

It was under his leadership—and that of the managing editor, Gene Roberts—that John Darnton as the cultural editor developed the daily *Arts* section that became a separate entity. Prior to that, the cultural news was the back part of the *Metro* section. The second important change—in September 1997—was to split the Friday *Weekend* section into two sections, with the first for movies and television and the second for fine arts. As Darnton, a worldly man with an institutional memory, recalled to me: "So there was a real push on cultural news in '96. . . . For the first time fine arts had its own front page so now in color you could splash an exhibit at the Met on the front page" (June 21, 2005).

Veteran reporter Clyde Haberman observed:

Joe [Lelyveld] is a bit more of a throwback to an earlier
era. He believes in reporters more than editors so he gave
people in the field a fair amount of freedom, more perhaps than his immediate predecessors. . . . If you speak to
midlevel editors, they probably wouldn't speak of him as
fondly. Part of my view is tainted because I'm friends with
these people so my views are not impartial. I heard a lot of
complaints that Joe just didn't value their opinions. He was
a reporter's editor. Were there great innovations under his
watch? Probably not. . . . Was he a steady, solid, straight-
as-can-be editor? Absolutely. That became reflected very
much when Howell [Raines] had to resign, and the next
morning it was announced that Joe was taking over. Joe's
return was just so desperately seized by staff people who
just wanted a reassuring figure. He provided that reassur-
ance. His contributions in those couple of months that he
was interim editor were as important as his contributions
before. (June 21, 2005)

To complete this historical overview, I briefly turn to the short-lived
executive editorship of Raines and his successor, Bill Keller. Raines's bête
noire was his predecessor, Joe Lelyveld, because Lelyveld represented
the status quo—cautious, risk-avoiding, trusting the reporters to take
the initiative—that is, he represented a path Raines wished to seriously modify. But if the Raines editorship taught the *Times* anything,
it was the need for a less authoritative, more cooperative, and more
self-effacing style of leadership. Undoubtedly, the day of the tyrannical
editor personifying the newspaper is over, and reporters and editors
no longer respond to strong-armed kinds of leadership any more than
faculty do at universities. Raines's editorship would not have lasted
long even if Jayson Blair's bogus articles had not existed.

Raines's successor in 2003, the soft-spoken and confident Bill
Keller, had lost out to Raines in the 2001 competition, but was welcomed
by the staff as the anti-Raines. Keller is attentive to human feelings
and the need for compliments and respect; he is aware that ambitious
and competitive men and women generate more than their fair share
of human tensions. It is not too much to say that Raines mistakenly

thought he could be Rosenthal in the latter's most imperious days, and Keller, especially at the outset, when he wished to be the anti-Raines, followed the examples of Frankel and Lelyveld.

In subsequent chapters, I discuss the contemporary *Times* and the revolutionary impact of the short reign of Raines and the counter-revolution of his successor, Keller. For now let me say that according to the dominant historical narrative in the Times building, Raines, despite his wonderful coverage of September 11, 2001, endangered the *Times* not only by jeopardizing its integrity with the Blair affair and the Miller misreporting of WMDs, both of which took place because of a system that allowed for gaps in editorial and institutional super-vision, but also by abusing his staff. Keller in turn rescued it and is now trying to find its twenty-first-century audience in a digital world. The emphasis is on nytimes.com as the revolutionary initiative that will save the *Times* in the twenty-first century—just as, according to the accepted history within the Times building, Rosenthal and Punch Sulzberger saved the *Times* in the last quarter of the twentieth century.

X. The *Sunday Times*

No brief survey of *Times* history would be complete without men-tioning the *Sunday Times*, in many ways the newspaper's centerpiece. Until 1964 when Punch Sulzberger put Catledge in charge of both the daily and Sunday news staff, the *Sunday Times* was virtually a sepa-rate newspaper, presided over for forty years by Sunday editor Leslie Markel. Markel had transformed the *Sunday Times* since 1923 into a large moneymaker with bountiful advertising and a larger circulation than the daily *Times*. From 1923 to 1948, the *Sunday Times*'s circulation grew from 546,000 to 1.1 million, whereas the daily *Times*'s circulation increased only from 337,000 to 539,000 (Talese, 317). According to Talese's 1969 history of the *Times*, the third floor newsroom residents were more bourgeois and their counterparts on the eighth floor, where the *Sunday Times* resided, were more artistic and bohemian. Certainly through the early 1960s under the leadership of Markel as Sunday editor, the Sunday sections allowed more imaginative analyses than the daily paper.

Catledge's assistant managing editor, Theodore Bernstein, clashed with Markel, whose fiefdom on the eighth floor of the old Times building was increasingly challenged in the later 1950s and 1960s by more interpretive reporting in the daily paper. Analyses had been, with infrequent exception, the exclusive province of *News of the Week* (launched in 1935), which eventually became the *Week in Review*. Markel felt that "Man in the News" pieces were either the province of longer background pieces in the *Sunday Magazine* or, alternatively, shorter pieces in *News of the Week*. By 1972, the daily *Times* had introduced "Reporter's Notebook" and "News Analysis" and "Man in the News" (or on rare occasion, "Woman in the News") to complement the straight news, and these features would on some occasions be on the first page.

Frankel assumed the Sunday editorship in 1972 and held it until 1976 when the daily and Sunday departments were completely merged under Rosenthal. By then the news department produced the *News, Sports, Business,* and *Real Estate* sections and the Sunday staff produced the *Sunday Magazine,* the *Book Review,* the *Week in Review, Arts & Leisure,* and *Travel.* Now that the news section, as Frankel put it, "welcomed analysis and valued polished writing," the need for a separation of editors was not necessary (359). Older readers of the *Times* looked to what was then called the *News of the Week* for context and trends, but now that the daily *Times* was doing the lion's share of contexts and trends, Frankel redesigned the *Week in Review* to include more interpretative articles by correspondents and divided the section into the *World,* the *Nation,* the *Region,* and *Ideas & Trends*—the basic shape it retained until July 2011: "We radically redesigned the section on the assumption its closest readers were news junkies rather than people looking to catch up on news they had missed during the week" (Frankel 367).

As Sunday editor, Frankel also wanted to update the *Sunday Magazine*—begun by Adolph Ochs soon after taking control of the *Times* in 1896—to include more topical political and cultural articles. Although he introduced color and upgraded paper, he doesn't claim much success in developing a serious magazine with topical articles and commentary that could claim a shelf life of more than one week. For example, during his editorship, J. Anthony Lukas's issue-length article on Watergate was a pale facsimile of the work of Bernstein and Woodward. The *Sunday Magazine* did have its successes, including some under Frankel's leadership and some under the editorship of his various successors. But because the *Sunday Magazine* is less read and discussed than it was a few decades ago, perhaps in response to more competition for Sunday's leisure hours, editor Gerald Marzorati—replaced in October 2010 by Hugo Lindgren—valiantly tried to reinvent it.

Frankel wanted to make Sunday's *Arts & Leisure,* which had stressed Broadway theater and some off-Broadway theater, more inclusive and to treat film, television, art, and photography. Gradually, *Arts & Leisure's* discussions of music began to go beyond just classical and include jazz and, later, rock and other popular forms such as hip-hop.

Anticipating Raines and Keller, Frankel wanted to make the *Book Review* more interesting to nonacademic readers and to choose suitable reviewers. The *Book Review's* importance and prestige plummeted when the *New York Review of Books* appeared during the 1962–1963 newspaper strike. With its long reviews by ranking stars, the *New York Review of Books* displaced the *Book Review* as the place where intellectuals turned for serious discussion of books and ideas. Of course what Frankel writes about the *Times's Book Review* also is true of the *New York Review of Books,* if not more so: "Too many of our reviewers turned out to be novelists promoting their own literary achievements or scholars parading their own expertise at a rival's expense" (3).

XI. Diversity at the *Times*

In 1966, Guy Talese, who worked on the *Times* for ten years, wrote in his brilliant but anecdotal *The Kingdom and the Power* of the culture of the *Times*: "There is a very agreeable sense of privilege about employment on the *Times* that can forever spoil an individual who identifies personally with corporate greatness and tradition" (240). Probably the same can be said today. What is different is the gender, ethnic, and socioeconomic mix. Talese was speaking about a time when reporters not only from the *Times* but also from other newspapers tended to be males from the lower middle class, often liberal Jews and more conservative Irish Catholics from the North, with a mix of what Talese calls "progressive Protestants" from the South and Midwest. There were a few Italians, very few women, and virtually no blacks. Characteristically, Talese offers no supporting statistics for this. Later, the *Times* hired Ivy League graduates as copy boys and waited for them to take the initiative and write articles for the *Times* to show that they deserved to be promoted to reporter. At the same time, the *Times* used other papers as a farm system, hiring away those editors and reporters that they deemed worthy, and they continue to follow this policy today.

But what has the *Times* done to achieve diversity? Rosenthal prided himself on opening the doors and windows to women and blacks, but he did not go far enough and he had inherited some major dissatisfaction. In *The Girls in the Balcony*, Nan Robertson chronicled how women in 1972 had rebelled against their lower pay and lower status, and in 1974 sued the *Times*, a suit that was not settled out of court until 1978 and then for a grand total of $350,000 plus the *Times*'s agreeing to an affirmative action plan that would be in effect for four years under court decree. When the women began their rebellion, no woman was on the masthead, no woman was a vice president or in position to become one, and only one woman was in a job traditionally held by men—Betsy Wade, editor of the foreign news desk. Male salaries were considerably higher. The *Times* had one woman star, foreign columnist Anne O'Hare McCormick, and an effective religion reporter, Rachel McDowell, who retired in 1949, but according to Robertson, the *Times* was particularly backward in hiring women journalists. Even during World War II, when more women were hired at other newspapers to replace the men at war, the *Times* was sparing in hiring women. In 1962, Clifton Daniel had reputedly told Eileen Shanahan, "no woman will ever be an editor" of the *Times* (Robertson 238).

In 1989, Carolyn Lee became the first female assistant managing editor for administration. She had the power to hire women and minorities and was the first woman from the newsroom on the masthead. Elise Ross, who ran the computers, was the other in 1991. As of July 2011, six women are on the sixteen-member editorial board, the deputy editor is Carla Anne Robbins, and the prior editorial editor was Gail Collins, whereas in 1972 none of eleven was a woman. By 1991, Robertson informs us in her concluding chapter, "Promises," the *Times* had shown considerable improvement.

I concur with Robertson's view that Anna Quindlen's columns on the op-ed page did much to present a women's perspective—in her case, a perspective that took into account family issues—and that of those who are outside the beltway. Quindlen was the third woman after McCormick and Flora Lewis to have a regular column but perhaps the most important because she spoke with a woman's voice about women's lives. Indeed, it is a shortcoming of the current *Times* that, notwithstanding segues into sexual politics and domestic matters by the tart and tough if not cynical and hyperbolic Maureen Dowd—hired by Quindlen when she was metropolitan editor—it now lacks such a voice. In 2007, Collins became a permanent columnist after her stint as editorial page editor, but her focus so far has been on politics.

According to statistics produced by the *Times* for the American Society of Newspaper Editors, which conducts an annual census measuring the ratio of women and minorities within American newsrooms, the *Times* has made progress in hiring minorities. In 1980, about 5 percent of the *Times* newsroom professional staff (i.e., reporters, editors, artists, photographers) was comprised of minorities, and about 22 percent were women. In 2005, minorities made up about 17.5 percent of the newsroom staff, and women accounted for about 37 percent.

Since 1980, according to recent statistics, the *Times* has almost doubled its minority reporters from 9.9 to 18 percent, more than doubled its minority copy editors from 5.5 to 13 percent, and more than tripled minority newsroom supervisors from 4.1 to 13.6 percent. Since 1980, not only have women copy editors increased from 25 to 41 percent and women supervisors from 16.5 to 40 percent, but according to the *Times*, about half of the department and section heads in the newsroom are women.

The *Times* has made commendable progress toward a diversified staff, although in December 2007 there was only one ethnic minority represented among the top thirteen editorial positions, namely Dean Baquet, who returned to the *Times* in March 2007 as one of nine assistant managing editors after a stint as editor of the *Los Angeles Times*. And in 2010 the same held true of fourteen masthead positions, including the opinion page editors.

As soon as Punch's son Arthur Jr. became publisher on January 16, 1992, he made diversity an important focus. He was committed to being the publisher who transformed the concept of *Timesmen* into *Timespeople* and brought gender and racial diversity to the newsroom. When Frankel was executive editor, and Lelyveld managing editor, Gerald Boyd, as assistant managing editor, became the first black person on the masthead, while Bob Herbert became the first black columnist and Margo Jefferson the first black critic. That Raines announced that he would pick Gerald Boyd as managing editor during the time when Sulzberger was deciding between him and Keller may have helped him convince Arthur Jr.—much committed to diversity—that Raines was the person for the position of executive editor (Mnookin 47).

XII. Conclusion

In the past, I doubt that the proud *Times* would have issued anything like its 2005 apology for its coverage of the war in Iraq. We need recall that the *Times* not only bought into the propaganda about WMDs but also accepted without enough skepticism the pronouncements about progress in Iraq from military and civilian leaders.

I have more to say about the actual apology later. What I want to stress now is how the *Times* had become increasingly skeptical about the administration's policy on Iraq and to note that that this skepticism followed an earlier history of acceptance that ended with the disillusionment that began with government obfuscation during the Cuban Missile Crisis and continued with the Vietnam War, the Pentagon Papers, and Watergate, climaxing in Iraq and now Afghanistan. Thus, the lead story on June 17, 2004, by Philip Shenon and Christopher Marquis, entitled "Panel Finds No Qaeda-Iraq Tie; Describes A Wider Plot for 9/11," begins: "The staff of the commission investigating the September 11 attacks sharply contradicted one of President Bush's justifications for the Iraq war, reporting on Wednesday that there does not appear to have been a 'collaborative relationship' between Al Qaeda and Saddam Hussein." In a hard-hitting lead editorial, entitled "The Plain Truth," the *Times* urged:

> Now President Bush should apologize to the American people, who were led to believe something different. Of all the ways Mr. Bush persuaded Americans to back the invasion of Iraq last year, the most plainly dishonest was his effort to link his war of choice with the battle against terrorists worldwide. . . . There are two unpleasant alternatives: either Mr. Bush knew he was not telling the truth, or he has a capacity for politically motivated self-deception that is terrifying in the post 9/11 world. (June 17, 2006)

Changes in the *Times* are more likely to be evolutionary rather than revolutionary. Each executive editor wants to put his stamp on the *Times*, and each department editor reporting to the executive editor wants the same. But there are strong internal elements of resistance to change in addition to the external resistance of readers and advertisers who tend, on the whole, to welcome the same product each morning and who complain about change.

Reminiscent of senior faculty at elite universities, validated writers and editors often are the most resistant to change. Many *Times* writers have a strong sense of being at the pinnacle of their profession and of working at an institution with a proud history and traditions.

Major *Times* writers are well-paid, highly regarded figures who have not only received recognition in their own fields but also from the other media. Many of the major *Times* writers now appear regularly on cable TV, NPR, and PBS. Op-ed columnists, cultural critics—those who critique books, art, music, and so on—and even the sports, business, and food writers have considerable spheres of influence.

Now many bylined articles within the diverse daily and Sunday sections have particular audiences in mind, but not so long ago the *Times* assumed that its newspaper would be read by an audience that shared important values and ideas. The *Times*'s assumption of homogenous American values and the ideal of one America reflected not only the concept of the Great Melting Pot and the Ochs-Sulzberger family's assimilationist mentality but also the experience of fighting two just wars in the twentieth century and the Cold War that ensued.

For much of the twentieth century, the *New York Times* was a repository of America's historical memories and cultural contexts as well as a record of how we saw ourselves and how the world saw us. Current and back issues of the *Times* are a diary of how our history unfolds from day to day. People who need or want to be informed still read the *Times* to learn what is going on in the geopolitical world and to be sure they know what other informed people know. Once the paper of historical record and what that implied, the *New York Times* is an evolving informational icon, a creator of taste in the arts, and a centerpiece not only of New York City but also of national—and global—intellectual and cultural life. It has had and still has immense social, political, and economic influence on America and the world. Even in the age of instant news on cable TV and the Internet, the *Times* probably contributes as much to how the world perceives American culture as any other news source.

3

Looking Backward

The (Failed) Raines Reformation

The *Times* badly needs to raise the level of its journalism and to do so quickly to survive and make the full transition to a digital age.

—Howell Raines, "My Times," *Atlantic Monthly*, May 2004

Howell [Raines] hurt the paper. . . . He troubled the *Times*. He wanted to revolutionize it, make it tougher. . . . Raines failed completely. The ridiculous affair with Jayson Blair. It's unbelievable what happened in the newsroom.

—Arthur Gelb, June 21, 2005

The brief history, basically, is [that] it was awful under Raines. A lot of damage was done, that kind of damage is not repaired overnight, even under the best of circumstances. And these aren't the best of circumstances because of the economic climate, because of this Miller stuff that popped up, so it was a very tough couple of years between . . . the worst of Raines and the post-Raines Keller period recovery, which I think has been substantial. . . . It's not as gloomy . . . as it was in the Miller period when the paper was just getting hammered and, frankly, people felt it was hard to defend. But, since then, we've had some big journalistic successes. Things have calmed down internally; some of the management things that take time to work out have been worked out. So it's better, but I don't want to minimize the concerns that people have living in this climate.

—Jonathan Landman, October 9, 2006

I. Howell Raines's Vision

Raines convinced Arthur Jr. that, as an unworthy successor to Max Frankel, Joe Lelyveld, Arthur Jr.'s first executive editor appointment, had diluted the front page and had neglected investigative reporting. In some ways, Raines was Sulzberger's Sulzberger, the proactive liberal populist who challenges the status quo and who is confident that he knows best despite what others might think. In the aftermath of September 11, 2001—which occurred in the week following Raines's becoming executive editor—the newsroom won seven Pulitzers and Raines's stress on what he calls "competitive metabolism" seemed to be validated. By spring 2003, when Jayson Blair's fabrications came to light, it was clear that Raines had disrupted the collegiality of the newsroom and, as Ken Auletta puts it, created "an atmosphere of fear and intimidation that eclipsed [Abe] Rosenthal's last years" ("The Inheritance," *The New Yorker*, December 19, 2005, 70).

Raines is a man with strong opinions and a clear vision of what he wishes to accomplish. Raines convinced Arthur Jr. that he—rather than Keller—was the man for the job of integrating the news and business sides of the *Times*, while at the same time developing a larger audience and improving the paper's quality. He convinced Sulzberger that by bringing the newsroom into more efficient shape, he would do well for the bottom line and would thus please the paper's business side. As Raines put it in an email that Auletta quotes, "My own view is that an editor in today's environment who doesn't understand the economics of the newspaper business is under-informed" (70). Wanting to put his own mark on the *Times*, Arthur Jr. chose as executive editor the provocative and comparative outsider Raines over the logical choice, then managing editor Bill Keller. Raines had been editor of the editorial page since January 1, 1993, a position that, as Raines tells it, made him in Arthur Jr.'s mind the most senior of the inner editorial circle, except for the executive editor. We need recall that when Arthur Jr. took over in 1992, Max Frankel was executive editor, and was succeeded in 1994 by Joe Lelyveld. Raines became executive editor in September 2001 at the age of fifty-eight. Given the *Times*'s mandatory retirement age of sixty-five, he knew he had to move quickly to make an impact. Given that he would only last two years, he didn't know how quickly.

Raines's editorship ended with the now well-chronicled revelation that stories about a spate of serial killings in Washington, D.C., filed by a young black reporter named Jayson Blair, were fictitious. Once the Blair scandal broke, the *Times*'s editors began to examine other reporters, and their attention turned to Pulitzer Prize–winning journalist Rick Bragg. A close friend of Raines, Bragg also was implicated in fraudulent reporting, relying on stringers to do his footwork. When writing about the impact of river development on the Gulf Coast oyster industry in the Florida Panhandle, Bragg not only disingenuously claimed a byline for an article given to him by an unpaid freelancer named J. Wes Yoder, but also specified the location as Apalachicola, Florida, a place he had visited only briefly. Bragg's long suit was writing about local color presumably based on his experience of the sights and sounds of the places he visited. While Raines was still editor—he resigned June 5, 2003—the *Times* published an editorial comment explaining Bragg's errors. Yoder's travel and living expenses were paid for by Bragg for the four days when Yoder interviewed the oystermen in the story. Bragg was suspended for two weeks before resigning under pressure in May 2003.

Emboldened by the disintegration of Raines's editorial leadership, *Times* editors and reporters who resented Bragg's arrogance—and believed that he had unlimited access to the front page without editorial control—began to express public outrage. Like Judith Miller, Bragg, who presided over a one-man Southern bureau, "boasted about how he operated by a different set of rules from everyone else's" (Mnookin, 199). To the delight of Bragg's many enemies on the *Times*, his stories on occasion needed serious factual corrections. *Times* correspondents sent letters to Jim Romenesko's media website—Romenesko.com— claiming Bragg's method was not characteristic of the *Times* and was in fact abhorrent. According to Bragg, Sulzberger at first backed him when his lapses in reporting were exposed, even going so far as calling Bragg to thank him for "taking one for the team" (Mnookin, 202).

According to a May 29, 2003, article by Jacques Steinberg, "Rick Bragg, a Pulitzer Prize-winning national correspondent for the *New York Times*, resigned yesterday, five days after the newspaper published an editors' note that said he had relied heavily on the reporting of a freelance journalist for an article about the oystermen of the Florida Gulf Coast." It is notable that the article—perhaps reflecting an unrevealed agreement with Bragg—highlights that he resigned on his own volition rather than being fired, a pattern repeated in the more flamboyant resignations of Raines himself and Judith Miller. The *Washington*

Post and other media had a field day with the Bragg revelation and his dismissal posing as resignation because it once again diminished the stature of the *Times*. After Raines's demise, the Bragg case became another catalyst leading to the tightening and codifying of the *Times*'s standards as soon as Keller succeeded him.

What Raines claims in his postmortem "My Times," published in the *Atlantic* after his resignation, says a good deal about how the *Times* sees itself: "The *Times* not only occupies a central place in our national civic life but also plays just as important a role as the ethical keystone of American journalism. . . . It is the indispensable newsletter of the United States' political, diplomatic, governmental, academic and professional communities, and the main link between those communities and their counterparts around the world" ("My Times," *The Atlantic Monthly*, May 2004). Not surprisingly Raines's sense of the *Times*'s importance echoes that of his predecessors, his successor, and past and present senior editors.

Each executive editor has his own vision and believes in some major ways that he can improve the *Times*. Convincing the publisher that his vision is the right one is the reason he is chosen for the position. In this sense Raines was no different from his predecessors. Where he differed was in his lack of people skills, a shortcoming that took the forms of egomania, arrogance, belittling the judgment and contribution of others, and a confrontational style. Yet Raines's postmortem, although often defensive in nature to the point of narcissism, speaks to issues still debated in 2011 in the *Times*'s offices.

Russell Baker, longtime former columnist of the *Times*, retrospectively observed: "With Sulzberger's choice of Raines, the publisher was making a stronger statement of ownership prerogative than the newsroom was in a mood to accept. The newsroom feeling was chilly before he stepped on the scene and turned surly as he began taking charge" ("A Bad Morning at the *New York Times*," *New York Review of Books*, April 29, 2010, 6–8).

In his May 2004 *Atlantic Monthly* piece "My Times," Raines rightly claimed that if the *Times* did not modernize in significant ways it would not only lose its place as the most important newspaper in America but cease to exist. In Raines's view, "The *Times* is its own country. . . . [I]t is a culture that requires mass allegiance to the idea that any change, no matter how beneficial on its surface is to be treated as a potential danger." With his characteristic sense that he is smarter and harder working than his colleagues, he spoke of his being brought in to "confront the newsroom's lethargy and complacency" and to "raise our competitive metabolism." Clearly, he still saw himself as the white knight appointed by Arthur Sulzberger to restore health to the wasteland in order to get "the *Times* off its glide path toward irrelevance," but now unjustifiably sent into exile.

Like Frankel—the editor who retired early in part to keep Raines from getting the editorship before his then close friend Joe Lelyveld—Raines was in the tradition of editors who wanted to transform the *Times* into a national newspaper, but Raines characteristically acted as if he were the first to think about this issue. Echoing Frankel, but without Frankel's skills in dealing with people, Raines saw his role as "stripping away the New York parochialism—and editing perspective—that made our national edition a matter more of cosmetics than of substance. Further, it meant aiming our papers at a national audience that was catholic in its interests and worldly in its tastes" (8).

How, Raines asked—and he was hardly the first to ask this question—could the *Times* attract as readers not only more smart and affluent people in the New York area, but a great deal more of those people in the entire country? Raines felt that the national edition was not sufficiently different from the New York edition and that it didn't meet the interests of the wider audience. For example, he thought that the Monday *Sports* delivered to the Atlanta readers should focus on the Atlanta Falcons not the New York Giants. Furthermore, he felt that the lack of business news meant the *Times* wasn't meeting its circulation potential in the New York area although two-thirds of its circulation came from New York.

My interviews, which took place from a more retrospective and considered vantage point, reinforce the view expressed in Mnookin's 2004 *Hard News* that Raines's demise owes more to his posturing and autocratic management style than to Jayson Blair's bogus articles. In his characteristically direct and straightforward style, Jonathan Landman concurs: "It's important to understand that the events of that period were not mainly about Blair. He became a catalyst for a staff rebellion against two of its leaders [Raines and managing editor Gerald Boyd]. They are both gone" ("Talk to the Newsroom," April 28, 2006). Or as Soma Golden Behr put it to me: "One of the worst things about Howell was that he was a dictator. After he got seven Pulitzers, our seven Pulitzers, he didn't listen to any voice of objection. Traitors—it was a terrible atmosphere. And finally it just blew us apart. I hope it never happens to this place again and I hope Arthur [Sulzberger, Jr.] is vigilant" (October 11, 2005).

It is worth remembering that an internal uprising far more than the Jayson Blair scandal undid Raines. To most of his employees, he was a megalomaniac. Senior women, many of whom asked for anonymity, felt he was a misogynist and that his commitment to diversity did not extend to women leaders unless, as one put it, "they had cleavage." As Gerald Marzorati put it to me in evaluating what went wrong with Raines's editorship: "The days of a generation where the editor of the New York Times could stand up and thunder and pound his desk and scare people, you can't manage that way anymore. The world doesn't work that way anymore" (April 18, 2005). Rosenthal got away with this modus operandi, especially in his later years, but this kind of management style no longer works in newspapers any more than it does in corporations or universities.

Gone are the days when one labored in anonymity waiting years for a byline. Editors must work with their reporters, some of whom are prima donnas who do not write as much or as often as the editors would wish. If not given some latitude and stroked regularly, the writers might take other positions. Indeed, as I got to know how the Times operates, I realized that the editors need the kind of diplomacy one sees in the administration of major universities and that coercion often gives way to stroking.

Where Raines went wrong was his dismissive attitude to many if not most of the Times editors and reporters. Many of these people took great pride in their accomplishments and work ethic, and had received considerable validation in the Times as well as the wider world of journalism. In his "My Times" Atlantic Monthly piece, Raines describes a situation in which "the motivation and energy of the staff were . . . low" and many staff members had virtual sinecures. According to Raines, "the culture of achievement" struggled with the "culture of complaint." He speaks of the "tribal pathology" of those in the newsroom: "As a group, they tend to be politically liberal in regard to the government's domestic policy, conservative in regard to the location of their desks, rebellious in regard to the Times stylebook, and anarchic in regard to the paper's management" (19). He barely contains his disdain for a group that did not adjust to his thinly disguised arrogant and autocratic style.

Some of Raines's ideas did have substantial impact. Raines rightly believed that the financial section had to be improved, that popular culture couldn't be ignored, and that hard news "could not drive circulation growth on the scale that was needed." He was also correct that electronic journalism had been neglected. In his post-mortem, he expressed his views with his characteristic self-confidence touched by his propensity for hyperbole: "Our coverage of culture, entertainment, style, and travel was in fact in shambles, under funded, unimaginative, and devoid of any unifying editorial sensibility." John Darnton, who once had been the *Times*'s cultural editor, spoke to me rather disdainfully of Raines's idea of culture in comparison with the ideas of earlier editors who respected high culture: "Under Howell that changed dramatically. He bought the argument that the *Times* could be sold in 40 million households if only it was more in tune with what he thought people wanted: pop music, country music, films, hip hop, and television" (June 21, 2005). Yet, Raines's ideas on cultural coverage seem to have prevailed and are very much part of the present *New York Times*. Certainly Keller's editorship carried on Raines's mandate for change in these categories.

In the face of Raines's and managing editor Gerald Boyd's resignations and the Blair scandal, the *Times* was faced with the issue of how to retain Sulzberger's and Raines's laudable goal of diversity and the use of affirmative action initiatives in hiring and training without sacrificing merit.

II. In Raines's Own Words: How He Understands the Raines's Reformation and Its Demise

It is December 13, 2005, and I am sitting in former *Times* executive editor Howell Raines's living room in front of his fireplace on his small farm in Henryville, Pennsylvania, after a delicious lunch of stewed chicken, which his wife cooked for us. He tells me that he has turned to novel writing and has sold his New York City home. Raines's house reflects his tastes, especially his interest in fly-fishing and hunting. Unlike most people I know, he has a hunting rifle mounted on the wall and has a hunting dog named Pointy.

Proud of his Southern heritage, he likes to talk about his family and displays in his home an elaborate family tree going back to a time

before the Civil War. In his view, being a Southerner is "an advantage. . . . It never hurts to be a little different. It gives me a bicultural
vision." He is an Alabamian whose family members fought on both
sides of the Civil War. He has a strong interest in that war, especially
Sherman's campaign that devastated much of the South. I found myself
thinking that, ironically, Raines's campaign to reform the *Times* had a
Shermanesque effect on the *Times*.

In my interview, it was clear that Raines wanted my good will and
was eager to rehabilitate his reputation. He claimed not to have met
with anyone the way he was meeting with me. "This is the only and
longest conversation since I left the paper and the most I have thought
about the *Times*." He has, he told me in 2005, recused himself from
the *Times* and claims to read it only occasionally. But what becomes
apparent to me is that he has been thinking a great deal about the
Times and what derailed him. Raines agrees with Sulzberger's view
that "local newspapers were dying." According to Raines, by the late
1990s, the market didn't then exist demographically for the current
paper and his evidence was that circulation was declining. His goal
was to get the paper into the hands of a broadly sophisticated audience
of professionals, business leaders, and academics across the country
without abandoning the tri-state base, which provided a microcosm
of the intended national audience. In his words, he wanted the *Times*
to be the "newsletter of ruling class."

Raines's postmortems, although often defensive in nature, give
voice to issues that were and still are regularly debated within the
Times's offices. Raines probably has reconstructed history to fit his
own psychological needs, but who doesn't? Although he has a gracious
manner and makes my wife and me feel comfortable, he takes few
questions and tells his own story. Talkative, outgoing, proud, genial,
casually dressed, paunchy, strongly opinioned, outspoken, grey-haired,
intellectually rigorous, Raines offers an impressive macrocosmic overview of the paper. He calls himself a populist—he graduated from
Birmingham-Southern College and has a certain suspicion of academic
elites—and a liberal. Much affected by the Civil Rights Movement, he
asserts, "I am a classic bleeding heart liberal." In his view, "Even our
worst presidents—Herbert Hoover, Calvin Coolidge—would have had
a plan to rebuild New Orleans [after Katrina]."

Raines often offered his analyses in the present tense as if to emphasize that Bill Keller's *Times* hasn't caught up with Raines's vision. Perhaps

another reason Raines speaks in the present tense as if he were still editor is that he cannot quite let go of the fact that he has been deposed.

As executive editor, Raines had, in his words, "no desire to preside" or be a "custodian." Indeed, he defines himself as "evangelical" in
furthering his beliefs. He understood, as he puts it, that "Newspapers are
dying because they are a technology that in some cases is still operating on nineteenth-century mechanisms, people rolling out papers and
putting bands on them. . . . The technology is dying and the audience
is aging." In his view, the future of newspapers hangs in the balance
because they have failed to habituate readers to the new conditions for
media. The *Times* had not yet learned how to address its audience—an
audience accustomed to quality—in a world now used to instantaneous
news. Like other newspapers, the *Times*, in his view, was before his
editorship and once again after his editorship not sure what newspapers
should be doing. He also believed that the *Times* was lagging in both
short- and long-term investigative journalism: "That is to say I wanted a
twin investigative potential: long term, people working on projects about
business or defense spending or something of that nature that would take
months, maybe even years to develop and a short-term capability where
there is a grand jury investigation, there is a business scandal, Enron,
you have people who have the reporting skills to go in and give short-
term capability, which is basically half what Woodward and Bernstein
did on Watergate." In Raines's view, his predecessor, Joe Lelyveld, had
not taken Frankel's lead in pursuing investigative journalism.

To be a national paper, Raines believed, the *Times* needed to
put money into non–New York news. Raines told me that he feels
he inherited a strong *Metro* section but that the *Times* needed to do
more with national news:

> What I was setting out to do is to build a *New York Times*
> and when I say I, this was Arthur, myself, Janet Robinson
> and the core management team around us, I would say a
> group of about eight to ten people around us, but what
> our common strategy was, it was this. It was to look at
> where we were financially. We were still strong enough in
> New York City to build a national newspaper. That national
> newspaper had to appeal to a broad range of people who
> were not defined by where they lived, [that is] Brooklyn,
> Queens, Westchester, but were defined by what they did,

professionals, governmental leaders and civil service, academics, people in finance, so our paper had to be as appealing to the associate history professor at Kansas State as it was to the female investment banker in Houston as it was to the film maker in LA as it was to Wall Street in New York. In other words, the problem was to make the paper more broadly sophisticated and to get it in the people's hands.

Raines's executive editor agenda stressed raising the quality of the journalism and focused on addressing what he believed should be the *Times*'s target audience, and that necessarily included finding "[a] younger audience by appealing to their interest." To raise the quality of journalism, he relied mostly on the so-called New Journalism, which he saw as a more elegant and stylish kind of writing than what he thought of as "stenography," that is merely reporting the facts. As he put it to me: "The earmark is sophistication, and you can write about anything within the *Times* context. . . . You need a body of knowledge and ability to think as well as ability to write."

Indeed, one of Raines's bugaboos is what he called, in an email two days after our interview, "stenographic style" or "a return to stenographic journalism," which would "hobble the growth the paper must have." In that same email, Raines expressed to me his belief that *Times* readers revel in the joys of a writerly performance and that that kind of writing is indispensable to the paper's growth:

> The new readers the *Times* has to find will be attracted by writing that informs and also delights with its elegance or sophistication of style, thought, and wit. The search for writers inside and outside the paper who could do that was what was underlying all the talk about a "star system." As long as there have been newspapers, reporters who write well have been pursued by editors and have been the object of envy in their newsrooms. Today there is, as there has to be in order to cover the demographic swath we discussed, an even greater premium on this kind of talent.

In defense of his star system, he claims to have raised the bar on salaries for the best reporters. Reporters, he asserts, were used to being "economic outsiders," and his predecessors believed in a narrow salary band. He takes credit for a higher salary cap, raising it from $150,000 to $200,000.

In some ways, Raines identifies with Abe Rosenthal, a Jew with a City College education: "[Rosenthal] is the most important editor of the twentieth century" (December 13, 2005). As I have noted, Rosenthal was something of an outsider, but one who was valued by friends and enemies as a great writer as well as a strong editor who imposed his will on the shape of the *Times* and breathed new life into the *Times* as an institution. If Rosenthal was Punch's dramatic choice to revivify the *Times*, Raines was Arthur Jr.'s bold choice. Rosenthal stressed the idea that reporters should combine knowledge with a lively style, a kind of literary revolution replacing "here's the news." Like Rosenthal, Raines's roots were in the newsroom, and he sees himself as an advocate of the newsroom and its reporters. He makes no apologies for his star system: "I am a creature of the newsroom. I've never known a newspaper where the best reporters are popular."

After the successes of 9/11, when the paper won seven Pulitzers—"the greatest journalistic period of my lifetime"—Raines felt he had the political capital to improve each section very rapidly and the confidence to heal wounds. I want to call attention to how, in the previous quotation, he describes the seven Pulitzers. He doesn't say the "greatest journalistic achievement of the *Times* in my lifetime"—that is, stress the Pulitzers for 9/11 as part of the *Times*'s narrative—but conflates the Pulitzers into something in his own life narrative, as if they belonged more to him rather than the *Times*. Raines doesn't second-guess his strategy or his decision to act when he had the opportunity:

> I felt that I had the political capital to go through the paper in a course of about a year and replace the editors who I knew needed to be replaced and to just work through the paper section by section taking basically good sections like business and sharpening their focus, taking other sections like culture and revitalizing them and reclaiming our heritage, taking sections like travel that had never been looked at, taking [the] book review which I felt had slid down the slope, to go through that very rapidly because I thought that I had the political capital coming out of those first six months to do it. . . . But there was a land mine and his name was Jayson Blair.

Raines knew that an additional problem was that "change scares people." He felt that he could reinvent the paper; he thought he had a window to make these changes:

> It was a rational plan. I covered national politics for my entire professional career and I knew that there was dissent and discomfort because I was changing [the newspaper] so rapidly. . . . I felt that we had an irreplaceable window of opportunity. I did not seek the job; I was not running for president of the eighth grade. I wanted to make the dynamic changes that I thought were needed for the survival and improvement of an indispensable American institution. . . . I am a gregarious person and made a calculated risk, thinking I could deal with personnel issues. I wanted to make the *Times* more meritocratic.

Although he is credited with insisting that Gerald Boyd be given the position of managing editor—and by many accounts Boyd was not a very effective one—he now says "I didn't build a managerial team. I didn't reform the antiquated personnel bureaucracy."

Although Seth Mnookin's *Hard News* narrates in detail the story of Raines's rise and fall, he does not discuss how the actual writing and the selection and arrangement of stories changed during Raines's leadership. Raines believed that the *Times* had been slow in recognizing big stories. Under Raines, the *Times* stressed massive coverage of some major stories at the expense of others, as well as what he called "all that is known" summary stories. To some extent, Raines wanted to refocus energy on the developing story and to do so with massive coverage. Thus he wanted strong focus on "breaking stories" such as the 9/11 disaster or the Washington sniper stories.

As executive editor, his great triumph was the *Times*'s response to 9/11. The *Times* excelled and won Pulitzers for its extended coverage, including succinct biographies of the individuals who died in the 9/11 attacks. How Raines handled 9/11 derived from his ideas about blanket coverage of major stories and, of course, the fact that the *Times* had its resources in Manhattan, where 9/11 took place. Because of the number and quality of the *Times*'s reporters as well as its budget, Raines believes the paper's coverage of major stories could overwhelm its media competitors: "We need to concentrate forces on point of attack—as Grant did in the Civil War. You pay a price for being late. It took twenty years to get back on track after Watergate. You need to see over the horizon and see where a story is going. Do saturation coverage." He thinks this is especially important for major international news: "I had covered the first Iraq war and watched Rumsfeld and Cheney insulate the news. . . . I wanted a team in Afghanistan who were not part of the Pentagon pool."

Raines believes international reporting is "the jewel in the [*Times*'s] crown." When I intervene and say that I think international reporting has slipped, in part because of the demands of the war in Iraq and in part because the number of nations we now think are important has expanded far more than the international staff has grown, he concedes that it has: "We need a larger news budget. . . . We need [at the *Times*] to budget more into reporting international and national news. Across the media, international reporting has been dismantled." Raines does concede that the focus on hot spots means ignoring others: "The crisis of moment shapes foreign news."

One key to understanding Raines is that he is intensely competitive:

> I think my idea is better than yours and I am going to work as hard as I can to beat you and that is the kind of world it is. . . . I was talking about making the *Times* more strictly meritocratic. Whenever you talk about doing that . . . you threaten the old boy network and you also surface great anxiety among a broad swath of people who are afraid that they can't compete at the high level, and so when you say you are going to raise the bar, and you know the charge against me was that I believed in the star system, yeah I believe in people who can write and think in a way that is superior to other people's ability.

Raines sees everything as a contest and his reference points are often Civil War battles and football rivalries. His competitiveness leads him to think of *Times* journalists in terms of levels of competence; he thus featured his small stable of star reporters at the expense of many equally capable, or even better, journalists. Sometimes it seems as if he were more concerned with winning—whether it be Pulitzers or outsmarting his rivals—than with truth: "One of the things I used to say was that the one thing the South figured out in the Civil War was that you needed to concentrate your forces at the point of attack. . . . I saw that the *Times* was a paper with superior resources that was constantly getting beaten because it was late to recognize what was happening and then piecemealing its resources and that by the time it was in a position to use its resources, the story had been trademarked by someone else."

It is as if, to Raines, journalism was a version of the Alabama–Auburn football game, and he was the coach of Alabama speaking about a game plan. Thus, he saw his mission in terms of scoring enough points to defeat his rivals. The *Times*, he stresses, needs to be competitive on many levels. It needs to compete with *USA Today* in sports because that paper had become the paper of record when it came to sports. He also wanted to remake the *Business* section, which he felt was not competitive with the *Wall Street Journal*. Although he knew that major developments in terms of mergers and acquisitions were the *Wall Street Journal*'s beat, he wanted to be aware of secondary stories in business and publishing that the *Wall Street Journal* might have underestimated, such as mergers under the $500 million level. The Sunday *Book Review* had ceded belle-lettres to the *New York Review of Books*, and needed to reclaim its position by treating books as cultural events. The now-cancelled *Escapes* section was invented under Raines by John Geddes, one of the two current managing editors, to steal the thunder from the *Wall Street Journal* weekend edition that was aimed in part at upscale professional women with children. As Raines said to me, "I don't know what they have done with [*Escapes*] since but it was lively and it stole some coverage journalism from the *Journal*."

If what comes through in conversation with Raines is his competitiveness, that competitiveness also is tinged with some bitterness about his demise as editor. When he speaks of working at the *Times* as "swimming with sharks," I smile to myself, thinking that I am with one. He describes Keller as someone who could be a "Machiavellian," although no one else I spoke to saw Keller in this way; if anything others fault Keller for being too nice. Raines doesn't work for Keller and maybe some of my interview subjects were being circumspect. Yet I have been in the Times building and spoken to enough senior staff to see that Keller is not regarded as a Machiavellian. Raines believes Lelyveld, for whom he doesn't have much regard, "dulled down the front page." He is explicitly critical of Keller's *Times*: "I don't see the theme in the pudding." Or as he put it later in our email correspondence: "My worry for the future is that targeting the same audience of habitual *Times* readers with the paper as it now exists is not a formula for longevity or for journalism of a higher literary and intellectual content" (December 28, 2005).

In Raines's mind, before he took over, cultural reporting at the *Times* had been deteriorating. Although he doesn't quite name Lelyveld, that is who he holds responsible, as he makes clear by praising Lelyveld's predecessors, Rosenthal and Frankel. Raines believed the *Times*'s segregation of low and high culture needed to be broken down. In his view, hip-hop needs to be understood in terms of what he calls the "cultural matrix, that is, gangsta rap is about cultures arguing over money. . . . It's not about two gangs calling each other ugly names, it is about an economic competition in which Sony and every other major communications organization is involved. You have to seek things I think in their socialized matrix" (December 13, 2005). One can see how Raines the populist also has a professorial side and a bent toward conceptual explanations that include jargon.

Raines believes in putting news in a sociological context: Max Frankel, whom he regards as the "smartest" previous executive editor of the *Times*, "took heat for bringing in 'sociological news' and started us down that road." Raines also believes the *Times* should do more passionate advocacy. An example is the now much-ridiculed front-page stories about why women should be admitted into Augusta National, the club sponsoring the Masters golf tournament. Raines sees himself as an outsider and his successor Keller as an insider and believes his focus on the Masters called on the carpet the hypocrisy of the haves who preached diversity in their public life but didn't practice it in their private lives: "[R]eporters in my generation were generally economic outsiders. . . . I don't know how Bill [Keller] would have covered it, but his father was president of a major oil company and I think he has a much more tender attitude towards corporations than I ever had or ever will." It is on class, sociological, and advocacy grounds that he defends his controversial coverage of the Masters tournament; for him the Masters is "a crucible for prejudice. First all white, then all male. It is a sociological test tube" and an instance of how as a populist he fought "pro-corporate bias."

Although many of his senior editors agreed with him on the Masters issue, they believed it was not suitable for a major crusade, given that the club would still be a playground for the wealthy, were women playing there. I concur with the senior editors, but I do think Raines has a point in believing sports commentary in the *Times* should follow the NPR model of relating sports to American culture. To be sure, the 2010–2011 *Times Sports* section edited by Tom Jolly has moved in that direction, and, most notably, William C. Rhoden does this often in his columns.

III. Raines and the WMDs Story

Coming to terms with Raines's editorship means coming to terms with bogus stories about WMDs in Iraq. Raines seems to have given Judith Miller free rein, unlike other reporters, in part because of his belief in the star system. For a populist, as my interview makes clear, Raines had a strong elitist strain.

In a February 26, 2004, *New York Review of Books* essay, Michael Massing discusses how the Bush administration manipulated reporters and especially Miller: "Especially controversial has been Miller's alleged reliance on [Ahmed] Chalabi and the defectors who were in touch with him" (43). Chalabi arranged many of the interviews on which her articles about WMDs were based: "By late summer of 2002, then, Miller had developed a circle of sources who claimed to have firsthand knowledge of Saddam's continued push for prohibited weapons" (44).

Michael R. Gordon and Judith Miller's September 8, 2002, lead *Times* article claimed that Iraq was making an effort to purchase "specifically designed aluminum tubes" for making atomic bombs in Iraq ("US says Hussein Intensifies Quest"): "The diameter, thickness and other technical specifications . . . had persuaded American intelligence experts that they were meant for Iraq's nuclear program." The same article also speaks of Hussein's efforts to "develop new types of chemical weapons" and speaks of how "an Iraqi opposition leader"— whom we now know with some certainty to be Chalabi—was passing information to American officials. The allegations in this article became accepted as truth in the administration's justification for going to war. On the morning of September 8, Colin Powell, Dick Cheney, and Condoleezza Rice all referred to this particular September 8 *Times* article, the source of which is "Bush administration officials." In other words, administration officials were basically citing either themselves or their own spokespeople.

The *Times* compensated for being gulled not only by printing its internal examination of its WMD stories (although on page 12 of the May 26, 2004, front section), but also by taking a strong editorial position on Bush's misleading the nation (and of course the *Times*). In a lead editorial following the publication of the Senate Intelligence Report on the prewar assessment of Iraqi weapons, the *Times* indignantly indicts Bush for prevaricating: "Put simply, the Bush administration's intelligence analysts cooked the books to give Congress and the public the impression that Saddam Hussein had chemical and biological weapons and was developing nuclear arms, that he was plotting to give such weapons to terrorists, and that he was an imminent threat" (July 10, 2004). On June 19, 2004, the lead editorial, entitled "Show Us the Proof," asks Cheney to give us evidence to support the tie between Iraq and Al Qaeda; the editorial angrily concludes: "[H]e wants us to trust him when he says there's more behind the scenes. So far, when it comes to Iraq, blind faith in this administration has been a losing strategy."

On May 26, 2004, the *Times* wrote a strong editorial self-critique entitled "The *Times* and Iraq" and referred readers to an online list of articles entitled "The *Times* and Iraq: A Sample of the Coverage." The *Times* notes: "On the subject of the meeting in Prague, a *Times* follow-up cast serious doubt" and cites an October 21, 2002, piece, "Prague Discounts An Iraqi Meeting." Because in his *Times* columns William Safire continued to insist that 9/11 hijacker Mohammed Atta met with an Iraqi intelligence agent in Prague—and, to my knowledge, never deviated from this position—Keller no doubt felt a special responsibility to revisit and debunk the alleged Prague meeting. Safire's columns fell within the purview of the then editorial page editor, Gail Collins. Still, we might recall Raines's belief that "The role of columnists is to raise hell and attract attention," a comment that emphasizes Raines's stress on selling newspapers at all costs, and may give us insight into why he left Judith Miller—although a reporter and not a columnist—unchecked to write sensational news stories (December 13, 2005).

On May 30, 2004, public editor Dan Okrent visited the subject of why the *Times* took so long to review its reporting on WMDs in Iraq and strongly takes the *Times* to task on this issue: "To anyone reading the paper between September 2002 and June 2003, the impression that Saddam Hussein possessed, or was acquiring, a frightening arsenal of WMD seemed unmistakable. . . . Some of the *Times*'s coverage in the months leading up to the invasion of Iraq was credulous; much of it was inappropriately italicized by lavish front-page display[s] and heavy-breathing headlines" ("Weapons of Mass Destruction? Or Mass Distraction?"). Okrent might have mentioned, too, Safire's continuing repetition of the false information that Hussein's operatives met with Al-Qaeda in Prague, for that raises the issue of when we can say opinion becomes misrepresentation of facts and when the *Times* op-ed editor needs to insist that a columnist admit his or her error.

Okrent particularly faults Judith Miller's April 21, 2003, front-page piece "Illicit Arms Kept Till Eve of War, an Iraqi Scientist Asserts." At one point the *Times* editors had stressed, "Don't get it first, get it right," but now—and especially with the WMD tales— Okrent implies the reverse may be true. He implies that under the leadership of Raines, the *Times*'s standard editing procedures were cast aside and "that a dysfunctional system enabled some reporters operating out of Washington and Baghdad to work outside the lines of customary bureau management." He implies that the *Times* was duped by its sources, including the former exile Ahmed Chalabi, an administration favorite who proved to be an unreliable and manipulative source.

Jack Shafer in *Slate* provided evidence to support Okrent's view. Citing the reporting of the *Washington Post*'s Howard Kurtz, Shafer wrote that a *New York Times* internal email memo from Miller to the *Times* Baghdad bureau chief John Burns stated: "[Chalabi] has provided most of the front page exclusives on WMD to our paper"; Miller added that the MET Alpha—a military outfit searching for WMD after the invasion—"is using Chalabi's intelligence and document network for its own WMD work" ("Reassessing Miller," May 29, 2003). Shafer convincingly concluded:

> None of Miller's wild WMD stories has panned out. From these embarrassing results, we can deduce that either [:]

1) Miller's sources were *right* about WMD, and it's just a matter of time before the United States finds evidence to back them up; 2) Miller's sources were *wrong* about WMD, and the United States will never find the evidence; 3) Miller's sources *played* her to help stoke a bogus war; or 4) Miller deliberately *weighted* the evidence she collected to benefit the hawks.

In retrospect, we can say that a combination of 2, 3, and 4 were at work.

After reporting on its news pages on May 22, 2003, that the CIA was reassessing its prewar intelligence about Iraq's weapons program, on May 26, 2003, the *Times* voiced concern about the WMD revelations on its own editorial pages: "The failure so far to find any weapons of mass destruction in Iraq, the prime justification for an immediate invasion, or definitive links between Saddam Hussein and Al Qaeda has raised serious questions about the quality of American intelligence and even dark hints that the data may have been manipulated to support a pre-emptive war." In Shafer's May 29, 2003, article, he offers a telling commentary: "If the government must re-examine whether data may have been 'manipulated' to support the war, surely the *Times* should conduct a similar postwar inquiry of its primary WMD reporter, Judith Miller. In the months running up to the war, Miller painted as grave a picture of Iraq's WMD potential as any U.S. intelligence agency, a take that often directly mirrored the Bush administration's view."

In 2011, Raines is still held responsible for not being enough of a gatekeeper where Miller was concerned and is blamed for letting her have free rein. He acknowledged to me that he should have done more, but justifies his own behavior and points his finger elsewhere. He conveyed a sense that he feels betrayed by his senior editors as much as by Miller herself:

> In this case because Judy was working for an editor that requested her, because we knew what the public parts of the White House . . . were saying, yes these stories [seemed] correct. To my regret I didn't ask those [questions.] I mean some of them common sense would tell you, you know, you're quoting Chalabi, you're quoting the Pentagon, you're quoting the White House, you know those are the sources. But, I did not . . . go through the exercise that I sometimes went through of asking who was the specific source. The reason

I didn't was that I felt our customary way of handling these stories was sufficiently strong at that time because I thought even knowing Judy's history as I did. . . . She had sort of reclaimed her position by virtue of winning the Pulitzer and getting in these other stories and I thought that she was under sufficient managerial control through the investigative cluster of the Washington bureau. (December 13, 2005)

In our interview, Raines denied that he knew Miller's sources despite Miller's contention to the contrary. Raines contended that the *Times* should reveal which editors were responsible for assigning and editing Miller's stories, although among current staff members he is credited with giving her free rein. He asserted that the *Times* so far has engaged in damage control in contrast to the full disclosure that took place under his leadership when the Blair scandal broke. Clearly, he strongly felt that just as he was held responsible for the Blair mess, so Keller should be held accountable for the Miller mess.

IV. After Raines's Departure:
The Counter-Reformation Under Bill Keller

After a brief interregnum during which Lelyveld returned for a few months, Raines was succeeded by the losing candidate for executive editor in 2001, Bill Keller, whom Raines had insisted be demoted from managing editor when he took over so Raines could install Gerald Boyd as the first minority managing editor. With more developed people skills than Raines, Keller's immediate task was to restore morale and he accomplished that in his first months. He has sought some of the same goals as Raines in emphasizing cultural coverage, but has emphasized evolution rather than revolution. As Keller put it to me:

To some extent I have never been comfortable with the notion that people who run things need a long term vision of the future and [someone] to lead them there. My job is to hire and promote good people and place them in a good environment so they can do their best work. It is more about evolution than leading an institution to some place and time. Our big issues are the same ones that all news organizations have: one is clearly about the migration away from print newspapers into other media and how to survive that evolution. Another issue is whether or not the next generation of readers will read newspapers at all. (October 11, 2004)

In 2005, with great disdain, then deputy managing editor and now cultural editor Jonathan Landman summarized the Raines editorship to me: "With Howell there was no reformation. It was all bullshit. It was all gas; he transformed nothing, though he talked about it a lot" (January 21, 2005). But when I asked, "How did they ever put Raines in charge? How did a guy like this whom everybody hated get this position?" Landman responded:

> Well it's not that simple. I worked for Howell in Washington when he was bureau chief there and I had a great experience. . . . I was deputy editor in the bureau, and he was at that time a terrific newsman, one of the best political journalists I have ever met, I learned a lot from him. He had his ticks and his grandiosity and so on, but all within the normal limits amongst the peculiar people who occupy the world of journalism—they are a quirky bunch. . . . [But] something happened, and these grandiose tendencies that were visible then had taken over and it was very, very destructive. It went much deeper than simply a matter of style—some people didn't like his style—but the substance was a big problem.

In chapters 6, 7, and 8 we take a hard look at Keller's *Times*. But it is fair to say that in his early years as executive editor, Keller gradually restored a good deal of the *Times*'s credibility, balance, and dispassionate stance toward news stories without sacrificing analyses or the widening parameters of personal writing that evolved in the past decades as part of the paper's signature style. He appointed the first standards editor, Allan M. Siegal, to pursue conflict of interest and ethical issues. It is the role of the journalistic standards editor to make sure that when the *Times* errs, it makes corrections, and to monitor whether the *Times* is practicing fairness in its presentation of issues. Keller—and indeed virtually every senior editor with whom

I spoke—is aware of the unprecedented suspicion under which the news media labors today. With increased scrutiny from blogs, Siegal claimed that "we have to explain ourselves and prove we mean well, and in ways that we wouldn't have had to before" (quoted in Calame, "Anonymity: Who Deserves it?" August 28, 2005).

Because of the latitude and respect Keller gives his senior staff, he began as a great favorite. Assistant managing editor Glenn Kramon explained the Keller counter-reformation to me:

> We went from a Stalinesque regime to something opposite. Bill is someone who listens so carefully and is so slow to express his own opinion by design that we've gone from being something like a dictatorship or absolute monarchy to [something] much more like Voltaire's benevolent despot in *Candide* where he is a very smart guy who listens and decides but he really depends on a large group of people to help [him] manage the organization, and he knows the strengths and weaknesses of those people, certain people for certain things. (June 22, 2005)

Although the current editors know that the *Times* always will be a competitive place with sharp elbows, there has been under Keller more emphasis on community and working together than during the Raines era. I do not think that this is just lip service from toadies but something felt in the newsroom by reporters and editors.

Until the 2005 issues of Judith Miller's imprisonment, testimony, and forced resignation, Keller was still enjoying a long internal honeymoon in the wake of Raines's despotism. To longtime staff writers such as Clyde Haberman, who in 2005 acknowledged to me that after two years as executive editor and four as managing editor, Keller was for him not an easy man to read: "What I haven't figured out about Keller is how much of some of the changes that have taken place . . . is a true vision he's had all along, and how much he had to be reactive to his immediate predecessor, Raines" (June 20, 2005). Others with whom I spoke in 2005–2006 noted Keller's remoteness and enigmatic nature. Gradually, some of the staff had begun to wonder if his laissez-faire policies were indicative of intellectual fuzziness and lack of strong leadership.

From the outset, Keller was aware that the *Times* from motives of fairness and self-interest needs to reach out to a larger audience; as

Kramon explained to me: "We try to do less judgmental journalism than our most liberal readers would want" (June 22, 2005). But Keller has given the individual section editors and writers unprecedented leeway and perhaps accelerated the descent into *Timeslite* and *Timestrash* in the back of the book. Keller focuses on a balance of hard news and magazine content. His concept of hard news is not the big story for its own sake, but a tendency to follow events when they need reporting until the big story, like Katrina, emerges. And his blanket coverage of that disaster was something of a triumph. But he would have probably done less with the sniper story in the Washington metropolitan area that undid Blair and finally helped undo Raines.

In contrast to the passionate liberalism of Raines, Keller, according to Kramon, wanted to show an awareness of the world beyond the liberal perspective and understands that "It's a more complicated world: it's not just us versus them" (June 22, 2005). In his early years, Keller did not appease either the conservative critics or those growing numbers who could not stand George W. Bush. Keller knew he couldn't please Karl Rove, Bush's political guru, who always saw biased coverage. But after meeting with Rove, Keller acknowledged with a generosity or foolishness that probably annoyed much of his senior staff: "I do think he was channeling a feeling [based on deep hostility to the liberal media] about the . . . *Times* that's out there in the land, that we should be concerned about, or at least aware of" (Lemann, 2005, 168). Keller knew how difficult it was to please an administration that glorified the coverage of the partisan and irresponsible Fox News at the expense of the more balanced coverage of the other and older networks—CBS, NBC, and ABC—as well as of the *Times* and the *Washington Post* and even the traditionally Republican *Chicago Tribune,* and gave scoops and interviews to Rush Limbaugh.

As a developing story with human interest implications, Hurricane Katrina was Keller's 9/11—that is, a major story with the potential to make his reputation—and for more than a month he titled pages of the national news "Storm and Crisis." At one point, fueled by testimony from the city's police commissioner and the New Orleans mayor, the media was dominated by stories of rape and murder, mostly by poor blacks. The *Times,* which sensationalized the story less than cable TV and much of the media, revisited the claims of violent crime in a front-page story "Fear Exceeded Crime's Reality in New Orleans" by Jim Dwyer and Christopher Drew (September 29, 2005). This investigation into past claims was not enterprise journalism at its best because even the retrospective look at what happened in New Orleans relied as much on hearsay as on facts, but it did begin the necessary process of correcting hysterical and hyperbolic claims by overwrought officials. As the years passed, a different story has emerged of racially motivated violence on the part of white vigilantes and police (Trymaine Lee, "Rumors to Fact in Tales of Post-Katrina Violence," August 26, 2010).

The *Times* took a mostly skeptical stance toward the federal government's behavior on 9/11, but it often effusively emphasized the competence of New York mayor Rudy Giuliani and the heroism of the rescue workers and firemen. (Senior staff members with whom I spoke in 2007–2008 regarded Giuliani as something of a clown when he ran for president.) By contrast, in 2005 the *Times* held the city government of New Orleans as equally culpable with the incompetent federal response. On September 26, 2005, its lead editorial was entitled "Faking the Katrina Inquiry" and began with a scathing indictment of "The White House and [the then] Republican-controlled Congress" for "resisting popular support for an independent, nonpartisan commission" while "remain[ing] determined to run self-serving bogus investigations." This editorial was characteristic of the increasing anger on the *Times*'s editorial page under Gail Collins toward an administration that the *Times* felt reeked of cronyism, deception, and incompetence.

Keller's front page supported the editorial page's indictment of George W. Bush's handling of Katrina. On the same day, the left lead story—"Many Contracts for Storm Work Raise Questions / Lack of Bidding Cited / Officials Say US Agencies Risk Waste, Fraud, and Political Favoritism"—claimed that contracts for storm work were being given out without bidding or with limited competition to political cronies (Eric Lipton and Ron Nixon, September 26, 2005). According to the inspector general for Homeland Security, "Bills have come in for deals that apparently were clinched with a handshake, with no documentation to back them up."

But the Lipton and Nixon story also reveals one of the problems Keller has been having trouble solving. Characteristic of the current *Times,* with its emphasis on narrative journalism, human interest, and magazine chattiness rather than core news, the story's third paragraph, rather than the first, carries the essence of the story: "A month late, a review of the available evidence now shows that some, though not all, of the most alarming stories that coursed through the city appear to be little more than figments of frightened imaginations, the product of chaotic circumstances that included no reliable communications, and perhaps the residue of the longstanding raw relations between some public officials and members of the police." The first two paragraphs describe the rumors of anarchy and "gangs that were raping women and children"—the gang-raping rumors proved untrue and anarchy rumors were grossly exaggerated—but I would argue that the real lead is the third paragraph.

Although Raines gave latitude to a few of his favorites, such as Rick Bragg, Keller gives more freedom to all his writers to write somewhat more self-dramatizing and performative pieces that reveal their personalities. This generated some fine coverage of Katrina from the viewpoint of the victims, but sometimes lost the larger threads of the story. Keller's Katrina coverage did not win a Pulitzer, and probably he could have better coordinated reporters by having someone write a daily analytic overview, but he did cover Katrina and its aftermath and implications quite well and solidify his reputation in many quarters as a worthy executive editor.

Readers of Keller's 2004–2005 *Times* saw a continuing process of change to the point that they did not know in terms of content or design what to expect. Do readers want to see that much change or do they want more continuity? Is a newspaper a kind of benchmark of stability? For example, did they want the quarterly *Sophisticated Travel* section to become a *"T"* magazine more on the order of the *"T"* style magazines with celebrity contributors? Do they want articles on nude hot-tubbing and nudist camps? Or on house rentals of $36,520 for two nights—even if one divides the cost among friends? Do they want Sunday *"T"* sections that are really sites for advertising more than information?

Let us return to the *Times* May 26, 2004, *mea culpa* piece. Keller—with, of course, the approval of Arthur Sulzberger Jr.—printed a remarkable apology for the *Times's* Iraq coverage. Although I found in the following self-examination almost as much self-justification as apology, I was impressed by the lack of arrogance and self-righteousness. Certainly, such an apology would not have been forthcoming under the Raines regime:

FROM THE EDITORS
The Times and Iraq
Published: May 26, 2004

[O]ver the last year this newspaper has shone the bright light of hindsight on decisions that led the United States into Iraq. We have examined the failings of American and allied intelligence, especially on the issue of Iraq's weapons and possible Iraqi connections to international terrorists. We have studied the allegations of official gullibility and hype. It is past time we turned the same light on ourselves.

In doing so—reviewing hundreds of articles written during the prelude to war and into the early stages of the occupation—we found an enormous amount of journalism that we are proud of. In most cases, what we reported was an accurate reflection of the state of our knowledge at the time, much of it painstakingly extracted from intelligence agencies that were themselves dependent on sketchy information. And where those articles included incomplete information or pointed in a wrong direction, they were later overtaken by more and stronger information. That is how news coverage normally unfolds.

But we have found a number of instances of coverage that was not as rigorous as it should have been. In some cases, information that was controversial then, and seems questionable now, was insufficiently qualified or allowed to stand unchallenged. Looking back, we wish we had been more aggressive in re-examining the claims as new evidence emerged—or failed to emerge.

The problematic articles varied in authorship and subject matter, but many shared a common feature. They depended at least in part on information from a circle of Iraqi informants, defectors, and exiles bent on "regime change" in Iraq, people whose credibility has come under increasing public debate in recent weeks. (The most prominent of the anti-Saddam campaigners, Ahmed Chalabi, has been named as an occasional source in *Times* articles since at least 1991, and has introduced reporters to other exiles. He became a favorite of hard-liners within the Bush administration and a paid broker of information from Iraqi exiles, until his payments were cut off last week.) Complicating matters for journalists, the accounts of these exiles were often eagerly confirmed by United States officials convinced of the need to intervene in Iraq. Administration officials now acknowledge that they sometimes fell for misinformation from these exile sources. So did many news organizations—in particular, this one.

Some critics of our coverage during that time have focused blame on individual reporters. Our examination, however, indicates that the problem was more complicated. Editors at several levels who should have been challenging reporters and pressing for more skepticism were perhaps too intent on rushing scoops into the paper. Accounts of Iraqi defectors were not always weighed against their strong desire to have Saddam Hussein ousted. Articles based on dire claims about Iraq tended to get prominent display, while follow-up articles that called the original ones into question were sometimes buried. In some cases, there was no follow-up at all.

On Oct. 26 and Nov. 8, 2001, for example, Page 1 articles cited Iraqi defectors who described a secret Iraqi camp where Islamic terrorists were trained and biological weapons produced. These accounts have never been independently verified.

On Dec. 20, 2001, another front-page article began, "An Iraqi defector who described himself as a civil engineer said he personally worked on renovations of secret facilities for biological, chemical and nuclear weapons in underground wells, private villas and under the Saddam Hussein Hospital in Baghdad as recently as a year ago." Knight Ridder Newspapers reported last week that American officials took that defector—his name is Adnan Ihsan Saeed al-Haideri—to Iraq earlier this year to point out the sites where he claimed to have worked, and that the officials failed to find evidence of their use for weapons programs. It is still possible that chemical or biological weapons will be unearthed in Iraq, but in this case it looks as if we, along with the administration, were taken in. And until now we have not reported that to our readers.

Yet the *Times* should have apologized for its coverage and identified the culprits much earlier. Keller later acknowledged that he should have moved faster. In an October 21, 2005, memo to staff, he blamed his slowness on the paper's having gone through the "major trauma" of the Blair episode, and its need "to regain its equilibrium." The *Times* did not name Judith Miller in the apology as the main culprit for most of the disinformation.

The Raines reformation left the *Times* in disarray and turmoil. To an extent, Keller's early years as executive editor—what I call the counter-reformation—was a serious and sometimes effective effort to put Humpty Dumpty back together again. Yet, as we shall see, due to a variety of business problems that were out of Keller's control—most notably the effect of the Internet plus rising costs—along with some problematic decisions well within his control, the *Times* in 2011 is in perpetual crisis.

4

Digital Revolution

www.nytimes.com

I don't think it's a given that the printed *Times* will be gone in twenty years . . . [I]t's possible that the *Times* will exist as a kind of collector's item, sort of a boutique product for some smaller population that likes it.

—Bill Keller, May 20, 2010

My role . . . was to erase the boundaries between print and online journalism and make it that everyone thinks not in terms of platform, but in terms of presentation and readers.

—Jonathan Landman, June 9, 2010

Welcome to what you have to do: you grow and you expand or you begin to contract and die, and there's no such thing as stability in life and there's no such thing as stability in business. You're either growing or you're dying. We're growing.

—Arthur Sulzberger Jr., October 10, 2005

People are coming to the newspaper for the same thing they always came for. I don't think that's terribly different although, obviously the newspaper's changed quite a bit in the last twenty, thirty years. I think people do come to the web with quite a different and broader range of expectations of what they are going to find. They come to read the news, same as the newspaper, but they also come transactionally, they come to find out what time the movie is [and how] they can buy [their] movie ticket. Increasingly, they come to participate themselves, on blogs and other things. The range of how they use [our website] is greater, the people who come from a search engine to one article, read it or don't read it and never come back. [There are] people who obsessively are on there all day and all night. I think in the case of the newspaper . . . there are people who read the whole thing and people who read part of it, but it's a narrower range [of experience].

—Jonathan Landman, October 11, 2007

There's friction because we're going through a state of turmoil. Turmoil meaning change. . . . We're going through a decided change. The web is growing, and the desire of the newsroom to participate in the production of news on line is growing. There's a lot of ongoing discussion about who should manage it.

—Jim Roberts, April 12, 2007

I. The *Times* on the Web: nytimes.com

The Internet is a response to the future, but the *Times* is not at all sure what that future is. Nothing illustrates the foregoing better than Arthur Sulzberger Jr.'s own 2005 words:

We will follow our readers where they take us. . . . If they want us in print, we will be there in print. If they want us on the Web, we will be there on the Web. If they want us on cell phones or downloaded, so they can hear us in audio, we must be there. . . . At the end of the day, it is the audience we collect and the quality of that audience that is the critical factor, not the means by which we collect it. (quoted in Katharine Q. Seelye, "At Newpapers, Some Clipping," October 10, 2005)

As its masthead figures and other luminaries openly acknowl-edged in 2004–2006 interviews, the *Times* was institutionally puzzled by the long-term effects of the Internet, and they were not sure how it should respond or how to plan for the future. The *Times* senior business and editorial figures knew that the role of print media was changing and that its potential audience got rapid and visual informa-tion from TV and the Internet. It took some time for the *Times* to become fully aware that it publishes in a world in which the Internet plays an important role for many readers. The *Times* continues to put enormous resources into its digital site, nytimes.com, where virtually everything but the print classifieds appear, although one can purchase classifieds that appear both online and in the newspaper.

On January 20, 2010, the *Times* announced plans to charge its website users for frequent access to its website. On March 28, 2011, the *Times* introduced a paywall and began charging for use of more than twenty items a month on its website, including articles, slide shows, and videos. The original offer started at $15 every four weeks, $195 a year, for unlimited access to web content and the *Times*'s smartphone app. For $20 every four weeks, or $260 a year, the package includes the *Times*'s iPad app and unlimited web content. To get both applications, the cost is $35 every four weeks, or $455 a year. The *Times* was soon offering an introductory rate of 99 cents on any package for the first four weeks.

For the past several years, the website has been increasingly conceived as crucial to the *Times*'s future. In the past decade, the *Times* has devoted a great deal of its energy to converting itself into an Internet newsgathering operation as well as to integrating the print edition with the digital edition, nytimes.com.

In March 2009, the *Times*'s website reached over 20 million unique visitors per month—although these figures vary widely depending on sources—whereas the the print edition reached 2.9 million readers Monday through Friday and 4 million Sunday readers. At that time, approximately 18 percent of the online audience read the newspaper once a month. In January 2011, the *Times* claimed more than 38 million unique users each month.

As former deputy managing editor Jonathan Landman, who was a pivotal figure in the development of the digital site between 2005 and 2009, told me, measuring Internet clicks is not an accurate science:

> [T]he apparent precision of [measuring use of] the Internet is a complete myth. I mean, it seems logically as if you ought to be able to measure every click, right? It's a click. The machine knows. But the fact is, if you look at the different agencies that count this stuff, they're not only different, they're wildly, improbably, ridiculously different. We have had at the same time a page view count by one methodology that puts it up at billion a month and another that puts it

at 150 million and they're both supposed to be respected methodologies. . . . It's all bullshit. (June 9, 2010)

Launched in 1996, the site originally simply printed selections from the *Times* without ads, but it did include the first discussion forums in which readers could post their comments on particular subjects. By 1998, the site was updating during the day, including the stock market, and was organized by subjects. By 2000, the site was updating more frequently; in Version 3 readers were talking to one another in Readers' Opinions and more forums. Version 4 introduced more search engines, and Version 5, the current one, introduced in 2006, made the site more user-friendly, adding "Public Editor," "Podcasts," "Multimedia," and "Blogs" to its categories, and linking the *Times* site more to the blogosphere and to other newspaper and magazine opinions and discussions. Indeed, as I have discussed, the *Times*'s reliance on its own blogs and its surveys of the blogosphere have become more and more pervasive between 2006 and 2009.

Throughout 1999–2009, nytimes.com was continually evolving, changing rapidly, and offering its readers more and more audio and visual material. Landman was appointed in the first half of 2006 as the *Times*'s deputy managing editor, overseeing digital journalism. (In September 2009, Landman became cultural editor.) He was the person with broad responsibility for the *Times*'s web operations. He supervised the digital operations—the nonprint journalism—including the website, TV, and audio. Leonard Apcar, the then editor-in-chief of nytimes.com, has been succeeded by Jim Roberts, who ran the continuous news desk and is now an assistant managing editor.

On June 30, 2006, Landman announced the integration of the continuous news desk and the web newsroom under the newly created post of editor of digital news, a post held by Roberts, who was a former national editor and reported to Landman. Originally, as Roberts explained it to me:

> The continuous news desk [was] a small group of report-
> ers and editors, most of whom work between the hours of
> five in the morning till eight at night, [and] sort of provide
> a bridge between the print news room and the web news
> room. It was set up in 1999 at a time when the website was
> in its infancy and there wasn't a lot of enthusiasm among
> the reporting staff—the day-to-day reporting staff—to con-

tribute stories for the web as they do for print. I think the continuous news desk is something of a transitional device. It probably won't exist in its current form in the next five years—five years from now because I think . . . that news departments will be able to do this kind of work on their own. (April 12, 2007)

Until the 2007 move to the new building, the continuous news desk was in an adjunct building rather than in the main Times building. Now a reporter specializing in updating the website sits at every major desk and there is far better integration between the printed paper and nytimes.com.

In 2011, the goal is to have an online paper with greater depth than the printed newspaper and with equal accuracy or, as Landman put it, "quality stories on a second-by-second deadline" (quoted in Calame, "Breaking News: Can Times Quality Be Preserved Online?" November 19, 2006). Sometimes the stories are from the AP, sometimes they are written by the staff. According to Roberts, "We use staff stories during the day when the news is significant enough AND when we can bring a level of reporting and analysis that will help readers better see and understand the event" (quoted in Calame, November 19, 2006). Richard J. Meislin, then associate for internet publishing, spoke to me of his role in integrating the technical and newsroom aspects of nytimes.com: "[W]hat we essentially were trying to create was a situation where the newsroom would have the same kind of control in making an excellent website as the . . . newsroom has traditionally had in making an excellent printed newspaper" (April 13, 2007).

On rare occasions, printed stories for various reasons need to be omitted from the web. Thus, on August 28, 2006, the *Times* withheld from its British audience an article on the top of its U.S. home page entitled "Details Emerge in British Terror Case." To avoid violating British laws that prohibit publishing prejudicial information about defendants before trial, the *Times* adapted technology that was intended to be used for target advertising and thus easily withheld the article from the British print version of the *International Herald Tribune*. In an August 29, 2006, article in the *Business* section, Tom Zeller reported how, by means of several hours of programming, this was done on the Internet. Citing Meislin as his source, Zeller wrote: "[The *Times*] could already discern the Internet address of users connecting to the site to deliver targeted marketing, and could therefore deliver targeted editorial content as well." (I assume Zeller's piece was available online in the United Kingdom, but am not sure.)

The *Times* has reached a point where its website is driving the newspaper. Because the website appears all day, it impacts what is in the newspaper the following morning. It is not an exaggeration to say that the *Times* believes its very survival depends on figuring out how to make its website profitable. In the seven years I have been working on this book—a period in which a good percentage of my own reading of the *Times* has gradually shifted to the website—the role of nytimes.com has dramatically increased in importance and has become as much if not more the focus for me as the daily newspaper. The archival date on an article now refers to when it was posted online, with small gray letters at the bottom of the article telling the reader when and where it appeared in the printed newspaper; for example, "A version of this article [on how the Democrats in Congress are addressing health care] appeared in print on July 18, 2009, on page A1 of the New York edition." When such a note is absent from an article, it means that the online article did not appear in print.

The *Times* has entered a brave new world where the emphasis is on giving readers a reason to enter its site and click on a story—any story. It wants to engage a generation of readers who rely on the Internet for news and for buying many of their essentials. In 2011, the *Times* fervently believes that this is the future, and clicks are monitored to see who is reading what and whether readers finish what they start.

But how can the *Times* integrate the newspaper and the website so readers will want to have access to both, and be willing some time in the future to pay for both? In March 2011, the *Times* offered three other services nonsubscribers can pay for:

1. Times Reader;

2. Replica Edition, which shows the newspaper online exactly as it appears in print; unlike the Times Reader, this electronic edition is not updated throughout the day; if downloaded it can be read off line; and

3. Premium Crosswords (the daily puzzle and crossword archives).

Times Reader costs $5 a week, or $260 a year. Replica Edition costs $14.99 a month or $179.88 per year for a Monday to Friday subscription. It costs $19.99 a month or $239.88 a year for a seven-day subscription. Premium Crosswords costs $6.95 a month or $39.95 a year.

Subscribers have access to all three of these products, although finding the Replica Edition takes some work. Excluding the revenue from its online products and subscriptions, the *Times* relies on advertising to pay its web costs. Subscribers can sign up for a once-a-day pdf TimesDigest, about nine pages long, including some major international and national articles; it lacks advertising and pictures and arrives about 2 a.m. in the Eastern time zone.

The problem the *Times* has is how to make the site create a necessary revenue stream. *TimesSelect*, charging for columns and puzzles, was a paywall failure, but it became obvious that something had to be done to complement online advertising revenue, which still lags behind expectations and does not pay the site costs. By the end of 2009, the *Wall Street Journal, Newsday,* the *Financial Times,* and some smaller papers were charging for content, and many other papers were looking into it and waiting for the *Times* to take the lead. But it is uncertain which, if any, major newspapers will follow the *Times*'s lead.

Under the new paywall system, subscribers, including those who subscribe only on Sunday, have unlimited access to nytimes.com on all days. Articles accessed through such search engines as Google and Yahoo! as well as social media such as Facebook are free. This system was designed to "have little effect on the millions of occasional visitors to the site, while trying to cash in on the loyalty of more devoted readers" (Richard Perez-Pena, "The Times to Charge for Frequent Access to Its Web Site," January 20, 2010). A number of other possibilities had been discussed, including a monthly fee. Fees of $5 for nonsubscribers and $2.50 for those who subscribe to the paper had been mentioned in a survey targeting existing subscribers. There had been talk of charging by usage, but that would take more complicated technology.

As 2010 closed, the question still remained, "How to balance the print and electronic edition?" As Richard Berke, assistant managing editor for news, explained to me:

> It's a constant question about how to balance the [website and the printed paper]. . . . [M]y job really is to spend most of my day thinking about page one in the next day's paper. What we're going to put on page one, and when and where and. . . . The website just makes those instantaneous decisions without all this deliberation. And then we'll think

we're making the page one decision in the newspaper. Well, that story has been on the website all day, how should that effect what we do with it in the printed paper. Or should it? Have people looked at our website? So all these questions sort of hover over everything and there's no real answer to some of these things because we're all kind of feeling our way to the future. (October 9, 2006)

Not surprisingly, the early evidence showed a somewhat reduced number of hits, but the evidence did not speak to a full monthly cycle. According to Heather Dougherty, director of research at Hitwise.com, there was a five to fifteen percent decrease in hits between the twelve days before the implementation of the *Times*'s paywall and the twelve days after. To get around the paywall, users can access articles through Google or social media, such as Facebook. This viewing does not count toward the monthly limit.

Sometimes the first appearance of web stories—especially those that pertain to the economy—are misleading, as when giant profits reported by Citicorps and Bank of America on July 17, 2009, turned out, as the day progressed, to be based on one-time assets sales that created a false impression of the return of good times. *Times* business writer Floyd Norris played an important role in reframing the story. The final article appearing online and in the printed paper the next day, "Citigroup and BofA [Bank of America] Profits Aided by Asset Sales," basically reversed the original headlines online: "While both banks said they were again turning handsome profits, the cheery headline figures masked a sober reality: the results were driven by one-time gains—bonanzas without which both banks would have lost billions" (Michael de la Merced, July 17, 2009). These errors have been occurring less frequently in recent years because, after the new Times building opened in 2007, the digital *Times* staff was completely integrated with the print staff.

Chuck Strum, associate managing editor and the then night editor, explained to me how the final rewritten story for the 10 p.m. close of the first edition is more authoritative than the ongoing web story: "One of the problems that we encounter, I think, is that you have a story on the web at two o'clock in the afternoon, and you know you're going into the paper at ten o'clock when it closes the first edition with a story that's substantially different or more enriched in a certain way that makes the two o'clock in the afternoon story or the three o'clock or the four o'clock in the afternoon story way out of date because we know more, and we reach more people, and there's been more reporting, or the circumstances have changed" (October 9, 2006). Strum compared the web with a 24-hour news radio show "You're a 24-hour news radio program in a way, except the web is our radio, if you will, and the paper is still the paper that comes out on your doorstep in the morning". But I think that the *Times* website is far more substantive and authoritative than 24-hour news radio and has far more international and political depth and range. Moreover, the *Times* website also often posts analyses and investigative stories earlier than the 10 p.m. edition.

II. Change in the Reader's Role

The website is a hypertext where, rather than reading sequentially, the reader can enter and depart when he or she wishes. To be more precise, nytimes.com is an example of *hypermedia*, a term used as a logical extension of the term *hypertext*, in which audio, video, plain text, and nonlinear hyperlinks intertwine—one might say, build on one another—to create a generally nonlinear medium of information. It is worth emphasizing that the actual newspaper itself has become more and more a hypertext in which most readers follow their own inkling, while fewer and fewer readers turn the pages the way I was taught to read the paper, making my way first through the A section, then the B, and on to *Business*, *Sports*, and the daily rotating magazine sections.

What this means is that readers become their own gatekeepers, whereas when one reads sequentially, the *Times* determines what its readers read first. When the *Times* introduced the multisection paper to replace the two-section paper, sequential reading gave way for most readers to pick-and-choose reading, but the *Times* still controlled what readers might learn. The newspaper used to be an informational sit-down dinner but now it is a smorgasbord. Put another way, the *Times* is inviting readers to open the door of their private world a crack and let the *Times* in. "All the news that's fit to print" becomes "What each and every reader wants to read."

An old joke about the *Times* credo, "All the News that's fit to Print" was "All the news that fits, we print." On the digital site there really is no space limit and the site can refer readers to other news resources and blogs or the reader can Google them himself or herself. The *Times* has created a newsgathering product that responds to individual reader demand rather than simply supplying one product for all. The concept of editorial gatekeeping has changed, and by participating in the blogosphere—really conceding that most of the blogosphere is accessible by just one more click to another site—the *Times* gives readers access to multiple interpretations of the news to complement, supplement, and contradict what it is providing.

With increasing frequency, the *Times* is relying on staff blogs with interactive features and links to other blogs to supplement the Internet coverage that replicates the newspaper. Relying often on such new media as YouTube, Twitter, Facebook, and cell phones for its sources, "The Lede" blog gave impressive coverage of the 2009 Iran election crisis even after its reporters were forced to leave. In this interactive universe, readers now can participate in blog discussions by having a conversation with the individual writers and with each other. Sometimes, readers think they have different information than appears in the newspaper when all they have is gossip or a spin on the information garnered elsewhere, but they nevertheless are encouraged to express their opinions.

Twitter is a service that allows users to give their followers updates about what they are doing by means of text-based messages called "tweets," which must be under 140 characters. Tweets can include links to other websites, videos, and pictures. Tweets are received as text messages, email, or on the Twitter website, where each user has his or her own profile. The *Times* has twitter.com/nytimes on which it posts news updates and for which it has more than three million followers. A few *Times* bloggers and many of the sports writers also use Twitter, the latter posting frequently on the sports pages and especially while important events are taking place.

Anyone or any organization can set up a Facebook page, and the *Times* has done so and invited anyone who wishes to join. Joiners are called fans. As of March 2011, the *Times* had 1,185,668 "likes" to whom it sends the same news updates. Individual blogs such as "City Room" also have established a fan base, but so far the *Times* bloggers have a relatively small fan following; "City Room" had 2,914 "likes" in March 2011.

By using Twitter and Facebook, the *Times* is reaching out to younger readers and trying to solidify a new subscriber and user base. Some under thirties and even older readers check Twitter and Facebook many times a day.

Let us return to standard blogs. It is worth noting that with occasional notable exceptions, virtually all independent blogs—those unattached to major media—that are focused on international and national issues rely on information gathered by mainstream media. Thus, many blog readers who think they are getting something special are only getting reprocessed versions of the same information—often with a polemical point of view. Of course there are notable exceptions, but what happens is that we have the illusion of a democratic informational system and one that speaks to our sense that postmodern reality is complex and only can be apprehended through multiple points of view. The illusion is of multiple sources. But in fact, the informational sources are all the same and what varies are the interpretive communities, most of which manipulate the news for their own polemical and sometimes materialistic ends.

Although not often acknowledged in the discussion of the Internet, the freedom the reader has within the blogosphere is limited by the actual information available, and so-called inside information often is speculative if not bogus. Thus, in the interactive Internet universe—and even on radio and television, which recycle the blogosphere when not contributing to its flow of skewed information—opinions are given more credence and facts less credence than they were traditionally in the best newspapers such as the *Times*.

Inviting readers to customize their own reading experience is a radical shift in the newspaper paradigm away from authoritative coverage toward radical democratization, for now the individual reader—as much as newspaper editors—decides what he or she needs to know. It is an acknowledgment that we live in our own world as well as in a shared one, and each of our stories is different. In past decades, it was almost as if the *Times* felt an obligation to take its readers into a public world of world affairs, politics, and culture. Paradoxically, the Internet reminds us that we live in a shared world and yet, as Joseph Conrad wrote in *Heart of Darkness*, "we live, as we dream—alone."

More than in the print edition, readers become their own gatekeepers on the web because they make the choice of what they read by a click. When turning pages something hitherto ignored might catch the reader's attention. As Landman put it, "One of the best things about reading a newspaper is serendipity. You turn pages and stumble across such interesting and unexpected things. . . . On the web, that's harder to do. The web diminishes the power of editors, and that's both good and bad. It's good because it lets readers pursue their own interests, ignoring editorial judgment that doesn't reflect their worldviews. It's bad because editorial judgment can sometimes challenge people's world-views in constructive ways" ("Talk to the Newsroom," April 28, 2006).

In the Project for Excellence in Journalism's annual report, *The State of the News Media 2006,* the unidentified authors write: "Power is moving away from journalists as gatekeepers over what the public knows. Citizens are assuming a more active role as assemblers, editors and even creators of their own news. Audiences are moving from old media such as television or newsprint to new media online."

Yet, even on the Internet *Times* editors are still gatekeepers, if in a more limited way, as they decide which stories to highlight and how to headline stories so as to grab attention. Variation in headline sizes and layout are still ways that the editors maintain some gate-keeping function. Editors still decide what information to present and how to package it, and how to make the Internet website innovative, interactive, and still the *Times.* For example, the website is more concerned with national and international news rather than metro news because, according to Landman, "People using our website visited more than half a billion pages in March. About 15 percent of those pages were visited by people in the New York area" ("Talk to the Newsroom," April 28, 2006).

One must add that glitches, as all users know, are not uncommon on the website, although they are far less frequent than they were even a few years ago. One could click on a story and get a message saying that the page is unavailable. Sometimes nothing happens at all or an entirely different story appears. On other occasions, particularly with following sports stories, some clicks don't access the site. These are not random but daily occurrences. For weeks in early 2008 professional basketball fans could not access "transactions" and were sent to the nytimes.com member center where they were told the page was "not found." On June 18, 2009, Bill Keller's podcast on Iran under the rubric "The Takeaway"— something of a scoop since the executive editor was in Tehran—was quite difficult to find; inaccessible under podcasts or in a search of the *Times* site, it turned up on the Middle East section of "World."

III. The *Times* on the Web:
What the *Times* Provides Electronically

To get the newspaper emailed to you everyday all you need to do is provide your email address to nytimes.com. At about 4 a.m. EST the *Times* mails Today's Headlines to anyone requesting them, and that includes a partial version of the printed newspaper and on occasion some material that is only online. Each day shortly after midnight, the *Times* makes available the entire printed paper on the Internet. Also, in addition to the daily headlines, you can choose which sections you want—*U.S., Politics, World, New York Region, Arts, Editorial, Op-Ed, Technology, Sports, Business, Daily Featured Section.* You can also get versions of Today's Headlines called European Morning and Asia Morning, which stress content from those areas.

The format for reader selection of News Alerts continues to become more user-friendly. Once a nytimes.com reader establishes an account, he or she can log into "My Account," decide which subjects he or she wants to receive alerts for—defined by keyword, subject, or a particular stock—and which of a number of stipulated categories he or she would like to receive email newsletters about.

Desperate for revenue streams, the 2011 *Times* has become a facsimile of a mall gift shop under the rubric the New York Times Store. Surprisingly, the *Times* advertises its widely diverse products—from such collectables and memorabilia as a Moon Page signed by Buzz Aldrin to Abraham Lincoln cuff links—far more in the print edition. Products include T-shirts and hats with the paper's logo and an Isaac Mizrahi–designed scarf and bag in the colors of the Times building and a medallion with a T. Also for sale are historically and culturally important front pages, such as the ones for Obama's inauguration and the death of Michael Jackson. (The choice of the pop culture icon Jackson is itself indicative of the change within the past decade in the *Times*'s focal audience and consequently the *Times*'s focal subjects.) Readers can buy these products online or by phone. Because the *Times* even has links to buying movie and theater tickets, I assume that this too is part of the grand revenue scheme that seems based on the theory that every little bit counts.

The *Times* also offers online personal development or professional enrichment classes taught by both *Times* people and the staff at differ-ent universities under the auspices of the New York Times Knowledge

Network. Because most of these classes have a fee, I assume that this is another product to help create revenue. It is worth noting that the *Times* is, in some cases, lending luster to small and perhaps less well known universities in the process.

From September 2005 to September 2007, the *Times* charged nytimes.com readers for a package called *TimesSelect,* which gave them access online to the *Times* columnists, to the *Times* archives back to 1851, and to special multimedia features. *TimesSelect* also gave the readers access to the *Times* blogs, to News Tracker, which provided alerts on twenty topics, and early access to the *Sunday Times*'s articles. *TimesSelect* readers could save articles to consult later. *TimesSelect,* was sold as a package at $49.95 per year; as of February 2006 university faculty and students received a discounted rate of $24.95 a year, but in the first quarter of 2007, the *Times* decided to make *TimesSelect* free to students and faculty.

In 2005–2006, many observers, including myself, assumed that eventually the *Times* would charge for the entire newspaper and thought that *TimesSelect,* which had several hundred thousand subscribers, was a harbinger of things to come. With continuing retrenchment and layoffs, any little bit of revenue would have been helpful. But Internet advertisers want to have the maximum number of viewers, and the *Times* decided to stop charging for all but its puzzles. In 2010, they began charging nonsubscribers for Times Reader and the Replica Edition in addition to the puzzles.

On March 14, 2007, the *Times* announced that it was releasing Times Reader as a subscription product, which displays the newspaper on a computer much as it appears in the print edition. Beginning March 27, 2007, it was available to subscribers free but was originally priced annually at $165 or $14.95 a month. On May 11, 2009, the *Times* launched Times Reader 2.0. The major feature of the later version is that the paper can be read offline, such as on an airplane or commuter train, when it might not be possible to read online. Although updates are not added as frequently as on nytimes.com, they are added regularly throughout the day.

Using a feature entitled My Times—now called "My Account"—a reader was able to customize the newspaper. When it was released in Beta in 2006, the *Times* described My Times as "a new service that lets you create a personalized page with what you like best in the *New York Times* and your favorite sites and blogs all over the Web."

"My Times" was, as Landman explained in an email to me, "a customizable platform. . . . In other words, a web page that you can instruct to send you feeds from any site that interests you. So if you want your foreign news from the BBC, your sports from ESPN, your [New York Times] culture critics and the Yankees fan site all on one page, you can have it. [I]t's like myyahoo or mygoogle" (December 5, 2006). Thus, the reader was able to create his or her own mini web page on the site with favorite links and sections/authors/columns of nytimes.com. A program called a feed reader or aggregator used something called RSS (Really Simple Syndication or Rich Site Summary). Personalizing the *Times*—as My Times did—meant a reader became the gatekeeper and decided what he or she wished to read. Supposedly, this spoke to the reader's interests and saved him or her the time that would be spent sifting through nytimes.com. But for me, the very serendipity of my odyssey of reading the *Times*—whether online or in the paper—continues to be a pleasure in itself and a source of learning.

In any case, the My Times version of a customized newspaper has been phased out. Using "My Account" seems to be a way for the reader to do some gatekeeping by choosing which alerts and email newsletters he or she receives.

I might also mention "Replica Edition," a digital reproduction of the daily *Times*, and "TimesMachine," which allows the reader to browse through the archives from 1850 to 1922 and access any day's paper, although as of summer 2011, the print can be difficult to read. *Times* subscribers have access to the archives from 1922 through the present.

Since 2006, the *Times* has put continuing emphasis on ways the reader can use the digital *Times* to customize the news that he or she receives. The feature on nytimes.com now called "My Alerts" was originally called "News Tracker." The *Times* once charged $19.95 for this feature, which is now free. Users define the subjects for which they want alerts and indicate whether they wish them instantaneously or once a day.

Another recent and evolving online feature, on the model of Facebook, is Times People, a social network for readers of the *Times*, made up of people who can share information with one another. Once the user registers, he or she can see what others on his or her lists are recommending. Appealing to younger readers, a member may follow the recommendations of *Times* editors, reporters, and columnists or recommend articles on his or her own.

What appears on Times People can be connected to and accessed on such social media as Facebook and Twitter. As of August 31, 2010, the *Times* began using "Facebook connect," which lets people log into nytimes.com with their Facebook account. In summer 2009, the *Times* introduced "Times Insight Lab," a survey and interview system designed to get feedback from readers and users of its products. Once a reader fills out some basic information on how often he or she reads the print edition and nytimes.com and for what purposes, "Times Insight Lab" will request feedback.

The *Times* continues to experiment with new formats for offering its products electronically. For those with mobile devices, the *Times* mobile site provides various free services, including text messages and downloads or apps (applications). Even Times Reader can be downloaded onto mobile devices. Those who own an Amazon Kindle can download the *Times* for $19.99 a month; however, Amazon keeps 65 percent of that sum. One possibility for the future is portable reading devices with big screens about the size of a standard sheet of paper that would enable the *Times*—and other newspapers and periodicals—to replicate editorial and advertising content in much the same format as they appear in print.

On January 25, 2010, in response to electronic reading devices such as the iPad, the *Times* announced that it had created a new segment, "reader applications," which would develop new versions of its products for such devices—with the hope, of course, of creating a new revenue stream—and named Yasmin Namini, senior vice president for marketing and circulation, to head it (Brad Stone and Stephanie Clifford, "With Apple Tablet, Print Media Hope for a Payday," January 25, 2010). The *Times*'s iPad app was prominently featured in the iPad's launch advertisements. The iPad app can be purchased with unlimited web content for $20 every four weeks.

Gradually, I am being weaned away from the print edition. Although I still read the print edition because I enjoy the tactile sense of reading a paper, the page-turning, and seeing an article presented visually on one page, I awake to the headlines when I turn on my computer at 6 a.m. and often consult the continuously updated web edition. By reading the website during the day, users can see the daily newspaper taking shape.

Although nytimes.com and the *Washington Post* Internet sites have much in common—the *Post* completed a major reconfiguring of its site in March 2011—nytimes.com not only offers more features such as alerts on news topics but also is more user-friendly than the *Post*'s site, where the lists of podcasts, videos, and blogs have been less accessible. Yet the *Washington Post* offers more opportunities for interactive discussion of news articles. More similar to nytimes.com in navigation is the *Wall Street Journal*, which offers different home pages for different geographical areas—the United States, Asia, and Europe—but charges $1.99 a week, or $103 per year, for full access to all complete articles.

IV. Martin Nisenholtz and His Internet Strategy

Martin Nisenholtz, senior vice president for digital operations and the founder of the Internet group dating back to 1995, ultimately is the person in charge of the nytimes.com site. The importance of the Internet was underlined by the placement of his office down the hall from the *Times*'s publisher's office on the prestigious and hallowed fourteenth floor of the old New York Times building. (In the new building he is on the seventeenth, well above the hum and buzz of the newsgathering operation, and Arthur is on the sixteenth). He is in charge of the Internet for the entire company; to be more precise, he supervises the business side of the New York Times Company's digital divisions: nytimes.com, about.com, boston.com, the regional papers, and the research and development group.

Nisenholtz was deputy managing editor Landman's business and technical counterpart. Landman reported to Keller and Nisenholtz reported to the New York Times Company, which means Sulzberger and CEO Janet Robinson. Vivian Schiller, the former general manager of nytimes.com, reported to Nisenholtz.

I met Nisenholtz prior to the major April 2006 launching of the revised nytimes.com site. Slim, short, and fiftyish, Nisenholtz sat in a large, well-appointed office in the old New York Times building on the same floor as the publisher and presided over a staff of 180. Nisenholtz made clear that he was head of nytimes.com. At first he seemed impressed with himself, rigid, humorless, defensive, and a bit arrogant; certainly not a man who suffers from false modesty, but when he saw that I had done my homework, he became a bit more relaxed and was actually extremely informative. He did not give the impression of someone who likes to kibitz about his favorite team or accept teasing or jokes about himself. After some mild head-butting, he acknowledged that nytimes.com is a work in progress.

Basically, in 2011 the *Times* is still extending the boundaries of its site from the world of the Times Company to the world beyond. As the *Times* approached the April 2006 launch—which was regarded as a crucial turning point in the *Times*'s development of its website— Nisenholtz commented to me:

> We have been principally a walled garden for the last ten years. In other words, when you go to the *Times* website you get the *Times*'s content. . . . But increasingly our users will be able to aggregate content from around the Internet. And we'll guide them as to what that content should be—or is—in terms of its efficacy, in terms of its trustworthiness. [We'll provide] human approaches so that the aggregation scheme allows the user to define his world of news and information, but with a guided presence from the *New York Times*. So that's a radical departure for us. It's the first truly new product that we've launched in a long time. That's number one.
>
> Number two: we've branched out considerably beyond text and photography. We're doing much more audio and video reporting now. In April when we launch version three of the website, which is in essence the third substantiation of this product over the last . . . eleven years, you'll see a video player for the first time on the home page. And the reason for that is that we think our users are mostly broadband connected now and want more than just text and graphics from us. I mean they come to us principally for the text report that appears in the newspaper, but over time that's going to change. So that, that is a second huge change for us.
>
> A third change is a much deeper focus on . . . what I would call the application layer, particularly . . . in the back of the book [non-hard news] sections of the site—sections like travel, movies, and other sections. . . . [For example], the travel section of the *Times* website was really mostly a reflection of what we were publishing in the newspaper.
>
> If you use travel sites you know that you want a lot more than what a newspaper publishes. You basically are

very focused on, mainly a destination. . . . You want as much information about that destination as you can get. You also want to be able to map it. You want to be able to potentially look at what other users or other readers have said about it, particularly if there's a hotel involved. So there is a mix of applications that converge in these back of the book or vertical sections of the site that we need to develop and add. And that's what we're doing this year. So I think what you'll see over the next year and going forward is much more, a much deeper integration of software and software thinking, application thinking into the content itself. So that you'll not only be able to read the content, you'll be able to use it or mix it up in some way. . . . So those are just three examples of where I think we're going to be going over the next year or so. (February 17, 2006)

Since 2006, the travel site has become extremely useful and progressively far more inclusive in providing hotels, restaurants, and sites for tourists. Moving through the site and its links reveals a variety of advertisers. Of course the *Travel* print section's raison d'être always included a strong advertising component and advertising-friendly content. But I wondered whether Nisenholtz realized that people also read the *Travel* section for the pleasures of remembering trips they have taken and for imagining sites they haven't seen. Nisenholtz stressed using the site for a specific purpose rather than for provoking memories or fulfillment of intellectual curiosity about a place and its history. That he placed a strong emphasis on information as utility—as practical knowledge—rather than on information as knowledge for its own sake was revealing about the direction the *Times* was going.

In 2006, Nisenholtz believed that the *Times* newspaper's readers are different from those reading its website:

[A] lot of people read the *Times* because it's an enjoyable, relaxing thing to do. And that I think is the principal use [of] . . . the paper. It's not, hey I'm going to go find a story in the *Times* today. [Rather] it's I read it because I enjoy it. It relaxes me. I feel better informed after I read it. . . . [I]t's a valuable part of my life. On the web, it's much more, it's much more deterministic. I mean we do have some users who kind of read the web like they might read the paper.

But most people read the web much more in a targeted way.

I am doubtful that this distinction holds true now for most readers. If in 2005 younger readers often read the *Times* on the web for information quite differently from the way dedicated older readers read the paper, I would say that in 2011 fewer dedicated readers have the kind of time or interest to spend hours reading the entire print *Times*. Surveys show that readers spend less time with their newspapers, and that includes the *Times*. What many younger—and even older— readers want from the *Times* print version is standard gatekeeping but perhaps a stripped-down version that would give them essential news, sports, business, and arts in thirty minutes.

As Nisenholtz told me, his 2006 model was to somewhat abandon gatekeeping and throw open the *Times* to the entire web:

> We're developing a product that will be much more inclusive of the rest of the Internet. In fact, completely inclusive. In survey after survey . . . [we learn] people want density and choice on the page. I mean I keep coming back to that because if you don't deliver that they will go elsewhere. . . . Most people want density. They want to be able to look out and see a variety of stories that they can choose from.

But he wanted to balance this with some controlled gatekeeping:

> Readers do turn to the print and even digital *Times* for gatekeeping, that is, selection and arrangement of the vast panorama of available information. If they wanted the entire web, they would turn to Google. With access to the infinite web and the blogosphere, they want something from the *Times* that reflects succinctly the essentials of the *Times* product in preference to a hypertext that takes them all over the web.

What was and is ironic in Nisenholtz's argument that readers of the web are different from those of the print newspaper is that the *Times* has, since 2006, made the paper readers increasingly dependent on the Internet. One argument for the elimination of stock tables and congressional votes is that they are web-accessible. Clearly, Nisenholtz was looking to the future when probably almost everyone would be on broadband; now a great many more people are. But, in 2006, there were still quite a few people reading the *Times* on the subway or commuter train who, when arriving home, did not have time or the facility to access the web. Not everyone then—or even now—had the tools and devices to access the web while holding a strap in the subway.

By fall 2010, the World category or site has become better organized and struck a balance between inclusiveness and gatekeeping. On the left are recent major and related articles (with a few words about each) that can be accessed with a click; in the center is "Multimedia," which has links to the *Times*'s videos and slide shows that focus on recent major events such as the Haiti earthquake in January 2010; "At War" features stories and blogs about the Afghanistan conflict, Pakistan, and Iraq. Under "Multimedia" and "At War," which seem to change places between the top and second item, is "The Lede," Robert Mackey's regular blog that adds information to important stories.

By the end of 2009, the focus and the availability of topics by country still created an accessible short-term archive. These subsections are far better organized now than in 2006 and 2007 in terms of a narrative introducing the country and highlighting major stories from the archives. While every country does not have such an elaborate, detailed, and updated site—for example, for Anguilla, the *Times* only has links to other sites—each country has a "Navigator" and "Other Resources" section.

V. The April 2006 Revised Version of nytimes.com

Until the newer version was released in spring 2006, nytimes.com was rather cluttered. It is now much improved and more aesthetically appealing. The font was changed from Times New Roman to Georgia for bigger and rounder letters that Khoi Vinh, the chief designer at the website, thinks improves readability. The site also improved in navigability, but at first the *Times* was constantly tinkering with the site. Writing a few weeks after launching, Landman observed:

> We have made about 125 changes in the weeks since our redesign, many in response to reader complaints, suggestions and observations. We've increased the type size in individual articles and restored the underscores on the links

within articles. We've made some headlines bigger, tweaked spacing, made some things darker. We're planning to adjust some of the home page captions because they are showing up in different sizes in different browsers, and we feel some are still too small. (April 28, 2006, nytimes.com)

The 2006 challenge was to design the site so that it balanced the needs of first-time and inexperienced users with those who were familiar with the site and were consulting it several times a day. The site needed to be more user-friendly especially for less-experienced (and generally older) users. Nisenholtz was very much aware of these problems, and continued to take steps to improve the site: "I thoroughly agree that we should be as clear as we can be and that we're often not, particularly for novice users. However, we have to design the site for all different kinds of users. And so we're . . . constantly trying to strike the right balance between a person who's coming in once to find an article or to do a little research, and then people who use the site . . . six, eight, ten times a day" (February 17, 2006).

In 2006, the *Times* began to assume that most readers also would be users of the website; for example, it offered advice to readers on how—when it vastly reduced its stock market daily charts—to supplement the newspaper with the website. On April 3, 2006, as part of its new website, the *Times* also launched its new interactive business and investment section whereby users could set up their own profiles, specifying under a section entitled "My Portfolio" which stocks they own, and be kept abreast of news and prices. If users click on any stock within the portfolio they can find out basic information about the company. I find this feature very helpful in managing my relatively small investment portfolio.

The *Times* will email users of this feature relevant information about their investments and allow them to track the stock prices. Additionally, a user can now set up hypothetical investment situations to research whether a particular investment will be useful. The online business section also has comprehensive information about companies' stock prices, research on the companies including forecasts of each company's future, different analysts' predictions, graphs of foreign exchange rates, and easily understandable graph comparisons of different companies. Because an investor or trader can do considerable investment research on nytimes.com, the site is competitive with the *Wall Street Journal* site and that is clearly its goal.

Although I felt the April 2006 version was more user-friendly, at the time of the change I consulted some students for input to confirm my opinion. Carolyn Byrne, an independent-study student working with me on my *Times* project at the time, thought that the new site had a "more easily navigable setup. . . . [T]he different font makes it easier to read. . . . Overall, the site is more conducive to browsing and in-depth research. I can choose what I want to look at rather than grasp at whatever stories come my way."

In a significant move toward transparency, the *Times* editors, beginning with Keller in spring 2006, began taking turns on the website being interviewed in a Q&A format in a series called "Talk to the Newsroom." To be sure, by the end of 2009, these interviews, sometimes with secondary editors, had become at times redundant.

But Keller's interview took place right after the April 2006 launching that was, as I have stressed, a turning point in foregrounding the website. Discussing the new website, Keller wrote:

> Within a day or so, I'd come to like it much better than the old version. The overall visual effect is a little calmer, but the energy comes from what it can do. There is a lot more stuff, and it is much easier to navigate. The home page uses the wider space to make clear what's important and what's less important. The tabs make it easier to flip from section to section. The Times Topics feature takes you quickly to an archive of clippings and reference materials on thousands of subjects, or lets you survey the work of a particular reporter. The Most Popular feature lets you know which articles have generated the most reader interest. . . . There's more and better video—and will be much more of that in the months ahead. And when the MyTimes feature is launched, any reader will be able to design a vibrant personal home page fed by the journalists of the *Times* and favorite material from elsewhere on the Web. ("Talk to the Newsroom," April 14, 2006)

After the launching of the new site in April 2006, then deputy managing editor Landman, who was in charge of the *Times*'s content on the web, answered online questions as the second participant in the "Talk to the Newsroom" series. He discussed issues concerning the website and the expectations the site created for its journalists, who now may post stories several times a day as new information becomes available in order to keep up with other websites and cable news. According to Landman,

> We (and others in our business) also created a new class of journalist, a "continuous news" reporter whose job it is to push the reporting forward aggressively for the web. So sometimes one reporter writes several versions of a story. . . . New journalistic forms like blogs and podcasts, and old ones that are new for newspapers, like video, also impose new demands. We now have a video unit in our newsroom, and many of our still photographers have learned to shoot video. Some reporters even carry their own video cameras. (April 28, 2006)

As Landman said to me: "The problem, the challenge was to enlarge the cut, to make editors understand that the palette of choices was greater than ever before" (June 9, 2010). Decisions about whether a reporter should do a video or an audio track or write for the web became part of the mix, and these decisions meant that editors had far more to manage.

With an eye on younger readers, the website stresses the visual—notably photography, videos, graphics, even comics—and audio. Podcasts enable readers to hear rather than read the news. After iTunes and similar products provided an inexpensive and accessible means of downloading radio-type recordings called podcasts, the *Times* put greater emphasis on its podcasts, which enables listeners to choose when and if they listen. They vary in length from less than one minute to more than eighteen minutes, and the recurring ones on occasion disappear and are replaced by others. As of September 2010, among the podcasts were the Monday through Friday "Front Page," where James Barron "summarizes the top headlines every weekday" as well as the weekly "Music Podcast" and "Ethicist," with then columnist Randy Cohen. One of the most effective podcasts is "Backstory," in which Jane Bornemeir, who oversees audio programming, talks Monday through Friday with *Times* reporters about the top stories of the day.

Videos enable the *Times* audience to see the news as if, supposedly, they were watching TV. More and more readers have broadband, which easily accesses videos posted on the website. Since April 2006, when videos began to play a prominent role on nytimes.com, they have continued to improve. That they are now accessible with the tab at the top of nytimes.com shows their importance. The *Times* also has a cooperative relationship with NBC, which enables it to use NBC videos. Videos were increasingly pivotal in the 2008 election coverage; the analytic videos on the day following Super Tuesday, February 5, 2008, were trenchant, well-produced, and informative discussions of the primaries and the direction in which the Democratic and Republican parties were going.

Often only a very few minutes in length, videos have the downside of offering oversimplifications that a nuanced article would avoid. For example, in summer 2006, various videos on the Israel–Arab conflict tended to be one-dimensional, adopting either the Israeli or Arab point of view. Inevitably, historical context is lacking; furthermore, in these videos, the pictures lead the story rather than vice versa.

For some viewers, Hassan Fatah's video "Attack on Ouzai, Lebanon," released on August 4, 2006, was heavily slanted to the Lebanese point of view, and did not take into account attacks on Israel or the kidnapping of Israeli troops. Later information revealed that Hezbollah had manipulated pictures of Ouzai and that Hezbollah fighters were embedded in the civilian population. On December 4, 2006, Greg Myre began a front-page article entitled, "Offering Video, Israel Answers Critics on War": "Israel's military, which has been accused of abuses in its war against Hezbollah this summer, has declassified photographs, video images and prisoner interrogations to buttress its accusation that Hezbollah systematically fired from civilian neighborhoods in southern Lebanon and took cover in those areas to shield itself from attack."

Videos played a crucial role in the presentation of the protests following the apparently fraudulent Iran election, such as Robert Mackey—the Lede blogger—and Vjai Singh's July 9, 2009, "More Protests in Iran" or the earlier "Roger Cohen on Iran: The Election and its Aftermath" in which he reports on his two weeks there. But this later video seems undated—a problem that I frequently observed in earlier years—and was at times inaccessible to the user. Nevertheless, the videos and slide shows—originally foregrounded and, in late July

2009, in chronological order on the Iran site within "World"—offer graphic evidence of the brutality of the Iranian authorities.

One of the more compelling video series was a substantive but intermittent one called "The Conversation," originally hosted by Calvin Sims and later hosted by others. He interviewed famous and important people who have made an impact, such as Elie Wiesel; the powerful black New York minister Calvin Butts, pastor of the Abyssinian Baptist Church in Harlem; 2006 Nobel Laureate in Literature, Orhan Pamuk; and Neil deGrasse Tyson, director of the Hayden Planetarium. Ten or twelve minutes in length and a little more when necessary, Sims's videos are excellent because he skillfully chooses his subjects and asks informed and pointed questions. The production values of Sims's interviews rival those of polished television shows; the only difference is that the small screen does make the speakers look a tad odd. Nicholas Kristof's January 24, 2009, "A Conversation with Bill Gates" about aid to developing countries matches interviewer and interviewee with excellent results.

Even in late 2009, "jamming" errors—when clicks do not open the video because the video does not load properly or the page is blank where the video should be—and video-accessing problems happened less frequently, but by no means have such errors been eliminated. Accessing the wrong videos can lead to moments of surprise, comedy, and incongruity. Unfortunately, on March 4, 2007, when I clicked on Sims's interview with Kareem Abdul-Jabbar, the former basketball player—and I clicked several times throughout the day—I accessed a video report on "Baghdad Borderlines." Indeed, such errors happen disproportionately on videos, but do occur throughout the site. On occasion, although less frequently with each passing year, I access blank pages.

In 2010, the *Times* introduced "Timescast," a Monday through Friday, six-minute informal video that addresses how the *Times* is covering three major stories, although often the stories are lightweight features such as the September 20, 2010, discussion on why we eat chili peppers.

VI. Forums: The Beginnings of the Interactive *Times*

The precursor to blogs and the seminal phase of the interactive *Times* were the forums. For a number of years, nytimes.com included a host of its own forums, open to all. The forums were reader discussion groups on a wide variety of topics, from international issues to sports and health; by July 2006, there were more than 37,000 postings on the Middle East. These forums, some lasting for five years, were a crucial part of earlier versions of the interactive *Times*, although, of course, only a small percentage of readers took part.

The forums date back to the early days of nytimes.com—a copy of a December 1996 home page includes a promo saying, "Join the discussion in the new forums." They were found under "Opinion" within a section called "Find a Reader Discussion."

What is the difference between a *Times* forum and a *Times* blog? A *Times* forum is a public site within nytimes.com where readers discuss a designated topic, whereas a *Times* blog normally refers to a website where the original comments come from one or perhaps a few voices presiding over the site. In *Times* blogs there is room for comments by visitors to the site. Forums, however, did not require a subscription to *TimesSelect* for access, they required that users register and provide an email address. The *Times* wanted those readers posting to identify themselves: "We ask you to complete the simple Forums registration to ensure that you have a valid email account and that you accept our terms and conditions. The registration process serves to facilitate the development of our online community, and ensure that members take responsibility for their writings."

By early 2007, the *Times* had hundreds of forums, with titles ranging from "Boxing" to "Urban Haiku," from "You're the Ethicist" to "Gay Rights," from "Owning and Renting a Home," to a forum on autos called "Motor Mouth." Some of the forums, such as those on opera and classical music, were, on the whole, quite impressive and contained a plethora of knowledgeable comments. That the discussion on the classical music forum revolved frequently around recent concerts in the New York area was limiting to those who lived beyond the metropolitan area, however.

On April 16, 2007, the *Times* posted a notice that most of the forums were being discontinued (April 23, 2007, email to the author from Rich Meislin). Although some of the forums became the basis for blogs and the forum concept was extremely important to the development of the interactive nytimes.com, the forums eventually all disappeared. Even the opera forum, one of the most successful, could no longer be accessed. The public editor's forum—which was one of the most notable in terms of content—has continued as a blog where Clark Hoyt and now Arthur Brisbane, current public editor, prints letters from readers.

What went wrong with the forums? Forum moderators might have done more to monitor content and civility. On the immigration forum, insults became the norm. On forums addressing complex issues where opinions are strongly held, what began as a substantive thread at times degenerated into an extremely parochial and heated argument among a few participants. This occurred even on what might seem the more innocuous contemporary education forum. Within many forums—and not only politically charged ones—rational participants backed off rather than get caught in the clutches of shrill and mean-spirited participants. Some readers found the negative tone so offensive that they not only ceased participating in a forum but also ceased reading it. At times, the forums devolved into iteration and some—especially, sports forums—often devolved into gibberish.

While I admired the democratic town-meeting quality of the forums that allowed anyone to express a viewpoint, the *Times* probably should have edited each forum on a weekly basis, only keeping comments that contributed to an ongoing community of inquiry. The standard for retaining comments for more than a week should have been higher—that is, only highly significant contributions should have been retained—and the standard for retaining comments for a month should have been even higher. Maybe the moderator should have posted weekly or monthly questions to give the discussions more shape; contributors need not have been bound by the questions but could have been encouraged to think about them.

VII. Blogs and the Blogosphere

Looking to the future, Sulzberger saw in 2005 a more interactive audience on the model of the proliferation of *Times* forums on the web:

> [W]e're going to have to recognize that our old way of operating, which was for us to talk to you, is only half the equation now. We have to give you the opportunity to talk back to us. And more importantly, to talk to your peers. Because the people who read the *New York Times* are people who think and are people who you want to get to know.

You want to begin to have that conversation with them. We
need to become the convener of conversations. (November
11, 2005, interview with Charlie Rose)

Interactive journalism raises problems of civility. As Hoyt asked,
"How does the august *Times*, which has long stood for dignified
authority, come to terms with the fractious, democratic culture of the
Internet, where readers expect to participate but sometimes do so in
coarse, bullying and misinformed ways?" ("Civil Discourse, Meet the
Internet," November 4, 2007).

By spring 2007 the *Times* had turned to blogs by regular staff as
the focal point of its interactive universe. The *Times* invested in the
blogosphere by hiring four full-time editors to screen reader submis-
sions before posting them. By 2008, the blogosphere had been fully
integrated into the *Times*. Along with the regular blogs, many columns
and some stories—especially stories in the *Sports* section—appear as
blogs with invitations for comments.

The *Times* allows readers to post comments on most blogs,
although a few that are not text based, like "Lens"—focusing on photo-
journalism—do not. At the end of a blogger's post, there is in most
cases a place for comments and a link to view the them. The reader
who wishes to comment must register with a user name, but need not
identify him- or herself with his or her actual name. Presently, those
wishing to comment must provide a bit more information to register,
including email, birth year, gender, country, and a zip code if in the
United States. Prospective commentators are asked for demographic
information about income and job title; however, they can click on
"prefer not to answer." The *Times* does insist that comments not be
abusive or incoherent or way off the topic.

Editorial control is much improved over the forums. We do not
know how much editing takes place, but the comments rarely are
offensive and only occasionally are uninformed. Comments are listed
from newest to oldest rather than organized by subject subheadings,
which might be a better alternative. Some bloggers respond to comments but, other than that, the bloggers do not usually make specific
recommendations about which comments are notable.

In addition to blogs, the *Times* offers other venues for reader
comments. Readers can comment on opinion pieces; the editors may
select comments they recommend or may reply to a comment. If

users recommend a comment, the comment is placed on the "Reader's Recommendations" page where recommendations are organized by the number of people recommending a comment rather than by subject subheadings, or quality of comments. Interactive intervention plays an important role on the movie site where nytimes.com prints short readers' responses to recently reviewed films.

At the end of July 2009 the *Times* not only began to open comment on analytic news articles, but to include more "Editors' Selections" and "Reader's Recommendations." An example was the piece on the implications of the arbitrary arrest of the distinguished black professor Henry Louis Gates in his own home: "Professor's Arrest Tests Beliefs on Racial Progress" (Susan Saluny and Robbie Brown, July 23, 2009). Following the example of the online *Washington Post* and *Wall Street Journal*, the *Times* now offers major news articles for comment. (See, for example, David Sanger, "Clinton Says Nuclear Aim of Iran Is Fruitless," July 26, 2009.)

I could imagine tighter gatekeeping of blogs. Reading through reader responses can be a tiresome task due to content repetition. It is as if a reporter interviewed 500 people and printed the views of all 500. And some readers re-enter a discussion to virtually repeat what they said already. I found this particularly true of the political blog "Caucus" during the height of the winter 2008 primary season.

In "Bad News," a July 31, 2005, essay in the *New York Times Book Review*, Richard Posner wrote about the virtues of bloggers who "dig into a story longer and deeper than the conventional media dare to, lest their reader become bored. . . . [A]lthough individual blogs have no warrant of accuracy, the blogosphere as a whole has a better error-correction machinery than the conventional media do." By contrast, Posner argues: "A serious newspaper, like the *Times*, is a large hierarchical commercial enterprise that interposes layers of review, revision and correction between the reporter and the published report and that to finance its large staff depends on advertising revenues and hence on the good will of advertisers and (because advertising revenues depend to a great extent on circulation) readers. These dependencies constrain newspapers in a variety of ways."

Posner claims blogs are not merely a challenge but a threat to the survival of newspapers. But he is assuming that a reader can trust amateurs and can read the continuing exchanges to find the actual facts. Posner seems to ignore the fragmentation of the blogosphere when he claims corrections are "disseminated almost instantaneously." He also ignores the idiosyncrasies and fixations of bloggers—qualities that produce not only obfuscations, distortions, and, at times, outright lies but also gossip and foolish theories, all of which get in the way of accuracy. Moreover, much of the information on the blogs comes from the same sources and the blogger often has the same interpretive relationship to original material as literary critics have to the original texts or historians to facts. In academic terms, the blogosphere often has an interpretive function in the world of punditry but it doesn't always add much to what is known.

Even though people read blogs, they do not necessarily trust them for hard information; as the Project for Excellence in Journalism stated in its 2006 annual report, "The appeal of the Web is its convenience, interactivity, diversity and control. Yet the more people use the Web, the less they trust it. The most trusted sites of all increasingly are those from the old-legacy media. Even people who enjoy blogs, for instance, are suspicious of them. They go for the energy, argument and authenticity they find there, not hard information. The public, it increasingly appears, accesses different parts of the Internet for different reasons."

Sulzberger has been very much aware of blogs, but believed— correctly I think, considering that a 2006 survey by the Pew Internet & Life Project reported that 12 million Americans keep blogs—that, although some are valuable, many are uninformed, unreliable, and quirky or have an axe to grind (Felicia R. Lee, "Survey of the Blogosphere Finds 12 Million Voices," July 20, 2006). I recall the perhaps hyperbolic, dismissive, and patronizing view of the blogosphere Sulzberger expressed to me on October 11, 2005: "99 percent . . . of the three or four million blogs that already exist . . . are worthless." Although he did, in that same interview, concede the need to pay attention to the other 1 percent, he strongly differentiated *Times* blogging from the rest of the blogosphere:

> We are a fact-based organization, and, so, we have a lot of challenges: how do we integrate blogging into what we do on the web, how do we integrate it in a way that makes sense . . . so that we are still giving our users the *New York Times* experience. [We give] trustworthy news . . . [with] the authoritative voice of our journalism. . . . We're not always perfect, we're humans too, we will make mistakes, but [we provide] trustworthy news and information where you own up to your mistakes and correct the process that led to the mistake.

With a strong investment in its own blogs and a realization that other blogs are at times reliable informational sources, the *Times* has integrated the blogosphere into its 2011 universe.

Since 2006, the *Times* has moved forcefully into the world of blogs, both by having *Times* staff do blogs on its site and by providing other recommended blogs that can be accessed by a click. Blogs supplement in important ways the interactive dialogue between readers and the print newspaper, which in the actual newspaper is still limited to a handful of letters. In July 2005, Rich Meislin provided on the *Times* site a crash course entitled "Blogs 101," which he updated to keep readers abreast of new sites beyond the *Times*'s own universe. As business editor Lawrence Ingrassia predicted, "Blogs will become increasingly important because they enable newspapers—which generally have had mass readership—to also reach specialized audiences. That's because many readers want 1) more depth, and more space, than we can devote to any single topic in the paper; and 2) to know more than what any one publication is reporting, because they may have a voracious appetite about everything important written on a specific subject" ("Talk to the Newsroom," May 26, 2006). On April 9, 2006, in an article entitled "The *Times*' New Blogs: More Information, Fewer Filters," then public editor Byron Calame discussed the newspaper's new explorations into the blog world. He explained, "blogs run by assigned staffers are posting opinions and information they consider insightful on topics such as dining, wine, real estate, and the financial world." Calame explained that the *Times* was slow to launch blogs on its website because of the possible unreliability of information: "Staffers directly posting their own thoughts or those of others that they found insightful . . . was a step to be taken with care at a serious paper."

By July 2006, the *Times* had, within its own universe—that is, blogs by its own staff members—fifteen or so functioning blog sites with a promise of more to come; in March 2007, the number increased to twenty-seven, including some that were clearly time-limited and some that were restricted to *TimesSelect*. By November 27, 2007, there were twenty-five regular blogs, but also such seasonal sports blogs as "The Fifth Down," devoted to professional football, and "The Quad," devoted to college football. In February 2008, the *Times* had approximately thirty blogs. By March 2011, if we include seasonal blogs, there were more than fifty blogs, including eight opinion blogs. Almost every blog has an interactive feature, allowing readers to submit comments as long as they are not abusive or obscene.

Let us examine the *Times* and the blogosphere. For Dan Okrent, Byron Calame, Clark Hoyt, and now Arthur Brisbane, the public editor's blog has been a useful complement to the public editor's columns. It gives readers a chance to respond to the column and enter into something of a dialogue with the public editor about the paper. To the *Times*'s publication of the revelation that the administration was examining the banking data of private citizens, Calame received intense and often negative responses and printed a "representative sampling" on June 26, 2006.

With his blog "On the Ground," Nicholas Kristof was the first of the op-ed columnists to enter the blogosphere. He supplemented his twice weekly op-ed columns with further reports on such places as Darfur and China, two of his main foci, and his account of the plight of the Pakistani women's rights activist, Mukhtaran Bibi. Kristof also uses short videos on his blog to show the horrifying situations he describes in his column.

Although the blogs are looked over by editors, Meislin conceded to me that the blogs are "not edited the same way as a 900-word story for the front page is going to be" (April 13, 2007). What Meislin said to me of the *Times* blogosphere in 2007 is still relevant today:

> It's a very eclectic collection; a lot of it came at the beginning, about a year ago, based on peoples' interests in actually doing them. . . . There are certain things that are done for a certain subjects [such as] cars and the auto shows. Those come and go, but for the most part we start one with the expectation that it's going to continue and we require a high level of commitment from the person who comes to us and says they want to do it. We inevitably tell them that it's going to be harder than they think to do it. They always say: "yes, yes it will be fine" and they come back in four weeks and say "this is harder than we thought." You know, these are all experiments, and one of the nice things about the web is that you can experiment in public in ways that aren't embarrassing.

Meislin somewhat overstated the stability of the *Times*'s blog list. Between November 2006 and summer 2011, the *Times* added and subtracted quite a few blogs, and that pattern will undoubtedly continue as staff assignments change.

The goal of the *Times* blogosphere is to appeal to as many interests as possible in order to attract as many nytimes.com hits as possible each day. At first, the *Times* had time-limited blogs, especially for sports. They were for such events as the 2006 World Cup, the World Series, or the NCAA college basketball championship ("The Bracket"). In fall 2006, the *Times* had a blog discussion of fantasy football as a strategic pursuit and social phenomenon. But by 2009, some of the seasonal blogs had expanded; "Bats" now follows the Mets and Yankees throughout the year. "Goal" covers soccer. "The Bracket" has been succeeded by "The Quad," which covers all college sports. "The Fifth Down" mostly focuses on the Jets and Giants and occasionally segues into fantasy football.

During the 2006 World Cup and even more so in 2010, the World Cup blog was especially appealing to the more multinational readership of the website. The blog was a potpourri of commentary, picture links, gossip, and real-time play-by-play reporting. During the winter run up to the 2006, 2007, 2008, and 2009 Oscar ceremonies, under the title "The Carpetbagger," David Carr—punning on his last name—covered the film awards. But what began as a special time-limited blog expanded to cover the film industry year round and also had links to other sites concerned with film. On June 3, 2009, "Carpetbagger" became part of a new blog, "Media Decoder," devoted to a "comprehensive" view of the media.

Basically, in 2011 the *Times* is still extending the boundaries of its site from the world of the Times Company to the world beyond. The blogs will continue to evolve. To give a further idea of what the *Times* is offering online, let us briefly mention some other blogs that continued into 2010. "Dealbook," edited by Andrew Ross Sorkin, is a summary of major business deals and presentation of important research on companies. Presenting major business news in the form of a daily newsletter, "Dealbook" is another effort to compete with the *Wall Street Journal*. By 2011, the provocative blog "Freakonomics"—which had been under the *Times*'s auspices since August 2007—had disappeared from the *Times*. The blog had been edited by Steven Levitt and Stephen Dubner and took off from Levitt's book *Freakonomics: A Rogue Economist Explores the Hidden Side of Everything*. The closest replacement is "Economix," a recent blog that uses economics as a lens to understand news and business. It is mainly written by economics reporter Catherine Rampell and Economic Scene columnist David Leonhardt. "The Lede" (a term for the opening sentence of news stories) follows up on details and implications of news stories; the main blogger, Robert Mackey, coordinated instant coverage of Iran's postelection turmoil in June and July 2009. "Pogue's Posts," with technology columnist David Pogue, discusses technology.

On June 22, 2006, Viriginia Heffernan introduced her blog with a mission statement; she contended that television and the Internet have merged and that Internet videos have become an important art form:

> [W]ith everyone creating and producing and uploading now, who is going to be on the downside, watching and savoring it all? All of that web video, viral video, user-driven video, custom interactive video, consumer-generated video, embedded video ads, web-based VOD, broadband television, dialogs, vcasts, vlogs, video podcasts, mobisodes, webisodes and mashups? Um, me? Yes, that's my idea. I'll watch. That's what Screens is for.

Redefined in 2007 as "The Medium: The Way We Watch Now," the blog discussed web video and media. In June 2009, "The Medium" became part of "ArtsBeat," the *Times*'s arts blog, to which Heffernan sometimes contributes.

Addressing younger readers, Heffernan reported on web videos—which, in 2006, Cornell undergraduate Meaghan Corbett called "procrastination tools for teenagers and college students"—and provided links to those she found most interesting. The goal is to attract young readers accustomed to *Rolling Stone* and Internet discussion of pop culture to the *Times* for discussions of hip-hop and rock festivals, but if my discussions with students are any criterion, that has not yet happened in great numbers.

One of the most notable of the *Times* blogs is "Opinionator," which is a Monday through Friday blog organized first in 2005 by Chris Suellentrop, much of whose journalistic experience had been with *Slate*. Suellentrop was later joined by Tobin Harshaw. Their own contribution was mostly a recapitulation of the views of others they had read, but by calling attention to their reading, they had considerable authority as gatekeepers in pulling together comments and opinions on important issues from other major domestic newspapers, magazines, and blogs. When one of my research students wrote Suellentrop because we were puzzled by what the site was doing (i.e., were we reading Suellentrop or excerpts from blogs), Suellentrop responded in an email: "I write the material that appears on the Opinionator page. But the material that I link to and quote from is written by others. So I'm highlighting opinions from around the Web, as well as framing them into the larger debate" (email to Nessia Sloane, February 12, 2006).

In the early days of "Opinionator," it was not always clear what the larger debate was; Suellentrop—joined by Harshaw in the months before the blog was entirely reinvented—did not provide enough historical and intellectual context and background. "Opinionater" surprisingly did not include foreign papers in its ken. Indeed, the *Times*'s own newspaper and online editorial page only post occasional editorials from foreign sources.

Recognizing that "Opinionater" needed some refurbishing, the *Times* relaunched it in November 2009. "Opinionator" now includes many of its regular online columnists: Stanley Fish, Olivia Judson, Timothy Egan, Judith Warner, Dick Cavett, Linda Greenhouse (the *Times*'s retired Supreme Court reporter), and "The Conversation" between Gail Collins and David Brooks. It added some recurring features such as "Living Rooms," exploring domestic life, and "The Stone," written by contemporary philosophers. But it no longer links to other websites. On Saturday, a feature called "The Thread" is very much like the old "Opinionater" in its effort to bring in opinions on major news developments.

Another important blog that appeared in 2010 was "Idea of the Day," compiled by Tom Kuntz and other editors of the *Sunday Week in Review*. Several times a week, this blog presented one interesting piece found on the web that addressed a major issue, such as the anniversary of the February 15, 1945, bombing of Dresden. Under the heading "More recommended reading," this blog also provided a bibliography of other interesting pieces that editors have been reading. "Idea of the Day" was discontinued in October 2010 when the *Times* decided to focus its resources elsewhere.

Certainly the centerpiece of the *Times* blog universe during the 2008 election in terms of written words and reader interest was "The Caucus," in which Kate Phillips—the site coordinator—and the *Times* politics staff, after analyzing the midterm elections, began extensive coverage in November 2006. As the 2008 campaign progressed, "The Caucus" presented a wide range of information and added new stories throughout the day.

Building on the large readership it attracted during the 2008 presidential election campaign, "The Caucus" has continued to be a crucial site for covering the Obama presidency and Congress. During the 2008 election year, "The Caucus" provided extensive daily reports in the paper, supplementary reports on the Internet, photographs in both venues, poll results regularly, videos, slide shows, and information on candidates, contributors, and finances. Online, "The Caucus" provided biographies, recent and back blog postings about candidates, and compared their positions on four major issues: health care, abortion, Iraq, and immigration. In 2008, a click within "The Caucus" site on finances enabled the reader to search by donors and geography. Readers could type in their zip code and see who was supporting whom if they had given $100 or more.

In the run-up to the 2010 election, Nate Silver's statistically inflected "FiveThirtyEight" blog has been foregrounded on "The Caucus." The 2010 Caucus site also included tweets from the people the blog follows on Twitter, articles that the blog's authors are reading, and connections to other blogs on its blogroll.

The *Times* election coverage is comparable to sports coverage, perhaps closer to an extended golf tournament or an almost endless ultra-marathon. Words like "race," "field," "contest," "strategy," and "challenge" are used frequently as a way of ratcheting up the continuing drama. Perhaps the *Times* believed that it could turn the 2008 presidential race for the nomination into a two-year sporting event that Americans would follow even as the Bush administration ebbed. In doing so, the *Times* gave authenticity to a two-year campaign and perhaps contributed to the public's expectations of early announcements and early primary results. Yet, to an extent, this early heated reporting of the preliminaries to the 2008 election was an example of the news media writing less for an engaged public than for each other and for the beltway insiders. With a great deal of space to fill, the *Times*, in its early 2008 election coverage, participated strongly in giving credence and value to what might only be called virtual events.

For example, in the August 11, 2007, Iowa GOP straw poll, a poll in which one paid $35 to vote, supporters were not only bused in and given free food, but many of them had the $35 fee paid for them by the candidate. Three of the four major contenders refused to participate. Is this event part of the exhibition season or does it count in the standings? Put another way, if such an election happened in a third-world country we would be laughing, and yet the *Times*—albeit with some irony—ran Adam Nagourney's front-page if low-keyed story August 13, 2007, after the Iowa straw poll as if it were a somewhat important event; "For a Joke-Telling Candidate, A Second Place Made of Straw" was the title given by a skeptical if not smirking headline writer, recalling one of the houses the big bad wolf blew down, because Mike Huckabee received 18 percent (2,587 votes) of 14,000 votes. The student government president or prom queen at large state universities might get this many votes. Huckabee had developed no real following and probably would have not officially entered the race had not the media—including the *Times*—decided (or pretended) that his second-place finish counted for something. In 2011, the Iowa straw poll received similar excessive coverage.

We know from polls—most notably the *Times* report on July 30, 2007, by Dahlia Sussman ("Poll: 'America Tuned In to the Campaign'") on its own New York Times/CBS poll, as if to justify its own verbal tsunami of election coverage—that the media was successful in arousing early interest. Thus, the *Times* was a major factor in turning the 2008 election into a mediathon of astonishing proportions. A mediathon is an event in which journalists—whether newspaper reporters or TV reporters—become major players. Originally the term applied to tabloid journalism and the soap-operatic presentation of narratives about gruesome crimes like the kidnapping and killing of the Lindbergh baby. But the infocircus is no longer limited to tabloids, especially now that photograph and videos are part of the information flow. (See Frank Rich, "The Age of the Mediathon," *New York Times Sunday Magazine*, October 29, 2000.) The *Times* stoked the mediathon fires by continuing to lavish vast quantities of words on the presidential race.

In January 2009, the *Times* launched "Room for Debate," an opinion site that is not considered a blog, but grew out of the former "Ideas" blog. "Room for Debate" gives commentary on a recent news story or current issue: "We hope these forums, by offering analysis and opinions from different perspectives, will give our readers context for the news. Sometimes our contributors will engage in back and forth with one another. Sometimes they will just share what they know." For the most part, "Room for Debate" has generated excellent discussions, including informed reader response.

Although the news analyses and discussion blogs have improved in quality, the *Times* needs to continue distinguishing blogs from its traditional news content, but that becomes harder to do when the bloggers are its own reporters and columnists. Blogs may appeal to readers interested in one specialized topic or another, but they represent a fundamental departure from the way in which the *Times* traditionally constructed its reports and disseminated information. Because blogs don't always deliver *Times*-quality news content—some of the "Fifth Down" blogging on New York Jets and Giants football resembles adolescent chatter—they may draw a different audience.

Moreover, by referencing other blogs—some of which are not above printing gossip and misinformation disguised as news—the *Times* is abandoning its traditional gatekeeping function and giving those blogs legitimacy. Craig Whitney, the *Times* standards editor who succeeded Al Siegal, the first standards editor, remarked to me: "It's a slippery slope you go down if you start linking to other sites, and you have to make clear that, when you do it, that you're not making any guarantees at all about vouching for the accuracy of the information there. . . . We're just allowing you the chance to go look at it. We're not vouching for it" (October 9, 2006).

Another negative feature of the *Times*'s own blogs is that the newspaper does not apply its usual prose standards to its own writers—although by summer 2009 there clearly was significant improvement from, say, 2007—to say nothing of the gibberish that some of its occasional contributors write. In a sense, the *Times* is abandoning its role as arbitrator of American style, although this devolution in writing has been going on for quite some time, most notably in the *Arts* section, especially but not exclusively in its reviews of pop music, and in the *Style* sections.

VIII. Reading, Listening to, Watching the *New York Times* on the Internet

In response to a survey released on July 10, 2004, by the National Endowment for the Arts that found that reading for pleasure has declined in America, Andrew Solomon wrote in an op-ed piece in the *New York Times*: "Reading is not an active expression like writing, but it is not a passive experience either. It requires effort, concentration, and attention. In exchange it offers the stimulus to, and the fruit of, thought and feeling" ("The Closing of the American Book," July 10, 2004). According to the report, "In 2002, those who do read and those who do not read literature watched about the same amount of TV per day—three hours' worth. The Internet, however, could have played a role. During the time period when the literature participation rates declined, home Internet use soared." Paradoxically, the survey shows readers are more active participants in the community—more likely to perform volunteer and charity works, go to museums and concerts, and attend sporting events than nonreaders. Solomon concluded: "There is a basic social divide between those for whom life is an accrual of fresh experience, and those for whom maturity is a process of mental atrophy." He argued, "You are what you read. If you read nothing, then your mind withers, and your ideals lose their vitality and sway. . . . We need to teach people not only how, but also why to read. The struggle is not to make people read more, but to make them want to read more."

Let us think about how reading on the Internet has become a more focused kind of reading than perusing a newspaper by turning the pages in succession. Using hypertext is easier than page-turning or even consulting tables of contents. With the Internet, the reader can immediately pick and choose in a way that is impossible on TV and radio.

Our desire for information is a function of how urgently we need to know, and on the web we can, with the help of Google, zero in on what we want more quickly than by turning pages of a newspaper. If we know we are driving in the Northeast, we need to know the weather and will take the time to find out about it. But if we are very busy, we can do without knowing about what is happening in Haiti. If we were a year from retirement, an article on retirement would be more urgent than, say, an article on teen anorexia, unless we had a very skinny child or grandchild.

What the website means is that the reader always has access to information because information remains on the Internet. Prior to the Internet, newspapers allowed much more choice than radio or TV and could be used—for a few days at least—more easily for searches or revisiting. We discard newspapers, perhaps after clipping a few articles that we often soon misplace. With the Internet, we needn't wait for a news broadcast, and we always have access to past information, thanks to Google and the *Times* archives. Of course, it always took longer to pick and choose with the physically imposing paper *Times* than, say,

The Economist. To be sure, a listener has the technical means to record what was heard on radio and a viewer can record what was seen on TV.

According to my Cornell colleague, Professor Geri Gay, research shows that people are more likely to skim stories online rather than read them carefully. For older readers who are used to setting aside a block of time to read the newspaper—accompanying breakfast coffee or while eating lunch at a desk or while on aerobic exercise machines like the treadmill or elliptical—the paper version may still have appeal. In contrast to former generations of newspaper readers, for whom reading the *Times* for pleasure was a daily ritual, younger readers read less for pleasure than information on nytimes.com. Skimming is easier on nytimes.com, where the contents are in front of the viewer rather than on a page of print, especially for those accustomed to the Internet (i.e., younger readers). Also—and this is a virtue for younger multitask-ers—one may access the Internet for five minutes and return to it later in the day to read another story or see if the headlines have changed.

For all its strengths and its continued improvements, the 2011 *Times* website, even far more than the paper itself—which I fault for not editing prolixity—seems dedicated to the principle that the more words it provides, the better. It is as if the gatekeeper had fallen asleep. I find a disturbing incongruity between the plethora of words and the comparative dearth of hard news, particularly foreign news. Many readers would appreciate a traditional gatekeeper to edit the flow of information, or maybe we should say, with some irony, of words.

Internet users can communicate with others who share even the oddest views and tastes, but is that what *Times* readers want? The elimi-nation of the forums and greater editing of reader input have brought somewhat more control to the interactive *Times*, yet silliness abounds, especially in readers' comments on the *Times* sports sites, although perhaps that is what some sports fans want. *Times* readers think of journalists as professionals whose job it is to give us information in quantity and quality that we can digest. In other words, they want the *Times* to select and organize its newsgathering into efficient form.

Like the paper *Times* itself, the current site tries to do too much— and at times not enough. The website is ideal for the kind of local and regional coverage that might clutter the *Times* national newspaper edition, an edition that has only begun to be tailored to a site-specific audience. Yet until 2010 the site did not have regional news for other areas of the country beyond the metropolitan New York area—news that might include articles on important political and business issues, cultural events, and sports in, say, Los Angeles, Miami, Washington, D.C., Atlanta, Boston, Chicago, and San Francisco. Recently, the *Times* has not only added Bay Area, Chicago, and Texas local news to its print edition in those places, but also to its choices on the top of its U.S. website. I assume this is the beginning of focusing on major population areas.

When videos are preceded by video ads, they can be frustrating to access, although we know Internet ads are essential to the survival of the *Times*. The ads preceding videos do change, but there seems to be little matching in terms of appropriate content, although Bill Pennington's golf videos do focus on golf resorts. Perhaps this is the only economically viable way that the *Times* can fund its videos, but it is disconcerting, almost as if after a headline, one began a bylined print story with an interpolated ad.

The videos should be properly dated so the reader can know when and for whom they were originally made. Many but not all are, although most produced by the *Times* itself are. Videos are an important supplement to written news, particularly for younger readers of the *Times*.

My experiences with the Haiti site—especially, but not exclusively its videos—are worth noting as a critique of the tendency of the "World" site to fail to update. Haiti is one of my lynchpins for judging the "World" site because it is a pivotal country in terms of both poverty and the politics of Central America. On August 27, 2006, I watched a powerful interview entitled "Democracy Undone" with the former ambassador of Haiti, Brian Dean Curran, but the interview was undated. Moreover, in mid-February 2008, the viewer was told that the video was "a preview of the Discovery Times documentary *Haiti: Democracy Undone.*"

In both my August 2006 and February 2008 visits to the Haiti site, I viewed an undated video in the multimedia section of the "Haiti" site entitled "Haiti's Twin Crisis" and captioned "The immense challenges facing the poorest country in the Western Hemisphere have been compounded by political instability and natural disaster." The video referred to Aristide's 2004 departure and a hurricane later that year, but were I not aware of Haitian contemporary history, I would have had to do some digging in the Haiti article section. When I returned to the Haiti site in summer 2009, I found that some of the videos and all the slide shows were still undated, and that some of them were a number of years old.

Since the January 2010 earthquake, the Haiti site has become foregrounded and has been given a great deal of attention, with major stories and recent blog commentary from "The Lede" and "Room for Debate" as well as "Headlines from around the Web" pertaining to Haiti. The site not only contains graphic pictures of the earthquake, but the historical and contextual material on Haiti was updated January 25, 2010, to include the earthquake. Moreover, all the posted articles on the left are about the earthquake and the aftermath. On the right side toward the bottom, the Haiti page includes "Haiti Navigator," directing the reader to "A list of resources about Haiti as selected by researchers and editors of *The New York Times*" as well as "Expert Recommended Resources" containing a list of books on Haiti recommended by the *Times*. The site even includes links to Haitian newspapers and a reference to a Facebook page entitled "Haiti's Earthquake Recovery" with "resources and news updates from NYT journalists on the ground in Port-au-Prince." Yet, when I looked at the site on September 10, 2010, I discovered the last updating of the country overview for this rapidly changing country was June 2010, notwithstanding the inclusion of some more recent headlines.

IX. Nytimes.com and Business Implications

More than his predecessors as executive editor, Keller was aware of profit and loss involved in the business of publishing the *Times*. In his online answer to those who objected to paying for *TimesSelect*, Keller wrote:

> We hope and believe the website—whether by selling ads or by selling subscriptions—will make more money. The long-range future of the NYT, and of quality journalism in general, depends on that. Our newspaper, because of its national market, is in sturdier financial health than many of our competitors, but the cost of everything we do is going up faster than the ad and circulation revenues that support our work. More and more, we will count on our digital journalism to pay a greater share of this amazing news organization.

> The proliferation of information on the Internet has
> given rise to a notion, almost a theology, that "informa-
> tion wants to be free"—or, at least, wants to be supported
> by advertisers rather than consumers. As a guy who has to
> manage tight budgets to support great journalism, I'm not
> so sure. One way or another, journalists have to be paid for
> their work. Maybe it will prove true that consumers won't
> pay directly for news, or not in sufficient numbers to mat-
> ter, and that advertising is the only way to go. ("Talk to the
> Newsroom," April 10, 2006)

By 2007, the realization that "advertising is the only way to go"—that is
to give advertisers the *Times*'s entire audience—was a factor in abandoning *TimesSelect*. The *Times* did continue to charge $39.95 for its puzzles.

Hoyt's June 20, 2009, public editor's column revealed one model
for charging for nytimes.com: "*Times* executives are studying possible
ways to charge readers for online content, an increasing focus in the
industry as the world moves to the Web. [*New York Times* president
and general manager Scott H.] Heekin-Canedy said options include
a so-called metered model, charging customers for how much they
read, and a membership model that would leave much content free but
give members benefits, like access to special events." Heekin-Canady
expected decisions "by mid to late summer" ("Putting a Price on
News"). While this model would not have necessarily excluded print
subscribers, presumably they could be charged less.

When the *Times*—and other newspapers—have followed the
example of such venues as craigslist.org (which "logs more than 2.5
billion page views a month") by selling Internet advertising, they basically exchanged a higher margin for a lower margin business (Jon Fine,
"Mediacentric," 2005, 24). The *Times* knew by 2005 that not only do
readers—especially younger readers—go online for information but
they also make transactional decisions based on Internet information.
However, the major problem facing the *Times* is compensating for lost
print advertising by convincing digital advertisers that they will find
an eager and financially viable purchasing audience and that they will
do so at a level that justifies higher fees than those they now charge.

In the category of lost help-wanted advertising revenue alone, the
Internet—with free or cheap advertising—cost newspapers $1.9 bil-
lion in revenue between 1996 and 2004 (Fine, 2005, 24). Interestingly,
Craigslist, which keeps its costs much lower than the *Times* is able to,

has continued to flourish since then and passed $100 million in revenue in 2009, while, according to a June 9, 2009, article by Brad Stone: "By contrast, classified advertising in newspapers in the United States declined by 29 percent last year, its worst drop in history, according to the Newspaper Association of America" ("Revenue at Craigslist Is Said to Top $100 Million"). For the *Times* to match Craigslist prices, it would need to offer online real estate classifieds ads (for brokered apartments) in New York City for $10 and in all other areas for free and offer classified ads for those seeking jobs and companies seeking workers for $25. Of course the *Times* does offer the prestige of its site, but Craigslist also has a cachet among the young.

In summer 2009, every conceivable advertisement is on the *Times* site—some embedded, others popping up; some static, some kinetic—for everything from plays and films to computers and credit cards. Presumably the *Times*—and other media sites, too, including that of the *Wall Street Journal*—are struggling with the issue of what they should make people pay for. The *Times* is used to a paper model where subscription and advertising are not such competing entities—indeed revenue from circulation enhances the appeal to advertisers—but on the web they are competing models. On the web, people are not used to paying, but rather are used to just surfing. The *Times* knows that its decision to charge for the site in March 2011 means its hits will drop; although it has surely done research on this issue, the specific drop is of course unknown.

At these rates—or even double—the *Times* isn't going to solve its financial problems. The *Times* does not want to scare away its audience and therefore scare away its advertisers, but it does need to generate revenue on a rapidly accelerated basis to meet lost advertising revenue from the newspaper and rapidly rising costs.

At a time of declining—or, at best, flat—revenue the *Times* needs to have the website make a greater contribution to its revenue stream than it is now doing. Newspaper ad revenue either is flat or declining as both readers and advertisers move to the Internet. The paradox is that the web drastically increases circulation—in terms of readers who see the *Times* (at least for a brief glimpse) each day—but it has not yet produced the necessary revenue. What Landman said in his April 2006 dialogue with readers is just as relevant today:

> The problem is that advertising on the web doesn't yet bring
> in enough money to cover the very high cost of producing

a first-class news report, with correspondents all over the
world, top-quality critics, deep and talented editing ranks
and staffs big enough to take on challenging long-term
assignments. . . . It's important to remember that while the
Internet has created tremendous business challenges, it has
also allowed us to reach more people. The readership of *The
Times*'s website is considerably bigger than the newspaper's
circulation. ("Talk to the Newsroom," April 28, 2006)

The reason web articles are divided into multiple pages is to provide
more space for advertising; as Landman explained to me: "We split
longer articles for a business reason: When you click twice, we get two
page views. This is important because page views are the virtual 'space'
that advertisers buy. Without them we have fewer advertising positions
to sell" (April 28, 2006). According to the 2006 report of the Project
for Excellence in Journalism: "At least two analysts, Paul Ginocchio of
Deutsche Bank Securities and Lauren Rich Fine of Merrill Lynch, have
estimated that when print advertising moves to online, newspapers
typically take in only 20 to 30 cents for each print dollar lost."

But where will advertising revenue be coming from now that
the *Times* believes its long-term future is its digital site? Simply put,
the *Times* does not yet get enough ads and does not get them at a
necessary price to support its website. We see blank spaces where
there could be ads, although if we include archives and blogs, it may
be that the *Times* does not have to fill all the blank spaces with ads
if it can find a formula to charge enough for ads and to charge its
users. Although the *Times* tries to match ads with content and to an
extent with users, my visual experience is that the matching often
does not work.

Basically, there are two kinds of advertising on the Internet,
which produce two revenue streams. Either the *Times* is paid a fee to
carry the ad, or the *Times* is paid per hit, or there is a combination
of both. Thus, there is display advertising where the *Times* gets paid
when it delivers the page to you; whether you click on it or not, the
Times gets paid. What Nisenholtz said to me in 2006 is no less true
now: "Online, the advertiser only pays when we deliver the page to
you with that ad. Now you can hypothesize that the ad may have no
effect, but it's being delivered" (February 17, 2006).

The second kind is pay-per-click advertising, which is the kind of advertising seen surrounding, for example, a Google search. The *Times* no longer sells advertising based on the number of clicks—that is, when a user accesses an ad—but rather on the number of times the ad is shown.

Like many aspects of nytimes.com, advertising is a work in progress. Like the paper copy, nytimes.com is filled with advertisements for several of its own products. I have yet to see advertisements on the web for historic photos and embossed pages to commemorate national or sports events, but I am sure they are there or soon to come. One also can subscribe to various email advertisements by category—travel, shopping, theater, and so on—and advertisers pay for this service.

Web advertising needs to produce significantly more revenue than it has so far. Thus, the *Times* has developed self-service advertising to help small businesses design ads and to choose when and where to place their ads on the site.

Google pays for ads it puts on the *Times* site. Google's ads are always site-specific; that is, they are matched to content on the screen. At one point, these ads were accompanied by the blurb "the website is not endorsed by the *NY Times*," but by summer 2009 these ads were in a gray-purple box labeled "Ads by Google." A "What's this?" link explains: "Ads by Google are keyword-targeted advertisements provided through the Google AdWords™ program. These listings are administered, sorted, and maintained by Google. For information about these Google ads, go to adwords.google.com." Presumably the source of the ads pays Google, and Google then pays the *Times* much but not all of their receipts from the ad.

Advertising on the web takes many forms, ranging from "Surround Sessions," in which the advertiser has an exclusive voice during a user session, to "Site Sessions," with the advertiser buying a site for a certain period of time on a specific date. An advertiser can decide what time of day an ad will appear; this is called "Day Parting." One can target an ad to readers consulting, say, the "Most Blogged Articles," "Most E-Mailed Articles," and "Most Watched Videos." In the *Times* online classified section, one can advertise for residential and commercial real estate, jobs, and autos. The *Times* is also selling web advertising based on audience behavioral patterns, registration at sites, and content contexts.

Technology has improved to now allow companies to gather information online about its users. Thus, the *Times* can find out which readers are using its site and what subsites they are accessing. The *Times* can then sell ads for a particular audience. Thus, the advertiser places an ad where it makes most sense to find its audience, whether it be sports, arts, science, education, or international news.

Tracking data about its readers helps the *Times* decide how to budget its resources. Online media's gatekeeping and presentation in terms of the placement of a story can be affected by web traffic metrics, as well as by the traditional editorial judgments concerning which news is most important. According to Keller, such metrics do affect which blogs the *Times* expands or eliminates, but does not affect how the *Times* pursues a story or the actual news presentation "because we believe readers come to us for our judgment, not the judgment of the crowd" (Jeremy W. Peters, "Some Newspapers Shift Coverage Based on What is Popular Online," September 6, 2010). Needless to say, a dotted line exists between what in the same article Jeremy W. Peters, citing Keller, calls "strategic decisions about its online report" and the actual news.

The *Times* once employed Tacoda to collect consumer information and target advertisements. Tacoda is a behavioral-based marketing website that targets groups, not specific persons. According to Tacoda, "the sites in the network collect information about your browsing behavior." By tracking IP (Internet Protocol) addresses—each Internet-connected computer has a unique IP address assigned for an Internet service provider—the *Times* can learn not only geographic information but other data about its users in terms of who is accessing what. As the *Times* explained on its site: "The *Times* is able to get a computer's IP address and keep logs of information on what it is accessing on its site. This way, it can gain information and target ads to the user even though they are not registered. . . . This allows for very narrow targeting of any visitor to the NYTimes.com site, whether that user is registered with us or not." The *Times* could respond to the reader's input by monitoring clicks the way Amazon posts a recommended page for customers by using a "cookie" or "tracker" to see which articles a reader clicks on and then determining which similar articles or subjects might interest the reader. When responding to the reader's click, the *Times* would send not only the article but ads likely to appeal to his or her interests. But this doesn't seem to be the *Times*'s current program.

X. Conclusion

In thinking about nytimes.com, we need to distinguish between problems inherent in presenting news on the web—less gatekeeping with instantaneous stories and links to the blogosphere, the nonlinear nature of a hypertext medium that means an essential contextual story may not be fully understood—and problems in the design of the site.

Nytimes.com is conceived for a generation used to the web, raised on search engines, videos, and computer games. Younger people—by whom I, age seventy, mean anyone under age forty-five or fifty—regard the computer as a source of both information and recreation. For these readers, browsing the web is a physical activity requiring some dexterity and hand–eye coordination. Making choices, discarding them, probing elsewhere, and following leads are part of the pleasure and challenge of the web. Searches can be like mini-detective stories where one follows clues until answers are found, and the search itself can be a source of pleasure. The combination of writing, audios (podcasts), and videos creates a kind of excitement and energy that those raised on television and the web find appealing.

The original targeted web audience was younger than the traditional *Times* readership and, the *Times* believed, more interested in soft news, features, and value-added journalism giving them life advice than in hard news. But in 2011, the web audience demography is more and more similar to the print audience.

Getting information from the web requires a different kind of attention span than reading a newspaper, but becoming adept at navigating the web is an acquired skill. My undergraduate research assistant, Jennifer Schlesinger, who is extremely adept at using the Internet, writes in an email: "The *NY Times* website can still be hard to navigate for me. I was trying to find House and Senate votes on health care and TARP and found it almost impossible" (September 23, 2010).

For postmodern readers who are skeptical that any source provides a univocal truth and/or believe the major media are untrustworthy, the blogosphere is appealing for two very different reasons. Whatever readers believe—from the notion that capitalistic interests manipulate major media to the fantasy that the mainstream journalism is part of a secular conspiracy to marginalize religion—these readers can find in the blogosphere validation for their own version of truth. If, instead, they believe that all truth is relative and a function of who is presenting a narrative, they can find multiple interpretations of the same events.

According to what Meislin told me, "Just short of twenty percent of web readers look at the printed newspaper; forty percent of our print audience looks at the website" (April 13, 2007). I am sure in 2011 far more readers integrate both into their daily routines. I now read the *Times* as much on the Internet as in the newspaper copy and probably more, but still prefer to complement the web with the daily newspaper. For the ever-increasing readership with broadband—which I have become part of these last few years—the videos and podcasts do add a dimension to the reading experience, and I use them more and more. But I still enjoy the physicality—turning the pages, the feel of paper in my hands—and the visual, even aesthetic experience of varying sizes of black newsprint on white printed paper.

But are the *Times*'s assumptions about the web audience correct? Is the *Times* worrying too much about losing a readership that, having invested nothing in purchasing access to the *Times*'s site, will move readily to another site if they are seeking gossip, titillation, and such foolishness as a June 4, 2006, *SundayStyles* piece—originally in the newspaper—entitled "Coveting Thy Neighbor's Ex" by Mireya Navarro? Or are they dumbing down without needing to because regular readers come to the *Times*'s site for hard information and useful knowledge? Advertisers will choose the *Times* site for the *Times* audience, and the *Times* needs to create an enlarged core audience of serious readers rather than, as it seems to be willing to do, pander to a hypothetical audience.

Users in various surveys generally give nytimes.com the highest marks for being a source for news and information and for information they can use in their lives, but this is somewhat tautological because these are the people who have chosen the site. Interestingly, a significantly lower percentage of the same readers is less likely to use the digital *Times* to make purchases (i.e., respond to advertisers). We don't know what the comparable figures for positively responding to advertiser's products by making purchases are for the newsprint edition but this differential is a problem that the *Times* has been trying to solve. As Meislin acknowledged to me in 2007, the *Times* is still figuring out how to integrate effective advertising into the nytimes.com site:

> We need to find ways to have this become a strong money-generating enterprise. So we work out our positions by bal-

ancing the effectiveness of the advertising with the editorial
needs. . . . But it's one of those areas where it's not as well
shaped as the newspaper, where everybody knows the ads
will be in a little well on the outside. Online, as you change,
maybe ads make sense where you haven't put them before.
(April 13, 2007)

With its archives and links, to say nothing of its daily product and its retention of recent material on its site, nytimes.com is a
remarkable resource. But it needs to differentiate breaking stories from
more complete stories. For one thing, many readers do not read the
final version in the print counterpart or the final version that appears
online. The *Times* needs to clearly indicate on its site what is still
being edited and fact-checked, perhaps by including the story within
a subsite called "Breaking Stories." Such a subsite would indicate that
the newsgathering process is continuing and perhaps indicate not only
what facts are known and how they are known but also what needs
to be known before the full story can be written. Bylined "Breaking
Stories" could have an analytic component as long as the story clearly
differentiated facts from surmises and stressed what facts were not
yet known. (One reader suggested this be called "New York Times
Online Raw" for news that hasn't solidified; letter to the public editor,
December 10, 2006.) By summer 2010, "Times Wire" was somewhat
helpful, but it still doesn't show whether the article is in progress or
if it is the final version.

The Internet poses problems balancing speed and accuracy. Staff
retraining involves teaching print editors to handle web stories and
teaching web producers how to deal with narrative. At times, there
are fewer levels of editing and fact checking. The following examples,
one positive and one negative, show how nytimes.com handled two
2009 stories.

On the web, the *Times* published unproven allegations about
Caroline Kennedy's reasons for withdrawing her candidacy as a possible
replacement for Sen. Hilary Clinton because of Kennedy's supposed tax
and nanny problems. The article appeared the day after she withdrew,
January 22, 2009, and quoted an anonymous source under the headline:
"Taxes and a Housekeeper Are Said to Derail Kennedy's Bid." As public
editor Hoyt wrote, "[The *Times* story] quoted the anonymous source
as saying that [Governor David] Paterson 'never had any intention of
picking Kennedy because it was clear that she wasn't ready for prime

time. She had botched her rollout. She was unprepared. She clearly had no policy experience and couldn't handle the pressure of the public stage.' The article had no more information about the tax and housekeeper problems than was in the headline." Using an anonymous quote to attack someone violates the *Times*'s ethics policy, as Craig Whitney, standards editor, remarked (Clark Hoyt, "Reporting in Real Time," February 7, 2009).

In a corrective article on February 4, 2009—well after damage was done to Kennedy's reputation—*Times* readers were told how Paterson's staff had scurrilously tried to manipulate the news. Danny Hakim and Nicholas Confessore reported that Paterson's administration had "released confidential information about Ms. Kennedy and misled reporters about its significance as part of an orchestrated effort to discredit her after she withdrew" ("In Attack on Kennedy, Echo of a Spitzer Tactic," February 3, 2009).

On the other hand, the web enabled brilliant real-time coverage of the US Airways flight that landed in the Hudson River in winter 2009, inviting witnesses to call in and be interviewed and to submit photos even while reporters were writing online (Hoyt, "A Balancing Act on the Web," February 14, 2009).

Another issue is whether the standards for editing blogs should be different from the standards for print media. Whitney wrote a February 2009 internal memo (which is posted online) exploring the difference:

> Contractions, colloquialisms and even slang are, generally speaking, more allowable in blogs than in print. . . . Writers and editors of blogs must also distinguish between personal tone and voice and unqualified personal opinion. . . . Moderating reader comments on blogs involves the same Times ethical and journalistic standards that apply to articles. . . . Blogs on the news side of NYTimes.com are not the personal, private blogs of the contributors, but blogs of Times employees, whose reputations depend on readers' trust in their impartiality. ("News Blogs and Online Columns")

Web-only features and blogs do not always meet the standards of the print edition, and that is a problem because it compromises the quality of the *Times*. What Nisenholtz acknowledged to me in 2006 is less true today, but often applicable:

In terms of stuff like Carpetbagger and Opinionater, five years ago these things would never have had any chance of getting online. . . . We would never have done them. They're web-only features. They didn't emanate out of the newsroom in a traditional way, and now we're doing them. . . . We're learning. We're testing, and. . . . we usually do figure out how to make this stuff right over time. But it's a different . . . underlying philosophy. . . . That's a fundamental change in the way we operate. . . . Sometimes the stuff isn't as well baked or as comprehensive, or as comprehensible. But the upside of it is we're doing a lot more and we're competing with guys like Yahoo, like Google. (February 17, 2006)

If the content of the website is not always up to the print standards of the *Times*, doesn't that somewhat eviscerate the reputation of the *Times*? Nisenholtz acknowledged that the site is more prone than the newspaper to experimentation and trial and error, although, to be sure, it has improved in accuracy since 2006:

We've taken a very different attitude at the website than we had traditionally taken in print. In print, you know, everything was perfected before it was launched. I mean you'd never see us do anything in print that wasn't vetted a thousand times and then put out there, because it costs so much to put something out there in the paper. Right? We're doing stuff now online that's going to look ridiculous, that's going to feel wrong . . . that's going be criticized, and in some cases for very legitimate reasons. . . . So it's a different philosophy on the website than it is in print. And I grant you in all seriousness that some of the stuff that we're doing, particularly on the blogging side, is marginal. I'd say that our podcasts are still marginal.

But if meeting the standards of the competitors is the goal—and those standards, particularly in the blogosphere, are heavily weighted with rumor, gossip, innuendo, prolixity, and reductive conclusions based on half-baked facts—we need ask how this "different attitude" affects the *Times*'s reputation? For Nisenholtz is articulating very different standards than those of Abe Rosenthal. These online standards—along with changing editorial policy for print and nytimes.com that allow for *Timeslite* and *Timestrash*—may undermine Sulzberger's articulated desire "to ensure that when the time comes for the next generation of leaders to take over the *New York Times* newspaper and company that they are handed as strong and as powerful an institution as I was handed in my time" (interview with Charlie Rose, PBS, November 10, 2005).

The Internet changes the way foreign news is received because many of the readers are not those in America but in the country about which the article is written. Thus, according to Anand Giridharadas:

> Foreign correspondents no longer cover one place for the exclusive benefit of readers somewhere else. In the Internet age, we cover each place for the benefit of all places, and the reported-on are among the most avid consumers of what we report. . . . According to data teased out of the Google Trends service, the phrases "New York Times India" and "Washington Post India" are searched eight times as much in India, as a proportion of all Indian searches, as the equivalent in the United States. By the same measure, "New York Times China" is searched more intensively in Beijing than in New York. ("These Days, No Reporting Behind a Nation's Back," March 15, 2009)

This audience change highlights the need for careful online reporting. By means of emails and blogs, readers in the foreign host countries are more likely to catch errors than a Western editor and to criticize oversimplifications. Authorities in autocracies can organize vitriolic attacks on correspondents. In the same *Times* piece Giridharadas reports on how Nicholas Kristof, the *Times* columnist, was detained because of a column he wrote while in Iran.

At times I have an imaginary dialogue between Schwarz alpha, trained to read the newspaper in the tradition of my father and grandfather, and Schwarz beta, living in the world of the Internet. Schwarz alpha sometimes finds the site too busy with insignificant magazine stories and long-winded unedited blogs—especially on sports—followed by iterative readers' comments.

For Schwarz alpha, an example of *Timeslite* is the web page category "Most Popular" and such subcategories as "Most Emailed,"

"Most Blogged"—articles most frequently linked to by bloggers on the web—and "Most Searched." In September 2010, the "Most Searched" were "Modern Love," "China," and "Ground Zero Mosque." One also can find lists of most emailed articles and most blogged in several additional categories.

Schwarz alpha worries about the "Most Popular" stories and thinks stories and subjects should not be rated in such terms, and certainly not on the home page, where he finds, to his dismay, stories that are not very significant. He worries about pandering to what readers want rather than what they need to know. Perhaps the implication is that if we do not read what others read, we are somehow not in the cultural mainstream. It is as if the *Times* were a reality TV show in which the audience votes for the best amateur singer or body and facial makeover, as if readers' interest was in itself sufficient validation that the *Times* is making the right decisions in deciding what is newsworthy, even it means dumbing down its digital site. For example, on March 23, 2007, the most emailed and second-most blogged article was about living for a year with little environmental impact on Manhattan (Penelope Green, "The Year Without Toilet Paper").

Schwarz beta has become increasingly less distracted by lists of the "Most Emailed stories," the "Most Blogged Sites," and the subjects that are "Most Searched." He now realizes that "Most Popular" reveals a great deal about culture and the *Times*'s readership. He is curious about what his fellow readers find interesting, and realizes that the *Times* is directing its product more to what its audience wants rather than in the past to what it thinks its audience needs. He also understands that "the most" categories can be a source of necessary advertising revenue because the *Times* can guarantee advertisers more readers. On June 24, 2009, the most emailed article was "And the Pursuit of Happiness: Time Wastes too Fast," a wonderful graphic about Thomas Jefferson by Maira Kalman. Schwarz beta appreciates such graphics.

Schwarz beta has become more of an online reader and less of a print reader with each passing year. He enjoys the videos, which continue to improve in their analyses and news worthiness, and is grateful that the *Times*—especially after it sold its 50 percent share in the Discovery Channel in 2006—began putting more resources into shorter videos on its website.

Notwithstanding his caveats and reservations about the digital *Times*, Schwarz alpha, with some reservations expressed above, might join Schwarz beta in concurring with what the ever-optimistic Landman, perhaps the person most responsible for integrating the digital and printed *Times,* said to me: "The [new] platforms for journalism require different kinds of journalism, right? And, the trick is to do those different kinds of journalism in a full, open, non-defensive way and express the same values. It's really hard and I think we've been pretty successful at it. That's very unusual. I think other news organizations, because of shrinkage and other reasons, have not been able to keep fundamental values . . . secure" (June 9, 2010).

5

Media Economics 101

The Business Crises of the *New York Times*

No institution can possibly survive if it needs geniuses or supermen to manage it. It must be organized in such a way as to be able to get along under a leadership composed of average human beings.

—Peter Drucker, *Concept of the Corporation*

It's not print paper that I value for itself of all things; it's the ability to keep in place this fantastic news gathering machine. If economics change enough, if people don't want print paper, then why should we put out a print paper?

—Jonathan Landman, June 9, 2010

In truth, the expansion of the *New York Times* when you include print, the web, and now, of course, television, it's been a remarkable success story. We are no longer bound by the word "paper" and "newspaper." We are bound by the word "news."

—Arthur Sulzberger Jr., October 11, 2005

Having squandered billions during the newspaper's fat years—buying up all that stock, buying up failing newspapers, building a gleaming new headquarters—Arthur is scrambling to keep up with interest payments on hundreds of millions in debt, much of it falling due within the next year. To do so, he is peddling assets on ruinous terms. Arthur recently borrowed $250 million from Carlos "Slim" Helú, the Mexican telecommunications billionaire, who owns the fourth largest stake in the Times Company. . . . What is increasingly clear is that the wrong person may be at the helm. Arthur Sulzberger's heart has always been in the right place, but

he assumed leadership from his father uniquely ill-equipped for
this crisis—not despite but *because* of his long apprenticeship. To
their credit, the Sulzbergers have long treated the *Times* less as
a business than as a public trust, and Arthur is steeped in that
tradition, rooted in it, trained by it, captive to it. Ever the dutiful
son, he has made it his life's mission to maintain the excellence
he inherited—to duplicate his father's achievement. He is a careful steward, when what the *Times* needs today is some wild-eyed
genius of an entrepreneur.

—Mark Bowden, "The Inheritance," *Vanity Fair,* May 2009

I. Serious Business

Rule No. 1: Virtually every change in the *Times* derives from
    the need to sell advertising and newspapers.
Rule No. 2: See Rule No. 1.

In an effort to remain profitable, the New York Times Company
has become more and more a media company, owning a host of regional
newspapers, including the *International Herald Tribune* and the *Boston
Globe*, and interests in other businesses, including the Boston Red Sox.
It also has a Broadcast Media Group with television and radio stations.
It bought About.com, an online information provider with the goal
of diversifying its advertising base and extending its Internet reach.
In 2002, the *Times* moved into the television business by buying half
the Discovery Channel, which it later sold.

Many of its critics in the business world believe that the Times
Company should focus on its flagship newspaper and especially its
digital site, nytimes.com. To an extent, that is the current strategy as
it continues to *radically* transform itself from a newspaper to a daily
magazine with a strong newspaper component, as well as into a newsgathering digital site with a print component.

The *Times* is and has been for the past several years in serious
financial trouble and is struggling for survival in the face of advertising downturn, rising costs, and digital challenges.

Although the *Times* often stresses that the editorial *Times* and
the news *Times* are not the same, for decades it also stressed—some
might say, pretended—that the news and editorial *Times* have been

traditionally separate from the business of the New York Times Company. Although it is a long-standing, articulated principle that the separation be complete, the current editorial editor, Andrew Rosenthal, former executive editor Bill Keller, Arthur Sulzberger Jr., Scott H. Heekin-Canedy (current president and general manager of the *Times*), and Martin Nisenholtz (senior vice president for digital operations of the New York Times Company) meet weekly. Heekin-Canedy replaced Russ Lewis in 2004 and, according to the *Times* site, "is responsible for all of the business operations of the *Times* newspaper, including advertising, circulation, marketing, production, systems, human resources, finance, strategic planning, labor relations and New York Times News Services."

In February 2010, the Times Company reported profits for the last quarter of 2009 and for the 2009 year. As a result of somewhat good news and the improving stock market, the stock was then in the $10–11 range, a long way from $50 but better than the less than $4 in the worst part of the 2008–2009 recession. While the $16.9 million profit was far better than the $57.8 million loss in 2008, Richard Perez-Pena noted that, "One-time factors made the year-over-year comparison appear rosier, including a gain from freezing pension plans and the sale of the radio station WQXR-FM. . . . Over the course of 2009, The Times Company significantly reduced its debt and pension obligations, and it cut operating costs by $475 million on the year, or 17.1 percent. The steps the company took to shed costs included closing a money-losing distribution subsidiary, City and Suburban, last January, and wringing some $20 million in yearly labor costs from the unions at the *Boston Globe* in bitter contract talks last spring" ("Times Company Reports Profit for Quarter and Year," February 10, 2010).

Exuding her characteristic optimism accompanying the more recent July 22, 2010, announcement of the Times Company's second-quarter results and announcing an 18 percent quarterly profit, president and CEO Janet L. Robinson commented: "These positive results continued to build on the momentum of the past few quarters as the Company was able to increase revenues and decrease operating costs." She acknowledged that its 21 percent gain in online advertising was offset by its 6 percent loss in print advertising. Because print advertising is more lucrative than online advertising, it is extremely difficult to make up online for lost print advertising. That the stock hovered between seven and a fraction and eight and a fraction since the announcement speaks to Wall Street's vote on the Times Company's optimism.

In the fourth quarter 2010, net income fell by 26.2 percent to $67.1 million, from $90.9 million in 2009. Revenues decreased by 2.9 percent. Advertising revenue fell by 3.1 percent despite an 11.1 percent increase in digital advertising. Print advertising fell by 7.2 percent, showing that online advertisements have not yet made up for losses in print advertisements.

Despite a poor fourth quarter, 2010 was a more successful year than 2009. The *Times* made $107.7 million compared to $19.9 million in 2009. According to Janet Robinson: "In 2010 we demonstrated further progress toward our long-term strategy of re-engineering our company" (cited in Jeremy W. Peters, February 3, 2011, "Income Falls 26% at The Times Company as Print Advertising Drops." In mid-2010, Peters succeeded Perez-Pena as the *Times* reporter writing about the *Times*).

Simply put, the *Times* needs to sell print newspaper and Internet advertising for nytimes.com as well as sell newspapers, and the *Times* business—and yes, news—departments continue to devote an increasing amount of its energy to those ends. Beginning in March 2011, as we have noted, a pay wall limited online access to non-subscribers. Although virtually all past and present *Times* editors claim to be oblivious to business considerations, the *Times* is much more concerned with profit now than in its earlier days because since 1969 the company has been a publicly traded company rather than a family business. In the early 2000s, the business downturn was largely confined to big metropolitan dailies, not small papers where the advertising base is more stable; consequently, the *Times* pursued a strategy of buying small regional newspapers, but the 2008–2009 recession hit especially hard those papers that depended on local advertising.

Reading the various memoirs and books about the *Times*, and speaking to the current publisher and many *Times* luminaries on both the editorial and business sides, I became very much aware that the *Times* is not a nonprofit organization and that its business needs have become increasingly important. As high-minded as it would like to be, the intake of dollars sustains its existence. Outspoken veteran newsman Clyde Haberman noted the paradox to me: "No, I don't only want to make money, but yes I do want to make money because without making a profit, we die. Who pays for Kristof to go to Darfur? Solicitations on the street? It's such a mindless thing. I get it in the building all the time. They say 'did you see the new *Style* section? there's not much in it." What's wrong with having a section that's light and fluffy all the time? It actually has content" (June 21, 2005).

Having evolved into a corporation rather than a family business, the *Times* is now driven by business decisions. On the March 2008 masthead, "The Business Management" shared co-billing with the "News Sections" and the "Opinion Pages"; fifteen names were listed under "The Business Management" and fifteen for both the other categories. And this did not include the inserted box in which twelve of the officers of "The New York Times Company" were listed. Perhaps with the intent of redressing the impression that newsgathering was sharing the focus with such exotic revenue sources as a *Times* wine club, the Business Management masthead had by September 2010 been reduced to eight, whereas the News and Opinion numbered fourteen and the Officers of the New York Times Company numbered eleven.

The basic question we need to ask is whether Wall Street's demands for quarterly profit growth are compatible with the ongoing reconfiguration of the newspaper business. As a publicly traded company, profitability is examined every quarter. Another important question is what are the current financial conditions under which Arthur Sulzberger Jr. and the *Times* newspaper and website—as well as the parent New York Times Company—operate and how much these shape the daily newspaper and website?

Finally, are the editors under pressure caused by the publisher's financial problems? Are reporters assigned stories primarily to bring in readers and advertisers? Are some stories put lower on the priority list because they might embarrass or offend advertisers, the directors of the New York Times Company, the Sulzberger family, or other major *Times* figures? Have the employees of the *Times* become, as former middle-level editor Linda Lee charged in an April 29, 2007, telephone interview with me, the victims of a top-down management style where pleasing the supervisor takes precedence over everything else? Does Arthur Jr. really rule with a heavier hand than his father and grandfather, and is that related to financial pressures?

Under Keller, what the newsroom calls soft sections have proliferated. As he put it, "We don't put out a daily newspaper; we put out a daily newspaper plus about fifty weekly magazines. Some of them are actual magazines. But a lot of them, although they're printed on newsprint, are still—in format, conception, and design—magazines" (cited in Byron Calame, "Can 'Magazines' of the *Times* Subsidize

News Coverage," October 22, 2006). Keller's justification is that these magazines generate revenue to support the core news reports—foreign, national, metro, business, sports, cultural. This additional revenue is a way of sustaining earnings to keep up the stock price and helping to fill stockholders' pockets as dividends. Without this revenue, share earnings would be lower, stock prices would drop, and dividends might not be sustained at the current level.

Allan M. Siegal, the first standards editor when that position was created in 2003 in the wake of the Blair scandal, made a defensive remark in 2005 that is still apropos: "The most contentious areas these days . . . are in the area of business-side relations, because the perception in the building is that revenue is so stressed and the competitive field is so demanding that we can't be as fussy as we used to be about certain fringe things" (cited in Calame, "A Conversation with the Standards Editor," August 28, 2005). If my interviews are any criteria, he was accurate about the increasing importance of business implications in the *Times*'s decision-making process.

An important part of the current standards editor's job—Craig Whitney succeeded Siegal in 2006 and in turn was succeeded by Phil Corbett—is to separate the business and editorial sides and to help, as Whitney put it in the same interview with Calame, "staff members navigate our [the *Times*'s] ethics and conflict-of-interest policies." In his August 14, 2005, column, Calame pointed out possible conflicts of interest between freelancers and enterprises with whom they worked on the issues on which they were writing. Moreover, it is gatekeepers on the business side who decide how much to charge for an ad and which ads to accept—as we learned in fall 2007 during the flap about the *Times*'s publishing an ad from the liberal advocacy group MoveOn that played on General Petraeus's name as General Betray US.

Long before it had an official standards editor in 2003, the *Times* historically enacted a conflict between responsibly responding to news and selling advertisements for toxic products. Cigarette ads were accepted long after the relation between smoking and lung cancer was established. Even now the *Times* carries ads for pharmaceuticals under investigation. Certainly, some of the product claims of its advertisers are not checked independently, even when scientific evidence begins to raise questions about efficacy. Moreover, the *Times* travel pages rarely if ever critique its advertisers, even though some travel businesses have a history of disappointing clients by canceling or rearranging trips.

The *Times*'s realization that it was in financial trouble has been a gradual process. The advertising base of the newspaper world has been shrinking, in part because of the merging and disappearance of big department stores that used to buy full-page ads, in part because advertising is going to other venues like the Internet and television, and in part because circulation is dropping.

Growing the national edition in the 1980s and 1990s was one early solution to the *Times*'s problems. Conceived as an urban paper, the *Times* had been slow to follow its readers into the suburbs and even slower to realize its potential elsewhere. The transformation into a national newspaper—one produced in several cities—was a calculated, earnest, and at times desperate effort to increase circulation and advertising by lowering the age and increasing the geographic, gender, and ethnic diversity of its readership.

During Max Frankel's editorship (1986–1994), sales of the national edition increased by 100,000, while sales in the northeast increased by 50,000 and New York City sales stayed static. As Frankel said (with perhaps a hint of the slightly arrogant elitism with which officials of the *Times* customarily speak and write): "Our kind of educated, curious, and affluent readers could be found not only in Manhattan, Scarsdale, and Southampton but also in Grosse Point, Atlanta, Dallas, and San Jose" (*The Times of My Life and My Life with the Times*, 509).

From 2005 to 2010, a steady series of gloomy announcements emanated from the New York Times Company. Katharine Q. Seelye paired the *Times*'s announcement of cuts with a similar one by Knight Ridder announcing a small cut of one hundred total in its Philadelphia operation, which publishes the *Philadelphia Inquirer* and the *Philadelphia Daily News*. Interestingly, the *Times* cut was five times as large as the Knight Ridder one, which the article failed to mention, although the percentage of news people lost at the *Times* was smaller because the staffs at those other papers were originally smaller ("Times Company Announces 500 Job Cuts," September 21, 2005). Continuing to make the *Times* look as good as possible, Seelye, while acknowledging some layoffs in other areas in combination with buyouts, summarized remarks by Keller, who said he hoped to achieve the newsroom cuts by severance deals and attrition and less use of temporary employees.

In the same 2005 article, Seelye reported that at the same time it announced job cuts, the *Times* also announced that profits for the third quarter would be lower than expected, 11 to 14 cents a share rather than the expected 25 cents and much lower than the 33 cents earned for the similar period in the previous year. It also announced circulation would be flat to down slightly in 2005 and advertising revenue would increase in the low single digits rather than, as it had predicted earlier, from the low to middle single digits. The only place where advertising was growing was in digital operations, but in 2005 Internet ads had brought in only a fraction of print revenue and were still quite cheap in comparison to print advertising. Although the *Times* clearly hoped it could vastly expand Internet advertising revenue because Internet advertising has increased dramatically, by October 2010 it was still not producing the necessary revenue stream. Furthermore, it does not help newspaper circulation or nytimes.com that Yahoo! and Google or the *Huffington Post* recycle news from media outlets—most notably the *New York Times*—and present it as their own content.

Addressing the loss of advertising in the newspaper, Seelye referred to both the consolidation of department stores and the movement to Internet advertising by the travel industry. She specifically mentioned Hertz, which had not advertised in the *Times* for six months, and the decline in movie ads. Major companies such as Ford already had moved a much larger percentage of its advertising budget online; by 2005, classified advertisers were increasingly using such sites as Craigslist and Ebay and that trend continued in fall 2011. Moreover, many advertisers used such social networking sites as Facebook.

We can look back from a 2010 vantage point and see how misleading Seelye's 2005–2006 analyses were. On January 26, 2006, Seelye wrote an article "Layoff Costs Pared Profit at Times Co in 4th Quarter." She put the best possible glow on the news that net income fell from $110.2 million or 75 cents a share to $64.8 million or 45 cents a share: "Total revenue . . . rose 3 percent to $931 million. . . . Excluding one-time items, the results beat estimates based on a forecast the company issued last month."

Although her article hewed close to the *Times* party line at the time, namely that newspapers were in a lull, we see in fall 2010 that things were worse than even the pessimists suspected. Seelye's articles often repeated—and repeated—the *Times*'s own bromides about its problems. Thus, in a sentence following the information that the *Times* would be raising its home delivery rate, Seelye wrote: "Newspaper companies have been struggling to maintain advertising and circulation in the face of competition from the Internet and must grapple with the rising price of newsprint" (January 26, 2006). Seelye usually was behind the curve in reporting her newspaper's bad news, and her articles often were little more than *Times* press releases.

To be fair, I could cite a few more-balanced articles by Seelye in which misplaced optimism gave way to reality. In the *Media* section of the *Times* Seelye had a headline for her "Advertising" column, "Lagging Sales Contribute to Earnings Decline at Newspaper Chains" (April 14, 2006). Even as newspaper companies reported "that their Internet activities were thriving," those activities had not compensated for the loss of revenue from stagnant advertising by such industries as entertainment and automobiles and the cost of severance packages for recent job cuts.

For several years, the *Times* tried in the face of evidence to the contrary to put the best possible spin on its data. For example, in 2005, Janet Robinson, chief executive of the New York Times Company, remarked, "Newspaper companies . . . are reinventing themselves" (cited in Seelye, "At Newspapers, Some Clipping," October 10, 2005). But Seelye also quoted in the same article those who are gloomier about the future of newspapers and skeptical that newspapers will be able to repackage themselves to become more "navigable" to younger readers or deliver a product that will be essential to their lives. Certainly, even the published version of the *Times*—which is now read by virtually all readers more like a hypertext than a progressively linear text—is not as navigable as it might be. Retrospectively, we see how prophetic Seelye was: "Industry wide, ad revenue is flat, costs are up and circulation is eroding. . . . Pessimism about the industry's ability to overcome these obstacles continues to drive down the price of newspaper stocks."

Were Robinson working for a company whose management structure was not privately controlled, her overly optimistic take on events since 2005 would be a matter of serious concern. By 2009 she was more likely to provide fluff than numerical predications: "As other newspapers cut back on international and national coverage, or cease operations, we believe there will be opportunities for the *Times* to fill that void" (Perez-Pena, "Resilient Strategy for Times Despite Toll of a Recession," February 8, 2009). Another example of Robinson's tendency to whistle in the dark: "In a conference call with analysts, Janet L. Robinson, the chief executive, said that in the second quarter, ad revenue was 'trending similar to what we're seeing in the first quarter,' but will not fall as quickly after that. In talking to advertisers, she said, it seemed that 'they are saving dollars in the first half to do possibly more in the second half'" (Perez-Pena, "Times Co. Reports Loss of $74 Million," April 21, 2009).

On July 23, 2009, Richard Perez-Pena, who succeeded Seelye in May 2007 as the principal *Times* person who writes about the *Times*—and other media news—wrote under the seemingly overly optimistic and somewhat misleading headline, "Times Company Turns a Profit": "The drop was about the same, 31.7 percent, at the company's New York Times Media Group, consisting primarily of the flagship *Times* newspaper—a departure from the pattern through most of the downturn, in which the *Times* has held up better than the other newspapers, including the *Boston Globe*." In other words, despite the spin of the headline and a nominal return to profitability, the *Times*'s ship is still floundering if not sinking: "A favorable tax adjustment inflated the earnings in the most recent quarter. But even discounting that factor, Thursday's results represented a return to profitability—albeit slight—after a first-quarter loss of $74.5 million." Typically, Robinson's usual whistling-in-the dark quotation is part of the article: "We believe the rate of decline will moderate slightly in the third quarter. . . . For the full year we expect to save $450 million. . . . That amounts to 16 percent of our 2008 cost base."

It is true that the *Times* had made cost-cutting strides, including on the newsroom side 5 percent temporary salary reductions—plus ten days unpaid leave—from April 1 to December 31, 2009. The Newspaper Guild Union—representing newsroom and "certain other employees"—accepted a 5 percent reduction that matched mandated salary reductions to non-union newsroom employees and management. The alleged reason was to avoid cuts of sixty to seventy people from the newsroom staff of almost 1,300, but by September 2010, the newsgathering staff was down to 1,140, and it is in July 2011 described as "over 1,100." The freelance budget has been cut from 10 to 15 percent. With such cuts, newsgathering has to be affected.

Its staff cutbacks to date have been less drastic than most other major newspapers and other media. For example, ABC News, like the other networks, has suffered audience erosion, and announced in February 2010 that they were cutting back the news division staff of 1,500 by 300 to 400 people.

In the largest cuts since 2001, when a 9 percent reduction of 13,750 jobs took place after the technology bubble burst, the *Times* announced on September 20, 2005, that it was cutting five hundred jobs, or about 4 percent of its workforce, in an effort to reduce costs, and that was on top of a two-hundred-person job cut earlier in 2005 from a workforce of 12,300 people at the end of 2004. In spring 2009, the *Times* announced layoffs of one hundred people on the business side of operations (Tim Arango, "Tentative Nod to a Pay Cut at The Times," April 28, 2009; Perez-Pena, "Times Co. Announces Temporary Salary Cuts," March 26, 2009).

To save money, sections have been consolidated; in May 2009 *Escapes* was integrated on Friday with *Fine Arts*. In October 2008, the *Metro* section was moved into the A section; on Sunday (as of May 2009) city and regional sections were replaced by a new *Metropolitan* section. The *Sports* section was combined with the *Business Day* section except for Monday, Saturday, and Sunday. Beginning May 10, 2009, the *New York Times Magazine* ceded fashion coverage to *T Magazine* and the *ThursdayStyles* and *SundayStyles* sections. Thus, the *Times* now has four sections Monday through Wednesday as well as Saturday (which didn't change). The national edition sections remained the same.

As Perez-Pena explained in his April 16, 2009, "Times Will Cut Sections to Lower Costs," the recently expanded guide would be cut back to its original form: "The guide to each day's newspaper, which is now printed on the second, third, and fourth pages of the first section, will be consolidated into a single page, much as it was until last year."

What was crucial, as Perez-Pena stressed in his July 23, 2009, article, is that the *Times* made strong strides in cutting operating costs by 20 percent within the previous year: "The company trimmed operating costs 20 percent from a year earlier, or by $140.5 million; $29 million of that reduction came from the closure early this year of City & Suburban, a money-losing newspaper and magazine distribution subsidiary" ("Times Company Turns a Profit," July 23, 2009). Yet is this good news? Dirk Smilie of Forbes doesn't think so: "Signs of green shoots? Hardly. To hit these numbers, the *Times* has slashed operating costs and capital expenditures, raised prices at *The New York Times* and the *Times'*-owned *Boston Globe*, divested itself of an Alabama newspaper and sold off New York classical music station WQXR for $45 million" ("Green Shoots For Grey Lady?" July 23, 2009).

On July 18, 2006, keeping with a trend established by its competitors, the *Wall Street Journal* and *USA Today*, the *Times* announced that by the second quarter of 2008, it would cut the width of its page size by

1.5 inches and that, because some pages would be added to compensate for the 11 percent reduction in space, the cut would result in a 5 percent reduction in news. On August 6, 2007—well before the second quarter of 2008—the *Times* did adopt the smaller format, cutting 1.5 inches from its width and, following the *Wall Street Journal,* the *Washington Post,* and the *Los Angeles Times,* moving to what has become the newspaper industry standard of 12 inches. The *Times* expected to save $10 million per year but there is no way to check this figure.

Making a virtue of necessity, as it characteristically does in its retrenchment announcements, the *Times* claimed that the paper would be more user-friendly and claimed "research has found that readers, particularly younger people and commuters, prefer the smaller size" ("NY Times to Reduce Page Size, Cut Jobs," Associated Press, online, July 18, 2006). The *Times* also announced the closing of a printing plant in New Jersey and a consolidation of newspaper production at its newer facility in Queens, a decision that it claimed would result not only in cost savings but also in the elimination of 250 of the then 800 production jobs. In January 2009, the *Times* closed the operations of its retail and newsstand delivery subsidiary called City & Suburban. According to Jonathan Landman, job cuts are not continuing in 2011 (email to author, March 5, 2011).

Many of Katharine Seelye's articles from 2005 to 2008 are hardly reporting at all but rather an optimistic spin based on corporate inter-pretation of events. We are accustomed to this fudging from spokes-people for politicians and businesses, but it doesn't add to the *Times*'s stature. Toward the very end of her July 18, 2006, article, Seelye quotes some doubts of a skeptical Merrill Lynch analyst: "The paper is getting relatively expensive." But this is hardly a trenchant commentary on the performance of the *Times* or on the cheerleading that had preceded it ("NY Times to Reduce Page Size and Close A Plant in 2008").

That Seelye and Perez-Pena work for the *Times* makes one wonder if the media reporter should occupy a place like the public editor, that is, a place, insulated from the editorial supervision and hierarchy of the *Times*. At times, Seelye seemed to know that she was glossing over or putting a bright face on bad news. In my judgment, rather than Seelye or anyone else who is on the *Times* reporting staff, someone who reports to the public editor or is assigned by him should be doing financial analyses of the company and writing about it in specially designated columns.

But neither Seelye nor her senior editors or publisher could put a finger in the dike to stop the flow of bad news. Thus, on October 20, 2006, the New York Times Company reported a 39 percent drop in profit compared with a year earlier, earning 10 cents a share compared with 16 cents a share, although total revenue was only down 2.4 percent. The *Boston Globe* of the Times New England Media group has been a particular drain, but advertising and circulation revenue was down in the New York Times Media Group, which includes the *New York Times* newspaper, nytimes.com, the *International Herald Tribune,* and IHT.com.

On January 5, 2007, the New York Times Company announced the sale of nine local television stations from its Broadcast Media Group. The Broadcast Media Group had been profitable, although only contributing 4 percent of total revenue. The idea was to focus on its newspapers, not only the *Times,* the *Boston Globe,* and the *International Herald Tribune,* but also fifteen local newspapers and its fifty websites, including nytimes.com, a radio station, and About.com.

As I followed the various quarterly and annual financial reports, I could see a downward spiral accompanied by a skewed and myopic view of the facts. For example, the New York Times Company's 2007 first-quarter report showed that revenue per share was down, although the April 19, 2007, release claimed that without "special items" revenue per share was the same as last year. Moreover, corporate costs increased 25.4 percent over the same period in the previous year.

To raise cash in an increasingly desperate economic environment for newspapers, the Times Company continued to divest itself of assets, and that included its New York City radio station. On July 14, 2009, the *Times* announced a sale agreement to sell WQXR-FM—a station it had owned since 1944 and that had contributed importantly to its identity in the New York metropolitan area—for $45 million. This announcement followed the 2006 selling of the *Times*'s AM station to Radio Disney.

The *Times*'s economic crisis has only accelerated. The Times Company ownership of the *Boston Globe* has been a particular problem in terms of circulation and advertising revenue, with a large number of its potential customers reading online—and what they choose to read online is not necessarily the *Boston Globe.* In 2008, the *Globe* lost $50 million, more than the $40.6 million lost by the entire New York Times Company. In April 2009, the Times Company threatened to close the *Globe* if drastic cuts were not made, and the various unions finally agreed to concessions worth $20 million per year.

On April 3, 2006, as mentioned earlier, the *Times* launched a new version of its website. It has been investing enormous resources in its website based on its belief that the web is where potential growth in revenue lies and where readers under the age of thirty-five—and even more so, their children when they become readers—will look for information. But there is no guarantee that this will create the necessary revenue stream. Whether those under age thirty-five are more or less vulnerable to the blandishments of advertisers is a reasonable question, but Madison Avenue continues to believe it can find new ways to reach fourteen- to thirty-four-year-olds. The *Times* has made an enormous effort to reach readers on its website—updating it every few minutes throughout the day—and the site includes pop-up advertising and video advertising.

Increasingly, the *Times* is creating products to find new readers and to make a profit. Trying to reach a younger audience is a major part of its outreach. Its website is one way of lowering the demographic age of its readers. The national edition is a way of finding a new core of influential professional, business, and academic readers. The result is a newspaper with its website trying to be all things to all people, or as former national editor Soma Golden Behr colorfully put it to me: "Max [Frankel] used to describe this place as a grocery store, or a shopping mall, something like that" in that it had something for everyone (October 11, 2005).

Looking for revenue streams, the *Times* has tried many strategies. How the *Times* now presents itself reflects the evolution not only of the political aspect of our culture—with its partisan and slanted discussion—but also the evolution of the Internet, cable television, social media, and other technology which helps define our culture. Some business decisions have improved the newspaper by producing a more reader-friendly newspaper and website and made both more responsive to the needs and interests of current readers. Business decisions have necessarily driven the *Times*'s propensity for more dramatic and visual writing; for more value-added journalism that helps readers make better life decisions about health, money, and travel; and for better and more photography and graphics, especially in advertising.

The *Times* has been doing some flailing about while trying to figure out how to use the Internet to raise revenue. As I have noted, its renewed efforts to charge readers online for nytimes.com began in March 2011. After exploring options, including a model of micropayments for individual articles that the *Financial Times* has been using, the *Times* enacted a pay wall, where users must pay for unlimited web content (Eric Pfanner, "New York Times, The Paper That Doesn't Want to Be Free," August 16, 2009; Perez-Pena, "Times Company Turns a Profit," July 23, 2009). For a while, as I discussed in chapter 4, it sold an Internet product called TimesSelect that gave subscribers access to columnists and archives, but that was abandoned in 2007 in order for its advertisers to reach a greater number of readers. By contrast, even after it was bought by Rupert Murdoch, the *Wall Street Journal* did not abandon its policy of charging for much of its website. The rationale is not only that its million paying subscribers create revenue, but also that advertisers will pay a premium to reach an elite high-income audience.

I discussed some of the *Times*'s Internet products in chapter 4 and will not repeat that discussion except to mention Times Reader, a digital newspaper that can be read online or offline from a computer and that has the same look as the physical newspaper. As I discussed in chapter 4, the New York Times Store not only sells copies of past front pages and past photos as well as inexpensive sports memorabilia, but also expensive sports memorabilia such as autographed baseballs selling from hundreds to more than $1,000 as well as autographed pictures of such luminaries as Mickey Mantle ($1,500) and Casey Stengel ($1,250). Under the auspices of *Times Talks*, the *Times* also sells tickets to various lectures and various programs that include its well-known journalists and editors. To those not subscribing to the newspaper, the *Times,* as of March 2011, was still selling the crossword puzzles—along with other games and puzzles—as Premium Crossword for $6.95 a month or $39.95 a year.

In 2006, the *Times* launched TimesPoints, a kind of incentive program modeled after the programs that hotels and airlines offer to frequent customers. By making certain purchases on a specified credit card that the cardholder already holds, he or she received credit for *Times* products or gift certificates with various merchants. By the end of 2007, the *Times* had closed this rather foolish option.

In 2009, in its continuing search for revenue, the *Times* launched the *New York Times* Wine Club. The August 13, 2009, article interestingly listed no authors, but included the following comment by Thomas K. Carley, senior vice president of strategic planning for the Times

Company: "Newspapers don't have the same revenue sources that they used to. . . . [W]hatever we do has to really resonate and reflect well on *The New York Times*" ("Times Company Creating a Wine Club," August 13, 2009). One might wonder snidely what is the next club: cheese, or coffee?

In 2007 the *Times* moved to its elegant new quarters. With Forest City Ratner Companies, the Times Company co-owned its world-class new building, designed by Renzo Piano. Located at 8th Avenue between 40th and 41st, and fifty-two stories high, it is tied with the Chrysler Building as the second tallest building in New York and the sixth tallest in the United States. The *Times* occupies the second through the twenty-seventh and part of the twenty-eighth floors and originally owned 58 percent, leasing six of its floors to other tenants. The building's announced purpose, according to what *Times* spokes-person Abbe Serphos told me in October 2007, was to enhance the way the *Times* works, underscore the *Times*'s place in Manhattan, and serve the New York Times Company's long-term business needs as the building's owner. Yet in early 2009, the Times Company was seeking to sell the nineteen floors it uses for $225 million with the right to buy the space back at a predetermined price when a ten-year lease expires. On March 9, 2009, twenty-one floors of the building were sold to W. P. Carey with the Times Company leasing the floors back and retain-ing an option to buy back its stake for $250 million. As Perez-Pena wrote: "The deal is back-loaded, with the repurchase price looming in 2019, and a relatively low starting lease payment of $24 million a year on 750,000 square feet of space" ("Times Building Deal Raises Cash," March 9, 2009).

As the *Times* entered 2009, it had not significantly stopped the bleeding of advertising or circulation. On January 22, 2009, shares of the New York Times Company closed at $5.75 a share, down almost 90 percent from its high in the low $50 range in the 2002–2004 period and from a price over $20 in spring 2008. It fell below $3.50 within a handful of weeks. It had cut its December 2008 dividend almost 75 percent, from 23 cents to 6 cents a share. Not seeing how it could sustain even that, I was hardly surprised that it suspended its dividend entirely on February 19, 2009.

Indeed, raising the dividend in spring 2007 from 17 to 23 cents was a major mistake that drained needed cash and another example of the Times Company's weak business acumen. The Times Company has been frantically trying to sell assets to meet its debt obligations; $1.1 billion in loans comes due in the next few years—most notably $400 million was due in May 2009, although the Times Company stresses that the $400 million is a credit line and not the amount it actually owes. Even if the company could use the $400 million credit line in 2011 to pay down the $400 million that was due in May 2009—which assumes that line had not been tapped—and even using their own optimistic figures, they needed $214 million in cash in 2009, $546 million in cash in 2010, and $500 million in 2011 (Henry Blodget, *Silicon Alley Insider*, December 9, 2008; Blodget uses figures obtained from the New York Times Company for his analyses, and I should stress that the Times Company figures have always been overly optimistic).

On January 19, 2009, the Times Company entered into an agreement with Carlos "Slim" Helú to borrow $250 million at more than 14 percent interest in the form of six-year notes with warrants that are convertible into common shares. "Slim" Helú owns 6.9 percent of the common or class A shares, and when he converts his six-year notes he will own 17 percent of those shares. As of February 2011, the *Times* plans on paying back this debt in early 2012, three years ahead of the due date, although we need note that the *Times* has been in the past overly optimistic about its finances. The Sulzbergers own 19 percent of the A shares but, as I explained earlier, control the B shares that elect the majority of the Board of Directors (Eric Dash, "Mexican Billionaire Invests in Times Company," January 19, 2009). If the Sulzbergers (some of whom surely cannot afford to lose the value of their shares if the Times Company goes bankrupt) capitulate and are willing to sell the B shares, "Slim" Helú, Rupert Murdoch, and Michael Bloomberg have the resources to purchase the *Times* at a bargain price of a $1.2 billion—the approximate net worth of the *Times* at the July 26, 2011, share price of $8.66—or even a premium price of $2 or $3 billion. But will they do so for the sake of adding the legendary *Times* name as a kind of trophy to their portfolio?

Additionally, the Times Company has been seeking to sell its stake in New England Sports Ventures, which owns the Boston Red Sox, Fenway Park, and 80 percent of the New England Sports Network, which broadcasts the Red Sox games. (The *Times* sold a little of its stake in the Red Sox in 2010, and more in 2011.) New England Sports Ventures could be worth $200 million, which would constitute a profit since the *Times* paid $75 million in 2002 for a 17.5 percent stake in

New England Sports Ventures (Perez-Pena, "Times Co. Seeking to Sell Its Stake in the Red Sox," December 24, 2008). The Times Company also could sell About.com, their money-earning web company. But no matter what, further large staff cuts loom in the future.

II. Arthur Sulzberger Jr. at the Helm

In the face of the business downturn and the editorial misjudgments already mentioned and discussed in detail later, publisher Arthur Sulzberger Jr. has been the target of withering criticism, much of it deserved, but some unfair. One example is in the Bowden quote that serves as one of this chapter's epigraphs.

Arthur Jr.'s father, Punch, tried to import modern management training to the *Times*. He commissioned Chris Argyris of Harvard to do an organizational behavior study and sought advice from consulting groups like McKinsey & Co. But, according to Harrison Salisbury, neither Argyris nor anyone else "could convince *Times* executives that the bottom line was what counted, that profits were more important than editorial integrity" (Salisbury, *Without Fear or Favor*, 67).

By Arthur Sulzberger Jr.'s time all that had changed, and money and profit mattered. Arthur felt great pressure to succeed as a businessman. After the 1987 recession the *Times* lost advertising—in part because of the merging of the retail store giants on which the *Times* depended for substantial advertising—even as it gained readers. In 1992, the *Times* actually lost 14 cents per share and needed to turn around its financial fortunes.

In part because he is accountable to shareholders other than family at a time when the revenue stream has been challenged and the stock has declined deeply, Arthur Jr. is more conscious of the *Times* as a business and wishes to, as former executive editor Joe Lelyveld said to me,

> impose a business ideology on the editorial side. We fought that off. Arthur Sulzberger was behind it in many ways and had to be dragged back to basic principles. I just don't know how that works now, but I do hear that there is a lot of pressure for revenue-driven editorial decisions, and you can see it at the paper: *Escapes* only exists to fight the

Saturday *Wall Street Journal* and to have competitive advertising. *ThursdayStyles* came into being because [the now
cancelled] *Circuits* ceased to get the advertising it hoped
for; it just stole *Science Times*'s advertising. Actually it was
a worthwhile thing, and *ThursdayStyles* is not a worthwhile
section. There are more and more junk sections, there are
more auto sections. . . . Arthur always has things in mind
when he makes selections of editors now, and I think he
has a high regard for me but I wasn't enough part of this
for his liking, and part of what Raines promised him was
greater collegiality with the business side, which he didn't
deliver, but was part of his campaign platform and Arthur
went for that. (June 22, 2005)

Howell Raines's hiring in 2001 was in part a business decision to
try to increase profitability. Circulation at that time was stalled at 1.1
million for years after peaking at 1.2 million in the early 1990s, with
the *Sunday Times* back to 1.7 million after slipping to 1.6 in 1998 from
a high of 1.8. Raines convinced Sulzberger that he, Raines, would make
a big splash and that he had an understanding of the web and business
models. According to Raines, with his customary hyperbole salted by
pique at being fired, "Our business side had harvested all the growth
it could from the paper we were given to peddle to subscribers and
advertisers. . . . The Sunday paper had a declining circulation because
for the previous four years its front page, and key sections, including
Arts & Leisure, had gone from predictable to dull to stultifying" ("My
Times," *Atlantic*, May 2004). Sulzberger believed that, among other
things, Raines could reinvent the *Business* section to compete with the
Wall Street Journal and therefore give ballast to the national edition.

Controversial, proactive, prickly, defensive, and self-confident to
the point where a listener wonders if he is a tad delusional, Sulzberger
has Pollyanna moments when he denies the *Times* is in crisis and
pretends all is well with circulation and advertising. When I spoke
to him on October 9, 2005, I would not have known from his words
that recent financial documents offered a mixed picture. He spoke
of the growth in advertising revenue on the Internet and growth of
numbers of hits on the site. As we now know this growth has, with
some lapses, continued but not at the necessary pace to compensate
for rising costs and lost revenue.

In 2005, Sulzberger flagrantly misread the future and our interview reads as if he were trying to convince himself that the gathering storm cloud didn't exist. He acted as if there were no declines in circulation or staff and as if the future readership were ensured. He trotted out the figures about the declining age of readership and assured me that the copies distributed on campus could count in circulation figures because student activity fees paid for them. (In 2010, the education rate for faculty and students was $.50 a copy, which is one-fourth of the usual rate.)

To be sure, many will agree with Mark Bowden that "Arthur Sulzberger has steered his inheritance into a ditch" ("The Inheritance," *Vanity Fair*, May 2009). Although at times Sulzberger seemed to exude optimism and imply that the *Times* was invulnerable, in our 2005 interview he grimly said there would be a *New York Times* in one hundred years even if it weren't in newsprint. At times, he seems to believe the *Times* as a Sulzberger property has a divine right to survive. Survival is the challenge facing the *Times*, and my book discusses some strategies for meeting that challenge.

III. The Challenge to *Times* Management

With a substantial decline in the stock price, the *Times* came under siege from unhappy investors. Hassan Elmasry, a money manager for Morgan Stanley, who heads its Global Franchise fund, led the first attack. After Elmasry gave up, a second attack was launched by two "vulture" hedge funds, Harbinger Capital Fund and Firebrand Partners.

What these large investors wanted to see was more aggressive behavior from the *Times*'s leadership in its struggle to maintain advertising and circulation in the face of declining newspaper readership and the challenge of the Internet. In its January 5, 2007, issue of Portfolio Strategist that examined stock market prospects for the coming year, Citicorp included the New York Times Company on its list of 2007 "Top Sells" along with eleven other stocks; by comparison it recommended sixty-two buys. Its analyst predicted a 30.2 percent decline from the $24.36 December 19, 2006, price, to $17. On the entire Citicorp Portfolio Strategist list, this was the largest predicted decline, and the stock price actually was as low as $3.44 in 2009. To be sure, the entire newspaper industry has been in grave trouble for the past few years, but, for comparison, the Russell 3000 index of newspaper publishing stocks has been down significantly less than that of the New York Times Company.

Since 2003, Elmasry had been critical of the *Times*'s expensive new building, its liberal option grants as compensation for senior executives, and what he considered neglect of its newsroom. His concern even then was the *Times*'s profit margin in comparison with its peers, including Knight Ridder. In 2005, he added to his concerns the dual-class structure—in effect since 1957, well before the company went public in 1969—which allowed the holders of the B shares, of which the then family owns 89 percent, to elect nine of thirteen board members, while the class A stock owned by the public (including Morgan Stanley's shares through its Global Franchise fund) elected only four. Put another way, the *Times* stewardship depends on a family trust that controls the B shares. To declassify the B shares or repeal the two classes would require a six to two vote of the eight voting members of the family trust, four of whom were among the nine directors elected by the B shareholders. Furthermore, the trust requires that one of the six voting for declassification or repeal be Arthur Sulzberger Jr.

In being controlled by a family, the *Times* is hardly unique among newspaper companies. The Washington Post Company is controlled by the Grahams and Dow Jones was controlled until recently by the Bancrofts, and is now controlled by the Murdochs. At the April 2006 annual shareholders meeting, 28 percent of the voting shares registered their dissatisfaction with the *Times*'s performance by not supporting its slate of directors. More important was that Morgan Stanley, which as of November 4, 2006, owned 7.6 percent of the stock, challenged the company's two classes of stock. According to Elmasry, "Despite significant underperformance, management's total compensation is substantial and has increased considerably over this period" (cited in Seelye, "28% of Votes Are Withheld at Times Company Meeting," April 19, 2006).

By November 2006, Morgan Stanley Investment Management had sent the board of the New York Times Company a report highly critical of its governance practice as part of an attempt to pressure it to change the dual-class structure. As summarized by the *Times*'s Landon Thomas Jr., the report concludes that the dual-class structure "puts the interests of the controlling family over those of other investors" ("Morgan Stanley Criticizes Stock Structure of Times Co.," November

4, 2006). In response, the Times Company board decided to sell its nine TV stations, which critics felt deflected the *Times* from its core business. Furthermore, Arthur Sulzberger Jr., as publisher and company chairman, and Michael Golden, as vice chairman, asked board members to reduce their own compensation for 2006 and 2007 by not taking their grants of stock and stock options. Finally, in the first quarter of 2007, the *Times* agreed to raise its dividend, a way of sharing profits with its shareholders.

The *Times* also commissioned its own report, which concluded that except for the dual-class structure—a big exception, we might note—the company's governance procedures were strong. As noted previously, only the family trust can change the capital structure and the family has shown no inclination to do so (see Landon Thomas, "Morgan Stanley Criticizes Stock Structure of Times Co.," November 4, 2006).

Sulzberger sought advice about the possibility of taking the company private—and perhaps making the newspaper a nonprofit trust—but eventually the board of the family trust rejected that idea because they didn't want a private equity group to have power.

Janet Robinson, CEO of the New York Times Company since 2004, categorically has denied that there would be any change in the *Times* dual-share stock structure. Without change, vulnerability to a takeover is minimal. Speculators had been buying the stock because of rumors that the company might go private, sell assets, or be sold itself. Robinson asserted that, "We have been very clear about our dual-class structure. . . . It was put in place for a very important reason—to protect the journalistic independence and integrity of the *Times*, . . . [especially] in times of stress and change" (cited in Seelye, "No Stock-Class Shift," December 7, 2006).

Before selling Morgan Stanley's stock in fall 2007, Elmasry's demands were to do away with the dual-class structure—or at least increase the power of the A-share directors—as well as to separate the role of publisher and chairman of the New York Times Company's flag-ship newspaper, the *New York Times*, both now held by Arthur Jr. (see Sarah Ellison, "How a Money Manager Battled the New York Times," *The Wall Street Journal*, March 21, 2007). Morgan Stanley Investment Management submitted a proposal for the spring 2007 shareholders meeting that recommended that the Times Company board put to a vote the dual-class share structure.

At the April 25, 2007, annual stockholders meeting, shareholders withheld 42 percent of the votes for board members as a protest against the *Times*'s investment performance and governance practices. Even if the change had passed, it would have only been advisory because the change in share structure only can be made by the Ochs-Sulzberger family.

Because the family owns almost 20 percent of the class A shares, the vote meant that the majority of nonfamily shareholders withheld support. As Landon Thomas Jr. said in his *Times* article, the vote "signaled that a growing component of the company's investors are becoming impatient with its management, financial performance and stagnant stock price" ("42% Withhold Votes for Times. Co. Directors," April 25, 2007). At the same meeting, Sulzberger also defended the $500 million cost of the new building. While mentioning the rising revenues in the digital side of the business, he acknowledged the decline in the print side of the business.

When Elmasry and Morgan Stanley withdrew from the battle, the *Times* and outside observers knew there would be future challenges. Two hedge funds—Harbinger Capital Fund and Firebrand Partners—working in tandem purchased more than 19 percent of the class A stock. Although they tried to elect a slate of four of their own directors at the April 22, 2008, meetings and threatened a public proxy fight, they ended up settling for two seats. In response to their board challenge and their complaints about the company's business management skill, the New York Times Company increased its board from thirteen to fifteen members (Stephanie Clifford, "Times Company Elects Two Outsiders to Board," April 23, 2008).

In February 2010, Scott Galloway, one of the two directors named by the Harbinger Investment Group to avoid a proxy fight, announced he was stepping down. This shrunk the board to thirteen from fourteen. Harbinger bought 28.5 million shares between late 2007 and early 2008 and sold them from September to December 2009 for less than half of what it paid. The Times Company also nominated to the board Carol D. Greenspon, the first member of the generation after the current publisher, Arthur Jr., and the great-great-granddaughter of Adolph Ochs, who bought the *Times* in 1896.

Forewarning potential investors and acknowledging that it is in a period of crisis, the *Times*'s own Investor Relations website listed as of August 29, 2010, a substantial a number of risk factors along with elaborate explanations. I have numbered them but excluded the *Times*'s extended explanations:

1. Economic weakness and uncertainty in the United States, in the regions in which we operate and in key advertising categories, has adversely affected and may continue to adversely affect our advertising revenues.

2. All of our businesses face substantial competition for advertisers.

3. The increasing popularity of digital media and the progressing shift in consumer habits and advertising expenditures from traditional to digital media may adversely affect our revenues if we are unable to successfully grow our digital businesses.

4. If we are unable to retain and grow our digital audience and advertiser base, our digital businesses will be adversely affected.

5. The dynamic and evolving digital environment presents multiple challenges that could adversely affect our efforts to further develop our digital businesses.

6. Decreases in circulation volume adversely affect our circulation and advertising revenues.

7. Events with short-term negative impact may have a disproportionate effect if they occur during a time of high seasonal demand.

8. Changes in our credit ratings or macroeconomic conditions may affect our liquidity, increasing borrowing costs and limiting our financing options.

9. If we are unable to execute cost-control measures successfully, our total operating costs may be greater than expected, which may adversely affect our profitability.

10. Sustained increases in costs of providing pension and employee health and welfare benefits and the underfunded status of our pension plans may adversely affect our operations, financial condition, and liquidity.

11. A significant number of our employees are unionized, and our business and results of operations could be adversely affected if labor negotiations or contracts were to further restrict our ability to maximize the efficiency of our operations.

12. Due to our participation in multiemployer pension plans, we have exposures under those plans that may extend beyond what our obligations would be with respect to our employees.

13. A significant increase in the price of newsprint, or limited availability of newsprint supply, would have an adverse effect on our operating results.

14. We may buy or sell different properties as a result of our evaluation of our portfolio of businesses. Such acquisitions or divestitures would affect our costs, revenues, profitability, and financial position.

15. We may not be able to protect intellectual property rights on which our business relies, and if we lose intellectual property protection, our assets may lose value.

16. Our class B Common Stock is principally held by descendants of Adolph S. Ochs, through a family trust, and this control could create conflicts of interest or inhibit potential changes of control.

17. Legislative and regulatory developments may result in increased costs and lower advertising revenue from our digital businesses.

The Securities and Exchange Commission (SEC) requires full disclosure. But given these substantive if not compelling reservations on the part of the New York Times Company, it would take a brave person to make a long-term investment in the company. I would assume such a frank list in the interests of transparency is at least in part the result of legal advice, because it seems unduly gloomy in terms of its effects on stock price or investor relations.

IV. Circulation Issues

Three important facts:

1. Newspaper readership as a percentage of population is declining.

2. Young people read newspapers less than their elders; readership for those over age 65 has barely declined.

3. Fewer people read newspapers every day and some have stopped altogether.

One must ask why, and that is one purpose of my book. There is no one answer. In the age of the Internet, cable television (with some sites devoted exclusively to sports or business), and all-talk radio, newspapers break fewer news scoops and therefore fail to produce exciting stories for a nation that spends less time reading than it once did. Both the accessibility of the Internet and the partisan role of cable news are factors, but so are different reading habits among age and ethnic groups. For example, according to the 2004 "State of the News Media" report by the Pew Research Center's Project for Excellence in Media, "Readership is lowest among the country's two fastest-growing minority populations—Asians and Hispanics—and many Hispanics prefer Spanish newspapers." Although the 2009 report had a slightly different inflexion that may bode better for an American audience that will be increasingly nonwhite in coming decades, it would be hard to get too excited:

> According to demographic data of newspaper readership by ethnicity, the group most likely to read newspapers—whites—declined to 47% from 49% the year before. African Americans and Asians, however, held their readership steady between the two years, at 42% and 41%, respectively. For African Americans, this broke a slow but steady decline in readership that began in 2002. Asians readership, which had been seeing slow but steady readership decreases, has held readership steady for the past three years, since 2006. And after a slight increase in readership in 2007, Hispanics—the group least likely to read a newspaper—showed a decline in

readership in 2008, down to 29% from 31% in 2007. ("The State of the News Media 2009," Journalism.org)

Let us look briefly at circulation figures. For the period ending December 27, 2009, the average twelve-month circulation was 959,200 for weekdays and 1,405,200 for Sundays. By contrast, 1994 circulation figures were as follows: Monday through Friday 1,209,225; Saturday 951,419; Sunday 1,762,015. (Source for circulation numbers: *N.W. Ayer and Sons Directory of Newspapers and Periodicals* until 1984 and then *Gale Directory of Publications and Broadcast Media* [formerly *Ayer's Directory of Publications*].)

Thus, the print circulation trend has been substantially downward with 2009 weekday circulation 250,000 lower than 1994 and Sunday more than 350,000 lower. To put the 2009 numbers in further perspective, figures in 2007 showed that the *Times*'s weekday circulation was 1,120,420 and for Sunday, 1,627,062, which meant most of the decline has been in the last few years. Within two years, from 2007 to 2009, weekday circulation dropped about 160,000 and Sunday circulation dropped more than 220,000.

Interestingly, in part because the *Times* increased its focus on national news and national distribution, its overall Sunday circulation increased from 1993 to 2006, from 660,043 to 917,112—a total of 157,000—but fell by more than 400,000 within the New York City market, for a net loss of almost 150,000. In the corresponding period, the daily edition of the *Times* rose 160,000 nationally, but lost more than 200,000 within the New York City market.

Is there a limit, even allowing for inflation and $4 lattes, that the *Times* can charge readers for a newspaper without its becoming only accessible to the relatively affluent? In June 1944, the month of the Normandy invasion, the daily *Times* cost 3 cents. It now costs $2. The summer 2010 price of the *Sunday Times*—$5 in New York, $6 elsewhere—rose proportionately. As a way of developing a new generation of readers and, ultimately, it hopes, a new source of circulation revenue, the *Times* now gives its paper free to many college students, although, to count in circulation figures, the student activity fee or the university must pay the *Times* a minimal amount.

Although almost half of the *Times* circulation is now outside the New York area, the *Times*, with its recent Chicago, Bay Area, and Texas editions, has only begun to add local contents for specific audiences. The *Times* now produces a New York edition, a northeast edition (published in Washington and Boston and with local weather and television listings), the national edition, and the digital edition (the New York edition on the web). As of late September 2010, the *Times* was being published in twenty-seven locations across the country.

By 2009, the *Times* was more prone to broadcast its electronic visitors; thus in March 2009, it claimed 20,118,000 unique visitors, whereas *USA Today* had more than 10.3 million visitors. However, they have since revised that figure to 17.1 million unique monthly visitors.

Recall from my chapter 4 that when speaking to me Landman was dismissive of such figures: "One thing I learned in [my] Internet period was that the apparent precision of the Internet is a complete myth" (June 9, 2010).

For the same reasons, we really do not know how much time each user spent with the site as compared with the reading time spent on a newspaper. *Editor & Publisher*, a trade magazine, reported that 17.5 million people visited nytimes.com in October 2007 and spent an average of more than thirty minutes reading its site compared with its nearest competitor *USA Today* where 9.5 million visitors spent an average of sixteen minutes (cited by Hoyt, "The Campaign and the Horse Race," November 18, 2007). I am a tad skeptical of this, knowing how often colleagues and my students visit the site for thirty seconds to check a reference or find a fact. Maybe diligent readers return several times a day and read their local newspaper online and thus raise the average.

In a July 2005 piece that bordered on an obituary for newspapers as we know them, Richard Posner claims, without citing his source, that the daily readership of newspapers in the United States declined from 52.6 percent of the adults in 1990 to 37.5 percent in 2000, and that the decline was much steeper among the twenty- to forty-nine-year-old age group that uses electronic media and the web ("Bad News," July 31, 2005).

Basically, there is strong evidence that interest in the news—print or online—is rapidly declining. In a March 2009 Rasmussen Report telephone survey, only 30 percent of Americans read the print version of the local newspaper daily or almost daily and only 15 percent of those under age forty did so. "Sixty-two percent, however, said they rarely or never read the online local newspaper, whereas 19 percent read it once a week or less." Only 8 percent of adults said they read the online version of their local newspaper every day or nearly every day, with another ten percent saying they do so several times a week. Although the *Times* clearly does have a select audience of loyal readers—most of its readers return day after day—since 1972 the percent of people aged thirty to thirty-nine who read a paper every day has dropped to 30 percent from 73 percent. Certainly, one crucial challenge to the *Times* is replacing its aging audience with a new generation of younger readers. Anecdotal evidence: at Cornell, where I teach, machines dispense the weekday *Times* and *USA Today* free to any student with a valid student card. I have watched carefully and am astonished how few students take advantage of either newspaper, although more seem to choose the *Times*.

For the purposes of attracting advertisers, the *Times* is fond of the number of its actual newspaper readers provided by Mediamark Research, Inc. This figure assumes several people share the same newspaper. Thus, the *Times* boasted it had 5.3 million adult readers for its 2005 Sunday circulation of 1.7 million, although we can assume that as circulation drops, readership correspondingly declines (Calame, "Turning the Tables: What the Times News Staff Thinks of You," October 9, 2006). The *Times* also likes to cite the Mendelsohn Affluent Head of Household Survey, which stresses median household income of its readers. In 2009, the median age for nytimes.com users was forty-eight—somewhat younger than its print readers—and 55.6 percent have household incomes over $75,000, with a mean income of almost $84,660; 62.6 percent of their readers were college graduates.

V. The New York Times Company, 2004–2009

As we have seen, advertising and circulation requirements drive many publishing decisions. The *Times* does not break down which of its profits comes from circulation and which from advertising, but according to Byron Calame, "advertising appears to account for about twice as much revenue as circulation does" ("Cracks in the Wall between Advertising and News," November 6, 2005).

We can trace the *Times*'s current economic crisis to 2005. In its third-quarter 2005 SEC filing, the Times Company reported a serious downturn in operating profit—in large part due to staff reductions. According to the Times Company's explanation in this SEC filing,

"The decreases at the News Media Group were primarily due to higher expenses related to staff reductions, higher wages and benefits, increased distribution and outside printing expense, increased promotion expense, incremental stock-based compensation expense and higher newsprint expense." This report sounded a recurring theme that has continued to this day.

As if to hide the financial situation of the *Times* and nytimes.com, the annual SEC reports filed by the New York Times Company recuse the financial information on the *Times* newspaper and nytimes.com within the News Media Group. This group also includes the *International Herald Tribune* and the Times News Service Division—which sells its articles, graphics, and photographs to other newspapers, magazines, and media—as well as the New York Times Index, Digital Archival Distribution, and the New York Metropolitan area newspaper delivery business it once owned. The News Media Group also includes the New England Media Group to which the *Boston Globe* and *Worcester Telegram & Gazette* belong, and the Regional Media Group, which in August 2009 owned fifteen newspapers, one of which was a weekly.

VI. Do Business Decisions Undermine the *Times* Product Quality?

When I conducted some interviews on October 11, 2005, right after Judith Miller was released from prison, Soma Golden Behr, the frank, retired assistant managing editor who was the first woman newsperson on the masthead, spoke of the atmosphere of gloom deriving from an announcement of a second set of staff cuts on the heels of Miller"s imprisonment and release and still not too many years past the Raines–Blair turmoil. She acknowledged, too, that the pressure on reporting staff to produce a story not only for the *Times* but on the same day for nytimes.com and the *International Herald Tribune* might result in lower staff morale and sloppy writing.

Profitability has been an issue for Arthur Jr. from the outset, but as I have noted, once the *Times* became a publicly traded company in January 1969, concern with the bottom line increased gradually. In *The Times of My Life and My Life with the Times*, Max Frankel speaks about how the triumvirate presiding over the *Times*—including himself, the publisher Arthur Sulzberger Jr. (who had succeeded his father, Punch in 1992), and Lance Primis (the newspaper's executive vice president and general manager)—"were all accountable to and manipulated by Walter Mattson, . . . the corporation's president and chief operating officer [from 1979 to 1992]" (506). Mattson pushed for decisions that made business sense. Understanding that one path to profitability was to upgrade facilities, Mattson was the person responsible for building "the country's most advanced four-color printing plants."

Although the *Times* has, for the most part, reflexively claimed that its editors go to great lengths to distance themselves from its business side, the fact is that Sunday *Arts & Leisure*, *Business*, and *Travel* have been for decades dependent on advertising in these areas. The Sunday travel ads appear among upbeat articles about various kinds of vacations. Before its demise, *Escapes* seemed to exist for full-page color ads for expensive real estate. Acknowledging this, Frankel, executive editor from 1986 to 1994, explains that although the news was relatively immune to advertiser's input, the "feature supplements operated under a looser standard than the regular news pages. Although rigorously honest in what they carried, they were nonetheless expected to be more pliable at the margins, in both the material they published and that which they avoided" (370). Although past senior editors and some present editors and journalists are embarrassed by the soft sections, especially by the 2005 addition of *ThursdayStyles* and *SundayStyles* but also by *Escapes* and *"T"* supplements to the *Sunday Magazine*, the outreach to readers looking for something other than hard news goes back a long way, to various versions of the *Automobile* sections. Nevertheless, the *Times*'s focus on the sensational, tawdry, and prurient, as well as its hagiographic coverage of the wealthy and famous, are different not merely in degree but in kind from in past decades.

Part of the challenge for the *Times* today is how to preserve the wall between advertising and news both in the paper and on the website at a time when newspapers in general and the *Times* in particular are pinched. Clearly, the invention of these magazine sections is part of a focus on the bottom line. When the quality in these sections is eviscerated by prolix articles—the main purpose of which is to fill volumes of columns that are necessary to attract advertising—then business decisions are driving the paper. The same can be said about the *"T"* sections, where iterative photographs, accompanied by scant prose, create articles that are hardly more than punctuations within endless pages of advertising. Furthermore, the articles in these soft sections often are written by freelancers, some of whom may have ties to commercial interests that their articles are supporting.

The Tony Awards coverage is an example of where the separation of business decisions and news decisions is murky. With more of a sense of outrage than usual, in May 2004 then public editor Dan Okrent chastised the *Times* for over-publicizing the awards because they are restricted to the theaters owned by three major groups and Lincoln Center—major advertisers in the *Times*—and do not consider off-Broadway theaters ("There's No Business Like Tony Awards Business," May 9, 2004).

Focusing on another dubious use of advertising, Okrent's successor as public editor, Byron Calame, pointed out in November 2005 how "watermark" or "shadow ads"—like the October 6, 2005, image of Prudential Financial's rock logo embedded in the financial pages—blurs the distinction between information and advertising even if it is at present limited to one ad a day and only on a business page devoted to financial tables (see "Cracks in the Wall Between Advertising and News," November 9, 2005). The nytimes.com site has an overlapping of news and ads: Should a pharmaceutical company ad refer readers to archives of *Times* articles related to health and cholesterol? Who chooses which ads pop up when one selects an article? And what about ads that look like news pages or news articles?

In January 2009, blatant incursion of display advertising—combining words and texts—on the front page of the *Times's* print edition was another troubling example of news taking a back seat to business. As Perez-Pena put it, "In its latest concession to the worst revenue slide since the Depression, the *New York Times* has begun selling display advertising on its front page, a step that has become increasingly common across the newspaper industry" ("The Times to Sell Display Ads on the Front Page," January 5, 2009). The July 14, 2009, print edition contained a disturbing example of the effects of the policy of taking front-page ads. The front-page box highlighted an article on Exxon investing in biofuels. On the bottom of the very same front page was an advertisement for Exxon.

Of course, business decisions also are made in relation to the competition of other media developments (radio, TV, the Internet, and other newspapers). The *Times* has had both a collaborative and rancorous relationship with other media. At the end of July 2007, for reasons that had a strong money-saving component, the *Times* and NBC

News agreed to supply each other with material and announced that NBC's producers and the *Times* political reporters would be in daily contact. The *Times* would give NBC stories, graphics, pictures, and the Caucus Blog, and NBC would give the *Times* videos and would not only feature the *Times*'s coverage on its MSNBC.com website, but a *Times* reporter would appear regularly on NBC and MSNBC (Jacques Steinberg, "The Times and NBC News Agree to Share Coverage," July 31, 2007). For the *Times* and NBC, this agreement not only enhanced 2008 election coverage, but also coverage of the 2009 Iranian election and its aftermath; in the latter case, the *Times*'s impressive coverage was complemented by its posting videos from NBC and MSNBC on its digital site.

Although this relationship with NBC, which continues to this day, may save costs and bring the *Times* some new readers by putting its material on another site, the relationship further blurs the difference between two major news outlets. Now that in early 2011 Comcast has received approval to buy NBC Universal, it remains to be seen how the relationship between the *Times* and NBC will evolve.

It is worth noting that ABC and CNN also shared 2008 election coverage. The *Times* already shares polling with CBS; CNN and CBS had serious partnership talks in 2010, but by October 2011 nothing had resulted.

The question of whether newspapers and television should be in a cooperative relationship for anything beyond polls is a real one. One can ask whether this homogenizing of news costs the news consumer—reader and viewer—an important independent news source. Certainly, in the past the *Times* and NBC had very different takes on events and political candidates.

Historically, the *Times* view of cable TV news has been extremely critical. For example, Alessandra Stanley, under the rubric "TV Watch," strongly takes cable TV to task in an August 24, 2004, piece entitled "On Cable, a Fog of Words about Kerry's War Record." Implicit in her criticism—indeed, her indictment—is that the *Times* is more thorough, accurate, and competent in questioning news sources than cable TV news: "There is the fog of war and then there is the fog of cable." Not without some smugness and one-upmanship, Stanley accurately characterized differences and made important distinctions between news and gossip; she criticized cable news as a site "where the premium is placed on speed and spirited banter rather than painstaking accuracy. . . . At their worst, cable news programs . . . amplify the loudest voices and blur complexities." On June 14, 2009, Brian Stelter wrote, "Cable news normally serves as the front line for breaking news, but the channels largely took the weekend off as Tehran exploded in protests after Iran's presidential election. . . . [T]he Tehran protests were not covered [by CNN] with rolling live coverage for hours at a time" ("Real-Time Criticism of CNN's Iran Coverage").

Yet the *Times*'s columnists and reporters serve as cable television guests. They supplement their income and help remind viewers of the relevance and importance of the *Times*. However, often because much talk television is conservative, when *Times* people have gone on cable TV—and talk radio—they are faced with adversarial interviewers more interested in expressing their political views than seeking information. On occasion, it seemed that the reporters themselves were also engaged more in self-advertising than news analyses. Indeed, not only Okrent but also former executive and managing editors wondered if it was a good idea for reporters—he excludes columnists and crit-ics—to appear on television shows, especially those in which they face tough interrogators (see Okrent, "Talking on the Air and Out of Turn: The Trouble with TV," February 6, 2005). On May 20, 2010, Okrent said to me: "I don't mind if [reporters and columnists] pick a few bucks for going on television. . . . We try to be very careful to police people from going on these shows that are essentially shout fests, where everybody is really angry and want you to predict the future or say what ought to happen. And I think that there have been occasions where people have kind of been sucked into that, but we're pretty good at policing that."

VII. Conclusion: Have Business Conditions Improved?

Where is the *Times* going? As then cultural editor Sam Sifton remarked in 2006 in one of the nytimes.com Newsroom Q&A: "Try selling a centuries-old technology like newspapers to 21st century teenagers who answer to ring tones adults literally cannot hear." Thinking about what to cover in terms of cultural events, the *Times*, Sifton writes, has in mind "a broad spectrum of readers old and young and in between." The fancy term for this is *multiple points of entry*, that is, opening doors and windows for diverse audiences of readers. We can see that this is now the policy for the entire newspaper and digital site.

Is it possible that the *Times* loses quite a number of potential readers because it produces too much product? I have been told by students and colleagues that the print *Times*—and even the digital site—seems overwhelming to someone who has finite time to give to a newspaper. Perhaps, as the *Times* has become more a daily magazine, it has become unwieldy in terms of its mission of reporting the news, and readers have turned elsewhere for value-added features and usable news.

Speaking before the launching in 2006 of the new web page, but thinking about the newspaper in ways that are still relevant, Frankel remarked to me:

> The *Times* has not figured out which way the future is going, even dealing with what I would call the diminished attention span of the audience. I think the *Times* has been too slow in adapting to contemporary readers. It's too big and clumsy a product for these days and for good reason because it needs to have all these sections for commercial reasons, but it is very difficult to navigate—to read a story that starts on page one and jumps to section H, until you find it and then when you open it up it's two pages and you say "not on a workday, I don't have time for this stuff." (April 16, 2005)

Is there too much information in the published newspaper? Is this why on college campuses, when free copies of *USA Today* are next to free copies of the *Times*, some campus readers choose *USA Today*—called by some "McNewspaper"—mostly for sports? The same reasons may be true in airports when both are available for purchase, although the price difference also may be a factor. Some business travelers who want a quick read before working in airports and on flights not only choose *USA Today* for sports but for its glimpse at business and its focus on business travel. Serious business readers who want more depth choose the *Wall Street Journal*.

How can the *Times* hold and expand its audience? Clearly, it addresses a specialized demographic in terms of education and economic comfort and needs to continue to find readers that want their product. What Ted Koppel has written of network news is applicable to other news media, including the *Times*: "The goal for the traditional broadcast networks now is to identify those segments of the audience considered most desirable by the advertising community and then cater to them. . . . It is not partisanship but profitability that shapes what you see" ("And Now, a Word for Our Demographic," January 29, 2006). He also speaks of the struggle to find "a new format that will somehow appeal to younger viewers."

The *Times* will always appeal to a cultural and economic elite, but it needs to renew its audience by locating younger readers who prefer to get their information online. What if educated young people want to get their news in diluted and comic form from Jon Stewart and Stephen Colbert rather than an objective source? The *Times* needs to educate young people to become its print and digital readers and to teach them about the value of its product, namely unslanted and reliable news as well as value-added magazine-type features.

The *Times* is now engaged in a desperate search for readers and advertising revenue at a time when the Internet and other media pose major challenges. What every one of my interviews with editors reveals, and the online Q&A "Talk to the Newsroom" with various editors confirms, is that the current *Times* is obsessed with developing a younger audience and that many of the decisions for both the printed newspaper and especially the nytimes.com site derive from this. This search for a younger audience is related to the issue of how to sell advertising, particularly on the web, but also to changes in reading habits, most notably how people get information.

The *Times*'s position as the leading newspaper in the United States, if not the world, has been based on the premise that readers wish to be informed and have accurate information about complex issues. But what if Richard Posner is correct that contemporary newspaper readers want to have their opinions confirmed, to be entertained, and "to learn of facts that bear directly and immediately on their lives" ("Bad News," July 31, 2005)? He believes most people like newspapers that support their existing beliefs more than they want newspapers that tell them the truth. That is, an increasingly balkanized American citizenry want to have their core beliefs reinforced by positions that echo their own. If this is true, it is part and parcel of the radical skepticism about the news fostered by both government behavior and the media performance. It explains why many people prefer one-dimensional blogs to more complex views of issues. Even in the 2008 presidential campaign, which did seem to be a pause in the inward turning to personal concerns of a politically cynical public, the desire for information often took a back seat to simplifications on the part of candidates and raucous pundits on talk radio and television.

6

Counter-Reformation or
the Way We Are (I)

New Bearings and Continuity in the
Contemporary *Times* Under Keller, 2003–2009

What I hope I'll be able to say when I get around to retiring, is that we got the paper through a really tough time when a lot of other papers didn't do so well, and put it on a strong footing so that the kind of journalism that we practice and admire and believe in will have sturdy roots in the new dominant media.

—Bill Keller, May 20, 2010

I think that [Bill Keller] came in under very difficult circumstances. . . . [M]y sense is that he calmed and focused the newsroom and the *Times*.

—Clark Hoyt, May 19, 2010

The pursuit of balance can create imbalance because sometimes something is true.

—Okrent's Law, articulated by
Dan Okrent, *New Yorker*, May 24, 2004

I. Introduction

Every executive editor worries about the graying of the readership and how to attract the next generation. Every executive editor of the *Times* thinks he or she presides over a cataclysmic change in the audience and the concept of the newspaper itself. Although it may be that his predecessors on occasion exaggerated the crises, current executive editor Keller was, as of 2010, captaining a ship that sometimes seemed to have no certain destination if we conceive of its destination as the long-term survival of the *Times* in print.

When I interviewed Bill Keller on May 20, 2010, I recalled his words during our October 11, 2004, conversation, fifteen months after he began as executive editor: "To some extent I have never been comfortable with the notion that people who run things need a long-term vision of the future and how to lead it there. My job is to hire and promote good people and place them in a good environment so they can do their best work."

Clearly, when he took over in September 2003, he brought calm and equilibrium to the newsroom. Although his hair is greyer and the lines in his face deeper, Keller still has a quiet confidence and poise and is comfortable in his own skin. Having been, by the time of my 2010 interview, editor for almost seven years and having weathered continuing storms of external criticism that his predecessors did not have to worry about in the days before the scrutiny created by the blogosphere, he seems to keep his balance by focusing on the here and now. He has presided over the transition to digital media that puts the *Times* in the front rank of Internet news sites. In May 2010, he believed that advertising would continue to recover from the recession. Yet he acknowledges the difficulty of finding the business model for both the advertising and the circulation components of digital media, and he knows that it is hard to predict the effects of charging for nytimes.com on both.

Keller's *Times* presents and enacts various cultural conflicts in the diversity of its views while still implicitly favoring Manhattan-centric (and certainly blue-state) assumptions about value issues. He has made the *Times* less Manhattan-centric and more open to points of view other than those that prevail on the Upper West Side, the Upper East Side, Lower Manhattan, and a few enclaves in Brooklyn, Long Island, and Westchester. He wants the *Times* to write about conservatives, the Midwest, and rural America as peoples and places other than curiosities, and tries to think about those outside New York City as Americans living in diverse worlds. I think he has made some progress in these areas, especially showing an awareness of red-state and conservative perspectives, but he has not changed the basic ethos of the paper.

Although Keller at first made a conscious effort to be less Manhattan-centric and to include diverse political, religious, and cultural perspectives, by 2010 he realized that his core audience is New Yorkers and those who visit New York and regard New York as America's cultural capital. As he put it to me on May 20, 2010, "I think that switch flipped awhile ago. I think that the *New York Times* has a sort of New York identity and that we're urban; a lot of the things that we cover like the arts, business, finance in particular, like the fashion industry. . . . New York is the capital of those things; so I think we're of New York in that sense. And I think that it's really good [for] a national paper to have roots somewhere. But I've always thought that at least in my time here that the *Times* is more defined by demography than geography."

In this and the next chapter I examine how the contemporary *Times* under Keller reflects its New York identity while seeking to have national appeal. I also discuss how the *Times* has responded to the challenges of instant news on the Internet and cable by providing more analyses, value-added news, investigatory journalism and cultural coverage than in the past. By integrating its website with the printed newspaper, the *Times* seeks to present an enriched product, which will appeal to a broad audience, especially younger readers.

In the period from 1999 to 2009, which corresponded with the rise of the Internet, the published *Times* changed its emphasis from reporting news to analysis and investigative journalism, relying on its website to keep readers abreast of what occurs in real time. Although the *Times*—and specifically Keller—knows that it will never achieve the iconic status it once held as the arbiter of what is fit to print and what constitutes news, it seeks in a turbulent and chaotic time for print media to define a place midway between a newspaper and a daily news maga- zine and to supplement that news magazine with features—including daily special sections—that widen its appeal. As Keller acknowledged as early as in our October 11, 2004, discussion: "Today, the *Times* is like a daily newspaper with grafted magazines (weekly food, housing, book review, etc.); some sections are packaged as magazines and some sections are 'magaziney' in the way they are written and designed."

No longer presuming cultural and regional homogeneity even in New York, the *Times* now is very much aware of identity politics and the heterogeneity of American culture. Keller recognizes that the

Times speaks to an extraordinarily diverse audience and—with its three satellite editions in the Bay Area, Chicago, and Texas—needs to address as much of the entire nation as possible. Trying to reach the diverse segments of its potential audience, the *Times* now writes about the heterogeneous cultures in New York and America and covers in detail popular culture events; for example, early in Keller's editorship, the *Times* reported in some detail the "last" concert tour of Phish in summer 2004.

The *Times* also has been consciously trying to reach target segments of its audience, especially upscale readers. For example, the June 6, 2004, issue of the *Sunday Magazine* focused on "money and the moral quandaries it presents," while on May 16, 2010, the focus of the *Sunday Magazine* was "What are you really worth?" For many years, special weekly sections for such areas as Westchester and Long Island, as well as the *Real Estate* and *Jobs* sections—sections not distributed nationally—retained the New York flavor for local readers. For cost savings, one *Metropolitan* section now covers the entire metropolitan area, albeit with some pages reserved for Westchester, Long Island, and other tri-state areas. On the Internet, the *Times* speaks to readers all over the world, but still retains some local flavor for the New York region.

Improving the *Business* and *Travel* sections and making them more user-friendly, value-added advice sections have been ways of reaching targeted audiences, most notably now on its digital site. *Times* publishers, senior editors, and advertisers would prefer that its readers read only the *Times* at a time when less and less time is spent with newspapers. Ideally, they would like the vast majority of their readers not to go to other newspapers for business (the *Wall Street Journal,* the *Financial News*) or sports (*USA Today* or the *New York Post* or the *New York Daily News*) or even sensationalism (the *New York Post* or the *New York Daily News*). The *Times*'s *Metro* section shares many qualities with the tabloids it once disdained, including an interest in sensational crime as well as organized crime (the Mafia). Under the leadership of a former *Wall Street Journal* senior editor, Lawrence Ingrassia, the *Times* coverage of business news has been modified to be more competitive with the *Wall Street Journal* as well as with cable stations focusing entirely on business news. Under Murdoch, the *Wall Street Journal* in recent years has expanded its reaches beyond business news and now has the largest circulation of any newspaper in the United States: more than 2.1 million, plus more than 350,000 online paid subscribers.

Under editorial-page editor Gail Collins, who held the position from 2001 to 2007, the editorial page had never been more liberal, and, indeed, as the *Times*'s disgust with the George W. Bush administration increased, seemed to inch leftward year by year. A paradigmatic example of the *Times*'s liberal views under Collins was the January 23, 2006, lead editorial, "Judge Alito's Radical Views," urging that the Senate vote against his confirmation: "[Alito] wants to reduce the rights and liberties of ordinary Americans. . . . If the far right takes over the Supreme Court, American law and life could change dramatically."

Replacing Collins in January 2007 was Andrew Rosenthal, son of the legendary *Times* editor Abe Rosenthal. Good-humored, loquacious, and open, Rosenthal's views are if anything more liberal than Collins, and the editorial page was at first most enthusiastic about Obama. The real story is not the liberalism of the editorials but the sense that the *Times* editorial page implicitly and explicitly contended that the Bush administration was incompetent, cynical, and a menace to the best interests of the nation. I am not sure this attitude toward an administration prevailed at the *Times* at any time other than the final days of the Nixon administration.

The *Times* under Keller continues to evolve while sustaining editorial precedent. In particular, the editorial positions depend on bedrock principles such as free trade, free press, passionate defense of the First Amendment, civil liberties, progressive taxation, reproductive rights, environmental protection, and internationalism (including commitment to cooperative international treaties and the United Nations). Setting itself at odds with the Bush administration, Keller's *Times* took a leadership position in its reporting on many aspects of the cultural wars, including gay marriage, stem cell research, and abortion. When the *Times* changes its editorial position on major issues, it explains why.

The editorial shifts to the left since 1993 under the self-described populist Howell Raines (1993–2001) and later—after Raines's appointment as executive editor in 2001—Gail Collins (2001–2007) and now Rosenthal is quite evident. These aforementioned editors of the editorial page represented a return to the liberal editorial policy of John Oakes (1961–1976). The shift reflects the fact that Arthur Sulzberger Jr.'s political bent is markedly more liberal than that of his father.

Paradoxically, this more liberal editorial bent has been balanced by an effort, under Keller's leadership, to cover the kind of things the "red" or Republican states would be interested in (such as the 2005

Billy Graham crusade) and to understand the conservative political perspective. In January 2004, the *Times* created a beat that focused on covering the conservative movement in religion, politics, and the media. The idea was to give a voice to those whose views had not received ample coverage in the *Times*, and the first writer assigned to the beat, David D. Kirkpatrick, had six of his first twenty articles appear on the front page, covering such topics as "the use of gay marriage as a tool to rally conservatives; a college for Christian home-schoolers that touted internships in Washington; a look at preparations by Christian booksellers for the climactic installment in the 'left behind' series of apocalyptic thrillers" (Byron Calame, "The Conservative Beat: Is it Working?" March 12, 2006).

Calame, the second public editor, thought this conservative "beat" was a good idea, especially because it opened conservative doors to Kirkpatrick on occasions where the liberal press was not wanted. Giving Kirkpatrick greater access to prominent conservatives helped him write about the conservative responses to the Supreme Court nominations of John Roberts, Samuel Alito, and the ill-fated Harriet Miers. He wrote with authority on the conservative strategies for confirmation, or in the case of Miers, the strategy on the part of some conservatives for sabotaging the nomination.

But skeptics recalling the history of the *Times* as the paper of record might question whether a "beat" should be assigned to a political point of view. Does the *Times* need to find better ways to get these stories and to understand the thinking of conservatives than designating a specific reporter to focus on reporting the views of one group?

In his June 23, 2005, staff memo entitled "Assuring Our Credibility," Keller not only wished to avoid using "moderate" as a positive term or "religious fundamentalists" to describe religious conservatives, but also to expand the "national conversation" and "to stretch beyond our predominantly urban, culturally liberal orientation." Keller endorsed the 2005 Credibility Committee's view that the *Times* should have diversity in reporters and editors, and added, "[W]e will make an extra effort to focus on diversity of religious upbringing and military experience, of region and class." Perhaps focusing on diversity in terms of class, religion, military background, and religion takes political correctness to a new level.

Hiring advocates for a particular perspective is quite different from the laudable policy of the *Times* stipulating staff diversity in terms of "gender, race, and ethnicity." The goal of having reporters with diverse life experiences is a worthy one but isn't the mark of a good journalist, whatever his or her background, to have the ability to see and hear diverse views and weigh their accuracy, fairness, and partiality? Keller's notion of bending over backward to see the view of those religious conservatives who have a monolithic perspective—and whose intolerance is not just another perspective—could be construed as giving aid and sustenance to active and belligerent forces opposed to civil liberties.

In more recent years, Keller seems to have pulled back from this desire to represent a conservative point of view and realized that accurate and fair reporting is itself a contribution to a national conversation that too often has become a shouting match between right and left, represented by Fox and MSNBC. Indeed, the *Times* was behind the curve in recognizing the rise of the Tea Party movement in 2009. Rather than another conservative reporter, what the *Times* needs is simply good reporting that ferrets out information and listens to reasonable perspectives.

On the op-ed page, edited by David Shipley, who reports to Rosenthal, the mantra is balance. This explained the controversial appointment of William Kristol to a one-year trial term as columnist beginning in January 2008, an appointment that ended in January 2009 in part because Kristol was one of Sarah Palin's 2008 campaign coaches. He was succeeded in April 2009 by the young conservative Ross G. Douthat, whose column appears online and in the paper once a week. Because of a dearth of conservative voices among its columnists, the *Times* has sought representative conservative commentary in those op-ed pieces it selects to run on a one-time basis. But given the commotion created by Fox News and its less influential liberal nemesis, MSNBC, the current *Times* seems less concerned with choosing partisan commentary for its own sake.

II. Keller's Editorship: Counter-Reformation

On his first day on the job in July 2003—and on the heels of the Blair fiasco—Keller announced the creation of the position of public editor, to which he, presumably in consultation with Sulzberger, appointed Daniel Okrent for a term of eighteen months. This was done to renew readers' trust and to rebuild readers' confidence in the newspaper, which even before Raines had suffered more than its share of embarrassments. In his review of Okrent's collection of his public editor columns, Harold Evans correctly notes that well before Raines, the *Times* was on shaky ground in a number of areas: "the intrusion of mean-spirited gossip into news articles; the unwillingness to correct the misleading scoop on the Clinton-Whitewater land deal; the proliferation of blind quotations" ("Eye on the *Times*," *New York Times Book Review*, June 18, 2006).

Evans could have added the *Times*'s less than satisfactory performance—under the editorship of Lelyveld—in the Wen Ho Lee episode when, before a formal indictment, the *Times* leaked the news on March 6, 1999, that Lee, a scientist at Los Alamos National Laboratory, was an atomic spy and did not, as the *Times* later acknowledged, give Lee "the benefit of the doubt" ("The Times and Wen Ho Lee," September 26, 2000). On June 3, 2006, threatened with contempt for protecting its sources, the *Times* along with our other major media companies—plus the federal government—settled a libel suit with Lee.

In September 2003, as another major part of the effort to restore readers' confidence, Keller also created the position of standards editor, held first by Allan M. Siegal, a position he had informally held for years, but which became a masthead position with the title "assistant managing editor." Upon retirement in 2006, Siegal was succeeded by Craig Whitney, who in turn was succeeded upon his September 2009 retirement by *Times* veteran Phillip Corbett. To help protect against a repetition of the Blair fiasco, which resulted in part from editors not reporting incompetence and nonfeasance to other editors, Glenn Kramon became career-development editor, before being appointed assistant managing editor with a focus on "enterprise" or investigatory journalism, an area which the *Times* wanted to be a centerpiece of its mission as its dominance in reporting actual news receded.

Unlike his authoritative predecessors Raines and Rosenthal, the better-tempered Keller runs a collegial senior staff where input and initiative are encouraged. Yet he keeps his own counsel and does not always open up to his staff. One does not get the sense that his subordinates are in awe of him or frightened by him, but instead some find him remote. Indeed, in contrast to the autocratic reign of Raines, Keller encourages each department's chief editor to think of himself or herself as presiding over a somewhat independent unit. Certainly in his early days, he successfully defused the anger and anxiety that existed among department editors and even more so among the staff. Keller placed loyalists, such as former deputy managing editor Jonathan Landman, in important positions and this helped shore up his support in the contentious newsroom, where ambitious men and women vie for promotion and recognition. Landman, once considered a possible heir to Keller by Timesologists, was appointed to the post of cultural editor in September 2009 and no longer appears on the masthead.

Keller has committed himself to greater transparency and accessibility. In the June 23, 2005, staff memo, "Assuring Our Credibility," Keller responded to the report of the Credibility Committee that had been examining the *Times*'s processes and procedures for ensuring accuracy, impartiality, fairness, and accountability—that is, the values that form the bases for the *Times* as an authoritative source. He offered specific measures, including online answers by senior editors to questions from readers. In mid-April 2006—ten months later—Keller, under the rubric "Talk to the Newsroom," launched an online Q&A with selected questions from readers, and he has been followed at intervals by quite a number of other important editors who take a turn at answering questions that pertain to their specific area of responsibility. Although the series has been on hold, with the single exception of a July 25, 2010, discussion of the recent publication of WikiLeaks documents about the Afghanistan war and the role of Pakistan's spy service in guiding the insurgency, this online Q&A series in which senior editors answer selected readers' questions is certainly a serious if controlled effort to communicate more with readers.

Calame had rightly written of the need for "improving openness to reader feedback," and openness to readers is one aspect of the transparency issue (March 26, 2006). Only a tiny fraction of letters to the editor are published in the daily paper, and they usually deal with very specific issues raised by recent articles. I would prefer—at least in abbreviated form—to have the valuable Q&A also appear in the newspaper lest the newspaper readers be consigned to second echelon position.

Although the *Times* institutionally fears probing outsiders, the aforementioned Q&A series is a positive move to alleviate that paranoia.

In mid-April 2006, Keller wrote:

> Over the past few years we've done several things to make the
> *Times* more open. We have created the position of the Public

Editor, whose job is to enhance our public accountability. We have opened new channels into the paper, including online email access to the reporters themselves (to send a message, click the reporter's byline while reading the story online). Editors and reporters make a more conscientious effort to submit themselves to the questions of the public. This week's Q&A, the first in what we hope will become a regular Web feature, is just the latest example. Over the past year scores of *Times* editors and reporters have accepted invitations to speak and be on panel discussions at universities and community meetings around the country. This greater transparency, I think, both serves as an additional corrective mechanism for the paper and bolsters our public credibility. ("Talk to the Newsroom," April 14, 2006)

Although I take issue with some of the foregoing, and on occasion have found some senior figures at the *Times* evasive, I do think many of its editors are trying to be more forthcoming. The responses of senior editors in online Q&A sessions and various blogs give readers a chance for interaction. Very infrequently, staff and editors respond online to readers' comments under the rubric of a "replies" tab.

In his June 23, 2005, memo responding to the Credibility Committee, Keller committed the *Times* to making clear when a journalist is commenting in a "news analysis" or "critic's notebook" as a way of making transparent the divide between news and opinion. I would add that the *Times*—which tends to assume every reader is a repeat reader who knows the customs of the *Times*—needs to have definitions of these terms on its website and in its daily paper. Keller also outlined plans for "more systematic" responses to public attacks and more public appearances by *Times* staff people in programs that are "designed" for "enlightenment" rather than for "gladiatorial combat." Unfortunately, some of the programs that promise the former can devolve into the latter, depending on both the moderator and other guests and the temperament of the *Times* staffer.

In the same June 23, 2005, memo, which was part of his transparency campaign, Keller promised to make *Times* reporters more email accessible. For a while, if a reader clicked on a reporter's byline on nytimes.com, a form appeared that allowed the reader to send an email. To be fully effective, this process needed two additional components: reporters had to read emails and also had to respond to at least some of them online. Reading readers' email might have sometimes given the *Times*'s staff different perspectives and different information that would improve stories, and I assume some reporters and editors do read some of them. By summer 2010, all online opinion articles, blogs, and some news articles allowed readers to comment, although reporters and editors very rarely respond, no doubt in part because responding is time-consuming and diverts them from their main tasks.

Finally, in the aforementioned June 23, 2005, staff memo, "Assuring our Credibility," Keller addressed the issue of accuracy. He insisted that reporters check and recheck information, often returning to sources to do so. Although he stressed using anonymous sources only as a last resort, I find using such sources common in reporting Beltway insider information.

Dan Okrent, the first public editor from December 2003 to May 2005, chided the *Times* for its use of anonymous sources—called "anonymice" by Jack Shafer of *Slate*—and spoke about the necessity of accurate quotations from sources it does identify. What the *Times*'s reliance on anonymous sources within the administration does is undermine readers' confidence and open the door to allegations—often not groundless—that the journalists and political figures are involved in an elaborate game of manipulation in which the journalists are often gulled into thinking they are providing scoops when they are only being used as conduits for Beltway gossip. At times, particularly in the period from 1999 to 2004, the Washington bureau has produced lightweight articles based on interviews with unnamed administration or congressional sources. In part because of Okrent's prodding—prodding that his successors, especially Hoyt, continued—the *Times* in recent years has made progress against unnecessary anonymous sources.

That the problems with sources persist is clear from Hoyt's August 15, 2009, column "Cloaked Identities, Even With Names": "The *Times* was again dealing with fallout from unidentified sources. If that were not enough, the newspaper ran into trouble with sources it did name, too. . . . An anonymous shot [at Michael Jackson's executor] violated the newspaper's written rule against letting unnamed sources make personal attacks." In the same piece Hoyt raised a different issue needing vigilance: certain named sources, who complained vociferously that technology had altered family routines, turned out to be people too closely connected to the *Times*.

More self-conscious about its behavior, in part as a result of the Jayson Blair scandal and the Howell Raines and Judith Miller turmoil, the *Times*'s editors by 2010 became much more prone to ask: "How do we at the *Times* deal with sources who refuse to be identified or who are using the *Times* to publish information that serves their own self-interests rather than the interests of the *Times* readership who seek truth and accuracy? Should the *Times* omit such material unless it impacts significantly on national security?"

III. Questions about Keller's Judgment and Gatekeeping Decisions

The executive editor ultimately is responsible for everything that appears in the newspaper. He or she is the ultimate gatekeeper, but of course reporters, editors, headline writers, and department editors make thousands of gatekeeping decisions everyday.

Early in his reign, Keller had a number of crises. Perhaps the most notable was his handling of the administration's warrantless wiretapping. He has never adequately explained why he withheld information until December 16, 2005, about the administration's warrantless wiretapping. Originally, the *Times* claimed it only had the information for a year, but in Keller's December 31, 2005, follow-up, the term "more than a year ago" appeared, and later in Keller's April 2006 "Talk to the Newsroom" Q&A with readers he revealed that he had the information before the 2004 election. Publishing this information, as well as the later information about government oversight of the banking data on persons and organizations, were important stories that served the American public. But if the *Times* had reported the first story before the election, it might have contributed to different results. In his August 13, 2006, response to the public editor, Keller claimed that he doubted his sources until December 2005 and that it would have been unfair days before the election to publish a negative story. Keller wouldn't answer questions about this matter posed by the public editor in January 2006.

Keller should have explained in December 2005 what he claimed in August 2006—namely that his sources had drastically improved: "We now had some new people who could in no way be characterized as disgruntled bureaucrats or war-on-terror doves saying we should publish. That was a big deal." But should the politics of the sources determine whether the story should be published? I don't agree with

Calame's notion that "candidates affected by a negative article deserve to have time—several days to a week—to get their response disseminated before voters head to the polls" ("Eavesdropping and the Election: An Answer on the Question of Timing," August 13, 2006). Do we not need to differentiate between a "negative" election article and a major revelation about the Bush administration's undermining of the Constitution? Didn't the *Times* sit on something essential and true that the public needed to know? Did Keller withhold from the electorate something necessary and sufficient for making an informed choice? Are we to have a news blackout the week before an election if a story might damage one of the candidates? Keller was not suppressing possible gossip, but a possible subversion of our legal system.

Keller gave no explanation for fudging the chronology. Furthermore, he claimed "I don't remember" to Calame's query about whether the election-day timing was discussed internally. Were Keller a reporter interviewing someone with these responses, he would have been—as I am—incredulous. But Calame gave Keller a virtual pass. Shouldn't Calame have noticed the casuistry in Keller's arguments and Keller's fundamental failure to explain to his readers one of the most important decisions he as executive editor (no doubt in consultation with the publisher, Arthur Sulzberger Jr.) had to make? Calame observed, "Mr. Keller declined to explain in detail his pre-election decision to hold the article, citing obligations to preserve confidentiality of sources. He has repeatedly indicated that a major reason for the publication delays was the administration's claim that everyone involved was satisfied with the program's legality" (August 13, 2006).

Isn't the role of the *Times* to investigate whether the administration's claims of legality are valid—to consult legal authorities—and wasn't Calame's role to call the *Times* to account, not simply to repeat Keller's views? Calame should have been all over Keller for his explanation of why in the December 16, 2005, article he claimed that the *Times* had delayed "publication for a year." Keller and Calame would be chuckling with their colleagues if an administration figure had said what Keller said to Calame: "It was probably inelegant wording. . . . I don't know what was in my head at the time."

But in this case, Keller and the *Times* should have been held accountable for not revealing information of vital importance to the American people. He had drafts of the December 16, 2005, wiretapping article weeks before the 2004 presidential election, according to what he told Calame. It seems as if the *Times* censored vital information. Even the appearance that the *Times* was in cahoots with the administration is damaging to the *Times*. As Jonathan Dixon's August 20, 2006, letter to the public editor in the *Times* stated, "Mr. Keller's job—specifically noted in our Constitution as a key safeguard of our democracy—is to provide accurate information to allow informed citizens to vote responsibly for the well-being of our country."

Another example of Keller's questionable gatekeeping, which raised serious questions about his judgment, was the decision not to print inflammatory cartoons that precipitated Muslim riots in winter 2006. These twelve editorial cartoons, most of which depicted the Islamic prophet Muhammad, were published in the Danish newspaper *Jyllands-Posten* on September 30, 2005. Keller's February 3, 2006, memo to staff on why the cartoons were not to be published points to how editors are gatekeepers:

> We've had a long and vigorous debate in the newsroom and concluded that publishing the cartoons is not essential to telling the story. On the one hand, we have abundant evidence that a significant number of people—some of them our readers—consider these cartoons deeply offensive and inflammatory. Indeed, to publish them after seeing the outrage and violence across the Islamic world could be perceived as a particularly deliberate insult. On the other hand, we feel we can adequately convey the nature of the cartoons by describing them. Like any decision to withhold elements of a story, this was not easy nor entirely satisfying, but it feels like the right thing to do.

I myself believe that the *Times* had an ethical obligation to publish these cartoons. I show Nazi anti-Semitic cartoons to my class on Holocaust narratives, in which many of the students are Jewish, as a way of demonstrating how racial hatred is fomented. By seeing racist caricatures, we become aware of the stereotypes that shape opinions that we may find distasteful. But I do realize that among the considerations in the *Times*'s decision on whether to publish the anti-Muslim caricatures are safety to its reporters in Iraq as well as those in other Arab countries and perhaps credibility and access in these countries.

A final important example of Keller's insufficient gatekeeping is the handling of the accusations by a black exotic dancer that three white Duke students raped her. Many of the *Times* senior staff were doubtful about the authenticity of this story. Yet the front-page, 5,600-word follow-up by Duff Wilson and Jonathan D. Glater, "Files from Duke Rape Case Give Details But No Answer" on August 26, 2005, seemed to keep alive the last shred of credibility in a rapidly eroding tale that both David Brooks—calling it a "witch hunt"—and Nicholas Kristof—comparing it to the 1931 Scottsboro Boys case—had debunked. Did the *Times* sufficiently examine the available evidence and the motives of district attorney Mike Nifong, whom the reporters never interviewed? Was the *Times* so eager to be politically correct that it accepted and believed a fabricated story that depended on white exploitation of people of color?

The *Times*'s editors need to be certain that its reporters know what they are talking about and that they are not zealously overreading data or being manipulated by sources. Even if 98 percent of their investigative stories are valid, their credibility is tarnished by the remaining 2 percent. In this period where for many truth takes a backseat to ideology, errors give the *Times*'s political enemies—especially those whose judgment or integrity the *Times* has questioned—an opportunity to discredit the *Times*. While much of the media jump with glee on the *Times*'s mistakes, the conservative media are always the shrillest.

Keller is often slow to recognize when the *Times* goes off track, perhaps because of its very size and perhaps because of an institutional self-importance that at times pervades the building and is especially inherent in its senior editors and journalists. For the most part, the *Times* is self-regulating and wants to do the right thing when it errs, but what the right thing *is* is often not clear to the decision makers. In the case of the infamous WMD story—to be discussed in detail in my chapter on the *Times* and the First Amendment—and the Wen Ho Lee case, the reporters and their editors for a long time became what Lars-Erik Nelson aptly described in the September 26, 2000, Online NewsHour as "captive to their sources."

We need to recognize that senior editors and the publisher often differ among themselves about both priorities and how to pursue them as well as how to behave when challenged or when mistakes are recognized. But neither Keller nor Sulzberger can hide behind such bromides as "human error" or "we publish a zillion words a week" or that "we issue corrections and apologies when necessary."

IV. Questions of Keller's Judgment in the 2008 Supposed "Exposé" of McCain's Relationship with a Lobbyist

On February 21, 2008, the *Times* published a controversial front-page story, based on the use of anonymous sources, implying that John McCain had, during the late 1990s, compromised his rectitude by writing letters on behalf of clients. The piece focused on Vicki Iseman, an attractive female lobbyist for telecommunications companies (Jim Rutenberg, Marilyn W. Thompson, David D. Kirkpatrick, and Stephen Labaton, "For McCain, Self-Confidence on Ethics Poses Its Own Risk").

According to the authors, some of McCain's top advisers warned Iseman during McCain's first presidential campaign in 2000 to stay away from McCain, with whom they believed she was romantically involved. The article looked back to favors McCain did for Charles Keating, one of his campaign contributors, who was involved in the Savings and Loan scandal in the late 1980s; McCain was ultimately reprimanded by the Senate Ethics Committee in 1991. In a crucial sentence on the first page, the article concludes: "Even as he has vowed to hold himself to the highest ethical standards, his confidence in his own integrity has sometimes seemed to blind him to potentially embarrassing conflicts of interest."

Keller was excoriated by an array of critics for bad judgment in allowing the story to appear. Conservatives were outraged at what McCain's campaign called a "hit-and-run" smear campaign, and many conservative pundits called for Keller's resignation. Furthermore, the timing was questioned because editorially the *Times* had strongly favored McCain over the other Republican candidates and now was printing the story after McCain had emerged as the nominee and his rival was almost certainly going to be Barack Obama.

The article's reliance on anonymous sources reduced claims about alleged conflict of interest with Iseman to rumor and innuendo. In a special February 21, 2008, "Talk to the Newsroom," Keller wrote: "*Times* standards were followed and senior editors knew the identities of the sources for the story, who provided detailed and consistent accounts about their concerns about the senator's relationship with a Washington lobbyist." But is knowing the sources enough? Don't we need to know more about their motives and character? John Weaver, an informal adviser and once a top McCain strategist—and one apparently who has feuded with other of McCain's top advisors—claims to have arranged a meeting where Iseman was told to keep her distance; he was willing to be identified and could, if one reads David Brooks's article carefully, have been one of the sources ("The McCain World Rift," February 22, 2008).

The article was presented as part of an intermittent series entitled "The Long Run" in which *Times* reporters take a step back from the campaign and look—at times quite critically—at important moments and issues in a candidate's career. According to Keller, "[I]f you refused to publish stories that included anonymously sourced information, most of the most important things we know about how our country is run would not published. There are things you just cannot find without being willing to protect your sources" (online interview with NPR on February 21, 2008). In the aforementioned "Talk to the Newsroom," Jill Abramson chimed in:

> Much as we prefer on-the-record (or even documentary) information, and editors and reporters push hard on sources to let us use their names, without the ability to protect sources newspapers would not have been able to report on important activities of the government and other powerful institutions, and political reporting would be much more a kind of event-driven stenography. . . . Our mission is to inform our readers, which includes giving as much information as possible about sources. In the case of two anonymous sources, the story said, "The two associates, who said that they had become disillusioned with the senator, spoke independently of each other and provided details that were corroborated by others." (February 21, 2008)

Given the subject and the foregrounding with a picture of a beautiful woman and the suggestion of sex, it seems naïve to think that the reader would believe that the real story was McCain's writing letters to a regulatory commission, especially because one had to plough through an entire article to get to the details and denials. As soon as the nuance of sex is introduced into a story, it becomes the story and to think otherwise is to believe in the tooth fairy.

The online picture of Iseman shows a great deal more of her elegant sleeveless dress than the print newspaper did, and, unlike in the newspaper, the photograph is in color. Did the *Times* use good judgment when it published in its exposé: "Both [former associates] said Mr. McCain acknowledged behaving inappropriately and pledged to keep his distance from Ms. Iseman"? Since McCain denies inappropriate intervention on the part of Iseman as a lobbyist, what does "behaving inappropriately" mean? An affair? The appearance of an affair in the form of flamboyant public flirtation and/or McCain and Iseman withdrawing together to private spaces?

As public editor Clark Hoyt wrote in his February 24, 2007, column: "The article was notable for what it did not say: It did not say what convinced the advisers that there was a romance. It did not make clear what McCain was admitting when he acknowledged behaving inappropriately—an affair or just an association with a lobbyist that could look bad. And it did not say whether Weaver, the only on-the-record source, believed there was a romance" ("What That McCain Article Didn't Say").

If sexual favors are being traded for influence, that needs be verified. But, if there are no improprieties in McCain's interventions for Iseman, whether she and McCain had sex is really their and the current Mrs. McCain's business, not ours.

Finally, reading between the lines, wasn't there something self-important if not boastful about aides telling reporters that "they" kept Iseman away, saving McCain from further indiscretion as if they were his keepers? Do we really believe that the codicil—to which Abramson points—about "associates, who said they had become disillusioned with the senator" tells readers anything useful in terms of identifying sources? Were they disillusioned in 1999 or at the time of the 2008 article? Are they aides who have been fired or pushed aside?

V. Keller's *Times*: An Overview

At times one feels that the 2011 *Times* is trying to be all things to all people. The *Times* was once a set-menu newspaper, choosing rather archly what to present to its loyal readers, but it now presents a smorgasbord. Put another way, the *Times* often follows the quite plausible theory that if it can find any way online or in the newspaper to catch a reader's interest and perhaps get him or her to read further, it will create a future reader.

Thus, in its focus on sensationalism, at times the former *Metro* "B" section—now reduced and part of the "A" section—tried (sometimes none too effectively) to be the *Daily News* and the *New York Post*. No one would argue that the sex scandals of New York's ex-governor Eliot Spitzer and the sometimes sordid shortcomings of his successor David Paterson and especially Paterson's senior aide David Johnson, accused of beating up his girlfriend, are anything but real news, but in its reporting, the *Times* tiptoed to the edge of tastelessness, especially in providing the details of Spitzer's sex life.

As the former metro-regional editor and now assistant managing editor Susan Edgerley said in my February 17, 2006, interview with her, there once was a tendency to say "this is not a *Times* story," particularly when it was about a sordid crime with sexual implications, like Robert Chambers strangling Jennifer Levin, the daughter of prominent parents, in a 1986 case that came to be known as "The Preppy Murder." But Edgerley makes clear that things have changed: "I think the *Times* had a bit of a reputation of too easily, too quickly saying, well, that's not a *Times* story. . . . You don't put [the Levin–Chambers] story in the paper because it's a story of violence. You put that story in the paper because it's such a huge statement of what was going on at the time." It was two days before the *Times* printed a story about the murder, and that delay would not happen today.

The *Times* now is more likely not only to cover violent events, including domestic violence and other murders, but to be more attentive to organized crime, and in particular the Mafia, because it understands that its readers are more interested in the Mafia in the wake of the *Godfather* films and the *Sopranos*.

The *Times*'s emphasis on sexuality as well as its occasional forays into yellow journalism, gossip, and even sensationalistic photography is another part of an effort to attract tabloid readers who have in the past found the *Times* priggish. Let me cite a recent example. On July 9, 2009, a banal article on porn films by Matt Richtel entitled "Lights, Camera, Lots of Action. Forget the Script" appeared on the front page of both the New York and national editions.

To attract diverse audiences, the *Times Sports* section—not without an eye on the sports gossip being reported by the New York tabloids—emulates *USA Today* in its coverage of sports; the *Business* section wishes to compete with the *Wall Street Journal*; and arts and entertainment coverage overlaps with *People Magazine* and *Rolling Stone*.

Keller's *Times* forgets on occasion that its core readers still want news and analyses, not a daily magazine. As a business strategy, the *Times* does not want any of its readers to feel they also have to spend more money and buy the *New York Daily News* or the *New York Post* to get metro crime stories or to buy the *Daily News* or *USA Today* for expanded sports coverage or *People* for celebrity gossip.

As I noted previously, since his early years, Keller has gradually moved from defining the *Times* as a truly national newspaper to defining the *Times* as a national newspaper with a strong New York cultural base. Yet it would be more accurate to say that the *Times* oscillates from one of these definitions to the other.

Intermittently, the urban and cosmopolitan bias of various *Times* editors conflicts with the *Times*'s desire to be a national newspaper. Frequently, the *Times*'s provincialism puts it in the position of viewing Manhattan (and a few areas of Brooklyn, Connecticut, Westchester, and Long Island) as the world. One prime example of this was Tom Wolfe's nasty rant against New York's Landmark Preservation Commission in the op-ed pages in the November 26, 2006, *Week in Review*—rather than, say in the *Metro* section, where even there it would be marginally interesting to those who live outside Manhattan. Wolfe objects to a builder named Aby Rosen building thirty additional floors at 980 Madison Avenue on top of a five-story building between 76th and 77th streets. He is equally exercised by the failure of the Landmark Commission, chaired by Robert B. Tierney, to share his objection. Entitled "The (Naked) City and the Undead," this piece may rank with the most parochial use of quality space in the *Times*'s long history.

Without a chance to respond to Wolfe's scurrilous accusations, Tierney, like Rosen, is raked over the coals. Wolfe's piece is filled with name-calling of people that no one outside of Manhattan has ever heard of. For most readers, Wolfe's diatribe might as well have been written in some as yet undeciphered ancient language for all it means to them. Perhaps the debate about whether the building should be declared a landmark is worth an objective article in the *Real Estate* section, which reaches only the metropolitan audience. Even as a letter to the editor, it is moot that this piece is sufficiently interesting to those living beyond the Upper East Side and maybe a few other of the wealthiest areas of Manhattan.

Indeed, this article is an example of the *Times*'s obsessive fascination with Manhattan's ostentatious spending class that increasingly dominates the pages of the *Times*. This is particularly true in *SundayStyles* and *ThursdayStyles* where the writing wears the mantles of *Timeslite* and *Timestrash*, and is thus frothy, insipid, pointless, and inane, but apparently also attractive to some advertisers.

Another example of the *Times*'s "Manhattan-think" was the coverage of Wendy Wasserstein's career and death on January 30, 2006. The *Times* transformed her from a well-received and talented but somewhat narrowly Manhattan-centric urban playwright into a major figure in American cultural history if not a cultural icon of the importance of Eugene O'Neill, Tennessee Williams, or Arthur Miller or a modernist on the order of Samuel Beckett, Tom Stoppard, or Harold Pinter. Wasserstein won a Pulitzer and a Tony with "The Heidi Chronicles"—a play that had a good run of 622 Broadway performances after opening in 1989—and had a second success in 1993 with "The Sisters Rosensweig," but the hagiography accompanying her death was an example of the power of the *Times* to create reality from a Manhattan-centric perspective.

Beginning with a front-page obituary on January 31, 2006, by Charles Isherwood, the *Times* began the process of canonizing a well-liked Manhattanite with a wide range of friendships in the theatrical and cultural community and a wealthy brother, Bruce Wasserstein, who is a player in the interrelated New York financial and political communities. Online, the then editorial page editor, Gail Collins, wrote in an appreciation ("Wendy Wasserstein Dies at 55; Her Plays Spoke to a Generation," January 31, 2006):

> Wendy was a charter member of the company of nice women, a river of accommodating humanity that flows through Manhattan just as it flows through Des Moines and Oneonta, N.Y., organizing library fund-raisers, running day care centers, ordering prescriptions for elderly parents, buying all the birthday presents and giving career counseling to the nephew of a very remote acquaintance who is trying to decide between making it big on Broadway and dentistry. . . . Wendy understood that being considerate in a society of self-involved strivers was not for wimps. It required a steely inner toughness that was the hallmark of many of her heroines.

Although written with conviction and generosity and perhaps truth, Collins's piece contains its share of platitudes and shows how a senior Timesperson can commandeer space.

Inadvertently belying Collins's claims of Wasserstein's universality, Virginia Heffernan's piece in the February 3, 2006, Friday *Weekend* gives us a strong clue to the reasons for this cultural hagiography by defining Wasserstein in terms of the politics of gender and the politics of wealth in New York: "She was the ultimate girl's girl, a woman whose presence in New York suggested the possibility of an unhostile and entirely female world, one open to no guys except her brother Bruce, the hedge-fund manager (he'd supply the capital), and gay men from the arts" ("Revisiting Wasserstein's TV, Where Female Stars Thrive"). Several worlds collide in the foregoing sentence, in which Heffernan alludes ironically to the importance of gay artists in the cultural world revolving around the stages of Lincoln Center and Playwrights Horizon. What Heffernan is implying is that in the aforementioned Manhattan special world—a world nourished and sustained by power brokers, gay and straight, who wield enormous monetary influence over aspects of New York cultural life—Wasserstein's operatic divas seemed to appeal to New York feminists within comfortable socioeconomic groups as well as to gay men, the latter finding these women to have the appeal of drag queens.

VI. Keller's Fine-Tuning

Okrent asked in the headline of his July 25, 2004, column, "Is The *New York Times* a Liberal Newspaper?" His opening one-sentence-paragraph answer took all of four words, "Of course it is." He continued: "If you're examining the paper's coverage . . . from a perspective that is neither urban nor Northeastern nor culturally seen-it-all . . . then a walk through this newspaper can make you feel you're traveling in a strange and forbidding world." He cited as evidence the editorial page, where only two of the then seven op-ed columnists were conservative—Brooks and William Safire—as well as the articles in the *Sunday Magazine*, the culture pages, the fashion coverage, *Sunday Styles*, even the *Sports* and *Metro* sections, and, alas, even the news pages.

Okrent claimed: "[I]f you think the *Times* plays it down the middle [on social issues: gay marriage, gun control, abortion, and environmental regulation] you've been reading the paper with your eyes closed. . . . [On gay marriage], *Times* editors have failed to provide the three-dimensional perspective [that] balanced journalism requires." Commenting on the fact that only 50 percent of the *Times*'s readership resides in metropolitan New York, he writes that although six years previously the *Times* owners decided to make the newspaper a national one, "the paper's heart, mind and habits remain embedded [in New York]. You can take the paper out of the city but without an effort to take the city and all its attendant provocations, experiments and attitudes out of the paper, readers with a different worldview will find the *Times* an alien beast."

Keller is conscious of the identity articulated by Okrent and has made some modest efforts to change it. Keller's politics are more conservative and less doctrinaire and also less identifiable than the populist Raines, but what is more important is that his temperament favors balanced perspectives and a commitment to air multiple sides of an issue, in contrast to Raines's crusading temperament.

Raines had a muckraking sensibility and responded intuitively to the possibility of turning events to his advantage. Raines's competitiveness was at work when he set out to cover 9/11, although it would be unfair to say that was his only motive. But the six Pulitzer Prizes for his coverage of 9/11 events and the aftermath—about which he speaks so proudly—reflects his zeal for recognition.

Keller is a positivist who looks at the overall picture from a rational if skeptical perspective and understands that decent people can differ on issues like abortion and gay marriage. In Keller's words,

> Conservatives feel estranged because they feel excluded. They do not always see themselves portrayed in the mainstream press as three-dimensional humans, and they don't see their ideas taken seriously or treated respectfully. This is something I've long felt we should correct, not to pander to red-state readers but because it's bad journalism to caricature anyone with reductionist portraits and crude shorthand. . . . Portraying conservatives fairly does not mean equal time for creationism. But it does mean, for example, writing about abortion in a way that does justice to the deep moral qualms most Americans have about it. It means trying to understand the thinking of people who

regard gay marriage as unacceptable, who worry that gun
controls represent an encroachment on their civil liberties."
(Lemann, "Fear and Favor," 174)

Under Keller, the *Times* has been trying to reach beyond its core
audience of socially liberal, urban, and sophisticated readers. Although
Raines was from Alabama and committed to civil rights, trying to
understand the thinking of people who didn't agree with him, whether
in the newsroom or within his potential readership, was not his strong
suit. By contrast, in his early years as executive editor, Keller reached
beyond the core in several ways. For example, that the *Times* covered
Billy Graham's summer 2005 New York crusade as a significant event—
rather than merely a curiosity—was a deliberate decision, as Glenn
Kramon revealed to me in a June 22, 2005, interview. This event would
not have made the front page in prior eras. Under Keller, Landman
(former acting cultural editor from 2004 to 2005 and now once again
cultural editor), and Sam Sifton (cultural editor from 2005 to summer
2009), the daily *Arts* section has become larger and more inclusive,
with more substantive articles on a wide range of subjects and with
a greater awareness of exhibits and performances beyond New York
and the Eastern corridor as well as world cultural issues, such as the
plans to redesign Les Halles in Paris (Nicolai Ouroussoff, "Rich Menus
to Choose From, but What Will Fill the 'Belly of Paris,'" January 6,
2005).

Not only has Keller been trying to include diverse perspectives in the *Times*, but in his years as editor he also has been trying to reach new audiences by changing and upgrading the format,
utility, and readability of both the printed paper and, especially, of
nytimes.com. Specifically, he has worked with Landman, who in 2005
became deputy managing editor with a special responsibility for digital
journalism. More and more valuable material appeared only on the
digital site. Thus, the 2006 Electoral Guide on the Internet showing
which seats were safely Democratic or Republican or leaning Democratic
or Republican or were a toss-up was helpful; such features became a
staple of the Internet political coverage, but usually were and are absent
from the printed newspaper.

The online additions demonstrate the value of the new media as
a teaching tool. Missing from the print edition are the valuable graphics in the "Inside Congress" feature within the *Politics* section of the

digital *Times*. Readers can click on a vote—for example a November 5, 2009, vote on extending unemployment benefits—and find out how many Democrats and Republicans voted for the bill, how specific legislators voted, and a map of the United States with the geography of the vote color-coded. Nytimes.com has helpful interactive time lines of the lives and careers of the subjects of its articles; an example is Michelle Obama's interactive family tree on October 8, 2009, which provided necessary context for the printed article. Another recent example is the time line of Intel's anti-trust history, which was posted November 4, 2009, when Intel's anti-trust behavior was foregrounded in the news. The nytimes.com Caucus blog has continued to improve; originally by Kate Phillips with contributions by the *Times*'s political reporters, it often was long on verbiage and short on substance and written from a tunnel-vision perspective. Now subtitled "The Politics and Government Blog of the Times," various staff writers rotate with more substantive and focused contributions.

In terms of the evolution of the *Politics* site on nytimes.com, the audio with Janet Elder, the poll editor, on the night before the 2006 election was excellent. Indeed, nytimes.com election coverage in 2006 was a turning point where online coverage was markedly superior to that of the newspaper, although the newspaper audience did get strong post-election analyses in a special section two days after the election. Still, much on the website never appeared in the paper. In summer 2009, most of the up-to-the-minute coverage on "the Lede" (the *Times* news blog) of Iran's postelection turmoil—based on such new media as Twitter, YouTube, cell phones, and blogs from those observing events inside Iran—did not appear in the printed newspaper; this coverage became even more important after the Western media were forced to leave Iran.

Under Keller's leadership, the use not only of photography but also of useful graphics has proliferated. More graphics appear on the Internet rather than in the newspaper. The use of graphics is another way the *Times* seeks to reach younger readers. Sometimes, graphic narratives also appear on the op-ed page, and older readers often ask why and for whom. Early in Keller's editorship, it seemed that he was finding his sea legs when it came to graphics and allowing his section editors free rein. Thus, the *Sunday Book Review* of June 6, 2004, contained a color cartoon sequence by Ross McDonald on the title page entitled "The Insult that Led to an Orgy of Guilt-Free Summer Reading" that plays upon the old Charles Atlas magazine ads that invited readers to mail in a coupon for muscle-building information; in the cartoon the reader is promised "Pounds of Brawny, Rippling Intellect!" That cartoon, continuing on page 3 above the contents and within the text over several of the headings, was a way of announcing that the *Book Review* was being jazzed up. The hope was that younger readers would be attracted to the new more graphically oriented *Sunday Book Review,* a section that Keller and the current editor Sam Tanenhaus thought that they needed to rescue from stodginess.

The line between features and commercialism continues to blur. On September 25, 2009, an article by Maura Egan entitled "Ornamentalism" and supposedly on Hue in the *Sunday "T" Magazine* devoted to travel was really as much about expensive objects of clothing such as shoes and purses (with prices displayed in the article). The subtitle "ELABORATE TEMPLES, KINGLY PALACES AND A FORBIDDEN CITY—VIETNAM'S IMPERIAL CAPITAL, HUE, HAS ALWAYS BEEN JUST FOR SHOW" was a stretch to link Hue with fashion.

Keller also has presided over a proliferation of *Timeslite,* a notable example of which was a front-page story by Dan Barry under the rubric "About New York" on Saturday, October 15, 2005, on umbrellas in New York during a rainy week (Dan Barry, "Over the Asphalt Rivers, the Source of the $3 Umbrella"). For traditionalist *Times* readers such a story is simply filler. Or how about a front-page story in the November 13, 2005, *Sunday Times* by Andy Newman on "grille-mounted stuffed animals" ("They're Soft and Cuddly, So Why Lash Them to the Front of a Truck," November 13, 2005)? The article is accompanied on the front page by three colored pictures captioned: "Like figureheads on the prow of ships, Stewie (the name of an evil baby from 'Family Guy') . . . and his friends travel through Brooklyn on delivery trucks, garbage trucks and pickups."

Under Keller's leadership, the *Times* has reinvented the back-of-the-book sections—a fungible term used to refer to the feature sections other than hard news—and permitted a plethora of self-performing writing that tells the reader more about the writer than the subject. He also has allowed the continued growth of the following:

1. sensational and hyperbolic reporting about violence and sex crimes (especially but not exclusively in the *Metro* section);

2. unsatisfactorily labeled and even staged photographs, something Calame, the second public editor, rightly criticized in his July 3, 2005, piece, "Pictures, Labels, Perception and Reality";

3. more tasteless articles that aim to titillate, to show that the *Times* is now hip; and

4. more tabloid gossip about celebrity culture.

VII. Jill Abramson, Managing Editor for News

Jill Abramson, since August 2003 the managing editor responsible for news and now incoming executive editor, gives the impression of being capable and extraordinarily tough-minded. She is marginally polite but guarded to the point of being impatient, humorless, and abrasive and, although she did agree to grant me an interview, made no secret of feeling an interview with me was an imposition on her time. Hired away from the *Wall Street Journal* in 1997, she was appointed Washington bureau chief on January 1, 2001, but she and Raines did not get along.

She is more strident and less modest than Keller, who seems to be comfortable with himself if reluctant to impose authority. Given the staff's dissatisfaction with Raines's rough style, I had some doubts that she would be chosen to succeed Keller. Yet she may be different with colleagues, and the whispers in the *Times* building did indicate that Sulzberger would favor choosing a woman as the next executive editor.

If Sulzberger has a sense of privilege by being the heir to the *Times*'s ownership family, Abramson has a sense of both privilege by competence and privilege by way of having graduated from Harvard. She believes in her own competence, and if Sulzberger is selling vision, she is selling nuts-and-bolts ability to turn out a paper. As she put it to me: "My job is managing editor for the news, and I focus on the news. I don't sit here philosophizing about who the reader should be. How do we get on top of a big story, get behind it, get extra value-added that no other newspaper or magazine or TV network or cable TV network [gets]. . . . How are we going to give the most multifaceted view of an important story is what I worry about" (October 11, 2005).

She was one of the figures instrumental in the overthrow of Raines and is loyal to Keller, who appointed her on July 31, 2003, as managing editor: "I think one of the hallmarks of Bill Keller's time as executive editor that has brought immense gratification to me is the return of real investigative reporting and the time it takes to do the real thing." This very well may have been a coded way of saying that the kind of investigative reporting that Judith Miller was doing under Raines was unsatisfactory. That Maureen Dowd is her best friend on the paper may explain why the attack on Miller in the paper was begun by Dowd's October 22, 2005, column, "Woman of Mass Destruction."

VIII. The Public Editor: Ombudsman or Reader's Representative

The first public editor, Daniel Okrent, began writing in December 2003 and held the position until May 2005. When Okrent's eighteen-month term ended, Byron Calame, a retired deputy managing editor for the *Wall Street Journal*, succeeded him. In May 2007, Clark Hoyt, a former Pulitzer Prize–winning reporter, editor, and vice president for the news for the Knight Ridder newspaper chain, succeeded Calame, and Hoyt has been succeeded by Arthur S. Brisbane.

The role of the public editor is to critique the *Times* on the pages of the *Week in Review*. In his first column, December 7, 2003, "An Advocate for *Times* Readers Introduces Himself," Okrent somewhat stridently defined himself as "the first person charged with publicly evaluating, criticizing, and otherwise commenting on the paper's integrity" and explained that by agreement with Keller, his eighteen-month term would end on May 29, 2005. Within his columns, his persona was that of a smart, savvy, shrewd, and witty if, on occasion, quixotic outsider to newsrooms, but also that of a sophisticated New York insider. Okrent wore the mantle of someone whose role is to keep a vigilant eye out for shenanigans. By contrast, Calame had more of a newspaper editor's background and saw himself more as an intermediary between reader and newspaper and as the moderating and low-key voice of experience and reason.

What Okrent did—and this was no small accomplishment—was to establish his independence and willingness to critique the *Times*; by doing so, he created a tradition on which his successors could build.

He wrote every other week and could have written more frequently if he wished. To further conversation, Okrent announced in the February 15, 2004, column that he would turn over the column periodically to letters from readers on subjects he addressed in his columns, and his successors have continued to do that. Thus, on weeks between his biweekly columns, Okrent printed a tiny fraction of the five hundred to one thousand letters he received weekly from readers. He answered a good many of the other letters personally or forwarded them to the appropriate editor, and he maintained a web journal to supplement his comments. Calame and Hoyt have followed his example, although Hoyt's journal consists mostly of letters to him.

Okrent thought of himself as an ombudsman who preferred "conversation" to "argument" ("It's Been 11 Weeks. Do You Know Where Your Ombudsman Is?" February 15, 2004). In his role of ombudsman, he explained, "I don't attend editorial meetings, engage in personal discussions or review anything before it gets into print—nor should I be able to." He took the *Times* to task when he thought its coverage was biased, myopic, or unsatisfactory. But as a former journalist, he also was aware that a newspaper selects and arranges stories and chooses the facts presented within each story. On February 1, 2004, he criticized the *Times* for not paying enough attention to three stories that appeared in other publications: revelations about a 1967 civilian massacre in Vietnam; the insights of former treasure secretary Paul O'Neill about the Bush administration; and a piece in the January 7, 2004, *Washington Post*, "Iraq's Arsenal Was Only On Paper," revealing that "the putative Iraqi arsenal didn't exist." Okrent asked, "[I]f the goal of newspapering is to inform the readers and create a historical record, shouldn't the editors be telling us about everything they think is important, no matter where they find it?"

Because he was the first public editor, Okrent defined the position. A central tenet was what has become known as Okrent's Law, quoted as an epigraph to this chapter: "The pursuit of balance can create imbalance because sometimes something is true" (*New Yorker*, May 24, 2004).

He inspired confidence by his willingness to question accepted practices and by his usually low-key tone, although he had occasional moments of bad judgment and ill temper, as when in his last column, on May 22, 2005, he uncharacteristically launched a mean-spirited attack on Paul Krugman. For the most part, Okrent eschewed shrillness and avoided righteousness, arrogance, or a sense that he was observing the *Times* from an iconoclastic steep and icy peak. He convinced us that he had the reader's interest in mind.

An important example of Okrent following Okrent's Law that "sometimes something is true" was in his March 28, 2003, column, "The Privileges of Opinion, the Obligation of Fact," which began: "Should opinion columnists be subject to the same corrections policy that governs the work of every other writer at the *Times*?" and his answer was clearly affirmative. In 2004, a new rule promulgated by the then editorial page editor Gail Collins and the publisher, Sulzberger, stipulated that columnists' errors must be acknowledged at the end of subsequent columns. Another issue that I would stress: Should columnists be called to account when they flagrantly stretch the truth or use misleading hyperbole? In other words, when does stretching and distorting facts need an editor's note?

Always fluent, Okrent's columns could be breezy and humorous and sometimes folksy. He had Runyonesque moments when he was bit of a New York smart aleck and/or when he had the very Manhattan-centric view of the world that he criticized in the *Times*. An example of his wisecracking sense of humor is his rejection of the argument by some *Times* editors that because liberals and conservatives complain, "the paper must therefore be doing things right. This makes as much sense as saying that a man with one foot on a block of ice and the other on a bed of hot coals must feel just fine" ("How Would Jackson Pollock Cover This Campaign?," October 10, 2004). The analogy really tells us very little but is an example of Okrent's enjoying being Okrent. A previous Okrent sentence is in the same vein: "A definition of irony: what an ombudsman or public editor must appreciate to survive this campaign."

Okrent's forte was synthesis and intelligent overviews, often presented without probing research, of exactly how the *Times* was or wasn't doing its work. He liked easy and funny analogies and on occasion called attention to himself more than necessary through flip jokes or reductive parallels. He sometimes self-absorbedly reveled in the sheer pleasure of being a wordsmith to the detriment of the gravitas his role demanded. Yet often he deftly employed analogies in the service of his teacherly bent. For example, from his January 23, 2005, column: "Numbers without context, especially large ones with many zeroes trailing behind, are about as intelligible as vowels without consonants."

Okrent critiqued the use of anonymous sources for news articles. In February 2004, the *Times* instituted "a requirement that a ranking editor must know the identity of a reporter's unnamed source," except when "sources face dire consequences if exposed" ("An Electrician from the Ukrainian Town of Lutsk," June 13, 2004). Yet Okrent still found the *Times* rife with anonymous sources, which means readers don't know where information comes from and have to take what is reported on faith. In a May 30, 2004, column, Okrent proposed that the reporter should tell the source that he or she would be exposed if the anonymous story turns out to be a lie. Furthermore, Okrent proposed that articles be written in the reporter's own voice, without blind quotes and meaningless attributions to unnamed officials, so that we could hold the writers themselves responsible for the accuracy of what they report. Somewhat disingenuously, he asked, two weeks later: "Isn't that the way it ought to be?" (June 13, 2004).

When Okrent published his collected columns in a 2006 volume entitled *Public Editor #1: The Collected Columns (with Reflections, Reconsiderations, and Even a Few Retractions) of the First Ombudsman of the New York Times*, I had a better sense of his persona and what he accomplished. What emerges is something of a West Side character, quick-witted, playful with words, a tad to the left, and well-read. Okrent's good-natured, high-spirited persona brought seriousness to the enterprise without his taking himself too seriously. He didn't pretend to know everything and was generally tolerant of diverse points of view, except when they became overwrought. He was conversational and chatty, at times to the point of being glib. He wanted very much to be liked, both by the *Times* and his readers. Yet, at times, by trying too hard and revealing too much about himself in a role that asks for detachment and objectivity, he became less an ombudsman than a personality with his own tics and idiosyncrasies.

Sometimes Okrent played picnic softball with the *Times*'s editors—to adopt his analogistic technique—rather than really taking them to task when they deserved it. Perhaps if he had had the more ample form of his recent book rather than a word limit within his column, he might have cited more examples of the abuse of quotation and included more discussion of the economic challenges facing the newspaper business and how they were being met.

The contrast between Okrent and his successor as public editor Byron—he prefers "Barney"—Calame is revealing. In terms of knowing the press and speaking in spare and lucid language, Calame was quite different from Okrent. Calame had an editorial eye on journalistic problems and was more of a nuts-and-bolts newspaperman than Okrent, who is really not a newspaperman but, like me, something of an outsider.

Put another way, Okrent was a practitioner of the New Journalism in which the author calls attention to himself, foregrounds his own opinions even when they are not essential—"I'll be voting for John Kerry next month" ("How would Jackson Pollock Cover This Campaign?" October 10, 2004)—writes a playful, writerly text that may be full of metaphors and analogies, and is prone to hyperbole. By contrast, Calame belonged to a world where accuracy, detachment, and understatement still matter. The question is which best suits the role of public editor and I am not sure we have a clear answer. Possibly both would work, but Calame simply was not critical enough.

Calame (whom I sometimes think of as Gentle Barney because I feel at times he needed to be more aggressive in calling the *Times* to account) often deferred to the *Times*'s editors without raising the larger issues. He was too gentle and too trusting and on many occasions needed to hold the *Times* to a higher standard than he did. He didn't pursue issues on behalf of the readers as aggressively as he should or probe deeply enough into the question of whether the *Times* was keeping in mind the best interests of its readers. After asking managing editor John Geddes, "How much of an idea can you give us about the amount of news content in a few feature sections—the weekly *Escapes*, for instance?" and learning that there were thirty-two columns allotted to content, Calame should have pushed Geddes by asking, "What do the thirty-two columns in *Escapes* actually do? Does *Escapes* have any purpose other than accommodating advertising?" (see Calame, "All the News That Fits the Allocated Space," January 29, 2006).

Calame should have asked Geddes what Geddes and his senior colleagues were doing by printing so much *Timeslite* and *Timestrash*. Geddes defined journalism as "about telling . . . what's important in the order of importance." But was the *Times* fulfilling Geddes's own definition with the prolixity of its eighty-five columns in *Arts & Leisure* on Sunday and the even more egregious example of wasted words in *ThursdayStyles* and *SundayStyles*? Calame's December 18, 2005, column in the *Sunday Book Review*—about the chapter on the Sunday magazines—is another example of his playing softball. He failed to ask the difficult questions such as who decides what is reviewed and whether the best possible reviewers were chosen ("The *Book Review*: Who Critiques Whom—and Why?").

Calame needed to be a more resistant ombudsman in questioning the *Times*'s editors and reporters and in accepting their explanations. In his October 22, 2006, column "Can 'Magazines' of the *Times* Subsidize News Coverage," he accepted Keller's explanation that the plethora of magazines were in the readers' interest because they subsidize the news operation without asking whether the additional revenue is really aimed at protecting the earnings and dividends—and thus the stock price—for shareholders, including the Sulzberger family. Certainly, the *Times* is neither a charity nor a nonprofit organization, but a business that needs to make money to pay its bills. But if new ventures are launched for other reasons than the best interests of the readers, shouldn't the ombudsman speak for the readers' interests and explain whose interests—if not theirs—are being served? Is there any evidence, as Calame claims, that "increased advertising revenue" has gone directly to "bolster the metro staff by replacing reporters who had volunteered for duty in Baghdad"? Why not ask Keller why the coverage of Iraq has meant less coverage of other foreign news? Or what the effect on the newspaper's gravitas is of what Calame called "often fluffy life-style coverage" (October 22, 2006)?

Within the *Times* offices in 2004–2005, I heard grudging acceptance of the necessity of the public editor's role even as I also heard the view that the *Times* was overly apologetic and defensive in the face of Okrent's criticisms. *Times* editors have been more comfortable with Calame and Hoyt not only because they regard them as sympathetic fellow journalists, but also because they are now accustomed to the public editor's position. During Calame's years as public editor (May 2005–May 2007), *Times* senior editors must have breathed a collective sigh of relief every other Sunday when they saw how sympathetic Calame was to the *Times*'s point of view and how uncritical he was.

Fully aware of how gentle Calame has been but also realizing that the reader's representative needs to be critical, Chuck Strum, an associate managing editor, expressed admiration for Okrent but told me on September 20, 2006—while Calame still held the position—that Calame was a "dreadful public editor" who was "rearranging the placemats on the *Titanic*" (September 20, 2006). Jack Shafer, media critic for *Slate,* also contended in a May 9, 2006, commentary that

Calame was a "dreadful" public editor. Shafer asserted, "Calame possesses a mandate that would allow him to boil the journalistic ocean if he so desired, but he usually elects to merely warm a teapot for his readers and pour out thimblefuls of weak chamomile. . . . The prime beneficiary of Calame's incompetence has been his predecessor as public editor, Daniel Okrent, who brought to the job the needed athleticism, pugnacity, and intellectual curiosity" ("The Public Editor as Duffer," *Slate*, May 9, 2006).

Clark Hoyt, the third public editor, was more skeptical than most of the mainstream media about the Bush administration's case for the conflict in Iraq. He was more critical than Calame but less speculative than Okrent. Like Calame, but unlike Okrent, Hoyt was reluctant to reveal much about himself and wanted to present himself as a kind of objective referee making judgments about the journalistic game. He began a three-year term in May 14, 2007, and wrote his last column on June 13, 2010; he has been succeeded by Arthur S. Brisbane, who has a Knight Ridder background and has been editor and publisher of the *Kansas City Star*.

Like Calame, Hoyt brought strong newspaper experience to the position. Combining skepticism, diligence, experience, insistence on nuts-and-bolts accuracy, and an ingrained belief that reporting and editing can always be better, he was more rigorous than Calame in holding the *Times* to the highest standards. The common thread that runs through Hoyt's critique is that the *Times* should be as accurate as possible and should put facts in a context that readers can understand. For example, in his December 2, 2007, column, "Fact and Fiction on the Campaign Trail," he chides the *Times* for not checking the claims of the presidential candidates: "Fact-checking the candidates has long been an important part of campaign coverage." Although he praises the *Times* for publishing nineteen examinations of political ads since Labor Day 2007, he also complains, with examples, that "The *Times* has also missed opportunities to set the record straight."

Hoyt was particularly responsive to readers' complaints. For example, on January 27, 2008, he examined the controversial series "War Torn," which began with a story dominating page 1 on January 13, 2008, about veterans of Iraq and Afghanistan who have been killed or charged with killings after returning home. According to Hoyt, "the first article used colorfully inflated language—'trail of death'—for a trend it could not reliably quantify, despite an attempt at statistical analysis using squishy numbers." The article did not make clear what its focus was. "Was it about killer vets, or about human tragedies involving a system that sometimes fails to spot and treat troubled souls returning from combat?" ("Stories that Speak for Themselves," January 27, 2008). His columns reflect a balanced and quiet reasonableness along with a strong sense of righteous probity about what should have been; in this case what was missing was statistical analysis: "I believe the *Times* tangled itself in numbers right at the start. Keller said the newsroom's computer-assisted reporting unit normally screens articles with statistical analyses. Some of the problems might have been avoided if someone in the unit had read the first article before it was published. But Terry Schwadron, the editor who oversees the unit, which created a database for the 121 cases, said that did not happen," apparently because the editor and the article's authors never asked for such a review (January 27, 2008).

On another occasion, Hoyt thought that the *Times* was negligent in not revealing that Linda Greenhouse had reported on a Supreme Court case in which her husband, Eugene Fidell, filed a brief on behalf of a Guantánamo Bay prisoner. He did not fault the *Times* for leaving her on the story and praised the fair-mindedness of her reporting on the case. But in January 2008, he quite rightly urged full disclosure of relations between reporters and those even tangentially involved in a story: "The *Times* should systematically disclose more about . . . the intersections between the personal and professional lives of its journalists" ("Public and Private Lives, Intersecting," January 20, 2008).

Responding to nearly seven hundred messages—only one of which was positive—about William Kristol's appointment as a columnist to the paper's op-ed page for one year, Hoyt took a balanced approach, even though he made clear that Kristol would not have been his choice for a second conservative columnist to join David Brooks because of a statement Kristol made about prosecuting the *Times*. On the June 25, 2006, broadcast of Fox *News Sunday,* Kristol had said—and Hoyt quoted Kristol—"I think the attorney general has an absolute obligation to consider prosecution of the *New York Times* for publishing an article that revealed a classified government program to sift the international banking transactions of thousands of Americans in a search for terrorists." Yet, notwithstanding Kristol's attack on the First Amendment and freedom of the press—core values of the *Times*—Hoyt believed that the reaction of readers was overwrought ("He May Be Unwelcome, but We'll Survive," January 13, 2008).

As the reader's representative, Hoyt was attuned to ethical questions. He took the *Times* to task on September 23, 2007, for accepting an ad from the liberal advocacy group MoveOn.org that was
headlined "General Petraeus or General Betray Us?": "I think the ad
violated The *Times*'s own written standards, and the paper now says
that the advertiser got a price break it was not entitled to. . . . For me,
two values collided here: the right of free speech—even if it's abusive
speech—and a strong personal revulsion toward the name-calling
and personal attacks that now pass for political dialogue, obscuring
rather than illuminating important policy issues. For the *Times*, there
is another value: the protection of its brand as a newspaper that sets
a high standard for civility" ("Betraying Its Own Best Interests"). Hoyt
could have been more critical of Sulzberger's claim that he didn't know
the ad would appear and his characteristically sanctimonious semi-
apology: "If we're going to err, it's better to err on the side of more
political dialogue. . . . Perhaps we did err in this case. If we did, we
erred with the intent of giving greater voice to people."

Hoyt is not a puritan but he does have some problems with
sexual titillation, as when he questioned in a December 16, 2007,
column the *Times*'s use of a semi-nude seventeen-year-old model
in the Sunday "*T*" section: "What counts for The *Times* is whether
photographs of a semi-nude teenager with a certain Lolita quality to
them are appropriate for the newspaper, regardless of their artistic
merit. . . . I was disturbed that the *Times* would place a teenager in
a 'sexualized context'" ("A Semi-Nude Minor? In the *Times*?"). In this
piece, he reminds readers that the "*T*" sections are a financial boon
and chides the *Times* for putting financial gain ahead of good taste: "In
an otherwise depressed newspaper world, where revenues are stagnant
and layoffs and buyouts are frequent, '*T*,' the fashion magazine of the
New York Times, is a spectacular success."

That Hoyt has been criticized from the left and right shows that
he has found a place in the middle. Yet, when he first took up the
public editorship, on occasion it seemed that he was frying small fish
and losing the larger picture. But toward the end of Hoyt's term, he
began focusing on larger issues. Thus, in his June 20, 2009, column,
"Putting a Price on News Copy," Hoyt wrote about the price increase
to $5 (or $6 outside the New York area) for the daily *Times* and $6
for the *Sunday Times* and how readers were paying more and getting
less: "In the last week, the newspaper has trimmed the dimensions

of its Sunday magazine and announced that it was eliminating a half page of financial tables and other features in Business Day. . . . In the face of a severe recession and a technological revolution luring readers away from print, the price of the ink-on-paper *Times* keeps going up and some content is reduced or disappears."

In his October 31, 2009, "Recession, Revolution and a Leaner *Times*," Hoyt succinctly described what is happening within the news industry and specifically the *Times*. He put in context the recent decision to cut 100 newsroom jobs at the *Times*, reducing the newsroom at the time to 1,250, still the largest staff by far in the United States:

> The *Times* has already made the easier decisions—reducing the support staff, cutting freelance budgets, capping expense-account meals, seeking bargain airfares and hotels, rotating foreign correspondents every five years instead of four, and housing some bureaus in correspondents' homes rather than downtown offices. . . . Technology, which has led to the flight of readers and advertisers from print, has also drastically reshaped the newsroom. For instance, there is no longer a photo lab with a dozen technicians developing film, but there are a dozen videographers shooting for the website.

As the reader's representative, the public editor might write an annual evaluative column on how the publisher is running the *Times* and whether that could be improved. And he might do the same about the executive editor. He could do both in the context of the economic challenges facing the newspaper. Indeed, the public editor could write a twice-yearly general column under the rubric, "How could the *Times* do better?" and/or "How is the *Times* responding to the rapidly changing economic environment and the challenge of the Internet?"

Because Brisbane, the fourth public editor, has yet to define himself, I don't know how conversant he is with digital journalism, but I would hope that he has more experience than his predecessors in this area.

IX. Foreign News Coverage (and Shortcomings) in the Contemporary *Times*

As other American news media do less and less with foreign news, coverage by the *Times* is increasingly important. Indeed, it often is the source of foreign news in other newspapers and even network cover-age. The *Times* has excelled in its coverage on the Iraq war after a slow start and has given the fullest picture of what is evolving in that war-torn country. It has shown the distinction between the military progress of the surge and the political chaos that still reigned in July 2008. I could cite hundreds of examples of rendering the reality of life in Iraq, but an eloquent one is a summer 2006 piece by Robert Semple: "Once there was only one Saddam, now there are many. . . . Everyone has their own reason to kill. . . . There is a new saying. . . . We are all sentenced to death but we don't know when. . . . Danger is too close, I can't manage it. . . . Before I could manage it" ("City of Dread: Where the Collateral Damage Is in the Mind," July 30, 2006). Such depth is hardly an exception, but too often major ongoing foreign news, after being featured for a week or so, begins to take a back seat to less compelling domestic news—often really Washington chit-chat—and magazine-type features.

Afghanistan has now become the focus of foreign coverage, while the still impressive Iraq coverage has been reduced as the U.S. troops have now achieved the withdrawal goal of combat forces by August 2010, with the goal of all troops out by December 2011.

In a way that reveals once more how the *Times* has been trying to find a new audience, foreign news editor Susan Chira explained to me the Keller philosophy of presenting a front-page smorgasbord and how that philosophy diminishes foreign news:

> The front page is a mix that should entice many readers and that can talk to many aspects of their lives and their world. So the definition has absolutely changed probably over time to make foreign news less completely dominant. . . . [T]he definition of what should be a front page story has changed a great deal in the sense that news about your life, trends about life . . . [are] legitimate. . . . Believe it or not, there are a lot of people in news who are indifferent to foreign news. I don't like that. One of my campaigns is to try to [interest] young readers . . . in foreign news. (February 17, 2006)

I think the *Times* can do much better in providing continuity, context, and overviews, and it could do so with sufficient gravitas. Chira acknowledged that reporting of foreign news is intermittent: "The news is episodic. That's a legitimate criticism. We're not a magazine like the *Economist* that sort of checks in regularly." The *Times* needs to provide an ongoing narrative of what is happening between foregrounded stories. As Jonathan Landman told me on October 9, 2006, "One of the shortcomings of journalism, as a form, is it has a short attention span. Journalism is not scholarship, even the very best journalism is not scholarship and one of its characteristics is, its attention span is short." But this is not a sufficient explanation for not keeping up its focus on major foreign news stories. Because the major networks no longer have substantial foreign news resources and tend to have little time for anything other than Iraq and Afghanistan, we count on the *Times* for in depth foreign news.

Even with twenty-five foreign bureaus (plus one at the United Nations), the *Times*'s foreign reporters have trouble covering breaking stories in more than two hundred countries. With a larger foreign staff, day-to-day coverage could be better. For example, although the January 29, 2006, coverage of Haiti was excellent as an example of investigative or enterprise journalism (Walt Bogdanich and Jenny Nordberg, "Mixed U.S. Signals Helped Tilt Haiti Toward Chaos"), wasn't it a bit late, after Haiti had descended into chaos, to write about how the Republican administration ousted Aristide by making common cause with rascals and criminals? Most of the information could have been ferreted out much earlier if Haiti had been a *Times* priority. In defense of such delays, Chira explained to me: "Some things take time because as the spotlight drifts away, people are more willing to talk" (February 17, 2006). Perhaps if a senior staff member were on the ground or had at least reliable stringers there, in the persons of Haitian journalists, the aforementioned article about U.S. manipulation of Haitian politics—with its whistle-blowing potential—would have appeared earlier. Until Marc Lacey's March 23, 2008, article, "Haiti's Poverty Stirs Nostalgia for Old Ghosts," the *Times* had not carried a substantive update for several months.

Haiti seems to be a place the *Times* visits intermittently without paying full attention. In 2010, Haiti received a great deal of *Times* attention, with commendable reporting after the terrible January earthquake but coverage of the disaster could have further stressed that the seeds of a dysfunctional response had been planted long ago.

Haiti appears and disappears from the screen; so, too, do Lebanon, Venezuela, and Zimbabwe; and major countries in our hemisphere such as Brazil and Argentina are covered intermittently and spasmodically, whereas smaller but important countries like Tunisia or Bolivia are almost neglected. For several years, even North Korea and Iran and their nuclear ambitions got intermittent attention, although in recent years that has received more focus, and the failed nuclear negotiations with Iran were a major story in 2009 and 2010.

The failure of the *Times* to follow up on a major story was emphasized for me by Michael Wines's November 12, 2006, piece on Zimbabwe in, of all places, the Sunday *Travel* section. Although the article mentioned but skirted many of that deeply torn nation's real political issues, wouldn't an article on Zimbabwe in the A section or *Week in Review* have been more appropriate?

Finally, with the world's most rampant inflation as the backdrop for Mugabe's re-election campaign—and the ensuing failure of Mugabe and his cronies to respect the outcome—Zimbabwe returned to the foreground in March, April, and May 2008. After receiving some coverage in summer 2007, the *Times* distinguished itself in covering the aftermath of the March 2008 presidential and parliamentary elections that devolved into chaos and fraud.

Indeed, in early April 2008, to intimidate Western news media trying to monitor the behavior of Mugabe's autocratic regime in the wake of its dismissive and illegal response to the election, a *Times* Pulitzer Prize–winning journalist, Barry Bearak, was arrested in Harare, the capital, on the grounds that he was unaccredited by the government, although the government accredits almost no reporters and until that time was allowing foreign reporters to enter on their own passports and report. On April 5, 2008, the *Times* ran an excellent podcast with Wines, another of the *Times* South Africa correspondents and the bureau chief there. Although Zimbabwe devolved into chaos as Mugabe tightened his dictatorial grip and intimidated those whom he suspected of voting for the opposition, the *Times* covered the events in some detail. But, to tell the full story, one would have needed to complement the *Times*'s coverage with BBC and Reuters articles that were on the *Times*'s website's Zimbabwe page under "World"; while this supplemental coverage was commendable, less than a third of *Times* readers—if my informal survey is any criterion—references articles this way.

The printed *Times* needs more updates and needs to provide a better sense of a narrative as important stories unfold. Although nytimes.com increasingly is doing this with its backlog of stories categorized by country and brief historical time lines next to stories like those on Zimbabwe, the printed newspaper does not do this as much as it should. If there are gaps of weeks or months, the return to the subject should include refresher paragraphs and some explanation of what has happened in the interim. The printed *Times* could do far more to stress ongoing continuity of a story, especially because its coverage of so many different stories makes its focus more diffuse. Perhaps the print story should refer back to specific dates because the earlier stories can be accessed online.

Although some readers are still holdouts against reading the digital *Times*, more and more readers of the printed *Times* consult nytimes.com, where the *Times* now provides a great deal of background information and information from other sources. As the *Times* has integrated the print paper and the website, the printed *Times* refers readers to nytimes.com, which may refer readers to other sites for additional information. Currently, nytimes.com has on its "World" page a helpful reference site called "Times Topics: Find the News by Country." For example, the Haiti and Zimbawbe sites under *Times* topics for countries include articles from other sources such as BBC and AP in addition to other print and online resources.

What the reader finds under each country is useful reference material about the country and a collection of old stories. Yet when, in November 2009, I referenced a crucial country like Cyprus, I found only three articles in 2009—and one was an op-ed piece—about the conflict between Greek and Turkish Cyprus; the most recent one, on October 29, 2009, by Stephen Castle, "President of Cyprus Pessimistic on Unity," had two sentences of necessary background information. Is this, I ask, really enough? Checking back in August 2010, I still found many articles lacking the necessary historical context, although a February 28, 2010, article by Alan Cowell, "Protest Mars U.N. Leader's Visit to Cyprus," had a bit of the information required for understanding the protest.

Rather than just report on crises, the printed *Times* needs to focus on the larger picture with each nation. As it is, the *Times* is like a fire department that puts out fires without thinking about the larger issues of why so many fires occur in one area and how they can be prevented. Perhaps one editor on the foreign desk should be in charge of maintenance reporting so readers do not lose the narrative thread of a country's story. In my February 17, 2006, interview with Chira, she acknowledged this is a problem: "We try to put in a reasonable amount of background but it is true that, you know, more background could be useful but you can't always fit it in." Some but not all of the background could be done on the individual country site on the Internet, but that still would not solve the problem for those who just read the paper.

Foreign news often seems breathless and caught up in the moment—especially on the website—and thus less trenchant than it might be. In Keller's years as executive editor, the *Times*, when not focused on the chaos in Iraq or Afghanistan, often was overrun with light features such as an October 17, 2006, piece by Elaine Sciolino on the sexual peccadilloes of French politicians ("A Tell-all's Tale: French Politicians Stray Early and Often"), as well as with a bevy of stories about French president Nicolas Sarkozy's marriage, divorce, and remarriage. The *Times*-owned *International Herald Tribune* often has more insightful and succinct foreign news coverage and more trenchant analyses than the *Times*.

Perhaps the *Times* could provide a brief weekly update on both the digital site and in the print newspaper (which I still believe will be a major *Times* focus going forward in the immediate future) on every country about which there has been a recent major story and a monthly update for all but the most insignificant ones. Attention could rotate on a daily half-page entitled "Foreign News Update." Perhaps each day we would have a few paragraphs—perhaps news with analyses on the order of articles in the *Economist*—on eight or ten major countries; these would be either major countries in the world's geopolitics or countries on which there had been a recent major story. Perhaps the *Times*'s international news coverage could adopt the model of *USA Today*'s daily update of news from every state and provide regular country updates, although what I have in mind here are more substantive updates—and updates with a narrative thread—than the ones in *USA Today*. Within a monthly rotation, I would include every country other than those that have tiny populations—and maybe even the latter could be mentioned every two or three months.

The *Times* should more frequently provide some historical context for foreign news. In his April 24, 2005, piece, "The Hottest Button: How the *Times* Covers Israel and Palestine," Okrent seemed to defend the fact that "the *Times* does not provide history lessons," as if the expectation that it should provide history lessons were unreasonable. Major hot-off-the-presses stories should be the focus, but what the *Times*'s foreign coverage needs more of is the longer overview that comes with substantive background. Although, as Okrent claims in the same piece, journalism is "not reality, but a version of reality, and both daily deadlines and limited space make even the best journalism a reductionist version of reality," journalism should, I believe, be a down payment on history.

Let me close this section by remarking on how, for the most part, domestic news is much easier to cover than foreign news. As I mentioned in chapter 1, covering events in Iraq, Afghanistan, Pakistan, or Lebanon is expensive. In such places, reporters need armed guards, interpreters, translators, and a network of sources. They have to be experienced reporters who know a great deal about the history and culture of the place they are covering and savvy enough to protect themselves against harm. They need to be courageous and brave and have an adventuresome spirit, but they are risking their lives, and the *Times*, knowing this, does not want to send more reporters than are absolutely necessary and certainly not those without experience into areas prone to violence.

By contrast, election reporting is extraordinarily simple. Thus, the news media, including the *Times*, compulsively focused on the presidential election between Election Day 2006 and Election Day 2008. Unlike much international and administration policy reporting, election reporting—especially in the early stages prior to the first primaries—is a low-stakes activity where errors can be corrected and the consequences are far greater for the candidates than the news media. The candidates' staffs control access to the candidates and the flow of information, and, yes, reporters need to do a good deal of investigatory reporting to discover who the candidates really are, and, yes, *Times* reporters tend to be more experienced and professional than many of their peers. But pre-election reporting, particularly during days before the first presidential primary when a host of candidates—some delusionary as to their chances—are competing, is far less factual than most reporting.

Particularly in the weeks and months leading up to primaries, stories are filed by a single reporter in Iowa or in New Hampshire who follows a candidate around; in many cases, the reporter is given access to the candidate only when the candidate chooses. The reporter may interview a handful of citizens each day, talk to a few members

of the candidate's staff—many of whom are not at the highest level of
the candidate's strategy team—and listen to a short speech plus a Q&A,
and then file a piece based on his or her impressions. Given human
nature, it often does not take long for a reporter covering a candidate
to develop empathy or antipathy and that empathy or antipathy might
develop from how easy it is to get access to candidates or whether
aides are forthright in providing information or access or even how
aides treat the reporter on the campaign bus.

X. The Columnists and Op-Ed Page

One place the *Times* tries to be a national newspaper is on its editorial
pages and its op-ed columns. Not only through its regular columnists
but also in its selection of op-ed pieces, the *Times* speaks to the fissures
in both U.S. and world society. On these pages and in its letters to the
editor, the *Times* gives voice to conflict, and that conflict is enacted in
shriller voices than in the past.

Except for Frank Rich's Sunday column and Ross Douthat, who
appeared Monday, and Charles Blow, who appeared Saturday, the 2010
Times, in terms of which day columnists appear, rotated its columnists
on the op-ed page. These columnists follow in the tradition of Arthur
Krock, James Reston, Tom Wicker, Anthony Lewis, and Cy Sulzberger.
Gravitas was expected from them. Readers expected that what was
written by the regular columnists of the Old Gray Lady reflected profound wisdom based on high-level contacts, a long and wise historical
view, and deep historical and philosophical reading. The models for
this were the columns of Walter Lippmann.

Although collectively more liberal than conservative, the op-ed
columnists represent a spectrum of views. Perhaps the best known are
the magisterial internationalist Thomas Friedman and the wry satirist
and at times pop psychologist—and often ill-natured—Maureen Dowd.
Representing conservative points of view have been the late stalwart
William Safire, whose column ran from 1973 to 2005; his successor,
libertarian John Tierney, whose column ran from March 2005 to
November 2006; and, currently, David Brooks and, since 2009, Douthat,
in his early thirties and the youngest columnist in the *Times*'s history,
who takes a reasoned if quite conservative approach to such issues as
building an Islamic cultural center near the 9/11 site or gay marriage.

More than Brooks, Douthat is likely to speak about political issues that are on the front burner.

With the 2011 departure of Frank Rich and Bob Herbert, the current liberals are Keynesian economist Paul Krugman as well as Nicholas Kristof and Bob Herbert. As expected, Gail Collins, former editorial page editor, whose column began in mid-2007, has a liberal perspective. Quite often, her focus was the 2008 election and then the 2010 election and its aftereffects.

The contemporary *Times* features the global perspective of Thomas Friedman, who began his column in 1994. In recent years his stature and prestige have been somewhat discredited by his optimistically embracing the U.S. invasion of Iraq. But he is still a respected voice to be reckoned with, although no longer the gold standard of gravitas and the heir to the authority attributed to such figures as Krock and Reston. Prior to Friedman's enthusiastically arguing for the disastrous Iraq invasion, he was arguably the most influential international columnist in the history of the *Times* because he was read all over the world in the paper and on the Internet and seemed to have the eyes and ears of world leaders all over the world. His backing of the Iraq invasion gave it respectability. To a much lesser extent, his later doubts about administration policy helped shape the evaporation of support among the nation's leaders.

That he has been chastened by the Iraq experience is illustrated by his being much more cautious in endorsing escalation in Afghanistan. Indeed, his October 27, 2009, column, "Don't Build Up," seemed to be something of a reversal: "We simply do not have the Afghan partners, the NATO allies, the domestic support, the financial resources or the national interests to justify an enlarged and prolonged nation-building effort in Afghanistan." He also has become more cautious about whether nation-building will work in Iraq, without totally abandoning his support for the invasion.

Friedman always takes a hard line on the need for Israel to return land to the Arabs. On June 13, 2004, he notably argued that it was in Israel's interest to withdraw from Gaza not halfway but to the "U.N. blessed international border," partly because its withdrawal from Lebanon in 2000 was in fact a strategic success: "With that U.N.-approved pullout, Israel completely reversed its situation. It went from holding the strategic and moral low ground, to holding the strategic and moral high ground." In a November 9, 2009, piece, "Call the White

House, Ask for Obama," he cogently argued in his characteristically lucid, reasonable voice that the U.S. government should withdraw from trying to broker a peace between Israel and the now divided Palestinians until both are ready.

Friedman lives at times in the world of sweeping generalizations but his strongly crafted sentences and commonsense reasonableness support his arguments. At his best, Friedman gives the impression of reading primary material all over the world, even quoting, when he finds it, Arab opinion to support his view that democracy, women's rights, and education are the only way for the Arab countries to lift themselves from the economic basement. He often intrudes his personal voice and anecdotal evidence—as when he visited India before discussing American outsourcing there and wrote about India's burgeoning technological industry—to give body to his logical and legalistic analyses. He has been in the forefront in understanding and arguing for economic globalization and the interdependence of national economies. His optimism about globalization is supported less by statistical evidence than by his own observations. In a moving 2008 Mother's Day column that revealed a more sentimental side than he often shows, he attributed his optimism to his mother ("Call Your Mother," May 11, 2008).

Given the success of *The World Is Flat: A Brief History of the Twenty-First Century* (2005), it is a mistake to write Friedman off. An advocate of free trade, reducing U.S. dependence on foreign oil, exporting democracy, and the idea of a global village in which we all participate, Friedman characteristically wrote in "Maids vs. Occupiers" about how India and China are moving forward, while the Arab countries—often governed by "ruling elites"—are standing still, although "There is an ocean of untapped brainpower, particularly among women" (June 17, 2004).

To be sure, even with his authoritative knowledge, at times Friedman wrote exactly the same things in 2010 as he wrote in 2004. Simply put, he has a tendency to repeat himself. Notwithstanding three Pulitzers, one wonders if he has run his course in writing the foreign affairs columns for seventeen years.

Let us turn to the edginess of the mercurial Maureen Dowd. Dowd's self-dramatized persona often is that of someone looking at the world from three perspectives: (1) the woman from an economically modest Irish and Roman Catholic family; (2) the Washington insider; and (3) the tough, supremely confident, and hip woman approaching sixty.

Her famous October 22, 2005, column on Judith Miller as a "Woman of Mass Destruction" raised the question for some observers of whether she was showing her independence, attacking someone she clearly disliked, or writing on behalf of such *Times* editors as her friend Jill Abramson. When I asked Andrew Rosenthal about her column on Miller, he responded: "I'm going to challenge anyone who ever claims to have influence over Maureen Dowd to prove it, because they're a liar. . . . Maureen does what Maureen wants to do" (April 13, 2007). It is worth noting that she is held in great esteem by most of the *Times* senior editors, who at times seem oblivious to her shortcomings.

To be fair, Dowd did win a 1999 Pulitzer Prize for her series of columns on the Monica Lewinsky scandal, a subject made for her ironical if gossipy intelligence, and before that in 1992 she won a Pulitzer for national reporting.

I often find Dowd—who has been a *Times* columnist since 1995—somewhat frivolous, and find her efforts to place politics in the context of popular culture and her pop psychology tiresome. She attributed the Iraq war to Bush's desire to revenge his father's defeat. As is clear from Dowd's collection of Bush columns, entitled *Bushworld*, she revels in broad strokes. As Jacob Weisberg somewhat facetiously remarked in his review of that book: "George W., long the family black sheep, is driven both by the need to win his father's respect and the desire to symbolically slay him" ("Three Ways of Looking at George W. Bush," *New York Times Book Review*, August 29, 2004).

In some columns, she often is unable or unwilling to disentangle personal reminiscences from political observation or propose a sustained argument linking the two. Dowd often embraces psychobabble. In "Smack that Cheney-Bot," Dowd characteristically discusses Bush and Cheney in terms of the Stepford wives (June 17, 2004). In "Because They Could," the analogy-loving Dowd compares Clinton's excuse for his affair with Lewinsky with Bush's Iraq war: "They went after Saddam just because they could." She has used the pejorative Nixon nickname "Tricky Dick" for Vice President Cheney and, after the Libby indictment, "Vice" (June 20, 2004). I think her columns that dwelled on Hillary Clinton's supposedly Nixonite strain were unfair and tasteless. Nor do I like how Dowd dramatized a hypothetical—that is, fictional—debate with Obama and Clinton in which Hillary continually raises the issue of Obama's earlier drug use: "Reefer Madness in Iowa" (December 16, 2007).

I would respect Dowd more if she didn't engage in persistent rhetorical bullying and name-calling that that includes "Rummy"— with its connotations of alcoholism—for Rumsfield and "Macaccawitz" for Senator George Allen, who not only used the slur "macacca" to describe a man of Indian descent who worked for his opponent but who also did everything possible to hide the Jewish side of his heritage. In a sense Macaccawitz and Rummy encrypt rhetorically irresponsible short-handed slurs.

Favorite targets for her vitriol are the Clintons, Gores, and now the Palins. I have never read in the *Times* more malicious columns than those Dowd has written about Hillary Clinton's 2007–2008 campaign. Referring to the Clintons taking some gifts that belonged to the White House and not to them, Dowd sarcastically gives one argument for Obama choosing Clinton as secretary of state: "On a positive note, maybe she could bring back all that stuff she pilfered on her way out" ("Is She a Trojan Rabbit?" May 11, 2008). Yes, she is a wordsmith, but at times she writes slanderous nonsense. Often when discussing the Clintons she devolves into psychological gibberish: "As [Hillary Clinton] makes a last frenzied and likely futile attempt to crush the butterfly [Obama], it's as though she's crushing the remnants of her own girlish innocence" ("Butterflies Aren't Free," May 7, 2008).

In "Pantsuits and the Presidency," public editor Clark Hoyt takes up the issue of whether sexism colored reporting of Hillary Clinton's campaign and focuses on the *Times* (June 22, 2008). Commenting on Katherine Q. Seelye's and Julia Bosman's June 13, 2008, *Times* front-page article, "Media Charged with Sexism in Clinton Coverage," Hoyt writes: "Dowd's columns about Clinton's campaign were so loaded with language painting her as a 50-foot woman with a suffocating embrace, a conniving film noir dame and a victim dependent on her husband that they could easily have been listed in that *Times* article on sexism."

Ever since Sarah Palin appeared on the national scene, she has become a favorite Dowd target. In her July 4, 2009, piece, "Now, Sarah's Folly," Dowd observed: "Caribou Barbie is one nutty puppy. . . . Even some conservative analysts admitted that the governor's move seemed ga-ga before venturing the spin that Palin might be 'crazy like a fox,' as Sarah's original cheerleader, Bill Kristol, put it." Four days later, assuming the persona of Palin in "Sarah's Secret Dairy," Dowd presents Palin as delusional, illiterate, and stupid: "It's the same old double standard. I am not one of those who would whine and cuss. It's just not how I'm wired!!! . . . And I know that I know that I know those crappy bloggers will put out more confliction stories" (July 8, 2009). By mirroring Palin's simplethink even while satirizing it, Dowd raises questions about her own stature.

With her riffs that are not arguments, her homogenizing proclivity to reduce different phenomena to one monolithic sketch, and her weird mix of satire and references to actual events, she may be the *Times*'s first postmodern columnist, deconstructing the news into verbal play. On June 13, 2004, Dowd compared Katherine Hepburn to Ronald Reagan: "Kate and Dutch were naturals who disdained introspection and suffered box office slumps, but they got better and better at playing themselves." This kind of *Timeslite* clearly appeals to some readers.

Even given the legendary latitude of *Times* columnists, I am puzzled that Andrew Rosenthal and his predecessor Gail Collins don't question Dowd's verbal legerdemain—with its far-fetched analogies, her rhetorical bullying, her name-calling, her acerbic half-truths and distortions, and her failure to provide evidence. Sometimes I think Dowd should read and think more and watch fewer movies. Although Dowd complained about the Bush administration's capacity for half-truths, doesn't her hyperbole cross the line into out and out prevarication? For Dowd, words are playthings and not necessarily referential to accuracy or truth.

For some reason, the *Times*'s publisher and senior editor turn their eyes and brains away from Dowd and pretend that on many days something is going on other than name-calling. Would the op-ed page be better without her outrageous and irresponsible columns or at least if she appeared less often?

Within the Sunday op-ed (expanded in April 2005), Rich's former 1,400-word column was always among the most gracefully written, meticulously researched, and cogently argued. It also was fiercely antagonistic to the political right. Seeing politics in terms of drama, and stressing how the George W. Bush administration theatrically staged what it wanted to present, even while withholding information and deluding themselves as to both the actuality and effects of what was going on—especially in Iraq—Rich was one of the past administration's harshest and most effective critics. His efficacy derives in large part from his extraordinarily trenchant writing skills and his close observation of how the Bush administration orchestrated its policies.

Rich consistently took an acerbic view of the willingness of the press to suspend its critical perspective on what he argued were Bush's machinations and failures. Rich understood how the Bush administration staged its theatrical events to deflect attention from what was actually happening and mastered the art of manipulating the news. He showed how Washington correspondents of major newspapers and TV networks were slow to grasp the Abu Ghraib story and to understand that American soldiers were torturing prisoners. Most of them gave the administration a pass on Guantánamo. As Rich put it, "A number of news organizations have owned up to their disasters and tried to learn from them. Yet old habits die hard: for too long the full weight of the scandal in the Gonzales Justice Department eluded some of the Washington media pack, just as Abu Ghraib and the C.I.A. leak case did" ("All the President's Press," April 29, 2007).

In the same piece, Rich spoke with disgust about the chummy relationship between the administration and the news media at the annual White House Correspondents Association dinner, to which the president is invited to make a "star turn" and tell some jokes. Rich evoked Joseph Alsop, "the now forgotten columnist (and Vietnam cheerleader)," as someone complicit with the White House, but he might have mentioned that the spirit of complicity extended to Arthur Krock and not infrequently to James Reston and the Sulzbergers ("All the President's Press," April 29, 2007). After the April 21, 2007, dinner to which Rich was referring, the *Times* decided to end its participation in such events.

Although the *Times* has now corrected its course, for far too long it was less than vigilant in responding to Bush's WMD claims and Iraq policy and in questioning various claims of progress in Iraq. Although in the aforementioned column Rich didn't explicitly mention the *Times*—as he probably should—it is hardly immune from his critique: "The press has enabled stunts from the manufactured threat of imminent 'mushroom clouds' to 'Saving Private Lynch' to 'Mission accomplished' . . . For all the recrimination, self-flagellation and reforms that followed these journalistic failures, it's far from clear that the entire profession yet understands why it has lost the public's faith."

Bringing the eyes and ears of a theater critic as well as his knowledge of American culture to the political realm, Rich not only does his homework in terms on digging for facts and therefore often questions the conventional wisdom of other pundits, but also has a wonderful synthesizing and conceptual intellect. His trenchant coverage of the 2008 election was among the most probing political analyses in the *Times*. The once-a-week double-size-column format gave him room to combine his sense of the performative aspects of politics with his strong command of facts. On May 11, 2008, he prophetically wrote, "The rise in black voters and young voters of all races in Democratic primaries is re-weighting the electorate. . . . [The anti-Obama vote] will be more than offset in November by mobilized young voters, blacks and women, among them many Clinton-supporting Democrats (and independents and Republicans) unlikely to entertain a G.O.P. candidate with a perfect record of voting against abortion rights" ("Party Like it's 2008"). Earlier than most, he understood major trends in the run up to the primaries and grasped the significance of Obama's hope-based campaign.

Rich has a cosmopolitan view of the relationship between culture and politics; he is particularly aware of how the media shapes and is shaped by political events. Many readers who thought he was giving vent to leftist paranoia now see that he was more often correct than not in his perception that the Bush administration engaged in a giant series of deceptions and cover-ups at the level of Watergate.

Although Rich was enthusiastic about Obama during the election and in the early days of the administration, he became increasingly critical, but without taking on anything like the vitriolic stance that he still assumes toward George W. Bush and the right-wing Republicans. For example, in his September 12, 2009, "Obama's Squandered Summer," he observed, "This was a silly summer, as wasteful in its way as the summer of 2001, when Washington dithered over the now-forgotten Gary Condit scandal while Al Qaeda plotted. The president deserves his share of the blame." His September 26, 2009, piece, "Obama at the Precipice," used the lessons of Vietnam to warn Obama against further entanglement in Afghanistan.

Bob Herbert, a former *Daily News* columnist and since 1993 the *Times*'s first black columnist, sees himself walking in the footsteps of Martin Luther King Jr. and Bobby Kennedy. For the past eighteen years, before stepping down on March 26, 2011, he appealed to America's conscience and believed in America's best impulses, even while high-lighting its worst racist and classist moments and attitudes.

Herbert frequently called attention to failures in government ser-vices, poverty in America—including inequities in our legal and health care systems—and to the plight of American soldiers serving in Iraq. His tone often is outrage and he is effective in marshalling facts and anecdotes. In August 2004 he wrote passionately about how Florida was trying to disenfranchise and intimidate black voters. In 2009 through early 2011, he focused on the plight of the unemployed, a disproportionate number of whom are black, Hispanic, lacking a college education, and young. Typical of his eloquent outrage is his November 13, 2009, "A Recovery for Some": "President Obama's strongest supporters during the presidential campaign were the young, the black and the poor—and they are among those who are being hammered unmercifully in this long and cruel economic downturn that the financial elites are telling us is over." In his September 18, 2009, "The Scourge Persists," Herbert is attentive to the persistence of racism in America: "For many white Americans, Barack Obama is nothing more than that black guy in the White House, and they want him out of there."

In terms of racial and economic politics, Herbert is an old-fashioned liberal—and something of an outraged muckraker—who believes in the promise of America. Herbert's controlled but pointed sense of outrage was focused by events of the past few years. He was passionate about describing the effects of the recession on the have-nots, with a special focus on the unemployed and underemployed blacks and youth, but he also paid attention to whites who have been economically marginalized. He despises our military policy in Iraq and Afghanistan, but characteristically stressed the effects of war on the American families who have suffered the loss of fathers and soldiers who have lost limbs and suffered psychological disabilities. He has written eloquently of "the damage being done to the American soul by the endless war in Iraq"; commenting on the obituary of an Army ranger who "had been deployed to Afghanistan and Iraq seven times," he asked in anger and sadness, "What does that tell us about our shared wartime sacrifices?" ("Overkill and Short Shrift," May 3, 2008).

As the 2008 primary season wound down and the Clintons became increasingly shrill in playing the race card against Obama, Herbert not only strongly chastised them but reminded his readers of former tacky Clinton behavior, including Bill's pardons in his last hours: "Their repertoire has always been deficient in grace and class. . . . The Clintons should be ashamed of themselves. But they long ago proved to the world that they have no shame" ("Seeds of Destruction," May 10, 2008).

From 1973 to 2005, William Safire—who never graduated from college and changed his name to the less Jewish Safire by adding an "e" to Safir—held the conservative portfolio among the columnists. A former speechwriter for Nixon, Safire saw himself not only as a libertarian and a wordsmith, but also something of a muckraker. (He continued to write his impressively intellectual and erudite "On Language" in the *Sunday Magazine* until his September 2009 death). Frequently expressing outrage in his columns, Safire never saw a hyperbole he didn't like. Yet, in part because of the erudition of his "On Language" columns, his longevity seemed to confer an in-house stature within the Times building.

In his columns, Safire spent a good deal of energy tying to rehabilitate Nixon as the genius of foreign policy and political acumen. Safire on occasion imagined himself interviewing Nixon in purgatory ("The View from Purgatory"), while having Nixon articulate Safire's own views: "[A]s we come out of the war, Bush comes out of his slump" (June 16, 2004). That he has a mean-spirited Nixon predict a Bush victory—attributing to Nixon the claim "the Hillary crowd, having done their bit for Kerry, won't cry at his potential defeat because it would open the way to the Clinton restoration in 2008"—does not disguise Safire's own Machiavellian enjoyment of inside politics. That we have no reason to believe that the Jewish Safire or the Quaker Nixon believed in purgatory makes the analogy all that more feckless. Safire revels in mild paranoia, finding complicated explanations and latent motives when simpler explanations will do. Often his columns revealed a thinly disguised bitterness at Nixon's political demise.

With the 2005 retirement of Safire, David Brooks, who began writing his column in 2003, assumed an important role as a conservative voice. Brooks likes to wear the mantle of a Burkean conservative sitting above partisan politics and taking the long view of passing events. In 2004, he contended that John Kerry represented the aristocracy of mind and George W. Bush the aristocracy of money. In writing about the 2004 election campaign, Brooks drew a number of distinctions between the two, some—like the one just cited—rather arbitrary.

At times, particularly early on, Brooks's apparent rationality often seemed a disguise for clichés. But over the years, Brooks has grown in depth and stature and has taken on an in-depth historical and philosophical perspective. Although Brooks began the 2008 campaign impressed by McCain, his considerable admiration of Obama and his presidency and his reasoned evaluation of Obama's administration have placed him at odds with the shrillness of partisan criticism on the right. He thinks the Democrats are stuck in what he calls "the globalization paradigm," while he prefers what he calls "the cognitive age paradigm," which emphasizes psychology, culture and pedagogy—the specific processes that foster learning ("The Cognitive Age," May 2, 2008). In 2010, he wrote thoughtfully about such widely different issues as how we might respond to slower economic growth and how we are born with an innate moral sense ("The Growth Imperative," July 30, 2010; "The Moral Naturalists," July 23, 2010).

Nicholas D. Kristof, who has been writing his *Times* column since 2001, is willing to travel off the beaten path to find out what is going on around the world and to uncover social ills and violations of human rights, including human trafficking at home and abroad and other issues of global health. Exposing outrages to human decency, often in little-known areas, he is the international counterpart of Herbert. Married to a Chinese intellectual, he lived in China during the Tiananmen Square uprising. Kristof is the boldest of the columnists, writing from Darfur and Cambodia about outrages to human dignity and genocidal atrocities, with special focus on violence perpetrated on women.

For many *Times* readers, Kristof plays the role of conscience—and ombudsman—of American foreign policy. He has stressed the damage done to America by the Guantánamo prison camp: "In reality, it would take an exceptional enemy to damage America's image and interests as much as President Bush and Mr. Cheney already have with Guantánamo" ("A Prison of Shame, and It's Ours," May 4, 2008). He has eloquently written about child prostitution in Cambodia, and he also has urged a long-range view on climate change, claiming that of Obama, Clinton, and McCain, all three have been unfocused on that issue: "[N]one of the candidates focus adequately on climate change. . . . [T]his will be one of humanity's great tests in the coming decades—and so far we're failing" ("Our Planet Favorite," April 20, 2008).

What I like about the investigative human rights reports of Kristof is that, rather than fly from world capitol to world capitol, he travels instead to the most dangerous and uncomfortable areas to report. And this gives him credibility. More than any other major media figure, Kristof has called attention to what has been happening for the past several years in Darfur and he does not let his readers forget it. In the early days of his campaign to expose genocide in Darfur, Kristof wrote about 320,000 victims of mass murder in the Darfur region of Sudan in a June 16, 2004, column entitled "Dare We Call It Genocide?" Characteristic of how he personalizes tragedy and disaster in a particular victim, he focused on a twenty-four-year-old widow who had a "great life" a few months before the Sudanese government authorized a paid militia "to slaughter and drive out members of the Zaghawa, Masalt, and Fur tribes." In his next column, he continued his expose of the Sudan genocide, entitling his piece "Sudan's Final Solution"; Kristof gave authenticity to his byline by locating the site from which he is reporting as "Along the Sudan-Chad Border" (June 19, 2004).

On November 22, 2005, Kristof's column on gang rape in Darfur as a genocidal weapon invited readers to see a video about one of the victims in "The Forgotten Genocide" at nytimes.com/kristof ("Sudan's Department of Gang Rape"). In November 2009, Susan Halpern observed: "Kristof earnestly takes up the cause of the poor and oppressed of the world, most of them women, and of those who work on their behalf" ("Breaking a Conspiracy of Silence," *NYR*, November 19, 2009).

Kristof might have been more careful in outing Stephen J. Hatfill as the source of deadly anthrax mailings, and that accusation has involved the *Times* in costly litigation. In fact the then deputy managing editor of the editorial page, Philip Taubman, tried to restrain him and did get Kristof to drop one paragraph (see Neil A. Lewis, "Editor's E-Mail May Be Used in Suit Against the *Times*," January 6, 2007). Hatfill reached a $5.8 million settlement with the U.S. government, but his libel suit against Kristof was dismissed.

Paul Krugman, 2008 Nobel Prize winner in economics and a neo-Keynesian liberal economist with a populist bent, is a professor at Princeton, and has been writing his *Times* column since 2000. Krugman usually has such a pessimistic view of the economy even in relatively good times that I think of him as Professor Gloomdoom. While Alan Greenspan was head of the Federal Reserve, Krugman often was Greenspan's dark *doppelganger* or double, envisioning the worst possible economic scenarios. He is gentler with his former colleague Ben Bernanke, who in 2010 was appointed to a second term as head of the Federal Reserve, than he was with Greenspan. He was a scathing critic of Bush's policies, holding his administration accountable for the current housing crisis and recession as well as for undermining the Constitution in the name of the war on terror. On June 15, 2004, he opened his column "Travesty of Justice" with the provocative formulation: "No question. John Ashcroft is the worst attorney general in history." His indictment of Ashcroft for suspending civil liberties while failing to get any successful terrorist prosecutions is scathing, angry, sarcastic, and, yes, partisan.

Although he assigns most of the blame for the current downturn to Bush, he is increasingly impatient with Obama, whom he wants to do more to confront the recession and whom he scolds for being too cautious. During the 2008 election, Krugman foregrounded the economic issues, favoring Hillary Clinton's proposals over Obama's and, as the latter's nomination became clear, warning the latter not to neglect the Democrats' working class constituency ("Party of Denial," May 2, 2008).

Writing on November 5, 2009, after the 2009 election in which the Democrats suffered some serious defeats, Krugman observed in "Obama Faces his Anzio": "Voters across America are in a bad mood, largely because of the still-grim economic situation. . . . Conventional wisdom in Washington seems to have congealed around the view that budget deficits preclude any further fiscal stimulus—a view that's all wrong on the economics."

After serving as editorial page editor, Gail Collins began her own column in mid-2007. Her prose is funny, pointed, aphoristic, and depends on a crystallizing anecdote or quote on which she builds her columns. She is particularly good at exposing the foibles and hypocrisy of politicians, including in 2009–2010 those in states like New York, Illinois, South Carolina, and Alabama where state government has become most dysfunctional.

Collins was the *Times* columnist most sympathetic to Hillary Clinton's presidential campaign. But toward the end of the primary season, when Hillary was, in Collins's view, abandoning principles to get votes by urging a suspension of the federal gasoline tax, she became far more critical: "Hillary Clinton, who jumped on the gas-tax holiday bandwagon posthaste, wants to pay for it with a windfall profits tax on oil companies. . . . There are few things more satisfying than taking a strong stand in favor of something that is never going to happen. Free pander!" ("Indiana Holiday," May 3, 2008).

In April 2008, Charles Blow—the *Times*'s second black regular columnist—was introduced as "the visual op-ed columnist" whose columns would appear every other Saturday; they now appear every Saturday. He uses visuals and data as well as words to illustrate political points, such as the absence of discussion on the environment in the presidential debates and major interviews involving Obama and Hillary Clinton "("All Atmospherics, No Climate," April 19, 2008). On May 29, 2010, he used poll data to show that Obama needs to convince the American public that he is empathetic and engaged ("Give Them Something They Can Feel"). Increasingly, he is revealing his own liberal perspective, as when on August 27, 2010, he expressed his outrage at Glenn Beck's "Restoring Honor" rally on the site of Martin Luther King Jr.'s "I Had a Dream" speech ("I Had a Nightmare").

Since 2007, Roger Cohen's foreign affairs columns for the *International Herald Tribune* were mostly found on nytimes.com, although on occasion they appeared in the printed newspaper. Now, in 2011, his twice-weekly column appears online and somewhat more frequently in print. Cohen often provides a perspective of considerable analytic and historical depth, derived from his European heritage and experience. Knowing Iran well, he has been excellent on the schism in Iran following the 2009 election. Cohen has a cosmopolitan and internationalist view of world politics and writes about a wide range of issues, from the 2011 Arab Spring to what he feels is Israeli's intransigence.

Under both Collins and Rosenthal and their deputy editors, the op-ed page has become more diverse by including articles by writers who are not *Times* columnists. Thus, on June 14, 2004, op-ed carried a substantive piece by Sylvia Lawson, "Regressive Politics in Australia," about the death of the Australian Aboriginal leader Djerrkura and Prime Minister John Howard's introduction of legislation (two days after Djerrkura's death) to abolish the Aboriginal and Torres Strait Commission. On February 5, 2007, Hisham Matara, a Libyan whose father, a dissident living in Cairo, disappeared in 1990, wrote about how the West has been duped by the Libyan strong man Qaddafi into believing that he has changed when he is still, in Matara's words, a dictator ("Seeing What We Want to See in Qaddafi").

Although the columnists do not report to Keller but are under the auspices of editorial page editor Rosenthal and, of course, ultimately the publisher, I have discussed them in some depth because they are very much part of the public face of the *Times*. Knowing the news already, many of the *Times*'s most seasoned readers—especially of the printed paper—begin with the op-ed page and use the columns as a point of departure for their thinking and conversations on politics and foreign affairs.

A final thought: I doubt whether any columnist can sustain himself or herself for decades and whether the *Times* should give any columnist more than a five-year term, renewable only in special circumstances after, say, two terms. Not surprisingly, columnists tend to stutter in paragraphs and repeat their central themes. It is as if a professor taught the same students in the same course every year and said virtually the same things each time.

7

The Way We Are (II)

The 2003–2009 *Times* Under Keller

[T]he authority of professional journalists is both a valuable convenience for readers without the time or inclination to manage a
tsunami of information on their own, and a civic good, in that a
democracy needs a shared base of trustworthy information upon
which to make its judgments. . . . It would be a mistake to senti-
mentalize the previous century's version of journalistic authority.
But it is probably fair to say that the cacophony of today's media—in
which rumor and invective often outpace truth-testing, in which
shouting heads drown out sober reflection, in which it is possible
for people to feel fully informed without ever encountering an
opinion that contradicts their prejudices—plays some role in the
polarizing of our politics, the dysfunction of our political system
and the increased cynicism of the American electorate.

—Keller, "Henry Luce, the Editor in Chief,"
New York Times Book Review, April 25, 2010

I think contrary to the image of the *New York Times* as the Gray
Lady, which implies a certain conservative, unchanging, and dull
quality, I think actually newsrooms seem to thrive on change. The
analogy I [use to describe] the culture of the newsroom [is] . . . the
world's largest . . . improvisational theater troop.

—Bill Keller, May 20, 2010

Keller has presided over a time of tremendous innovation, enormous change. I think one thing Keller has always had [from those
working with him] is great respect for his intellect and judgment,
and utter confidence in his integrity. People have it [confidence]

in him. You could not successfully preside over a period of really disconcerting change unless those fundamentals were really powerful. Because fundamentally if Bill Keller [said we had] to do something differently, you can have complete confidence that that is an honest and trustworthy impulse that's worth following. With many people you would wonder what the hidden agendas are and so on. That's not a problem with Keller.

—Jonathan Landman, June 9, 2010

In this chapter, I continue examining both the contemporary print *Times,* which has reinvented itself as a daily magazine, with news analyses and features occupying most of its print space, and the digital edition, which provides instant news in addition to the analyses and features of a daily magazine and which has—with its virtually infinite borders—much less gatekeeping.

Very much in keeping with the philosophy that a daily newspaper now must provide information relevant to its readers' personal concerns—health, finances, relationships—the contemporary *Times* provides a continual manual on how to live, and it does not restrict this manual to the "back of the book" but flaunts it on the front page. Value-added journalism plays an ever more important role in its online blogs.

I. The 2009 Iranian Turmoil and the Information Revolution: The Indispensability of the *Times* and the Argument for Survival

Let us consider how, in 2009, the *Times* covered major events in Iran and how it used blanket coverage (the Raines legacy), although on a smaller scale than 9/11 and with different technical sources. The difference—including the inability to blanket the site on the ground—is instructive in terms of both media and *New York Times*'s transformation.

We witnessed an information revolution as well as a political one. The Iranian government had beaten and arrested Iranian journalists and impeded the work of other Iranian and foreign journalists by warning them to stay away. They also let the visas and credentials of foreign journalists expire. Indeed, one important aspect of this incredible story was the Iranian opposition's efforts to open informational doors and windows to the world's eyes and thus avoid a worse massacre.

News arrived in bits and snips because Iran was trying to put up a cyberwall to block information from flowing among its citizens—particularly the huge dissident movement that protested the 2009 presidential election—and beyond its borders. Simply put, the government was trying to shut down electronic communication. Using personal computers, blogging, YouTube, independent short videos, text-messaging, Twitter, Facebook, cell phones, and hidden cameras in the absence of traditional information sources, the New Media sources were vital not only to communication within the protest community, but also to foreign and Iranian news coverage. With these electronic postings comes a media sharing of news almost instantly—see the *Times*'s "The Lede"—that makes scoops and a monopoly on breaking news impossible.

But as the Iranian story unfolded, it became clear that first and foremost, guns and other shows of force beat tweets and that by both interrupting the New Media with its cyberwall and exerting its control of more traditional media, the government regained the upper hand in communication. As Nazila Fathi and Michael Slackman wrote on June 26, 2009:

> While protesters were aided at first by technology—primarily the Internet and text messaging—the government deployed its control of state television and news outlets to sweep away competing narratives.
>
> "It is still possible that the information age will crack authoritarian structures in Iran," wrote Jon B. Alterman, director of the Middle East program for the Center for Strategic and International Studies in Washington. "But it is far more likely that the government will be able to use that technology to secure its own rule." ("Leaders Press End to Iranian Protest Over Election")

Among its vulnerabilities, a limitation of the New Media is that some of these personal and often virtually anonymous reports cannot be confirmed. For example, the claims of size of protest crowds—and even some claims of violence—may be true, but cannot be confirmed by reporters who have been banned from events. As Robert Mackey of "The Lede" suggested online on June 19: "Given that anonymous supporters of Iran's opposition movement are responsible for almost all of the video, photographs and text messages uploaded to the web this week on the protests, no doubt some of what has appeared online is not what its makers say it is." Noam Cohen reminded us: "An article published by the website True/Slant highlighted some of the biggest errors on Twitter that were quickly repeated and amplified by bloggers: that three million protested in Tehran last weekend (more like a few hundred thousand); that the opposition candidate Mir Hussein Moussavi was under house arrest (he was being watched); that the president of the election monitoring committee declared the election invalid last Saturday (not so)" ("Twitter on the Barricades in Iran: Six Lessons Learned," June 20, 2009). To be sure, an aggregation of parallel New Media sources does go some way to establishing objective reality, but what if they are repeating the same rumor?

Providing some of the excellent *Times* Iran coverage before he was expelled, Roger Cohen wisely and eloquently wrote online on behalf of traditional journalism:

> [T]he mainstream media—expelled, imprisoned, vilified—is missed. Iran has gone opaque. Its crisis is seen through a glass darkly. Its cries are muffled, its anguish subdued. . . . To be a journalist is to bear witness. The rest is no more than ornamentation. To bear witness means being there—and that's not free. No search engine gives you the smell of a crime, the tremor in the air, the eyes that smolder, or the cadence of a scream. . . . Technology has enriched journalism by expanding the means to deliver it and the raw material on which it is based. But technology has also diminished the incentive—and the revenue—to get out of the office. ("New Tweets, Old Needs," September 9, 2009)

Not only in print but even within the online universe, rapid analyses and syntheses of Iranian developments became a crucial product, and the *Times* was and is in a unique position to put out the best product. Thus, notwithstanding the New Media, the *Times* made the best case for its own indispensability and survival. The *Times* excelled in its analytic and synthesizing coverage because it has retained—despite the especially dark 2008–2009 financial days—experienced and knowledgeable foreign affairs reporters and editors. Some have been in Tehran, including Keller (who was uncharacteristically reporting on foreign affairs—for the first time since assuming the executive editorship—with the full weight of his authority); by September 2010, many more were continually sifting through the informational flow of electronic information.

A typical article after the expulsion of foreign reporters was the *Times*'s synthesizing and analytic June 18, 2009, article by Fathi and Slackman, "As Confrontation Deepens, Iran's Path Is Unclear." It was followed by a note in italics showing us the range and location of contributors: *Nazila Fathi reported from Tehran, and Michael Slackman from Cairo. Alan Cowell contributed reporting from Paris, and Neil MacFarquhar and Sharon Otterman from New York.* The *Times* chief UN correspondent, MacFarquhar, an expert in the Middle East, to which he was assigned by the *Times* for five years, 2001–2005, has written among the most probing pieces to date about the inner workings of the Iranian ruling politicians and clergy and the power—including quasi-legal forces—at their disposal.

The *Times* had as resources for its Iran coverage both of its Pulitzer-winning international correspondents, Thomas Friedman and Nicholas Kristof. Most importantly, the *Times* had cultivated sources within Iran. Its reporters have much quicker access to the language of those senior officials who speak Farsi rather than English—some of its Tehran staff speak both Farsi and Arabic—and thus its contextual analyses of what was occurring were more substantive than those of its media rivals.

II. The *Times* and Business Coverage

To understand the importance of the *Times*'s business coverage in 2010, we need to remember that the *Wall Street Journal* has the largest newspaper circulation—more than twice that of the daily *Times*—followed by *USA Today*; since 2008 the *Journal* under Rupert Murdoch, has been expanding its coverage beyond business.

Until the stock market boom of the 1980s and 1990s, serious business news was something of an afterthought, written for corporate executives, stockbrokers, and the relatively small portion of readers who had an active interest in stocks and bonds. Indeed, until 1978 there wasn't a separate business section of the *New York Times*; stock prices were included with sports in the second of two sections.

Hired away from the *Wall Street Journal* in January 2004 (where he had been assistant managing editor), current business and financial editor and assistant managing editor Lawrence Ingrassia explained to me how he put into action in both the daily and Sunday *Times* his belief that the relevance of business news to a larger audience changed during the 1980s and 1990s: "What was happening in the business world actually impacted [our readers'] lives. You had deregulation of financial markets, money markets. You had world trade increasing and trade barriers falling, so with the imports all of a sudden people's jobs were at risk and at stake. With IRAs and 401(k)s, people were investors for the first time. And then you had huge inflation. It was affecting people's pocketbooks in ways that it hadn't before. I think [before] that a lot of workers didn't feel connected to what was going on in the business world" (April 18, 2005).

In part to compete with the *Wall Street Journal* and the *Financial News*, and in part to meet the needs of an audience for whom business and financial news are more important now that more people manage their own pensions in 401(k) and 403(b) accounts, the *Times* has put a much greater stress on business news that affects people's pocketbooks. As Ingrassia put it, "[We need to be] there on a regular basis with the news that you really need to know to inform you about what is going on in the world around you and occasionally help you make decisions. . . . To me, [that] journalistic quality and focus can help us sell newspapers, which in the end is what we need to do especially in the current environment where newspapers aren't doing very well" (April 18, 2005).

By April 2006, the daily stock tables were virtually eliminated from the print edition so as to save the cost of newsprint; according to Keller in his online Q&A responses to readers the week of April 10: "Like everyone else in this business, we're under some pressure to hold down costs, and I'd a whole lot rather do it by eliminating machine-generated lists of raw data than losing live, observant, thinking journalists who can break real news. In the day of almost universal Internet access, it just feels wasteful to expend acres of paper on columns of data." For those with Internet access, getting quotes in 2006 was quite simple. But in fact, even though Internet use was growing daily, every reader in 2006 did not have universal Internet access and many readers preferred to read the paper, particularly readers in their later years—and I know lots of baby boomers not fond of reading the *Times* on the Internet. The *Times* readership is mobile, and many people do not take along their computers or access the Internet at hotels or in their hosts' homes. Nor does everyone have an iPhone or Blackberry. In a sense, by diluting the *Times's* stock coverage, the *Times*—at least for some older readers—undermined one reason for buying its print product.

In a post-Watergate world and indeed in a post-Vietnam War world, the press—including the business press—has become more aggressive in exposing scandals and questioning official explanations of events. And this skepticism has extended to business pages. This was all the more true in the face of the 2008–2009 economic crisis, which the *Times* covered with as much clarity as any news source. The majority of American families were touched by the erosion of the value of their homes and stock portfolios, to say nothing of the large number of families touched in some way by widespread unemployment, foreclosures, and bankruptcy.

Although not oblivious to the lifestyles of the rich and famous, the business pages, under the editorship of Ingrassia and, to an extent, his predecessors such as Glenn Kramon and John Geddes, have pursued—with many notable exceptions—a somewhat more populist course than *Styles* and *Travel*.

Ingrassia recognized that the audience needed a different, more value-added product, and that that changes the process of delivering business news. Thus the *Times* has invented "DealBook"—which is what was originally called a "smart aggregation" blog and is now a financial news service edited by Andrew Ross Sorkin and produced by the *Times*—pulling together information about deals and acquisitions. As Ingrassia wrote online in response to a reader's question, "[R]eporters and editors at *The Times* who specialize in these topics are sifting through all the major news and picking out what really matters. That's so you don't have to, thus saving you loads of time. And as we know, time is money (make that lots of money for people in the world of finance)" (May 26, 2006).

Several of the business columnists take a populist perspective. For, example, Floyd Norris, the chief financial correspondent and columnist for the *Times Business* section, has long understood the effect of financial manipulation and stock bubbles on small stockholders. The daily and Sunday *Business* sections helped blow the whistle on subprime lending, just as it had on CEO abuses and concomitant outsized salaries and, before that, on the 2001 Enron scandal. The *Business* sections stressed the outrageous lack of supervision over the pay package of Richard Grasso, former president of the New York Stock Exchange (NYSE), who set himself—with the collusion of friends on the board—a nine-figure compensation package. An April 3, 2005, article by Claudia H. Deutsch, "My Big Fat C.E.O. Paycheck," is a case in point.

With the goal of increasing business coverage and this making the *Times* more appealing to a segment of readers and advertisers, Ingrassia was hired. As he said to me: "It is increasingly important to us in my view to produce a newspaper that is relevant to the people around this country because given the difficult nature of this business, if we're going to win readers we're going to have to provide them with news they are interested in and need to know. And that includes businesses because again what's happening in the economy is large and hugely important to them" (April 18, 2005). For business executives or stockbrokers, the *Times Business Day* is not going to replace the *Wall Street Journal* or *Financial Times*. But the goal of the *Times*'s business coverage is to provide a necessary and sufficient source of information in its newspaper or on its website for those who are interested in business news as part of a medley of needed information. And as was learned in the recession of 2008–2009, business news can become the most important news.

Conceiving itself more as a national newspaper, the *Times* felt an increasing need to explain business-related issues and, to accomplish this, increased its business staff mid-decade. In the face of its own economic difficulties, the *Times* in October 2009 combined the *Business* and *Sports* sections on Tuesday through Friday, although it continued to fine-tune its business news at nytimes.com.

More pointedly, if educated and influential readers read their local newspaper and one other newspaper (or website), the *Times* wants to be sure it is the *Times* and not the *Wall Street Journal* or *USA Today*. Or as Ingrassia put it, "I want to make sure that when you're out there you don't feel that you need to read the *Wall Street Journal* to get your major business news of the day and your major business trends of the day" (April 18, 2005). The reader of the *Des Moines Register* isn't going to get the major business news from that paper and Ingrassia wants to make sure that such a reader also will read the *Times* so as not to "[miss] any major developments."

But Ingrassia also conceives of the business news as having another function: "[Our] mission is to write stories that get ahead of the curve. . . . We want to set the agenda on issue stories. For example, the problems of public pensions and private, company pensions. How that's changing and how that's affecting people's lives. In various iterations the intersection of business and government is the great strength that I think the *Times* has" (April 18, 2005). Thus, Walt Bogdanovich, once a Pulitzer-winning journalist for the *Wall Street Journal*, while working for the *Times*'s investigative unit won a 2006 Pulitzer Prize for his stories about the lack of safety at railroad crossings—certainly an area with business implications—and a 2008 Pulitzer for his report on contamination of medicine imported from China.

From September 28 to December 28, 2009, various members of the *Times* financial staff contributed to an important series of articles called "The Reckoning" on the causes of the financial meltdown, and that series won a Pulitzer Prize for public service. In his June 8, 2009, "Talk to the Newsroom," Ingrassia spoke eloquently about how the downturn in the *New York Times*'s business conditions affected his perspective:

> Most editors and reporters got into the news business because they have a passion for exploring the important issues of our time, in all their complexity. For most of our lives, we didn't even think of it as a business. Our revenue and profits were generally so stable that pay reductions and layoffs and benefit cutbacks were things that happened at companies in other industries, not ours. Wow, has that changed. As I'm sure you know, even before the great recession hit, the newspaper (and magazine) business has started going through tectonic change. We're not just reporting the story, we're part of the story.
>
> The Internet has changed our comfortable business model. Many papers are slashing their staffs. A few have even closed, or become online only publications. I firmly believe the *Times* will thrive, because we've embraced the web—hey, Talk to the Newsroom is just one of many things we do online that we couldn't easily do in print!—and we

continue to do the kind of quality journalism that it's hard
to get in many other places. But, make no mistake, these are
difficult times, and they give us a better insight than ever into
what people in other troubled industries are going through.

Ingrassia makes a distinction between what he calls "commodity
news" and "value-added news." Commodity news is the raw material—the actual facts that appear almost instantly on the Internet—and
value-added news is both the interpretation and the application of
what concerns readers. He believes that the *Times* must provide value-
added news in its business coverage, including guidance for its readers
in making their economic decisions. It is as if he were differentiating
between crude oil and processed gasoline or pure 24-carat gold and fine
gold jewelry. As he remarked to me in our April 18, 2005, interview:

> Most of our readers know what the news was before they
> would pick up the paper, so we need to be much more into
> what that news means. . . . What's going to sell newspapers
> is what is going to make you feel that you need to read
> the newspaper. It's the news behind the news. . . . [W]e
> have stories that . . . help you live your life better. More
> magazinier [*sic*]. Whether it's [stories] like "what laptop
> should I buy?" "What cell phone package is the best one?"
> "What are the issues that I should consider in making an
> investment?", we want to help you; we want to give you the
> information to help you make those decisions. Again, the
> difference between today and fifty years ago is that I think
> most people have less time today and in some ways there
> are more choices.

At its best, the *Times* 2010–2011 business section entitled *Business
Day* integrates international news and business news, offers practical
investing and spending advice, and becomes the consumer's ombudsman. As ombudsman, it exposes outrageous executive salaries and
self-serving business practices in industries that supposedly serve the
consumers, like the mutual fund industry and the insurance industry.
Columns by Floyd Norris, Gretchen Morgenson, Joe Nocera, Ron Lieber,
and Andrew Ross Sorkin (the *Times*'s chief merger and acquisitions

reporter) provide informative and savvy economic and business analyses and blow the whistle on outrageous business practices.

Under the rubric of value-added news, the *Times* has become more of a daily magazine, and this is especially true of the *Business* section, which mixes advice and hard business news. With its wide range of information, career and financial advice, and analysis, the *Business* section offers value-added features and news as well as any other section, except perhaps for the *Science Times*.

Beginning in 2004–2005, one could see an increased focus on value-added business news. For example, Barbara Whitaker's "Managing Retirement, After You Really Retire" discusses how to make the most of retirement savings and explains various strategies to comply with withdrawal requirements and tax responsibilities (October 16, 2005). The *SundayMoney* rubric offers practical financial advice in the mode of Jane Brody's "Personal Health" column in Tuesday's *Science Times*. Thus, Susan B. Garland wrote a lucid article on long-term care, which advises consumers on what type of policy to buy (a shorter benefit period with a higher deductible) and who should and should not buy such insurance (July 24, 2005). In May 2008, Ron Lieber took on Saturday's "Your Money" and began with the advice: "[B]esting the overall market in most investment classes is nearly impossible over long periods of time" (May 17, 2008).

Hiring Joe Nocera in 2005 to write "Talking Business," a wide-ranging column that focused on the implications for the individual of business and investing, is another example of Ingrassia's effort to build a bridge between abstract business statistics and the impact of business trends on individual readers. A characteristic Nocera column "Passions Run High on Indexing" carefully differentiated "fundamentally weighted" index funds—funds taking into account revenue, earnings, dividends, and book value—from traditional index funds and explained how the former are really not index funds (May 17, 2008).

The business editor—or his deputy—is part of the group that meets twice daily with the executive editor and pitches to him or his deputy what goes on the front page. Yet, although business news is much more likely than in the past to find a cherished spot on the front page, at times a seemingly important story can in retrospect seem frivolous; an example is the April 18, 2005, lead story on page 1 by Jonathan Fuerbringer, "As Stocks Slide, Investors Hope for Positive

Earnings Reports." It was clear in a few weeks that by foregrounding the stock market at a time when really nothing much was happening—the stock market was at that time near the low of eight months of fluctuations within a narrow trading range—the *Times* was not reflecting but creating reality. Why was this nonevent recognized as something deserving of great attention by the editors on behalf of *Times* readers? Such a story has the effect of the *Times* crying wolf and undermines the ensuing occasions when an important article about stock market trends appears. The percentage of fluff in the 2010 business section has declined, although Tuesday's *Itineraries* on occasion contains value-added lite, and we do find articles that go on longer than necessary.

In the early years of Ingrassia's editorship, the *Times*'s business sections seemed to have too many pages to fill and many of the articles were inordinately long rather than thorough. At times, business stories had difficulty separating human interest stories from hard business news and drifted into *Timeslite* and even *Timestrash*. For example, how important was H&M's dismissal of model Kate Moss for cocaine use? Is this really, we might ask, a front-page business story or mere sensationalism posing as serious journalism (Guy Trebay and Eric Wilson, "Kate Moss is Dismissed by H&M After a Furor Over Cocaine," September 21, 2005)? Even now on occasion, the *Times*'s business news is not about interest rates or oil prices or market trends or changes in direction of major industries or corporations but human interest stories, some of which seem more appropriate for tabloids and *People* magazine, but surely worth little more than a note rather than the efforts of two or more reporters. Or take a 2009 example with pictures of women in small bikinis: "Apple Bans Some Apps for Lascivious Content," which appeared online as "Apple Bans Some Apps for Sex-Tinged Content" (February 23, 2009).

In keeping with the philosophy of creating a new reader who consults both the digital site and the print newspaper, *Business Day* was among the first *Times* sections to integrate the print newspaper with *Times*'s digital site.

When asked in his June 8, 2009, "Talk to the Newsroom" online discussion about how the *Times* differs from the *Wall Street Journal*, the *Financial Times*, and other competitors, Ingrassia basically repeated what he had told me in 2005:

I figure you mostly want to know how we stack up vis-à-vis business coverage, but that is only part—albeit an important part—of a package the *Times* offers that is more comprehensive than any other newspaper. We cover international news, politics, national affairs, sports, science, the arts and lifestyles, as well as the New York region. . . . At the *Times*, we make it the highest priority to cover the big issues in the economy, business and finance. Coverage of companies matters to us, of course, but we are especially proud when we shed light on how the economy really works, when we highlight important public policy issues and when we raise questions about dubious business practices that warrant scrutiny. . . . Our mission isn't to write incremental stories, or routine "commodity" news that you can get elsewhere, but we do endeavor to cover everything important that an informed reader might want to know, which means being highly competitive on major breaking news, too.

Ingrassia's goal has been to define business news in the broadest context to include how, in a global economy, politics and economics are interrelated and how that relationship impacts our everyday economic life. Early in his *Times* tenure, he remarked to me: "I know the *Journal* in some ways better than I know the *Times* because I know everybody there and I was involved in a lot of the coverage decision making." He concluded, revealingly: "I think the *Journal* does a very good job," for that was his background and point of reference. His goal at the *Times* has been "to make sure that we're writing every story ideally understandable to Main Street but sophisticated for Wall Street. That's the challenge" (April 18, 2005).

Because he wanted to speak to a more diverse audience, Ingrassia hired generalists whom he regards as good writers rather than specialists: "[W]hat I'm really hiring is someone who is smart, aggressive, fearless, knows how to source and get inside, get people to tell something so we can break the news, and who can write in a way that is very successful." Yet he also realizes that he needs to have reporters familiar with each industry. "We have reporters who write about the food industry. We have reporters who write about Wall Street mostly. We have reporters who write about the pharmaceutical industry, health care industry" (April 18, 2005). At times, however, this has resulted in articles that do not speak to an audience unfamiliar with the issues within an industry.

In 2005, Ingrassia, not surprisingly, seemed more conscious of marketing and costs than many other *Times* editors I interviewed at that time and more frank about discussing the economic bases for decisions. When the *World Business* section was "folded back" into *Business Day*, the decision was an economic one rather than an editorial one. As Ingrassia put it, "That was an economic decision. That was not so much an editorial decision. Advertising has been tight" (April 18, 2005). Another savings came from cutting back details on stock and bond coverage in the print edition; first, the opening, high, and low of each stock on the NYSE was eliminated and not so long thereafter almost the entire stock tables disappeared except for some drastically reduced tables on Sundays and the quarterly mutual fund special section. These tables and other financial tools, such as the ability to track one's own portfolio, now exist on the *Business* section's website.

Ingrassia explained, "[I]t costs a lot in newsprint . . . to print the tables and what I know of the research that has been done is that a smaller percentage of people read the stock tables than they did five years ago because they're getting more of it online. . . . These are tough decisions that we have to make and to some extent we have to cut something that a small percentage of our readers use or have to not fill positions of staff—reporter positions—because you could save a hundred thousand here or a hundred thousand there. I'd rather save that one hundred thousand there" (April 18, 2005). That Ingrassia stressed that complaints about truncated stock tables come in the form of typewritten and handwritten notes from older readers gives some clue to the *Times*'s attentiveness to demography, but may also show how somewhat younger editors at that time seemed to patronize the base of older readers before that group was Internet savvy, as probably most of them are now.

Ingrassia's goal has been to provide essential business news for a larger audience and to avoid articles aimed at small niches and MBA wonks. Ingrassia explained in his May 26, 2006, "Talk to the Newsroom" summary of his Q&A Internet dialogue with readers, "We no longer can just do a good job of writing what I call 'commodity' news, or news that is available many other places. It doesn't mean that we don't cover major breaking news, but it does mean that we have to go beyond the news in writing about it, by spinning it forward to say what it means and why. And it means that we place a higher premium on exclusive stories, like the M&A (Merger and Acquisitions) scoops that Andrew Ross Sorkin frequently reports, such as his February 2005 story about Univisión Communications, the Spanish-language media company, considering putting itself up for sale."

In part, the *Times* itself has not only become more adversarial in relation to business but has, by reporting its revelations, helped create the deserved skepticism toward business that, especially after the government bailouts of 2008 and 2009, pervades the culture as a whole. Ingrassia explained to me: "It's interesting that certain journalists were known as muckrakers. And that's probably in part because they stood out so much from what other journalists were doing, which in some way, shape, or form was recording the facts in the way they were presented to them by official organizations and not as critically questioned" (April 18, 2005). *Muckraking* was originally a pejorative term, and muckrakers were considered zealots who devoted too much energy to exposing corruption. More balanced and objective journalists and editors—such as those who wrote for the *Times*—patronized muckrakers. But the *Times* now has a large staff of investigative reporters, and, in the age of the Internet, it could be argued that digging beyond the surface facts and the public face of business—as well as government, politics, foreign affairs, and even sports—has become a major function of the 2011 *Times*.

Let us briefly turn our attention to the *Sunday Business* section. Good examples of the kind of value-added piece Ingrassia favors are those that are about saving for retirement. Such a piece is Paul J. Lim's May 11, 2008, "SundayMoney" column, "How to Tell if a Rally is for Real." Mark Hulbert's "Strategies" focuses on the stock market, often debunking common myths, such as the view held by many investors that they can beat an index fund ("Can You Beat the Market? It's a $100 Billion Question," March 9, 2008). For many readers, Hulbert's advice might seem to be a tad esoteric, but his actual advice is simple and homespun.

In her role of informal investor ombudsman, Gretchen Morgenson's columns focus on major economic issues, sometimes with ethical implications. Morgenson often has focused on how stock analysts sugarcoat bad news and how independent investors need to cast a wary eye on their reports. She focused on Dell's using its subsidiary Dell Financial Services to finance its sales ("Dude, You're Getting a Loan," July 17, 2005). In her May 11, 2008, "Big Rescues Can Work. Just Ask New

York," she bemoans the lack of an "intelligent and comprehensive plan for dealing with mass foreclosures and the economic consequences associated with the [2008 financial] debacle" and presents a historical perspective on how New York City was rescued by imaginative leadership."

The *Sunday Business* section is not immune to the siren call of pop culture and to articles five times their necessary length; one notorious 2005 example was Tracie Rozhon's "The Rap on Puffy's Empire" (July 24, 2005), which goes on for more than a full page (including pictures) about Sean Jean Combs ("Puff Daddy"). Supposedly about a struggling company, the article is really more of a biography of a popular rap figure and his hope of becoming a business mogul by marketing a line of clothing. The article, which cries out for rewriting in terms of trimming, organization, and argument, includes such nuggets as: "In the end the empire is only as strong as its emperor—Sean Combs or Puff Daddy or P. Diddy."

Perhaps even more disappointing are some of the lengthy and repetitive lead articles in the *Business* section, where we expect something other than gossip and trivia. An example was a piece on the bankruptcy of a private ski club/resort for the superrich and the divorce of the founding couple, Tim and Era Blisexth. On the borderline between *Timeslite* and *Timestrash*, the article (with pictures) takes up most of the front page and all of pages 6 and 7. In the guise of discussing the effects of the worldwide recession, it is in the genre of economic voyeurism; foregrounding excess, it is the *Times* at its worst (Amy Wallace, "Checkmate at the Yellowstone Club: Bankruptcies at Ski Haven for Superrich," June 14, 2009).

Yet by 2010, *Sunday Business* seemed on the whole to be somewhat less prone than many other sections to *Timeslite* and to provide more historical perspective, as when Peter Bernstein's May 11, 2008, piece, "When Should the Fed Crash the Party?" considers past pro and con arguments for intervention in the current credit crisis and comes down on the sides of both "managing prosperity" and "managing recession."

III. Sports

Under Keller, the *Sports* section has become more of a feature section and less of a section devoted to hard sports news. With sports results instantly available on the Internet and 24-hour sports cable television, daily sports news in the *Times* has taken a back seat to sports magazine analyses. Contemporary *Times* sports coverage is much more about the backgrounds and psyches of professional athletes, team dynamics, media presentation of events, and legal issues, including substance abuse and the business of sports.

As with the printed *Business* section, the *Sports* section, combined four days a week (Tuesday through Friday) with *Business* in the "B" section, has become shorter, with fewer statistics, whereas the online version contains statistics and even more discussion, much of it in the form of reader comments and, in the case of college sports, blogs from players and others. For example, since 2008, Doug Glanville, a former Major League player, has been writing a blog with exceptional in-depth commentary on the life of a professional baseball player.

One change in the past decade or so has been more of an interest in world sports, especially the 2010 World Cup in response to greater interest in American soccer and the Tour de France because of Lance Armstrong's seven consecutive victories beginning in 2009. Under the shadow of a rising tide of evidence that Armstrong may have used performance-enhancing drugs, these victories were revisited by the *Times* in 2010.

In my October 9, 2005, interview with Tom Jolly, sports editor since 2003, he defined his sense of the mission of the *Times* sports page: "The coverage that we do is kind of split in two—we're reporting breaking news with an eye toward putting it on the Internet right away as opposed to waiting until the next morning's news cycle, but we're also looking to when we do report the news for the next morning's paper, we want to do it in a way that puts it in perspective or gives readers a broader sense of what's going on with enterprise stories, investigative stories, and that kind of thing."

The *Times* somewhat inflects the Ivy League, as in its coverage of Cornell's Cinderella 2010 NCAA basketball run. Pete Thamel's March 2, 2008, article on Harvard's missteps in basketball recruiting is an example of Ivy emphasis, as is the follow-up on March 5, "Harvard and Ivy League Will Review Recruiting." Indeed, where the *Times* sports coverage often excels is in its investigatory coverage and the ensuing follow-up. For example, Katie Thomas's November 17, 2009, piece, "SUNY Weighs the Value of Division I Sports," discussed larger college sports issues in the wake of a scandal at the State University of

New York at Binghamton in which academic standards were abandoned for the purpose of building a prestigious basketball program: "The scandal at Binghamton highlights the way intangible sports benefits so sought after by university administrators—like increased visibility and buzz—can backfire." In September 2006, the *Times* began to leave out some baseball box scores of also-rans, something sacrosanct to rabid baseball fans, to whom statistics are breath itself, and that trend of reducing the box scores has continued. By 2010 increasing numbers of box scores and sports statistics could be found only on the website, but the range of information that could be accessed with Google from the website—including access to historic and lifetime statistics for each baseball player—was much greater than anything that ever appeared in the printed paper.

Between 1999 and 2009, sports coverage became weightier in some ways and more gossipy and lightweight in others. Following the tabloids, especially the *Daily News* and the *New York Post*, the *Times* puts more stress on the personal lives of sports figures and the some-times sordid scandals surrounding them—including Roger Clemens's probable use of illegal substances and his adultery—although the *Times* falls well short of the tabloids in its use of sordid sensationalism in sports coverage. Certainly, the *Times* was more restrained in covering the 2009 Tiger Woods sex scandal than most of the media, although, in 2010, it did not cringe from covering the effect of his personal life on his deteriorating golf results.

Reading about sports in the *Times* used to be a kind of half-hour Crusoeism away from the real world. Sports coverage in the *Times* and elsewhere has come to include wide-ranging discussions about the public behavior and the personal lives of the athletes, owners, and coaches. Sports sections reflect the culture at large, including its conflicts and fissures: race relationships, fairness in hiring minorities, use of performance-enhancing drugs, squabbles among players and between players and coaches, arrests of sports stars, and so on.

The 2010 *Times* sports coverage was much improved from three or four decades ago in terms of many more pages and in-depth analyses. But frequently, the athletic contests take a back seat to analyses of the emotional lives of sports figures—often in terms of pop psychology. In the September 30, 2004, issue, one article asked whether the Yankees are a team of depressives affected by a compulsive owner who takes the joy out of team sports. And this was before the Yankees, in a memorable collapse, lost the 2004 playoff series to their archrivals, the Boston Red Sox, four games to three after taking a 3–0 lead in games.

On September 20, 2004, one could read about self-destructive sociopathic behavior of a Los Angeles outfielder named Milton Bradley, who in 2009 was still behaving the same way, or Anaheim outfielder José Guillén and a Texas pitcher named Frank Francisco, who threw chairs at fans. Or one could have read about whether the New York Knick's ostentatiously overpaid guard Allen Houston was afraid to commit to a date when he could play because of his prior season's disappointment when he failed to recover from injuries.

What is the essence of sports coverage today? We no longer see sports figures—or entertainment figures—as icons separate from larger social issues or insulated from examination of how they live their lives. We know that sports performance is affected not only by larger social issues but also by very delicate psychological issues that are best discussed in terms that transcend simple pop psychology. Perhaps the *Times* should have a regular column by a sports psychiatrist since much of the sports section is about the psyche of athletes. For example, when I interviewed Jolly immediately after another Yankee playoff failure in October 2006, marked in particular by the ineptitude of third baseman Alex Rodriguez ("A-Rod"), he noted: "One of our stories right now is what's going on with the Yankees, and why did they fail in the playoffs. . . . We've written extensively about A-Rod and his apparent confidence issues or self-confidence issues, and he's acknowledged going to see a therapist himself" (October 9, 2006). Of course he could have said the same thing after the Yankees lost in the 2007 or 2011 playoffs.

The *Times* might do more behavioral analyses and discuss why athletes perform as they do. I'm not sure anyone has written the story that I would have wanted to read both before and after the early 2009 revelation of Alex Rodriguez's use of performance-enhancing drugs. That story would have framed Rodriguez's annual playoff performance (and sometimes even in crucial games during the season)—his failure to respond in the defining moments of his most important at bats and sometimes fielding opportunities—in terms of his background, psychological health, and his relationship with Yankee players. Simply put, why in crucial situations had his physical skills deteriorated to the point of virtual paralyses in public? (To be sure he somewhat redeemed himself in the 2009 playoffs, but that could have been the basis for a coda to the original story.) Wouldn't professional analyses of team and individual psychology be a strong addition to the *Times*'s coverage? To take another case with New York resonance, did the admission of performance supplement use hurt Andy Pettitte's 2008 performance?

Analysis from a distance is a risky business, but as long as the *Times* emphasized that a professional psychiatrist was commenting on the public behavior he observed and the data that was available, I think such psychological analyses would be interesting to a wide audience.

In preseason 2008, the sports focus was on the now late George Steinbrenner's sons as successors (Jonathan Mahler, "Oedipus Bronx," *Play*, March 2, 2008), as well as on the efforts by the Knicks to resurrect themselves by hiring Donnie Walsh and Mike D'Antoni to replace Isaiah Thomas as team president and coach. Throughout the 2007–2008 basketball season, the *Times* focused on the daily symptoms of the dysfunctional Knicks and the trials of the coach, but sometimes synthesizing articles were missing. When the Yankees got off to a mediocre first quarter in 2008, I looked for more trenchant analyses of what was happening than I found. What kind of bad decision making and inept talent had left the team with the highest payroll in the major leagues, without the required number of starting pitchers, and with reserves who couldn't play for other major league teams? When the extraordinarily well-informed Murray Chass retired from the *Times* in May 2008, baseball discussion at first seemed more statistically driven by younger writers with great faith in what sometimes seems statistical gibberish, but more recently the balance between statistics and other forms of analyses has been partially restored.

As with foreign news, more context and history are needed for readers who do not read the "BATS" blog and every word every day online or in the newspaper. Sports coverage needs more continuity in terms of an ongoing narrative, especially because committed fans already know the results. The best of *SportsSunday* are often articles that take the long view of the evolving professional seasons or trends in physical breakdowns such as concussions or arm injuries to pitchers, but there could be more of them. By contrast, *Times* sportswriters have joined the Twitter world; Twitter lends itself to the kind of mini-insights and recollected information that sports fan like.

Notwithstanding William C. Rhoden's columns that often focus on racism in sports, the *Times* could go further in relating sports to larger cultural developments, perhaps with a double column on Sunday on the model of Frank Rich's former weekly cultural commentary in the Sunday *Arts & Leisure* section, which discussed art in the context of larger cultural implications, or his later Sunday *Week in Review* column, which discusses political and international news as theater.

IV. *Science Times* and Special Health Sections

The section that most embodies the *Times* as a national magazine rather than a Manhattan or even urban newspaper-magazine is the Tuesday *Science Times*. The *Science Times* is *Scientific American* lite, but it brings science and health issues to the forefront. For the lay reader, the *Science Times* presents an array of lucid articles on recent research in astronomy, archeology, anthropology, medicine, epidemiology, biology, chemistry, physics—indeed, virtually any scientific field, that might have an impact on, or hold interest for, an educated audience.

Since I have looked at the *Times* coverage of the Normandy invasion in June 1944 and discussed briefly what the newspaper looked like then, let me choose an arbitrary day about sixty years after the Normandy invasion to examine the *Science Times*. On June 15, 2004, the magnificent science stalwart John Noble Wilford had a wonderful piece about how the Cassini spacecraft, launched in 1997 would enter Saturn's orbit on June 30 and, while visiting for four years, enable scientists to observe the thirty-one moons around Saturn ("31 Moons, Now Close Enough to Touch"). Eschewing jargon, Wilford captured the excitement of space exploration for even those who have become jaded. An accompanying chart showed how Cassini would slow down. Wilford eloquently concluded his wonderfully written piece: "[T]he 250 science investigators . . . wait expectantly and eagerly for a spacecraft, seven years from home, to find its way through a gate in the rings of Saturn and emerge with wonders to report and pictures to post of places as never seen before."

Interestingly, Wilford had no prior background in science and neither did the *Times*'s first prominent science writer, Walter Sullivan. However, Laura Chang, science editor since 2004, favors hiring writers with a scientific background, thinks much of journalism requires specialized knowledge, and stresses the value of experience ("Talk to the Newsroom," May 12, 2006).

Speaking of the problem of evaluating contradictory medical studies, Chang notes: "Though our reporters don't pretend to be scientists, they are part of this filtering system, to the extent that they pore over the numbers, consult knowledgeable people in the field and try to put the findings in historical perspective." Chang does not believe the *Science* section needs to pay attention to the arguments about intelligent design or the aspects of the war on science when "one side has no solid evidence to stand on"; yet she believes the section needs to show an awareness of opposing points of view and why significant portions of the American public reject scientific evidence on evolution (May 12, 2006).

Even *Science Times* occasionally has prolix and lightweight stories that need editing or are given a prominence they don't deserve. On June 15, 2004, the lead story in the *Science Times* was a disappointing lengthy discussion of "hair restoration" by Dan Hurley entitled "Does He or Doesn't He? It's Harder to Tell." Reinforced by a teasing headline that would rouse the interest of all men who had lost or were losing or feared losing their hair, the story earned its lead no doubt because of its subject, not its importance. The article seemed to belong in the occasional *Men's Health* section or in the *SundayStyles* section.

Chang strongly takes issue with the perception—a perception I share on occasion—that the *Science Times* has been dumbed down: "We must recognize that the Internet has affected the way many people read and how they respond to visual cues. So we are striving to make stories as comprehensible as possible, but also briefer when sensible [so as] to pitch them to intelligent laypeople rather than specialists, and to present them with a modern flair. . . . A thoughtful lightness does not equal lightweight thought" (May 12, 2006). The expansion into health news has not undermined the coverage of cutting age science, but many of the more scientific articles do seem briefer and less teacherly. What is interesting is that Chang's goals are very much the same as business editor Ingrassia's—to write for the widest possible audience even if gravitas as perceived by the cognoscenti is sacrificed.

Since 2004, the *Science Times*, especially on the website, has been improving its graphics and added further to its information on how to live healthy. In other words, the emphasis more and more is on value-added journalism rather than hard science, although one still finds splendid pieces on archeology and astronomy.

Using again the sixtieth anniversary of the Normandy invasion as a benchmark to measure how Keller's *Times* began evolving more and more into a value-added magazine, we might take the subsection of the June 15, 2004, *Science Times* called "Health and Fitness." Jane Brody's "Personal Health" column discusses how one can eat healthy— saving calories and, if desired, maintaining a vegetarian diet—while traveling and recommends a book for that purpose: *Healthy Highways: The Traveller's Guide to Healthy Eating*. In the same section, Dr. Lawrence Altman's regular column, "The Doctor's World," discusses in "A Recollection of Early Questions about Reagan's Health" whether Ronald Reagan, whose elaborate funeral had just taken place, had Alzheimer's disease while he was president and concludes that it was unlikely. Altman is a wonderful writer who uses anecdotes to support his conclusion, and who integrates consultations with experts with experience from his own 1980 interview with Reagan, who at age sixty-nine was the oldest elected president. With an eye to family health and the need for vigilance, the June 15, 2006, "Health and Fitness" section included a substantial admonitory piece by Mindy Sink entitled "Now at Your Drugstore: A Cheap and Dangerous High," which discusses students who get high on cough and cold medications containing dextromethorphan.

Brody, the *Times*'s longtime health columnist, writes a lucid and succinct health column in the *Science Times* that has a huge following. Her columns synthesize a wide range of research and information. She advocates exercise, nutrition, proactive preventive measures, a relatively abstemious lifestyle, surgery for injuries limiting mobility or constraining activity, and patient involvement in treatment for major illnesses. Her April 29, 2008, column, "You Name It, and Exercise Helps It," is characteristic of her belief in "the inestimable value to . . . physical and emotional well-being of regular physical exercise." At times, she can be almost preachy—"Do as I do and you'll be ok"—and is not beyond describing her own rigorous exercise program and her personal health issues.

Brody's optimism about overcoming obstacles and her full embrace of life are attractive qualities to readers. One notable column discussed sexuality in those over age fifty and considered whether and why sexual desire wanes as we age and what people can do about it: "I have no studies to corroborate this idea, but I strongly suspect that older people who stay in shape physically, keep their brains stimulated and remain interested in a variety of activities are likely to feel more attractive and be more attractive" ("A Lively Libido Isn't Reserved for the Young," April 10, 2007).

On occasion, the *Times* has published special value-added sections entitled *Men's Health* and *Women's Health*. The June 21, 2004, printed *Times* included a special "F" section, *Men's Health*, dominated by a discussion of Viagra, Levitra, and Cialis. David Tuller's "Gentleman, Start Your Engines? Racing for Sales, Drugmakers Cast Erectile Dysfunction in Youthful Terms" was the lead article in this section. There also were articles about needless tests for cancer as well as on the Achilles heel, hip replacement, and knee replacement. *Men's Health* followed by a few weeks the *Times's* special section *Women's Health,* on Sunday, June 6, 2004. The lead headline of this section was "Diabetes: Faces of an Epidemic," with an autobiographical piece, "The Morning I'll Never Remember," by novelist Anne Rice, about type 1, diabetes and a piece by Mary Donald on type 2 diabetes, "From Mother to Daughter, Shared Genes and a Burden." Also on page 1 was an article by Leslie Berger about hormone replacement therapy for menopausal women: "On Hormone Therapy, the Dust Is Still Settling."

By 2010, the *Times* had further ratcheted up its health coverage. Tara Parker-Pope, author of the weekly column "Well" since moving from the *Wall Street Journal* to the *Times* in 2007, presented an entire special section entitled "Well," which contained succinct and informed discussions of fourteen body parts. In her introduction she wrote, "Whether it's practical advice for keeping your brain active or relief for aching feet, you'll find answers to pressing medical questions and gain insights into healthy aging" ("A Guided Tour of Your Body," May 13, 2008). This was accompanied by a more elaborate interactive site online.

Parker-Pope's weekly column complements Brody's by presenting recent research with medical implications. In "Vitamin D, Miracle Drug: Is It Science, or Just Talk?" she explored claims that vitamin D could be a wonder supplement and admonished, "But don't start gobbling down vitamin D supplements just yet. The excitement about their health potential is still far ahead of the science" (February 1, 2010).

Parker-Pope is a teacher much like Brody. Thus we learn that studies of mice show that a "Low-Fat Diet May Cut Prostate Cancer Risk" (May 16, 2008). Readers are invited to join her blog "as she sifts through medical research and expert opinions for practical advice to help readers take control of their health and live well every day." Her blog is the quintessence of value-added journalism: Read me and be healthier.

On February 5, 2008, she wrote a fine *Science Times* piece on treatments for prostate cancer, reporting from research by the Agency for Healthcare Research and Quality that nobody can tell what type of treatment is most likely to save their lives ("No Answers for Men With Prostate Cancer"). On February 13, 2008, she took up rumors about side effects of statins, particularly Lipitor, on her blog: "Do Statins Make

You Stupid?" "Over the years, there's been a lot of discussion about whether statins affect thinking and memory, but drug makers point out that hundreds of studies haven't shown a causal link between statins and memory problems. However, anecdotal reports continue to suggest that some patients do develop memory loss while taking the drugs." During the fall 2009 flu epidemic, Parker-Pope wrote about seasonal and H1N1 flu vaccines ("As Flu Vaccine Arrives for the Season, Some Questions and Answers," October 9, 2010).

The *Times* does not limit coverage of health issues to the *Science Times*. Major stories appear on the front page. Since 2004, the *Times* has been especially conscientious in reporting on cancer, a disease that affects virtually every family at one time or another. On June 6, 2004, a series entitled "Redefining Cancer" began; the first article, by Andrew Pollack, was the lead for columns 1 and 2 on page 1 of the first section: "No Cure, but Drugs May Turn Cancer Into Manageable Illness."

Characteristic of the *Times* in 2004, Pollack begins with a paradigmatic dramatic anecdote that conveys the quintessence of one particular person's dilemma:

> Bruce Smith, the father of two young children, was only 26 three months ago when he was found to have advanced melanoma, a deadly skin disease. Several drugs failed to stop the cancer, while leaving him frail, depleted and ill.
>
> But two years ago Mr. Smith began taking an experimental pill along with chemotherapy, and his tumors disappeared. He dropped the chemotherapy nearly a year ago but still takes the pill twice a day. And his disease, though it may return one day, is still at bay.

Pollack gave us the background information in the first paragraph. The dramatic reversal in the second paragraph—after the opening emphasis on the seriousness of Smith's illness—not only catches the reader off guard, but draws him into a rhetoric of hopefulness at odds with his or her expectations about cancer. Pollack's anecdote and others like it have a cinematic quality, appealing to our tendency, cultivated by a lifetime of television, to visualize.

Although it might be objected that this is another example of a *Times* articles that fails to give us the main points in its opening, Pollack's nuanced essay-article turns out to also have an argument, namely that cancer has become for many a manageable chronic disease rather than a fatal illness. The articles also have more caveats than the attention-grabbing headline and the first anecdote would indicate. For one thing, the drugs only work for a minority of patients. For another, who is going pay for expensive drugs, some of which cost tens of thousands of dollars for a course of treatment?

Some articles from the excellent 2009 series, "Forty Years' War," about the efforts to defeat cancer, appeared on the front page. Noteworthy in the "Forty Years' War" were tightly written synthesizing articles with fewer of the personal anecdotes that characterized such pieces a few years earlier and, based on scientific evidence, more informative and useful material on recent research and treatments. Exemplary is Gina Kolata's November 12, 2009, closing piece in the series, "Medicines to Deter Some Cancers Are Not Taken."

An excellent 2010 *Science Times* article about whether sustaining quality of life can become a better choice for the terminally ill than focusing only on extending life was Donald G. McNeil Jr.'s "Palliative Care Extends Life, Study Shows," which informed readers that "patients with terminal lung cancer who began receiving palliative care immediately upon diagnosis not only were happier, more mobile and in less pain as the end neared—but they also lived nearly three months longer" (August 18, 2010).

V. Feature Sections: Style, Dining, House and Home

Under former style editor Barbara Graustark's leadership, the *ThursdayStyles* and *SundayStyles* sections became more prominent. (She also edited *Dining* on Wednesday and *House and Home* on Thursday.)

In my interview, which took place before she departed from the position she held for five years and was appointed editor-at-large in spring 2006, Graustark was quite defensive about her role. She would not like my epithet Queen of *Timeslite*. She resents the term "back of the book" as "a little bit derogatory because what we do is . . . journalism. It's news, it's not just service." According to her, she had as many columns to fill as the news department: "We have a news hole of about 120 columns which can go up to 140 columns a week when we have fashion shows. With a reporter pool of twenty people you can see how small we really are. The national news hole is about, they'll correct me if I'm wrong on this and that's the only reason I'm looking at my notes, I think the national news hole is 15 columns daily or 105 columns a week, not counting hurricane coverage, not counting special Iraq coverage" (October 11, 2005).

Graustark believed her mandate extended well beyond traditional notions of style and was rather defensive about the perception that she was presiding over soft or filler articles: "The style department is really about society, it's not about fashion. It's about that, too, and I don't want to underplay that we don't cover certain fashion trends. But look at us as covering social trends. Now [social trend] coverage is throughout the newspaper but our reporters have to kick it deep because they're interested in it and very enterprising."

Timeslite (another apt name would be *Timesfluff*) has flourished in the various daily sections that fall under the *Style* rubric, and in 2010 it found a central place in the *Metropolitan* section in such features as the "Sunday Routine" of New York celebrities and "Neighborhood Joint," which on September 5, 2010, featured a Rockaway bar with pictures of two women drinking while wearing bikinis (Alan Feuer, "Drinks, Breezes, Groaners").

Let me cite some examples of silly articles in the October 23, 2005, *SundayStyles*: Howie Kahn's "Modern Love: The Third Half of a Couple," about a friend of a couple who has "a nonsexual relationship with them," is virtually devoid of content. Alex Williams's "My Big Fat 80's Bar Mitzvah" is about the transformation of bar mitzvahs into social spectacles. While eliciting reader curiosity and playing on the title of a 2002 courtship film with a similar name (*My Big Fat Greek Wedding*), perhaps Williams's article had the potential to be substantive, but in this case wasn't. It is as if no topic was too trivial for the sections under Graustark's wing, and some of the senior staff were cognizant of her shortcomings.

Tough-minded managing editor Jill Abramson does not like to talk about shortcomings of the *Times*, but she acknowledged to me in 2005 that stories in the back of the book often are too long. "I wouldn't disagree with you that some of the stories are too long, I think . . . part of that is that some of those sections depend a lot on freelance assignments and, it's more difficult to put a section together if you're mainly dependent on freelancers than if you have a multiplicity of assignments any given week, and that may sometimes result negatively in a single story going on too long" (October 11, 2005). But clearly it is the responsibility of the masthead editors to see that these back-of-the-book sections of the daily paper are up to the standards of the rest of the newspaper.

Keller reorganized the *Style* editorship in spring 2006, giving Trish Hall the editorship of *House and Home* and *Dining*, and letting Trip Gabriel, who had edited *Style* but reported to Graustark, be what Keller called in his revealing March 2006 staff memo "sole proprietor" of *ThursdayStyles* and *SundayStyles*: "Trip has managed the extraordinary feat of putting out two sections that deal in fashion, night life, romance, fitness, shopping, beauty, lifestyle, sexual mores and all things cool—subjects that, in the *Times*, can sometimes flirt with self-parody." Gabriel and Hall reported to the masthead editors.

If his editorship of the *Style* sections under Graustark were any criteria, Gabriel often thought he was being hip when he was only being silly, edgy when he was being trashy, and classy when he was being economically and socially voyeuristic.

After Gabriel assumed leadership in 2006, I detected some movement to more serious subjects in the *Thursday* and *Sunday Style* sections, although their proclivity for lightweight content continues. A recent *Timeslite* article from October 28, 2009, was entitled "To Harvest Squash, Click Here" and focused on FarmVille, a Facebook game that had recently become very popular. Even more pointless and prolix was the thirty-paragraph piece about the current acceptability among the young of chipped nail polish (Melena Ryzik, "I Love What You Didn't Do to Your Chipped Nails," May 22, 2008). Ryzik's online video of the 2007 National Book Awards dinner was characteristic not only of the way a serious subject is trivialized but also of her often snide and condescending tone.

Part of *Style*, Lisa Belkin's biweekly "Life's Work" column discussed workplace issues, with a focus on women in the workplace more often than not. A characteristic column might examine the difficulties faced by women in technical fields; it drew on serious research done by the Center for Work-Life Policy ("Diversity Isn't Rocket Science, Is It?" May 15, 2008). At times needlessly chatty, Belken's column ran nine years. (Her last column was on October 15, 2008, and she has been writing the "Motherlode" for the *Sunday Magazine*).

Under Gabriel, many of the articles in the *SundayStyles* and *ThursdayStyles* sections are still far too long to the point where they become mere space fillers. A December 2007 Natasha Singer article (with pictures) entitled "Rubles Are a Girl's Best Friend," about the daughters of Russian celebrities living the high life, is an example (December 9, 2007).

In summer 2010, one could find articles about former Illinois governor Rod Blagojevich's and his wife's taste for high-end clothes, including expensive ties (Emma Graves Fitzsimmons, "A Dapper Defendant's Penchant for Ties," August 18, 2010), and various references to the sluttish and childish Snooki from *Jersey Shore,* such as Cathy Horyn's "Snooki's Time," July 23, 2010: "But trying to hold a conversation with Snooki is a little like getting down on your hands and knees with a child. You have to come down to her level, and sometimes you almost think you need to bribe her with a piece of candy to coax her to be more responsive." Surely Snooki's behavior had no place in my father's *Times.*

In my 2005 interview with Graustark, she deflected me from questions about the preponderance of fluff and, on occasion *Timestrash,* in *ThursdayStyles* and *SundayStyles.* She stressed that thirty-five of her articles made it to the front page—one might question whether they were all worthy of that placement—and that important stories are generated by her reporters. She particularly praised the work of Jane Gross, who was a *Style* reporter working under her.

The recently retired Gross is a splendid reporter, as demonstrated by her important series on assisted living and on Alzheimer's disease, both of which began as front-page stories, and by her splendid articles and blog on the elderly. But if these stories were run elsewhere in the newspaper as what the *Times* calls "enterprise stories"—or investigative stories—isn't it because *Style* reporters were doing something beyond the boundaries of the *Timeslite* that the *Style* sections usually feature? In other words, they were not *Style* stories but news and feature stories originating with reporters nominally assigned to *Style,* but outside the limited scale of importance on which *Style* concentrates. Thus, Gross's article on less-aggressive and less-costly care for those suffering "the inevitable erosion of advanced age" rather than "treatable illnesses" appeared in the "Health" section of *Science Times* ("For the Elderly, Being Heard About Life's End," May 5, 2008).

Often in the *Style* sections, because the *Times*'s editors fail to insist on logical, forward moving succinct articles with a narrative thread, stories are excessively long and poorly organized. All too often we find in the *Times* aggregations of paragraphs with little substance.

Thus, the author uses first-person present-tense leads to set a scene, begins by adopting the viewpoint of a human subject for a paragraph or two, and is off on a roller coaster peregrination—eventually importing some larger cultural context and returning on occasion to the subject's point of view—without topic sentences or argument or an editor who restrains him or her. One longs for editors who ask the writer, "To whom are you writing and why?" "What is the intended effect of your piece?" And the editors seem to do little more than correct (most of the time) grammatical errors.

Although *SundayStyles* and *ThursdayStyles* have had some fine features, they are—more frequently than any other sections—home to *Timestrash*. The second most prominent story in the January 8, 2006, section is about Heidi Fleiss's plan to open an all-male brothel in Nevada. Fleiss is identified as an "ex-Hollywood madam who served time in prison in the late 1990s on federal charges related to a high-end call-girl business" (Mireya Navarro, "The West Gets Wilder"). Navarro evokes a racy setting: "Picture a pleasure oasis in the Nevada desert, a collection of luxurious bungalows featuring bedrooms with fireplaces where sexual fantasies and desires are catered to. Starting at $250 an hour." In the guise of exploring whether women are ready for such a place, she gets in a fair amount of sex talk. The article includes a picture of—and an interview with—the man the article calls Fleiss's "first 'stud.'" The *SundayStyles* section's lead story the same day is entitled "Love and (Leave) Thy Neighbor," by Allen Salkin, about the mating habits of a group of young men and women who live at 126 Rivington Place in Manhattan. The article has a strong emphasis on what the author calls "sexual relationships." Certainly, the *Times* now foregrounds sex talk, although Michael Winerip's November 27, 2009, "In Search of Their Own Elixir of Love," about the quest of some mature women for medical help to rediscover their sexuality, while perhaps too anecdotal, seemed more tasteful than some leering mid-decade articles on sexuality.

Yet, to show that *Timestrash* is still living and still prone to heavy breathing, the June 14, 2009, *SundayStyles* section had a story on a sex fetishist who enjoys wrapping himself in a carpet and going to New York bars and clubs where people step on him; while in recent years he is charging a $200 fee, his main motive seems to be the pleasure of being stepped on (Kirk Semple, "Bartender; Make it a Stiletto," June 14, 2009). In the same issue, marginally more substantive, is the repetitious and frothy lead article on Ruth Madoff, now socially ostracized due to her husband's larceny and disgrace (Lynnley Browning, "The Loneliest Woman in New York," June 14, 2009).

But then again *Timeslite* has not for some years been limited to the back-of-the-book sections, but can even turn up on the op-ed page in the form of Carol McD. Wallace's "We're all Preppies Now," which is about the revival of preppy fashions (October 24, 2005), and Elisabeth Eaves's "The Lap of Luxury" about what strippers are selling, namely an illusion of "sexual prowess"—as if this were news—and, consequently, that the customer is paying steeply for the luxury of that illusion just as he pays for other luxury goods. Eaves is identified as the author of *Bare: The Naked Truth About Stripping*. This misuse of the op-ed page space occurred while the news was dominated by the revelation that Syria had arranged the murder of the former prime minister of Lebanon; the continuing morass in Iraq, which at that time had yielded 2,000 American military deaths; the upcoming Libby indictment; the pending Harriet Miers hearing; and, at the *Times*, the embarrassing Judith Miller scandal.

VI. Lifestyles of the Rich and Famous

Whether because, in response to Raines, Keller gives too much editorial freedom to section editors, or whether Keller himself believes his job is to raise circulation no matter what the price in terms of quality, his *Times* focuses excessively on the lifestyles of the rich and famous in the back-of-the-book sections.

As the *Times* has become a national newspaper, it has tried to find the right balance between catering to the economic elite, that is, the well-to-do and usually highly educated in communities across the country, while retaining its core audience of well-informed upper-middle-class New Yorkers and reaching out to the young and minorities. Yet, too often "Gee Whiz, How Great It Is to Be Rich and Superrich" articles appear throughout the paper. Whereas the *Times* used to speak to intellectuals and the very well informed—some of whom were upper income and most of whom closely followed the news—the *Times* now often plays more blatantly to those who value money above knowledge. Thus, we have articles about the richest of the rich, as in a 2005 article in the Sunday travel section on $1,000 a day in Anguilla (Julie Macur,

"On Anguilla, High Rubs with Low: $1,000 a Day/'Roughing it' at a chic resort: a chilly seaweed wrap and kids in the hot tub," February 27, 2005). Although generally excellent, perhaps the coverage of the 2009 Bernie Madoff scandal—and his cheating of mostly wealthy clients in an elaborate Ponzi scheme—sometimes veered into the ways the superrich live and their presumptive sense of privilege.

Clearly, one motive for focusing on the wealthy is to attract advertising from expensive products—upscale condominiums, cars, jewelry, and vacations—with large advertising budgets. But the *Times* is not only speaking to the rich but to a materialistic culture where fantasies take the form of living like the superrich, just as *Vogue* shows designer clothes but not only sells copies in the middle-class neighborhood grocery to consumers who only fantasize about wearing such clothes but also carries advertisements for the less-expensive clothing and cosmetics that most of their readers are more likely to wear.

In this vein of tapping into American economic voyeurism, in fall 2006, the *Times* began publishing an entire series, entitled "Gilded Paychecks: New Paths to a Windfall," about the superrich. These are people with annual incomes in the million-dollar range and sometimes much more and with eight or nine or ten figures net worth. Louis Uchitelle wrote the third of the series, "Very Rich Are Leaving the Merely Rich Behind" (November 27, 2006). To be fair, the series was double-edged and included such critical pieces on the superrich as Gretchen Morgenson's characteristically pointed and somewhat outraged "Peer Pressure: Inflating Executive Pay" (November 26, 2006) and Geraldine Fabricant's "Diller Takes the Prize for Highest Paid," explaining how Barry Diller made $295 million in 2005 (October 28, 2006).

While exploring how it is possible to make enormous salaries and be rewarded with unfathomably huge perks, there was a "gee whiz" quality about the series. More and more articles are either aimed at those who live in homes worth millions and have the means to rent summer vacation homes for six figures or those who fantasize about such a lifestyle. Another example in Sunday's *Travel* section was Jane Perlez's discussion of a hotel in Siem Reap—the Amansara—which costs, with service charge and tax, more than $925 a night with breakfast and either lunch or dinner included (July 10, 2005). This may be fine for R. W. Apple's expense account, but what percentage of readers can afford this or would elect to spend that much money in a place where luxury rooms can be had—as I know from my own experience—for a fraction of the cost?

I find more than a touch of economic condescension and economic voyeurism in articles such as Ralph Gardner Jr.'s "Bypass that Pesky Board" in the *House and Home* Section of March 17, 2005. The article discusses mansions in the 14,000- to 20,000-square-foot range that cost between $14 and $20 million (and that often is before renovation). We are told, "Buyers in the mansion market tend to be younger families in their 30s and 40s who have made a substantial amount of money at an early age and do not want to leave Manhattan for the suburbs." But we might ask how many readers are in the category where such real estate purchases are possible? Are we to assume that the *Times* believes that a large number of its readers are voyeuristically obsessed with superrich? Is this, I wonder, true?

In an annual rite, the *Times* focuses on expensive summer rentals in the Hamptons. For example, Lisa Kalis's "Going to Greater Length" in the *Escapes* section of April 1, 2006, informed readers about Hampton summer rentals in the $100,000 to $300,000 range, weekly rentals in Martha's Vineyard for $75,000, and other extravagant summer rentals beyond the means of most of us, although to be fair there is some discussion of more modest summer rentals. Yet even when discussing the low-price alternatives in the Hamptons in the form of Hampton Bay, Ms. Kalis cannot resist mentioning a rental for $80,000 and a more modest one for $35,000. Lest we think only New Yorkers pay lavish prices, we are told about a lower-priced alternative in the Outer Banks in North Carolina where a house rents for a mere $16,000 per week. One could imagine an article that kept in mind those whose family incomes are in the $75,000 to $100,000 range as well as those who might make considerably less.

Although during the worst of the 2008–2009 recession I thought I noticed some abatement in the penchant to describe excess, there was still Jennifer Kingston's "The Six-Figure Fish Tank Catches On," which with pictures sprawled across three pages of the August 19, 2010, *Home* section would take its place among legendary *Timeslite* in terms of economic voyeurism and triviality.

The Wednesday *Dining* section often reviews the restaurants patronized by the rich and famous or Wall Street managers or those in corporate or political America who eat on expense accounts. Yes, there is a second review for the rest of us entitled "$25 and Under," although the location of these places often is in out-of-the-way neighborhoods in Queens and Brooklyn where visitors and, from what I gather from friends, most Manhattan residents rarely visit. But one can imagine more stress on restaurants for those whose incomes are less than $500,000. We, too, take vacations and eat out.

Particularly disappointing is the social voyeurism in the *Arts* section, where the doings of Britney Spears, Paris Hilton, and Nicole Richie are given tabloid attention. "Arts, Briefly" at times has become an expanded version of the departed and hardly lamented "Boldface Names" gossip column. On February 19, 2007, three of "Arts, Briefly"'s one-paragraph articles—the length of all its articles—dealt with alcoholic and/or sociopathic behavior by, respectively, three troubled pop figures—Spears, Richie, and Foxy Brown—as if there were hardly any real art news to report; the sophomoric titles of the pieces were "Arrested Development (I) and "Arrested Development (II)" to stress that both Richie (DUI) and Brown (abusive behavior in a beauty supply shop) were arrested.

Nor was February 19, 2007, a fluke. The very next day in "Arts, Briefly", one of the stories was about the DUI arrest of the actor Ray Liotta, who is hardly a household word. And on February 21, 2007, we have in "Arts, Briefly" another one-paragraph story about Spears—"Britney Spears in Rehab"—and one about a judge's ruling on how O. J. Simpson's earnings will be divided to pay the civil judgment against him for the slaying of Ron Goldman. Isn't it Keller's job to supervise whomever is editing this column and remind that person what an *Arts* column is?

More recently, the focus of "Arts, Briefly" seems to be more on serious art and sometimes media news and less on tabloid figures such as Spears and Hilton. For example, in the first months of 2010, typical stories were on Lorin Stein being named editor of *The Paris Review* (March 5, 2010) or *American Idol* getting better ratings than the Olympics on NBC (February 25, 2010).

The quintessence of economic voyeurism—that is, the focus on lifestyles of the rich and famous—may be the Sunday "*T*" sections, where the ratio of substance to ads is very low. Indeed, these sections—which I discuss in the next chapter—contain hardly any substantive articles.

VII. The *Times* goes Pomo (Postmodern): Usher, Jay-Z, and the *Times*'s Giant Step Into Pop Culture—and Trash Culture

It is an often-repeated canard that the *Times* ignored cultural criticism until recent decades. Yet cultural criticism is an area in which the *Times* has excelled for decades. Brooks Atkinson and before him George S.

Kaufman were prestigious drama critics who could make or break plays, and the influence of reviews by Harold Schonberg and Howard Taubman on music and Bosley Crowther on film extended far beyond the *Times's* readership. John Martin wrote dance criticism from 1927 to 1962, and Anna Kissellgoff was the chief dance critic for decades. The *Times* had great architecture writing from Herbert Muschamp and Paul Goldberger. Because there were fewer major outlets for serious critics, these aforementioned figures shaped American culture even more than is possible for one critic to do today.

Under Turner Catledge in 1962 and during Orvil Dryfoos's short tenure as publisher (he served less than two years as publisher before a premature death from a heart condition), the *Times* appointed its first cultural news editor and began to consolidate the arts under a single department to replace the balkanization of the arts in enclaves. The coverage of the arts also gradually expanded; Arthur Gelb covered nightclub figures, off Broadway, and other aspects of the downtown cultural scene as early as the late 1950s. Indeed, Gelb may have done more than anyone else to expand the horizons of the *Times* cultural coverage and to understand the potential of the so-called New Journalism for *Times* reviews.

With some exceptions, the culture covered by the *Times* was primarily high culture—and certainly Manhattan culture—unless a particular figure or group became a social curiosity on the order of Elvis or the Beatles. In fact, it seems as if every executive editor of the *Times* at the outset of assuming leadership articulates a greater commitment than his or her predecessor to cultural coverage in the daily editions, and most if not all live up to that commitment to an extent.

Cultural criticism is a strong point of the contemporary *Times*, but the definition of culture has evolved. No longer does the *Times* have one ideal reader in mind. As Keller said to me, "In 2004 . . . we reorganized the culture department and in the process did a lot of hiring. Particularly at that point we felt like we were strong on critics but we needed more reporting in the culture department and we hired a bunch of reporters and we have not cut back on that" (May 20, 2010).

Under Keller and his cultural editor—most notably Sam Sifton, cultural editor from 2005 to 2009, but also in 2010 his successor, Jonathan Landman, who was acting cultural editor from 2004 to 2005—the *Arts* section has became larger and more inclusive. The *Arts* sections now contain more substantive articles on a wide range of subjects and these articles often show a greater awareness of world cultural issues, such as the plans to redesign Les Halles in Paris (Nicolai Ouroussoff, "Rich Menus to Choose From, but What Will Fill the 'Belly of Paris'?'" January 6, 2005). Keller made clear to me that he knew that this willingness to allow latitude for individual voices and independent section and deputy section editors has occasionally given cultural reviews a narcissistic bent:

> Writing on culture should aim to achieve the same straddle that we expect stories in other sections of the paper to achieve—meaning it ought to be authoritative enough that someone who knows the subject well will respect it, but accessible enough that someone who doesn't know as much about the subject can take something significant away from it too. That's why it is not good when critics get too knowing in their writing and when they assume a high level of specialized knowledge that tends to exclude readers who would've otherwise been interested in the subject. Then the writing becomes self-indulgent and sometimes self-dramatizing. (October 11, 2004)

That the 2004–2010 *Times* targeted different audiences in terms of ethnicity, age, and income and was aware of multiple cultural enclaves was both a business decision and a philosophic recognition of audience diversity. Sifton had a strong interest in popular culture, but even before he stepped down in the later months of 2009, the *Times* had backed off from trying to keep up with every development in the popular music industry.

By giving hip-hop serious coverage on the *Arts* pages, the *Times* confers on that aspect of popular culture legitimacy and stature for those in its readership who might otherwise look down on hip-hop. At the same time covering such a subject is an effort to make the *Times* appealing to a younger audience.

In 2004–2005, Landman was brought in to put daily and Sunday cultural coverage under one roof and to bring consistency to the conception of culture informing both the daily and *Sunday Times*. The *Sunday Times* was slower than the daily *Times* in abandoning elitism and becoming more inclusive. Perhaps Landman leans a bit more toward theater, dance, and serious cinema than to popular culture.

One place the *Times* has had great cultural influence is in the shaping of language, especially but not exclusively through the late

William Safire's long-running column "On Language," but also in its editorial policies. (After he died, "On Language" was written by different writers, but Ben Zimmer took over on March 21, 2010, until the column was dropped in 2011 by the new *Sunday Magazone* editor.) Among other back-of-the-book sections, the cultural pages of the *Times* brought "deconstruct" and "deconstruction" from the rarified air of the academy into popular speech and changed the scholarly meaning of deconstruction from questioning the concept of any one unified monolithic interpretive perspective to analyzing something and the verb "to deconstruct" into "to analyze."

In the early months of 2005, at a time when the *Times* was already feeling the pinch of financial exigency (although nothing like the crisis in 2008–2009), the *Times* hired more cultural reporters to supplement traditional and popular cultural criticism and news. This focus on cultural reporting has provided the Sunday *Arts & Leisure* section with such informative pieces as one on the careers of those who graduated from the Julliard School some years ago and another on behind-the-scenes customs of classical orchestras.

Let us examine the contemporary *Times* coverage of cultural events. In Friday's *Weekend* Michael Kimmelman, Roberta Smith, Karen Rosenberg, and Holland Cotter provide superb coverage of the visual arts, and until 2008, so did Grace Glueck.

The *Times*'s obituaries of important cultural figures are among the most important aspects of its cultural coverage. No better example can be cited than Michael Kimmelman's May 2008 full-page overview of painter Robert Rauschenberg's career—with a few color illustrations (supplemented by an online slide show)—which began on page 1 and which was comprehensive and comprehensible to the lay reader without sacrificing erudition, sophistication, and subtlety.

The pages in *Weekend* called "The Listings," with their brief abstracts of prior cultural reviews, not only recall the substance of the original reviews but also speak well for the range of cultural coverage. Knowledgeable critics cover dance, as they have for decades. Appointed in 2004 as successor to the brilliant Herbert Muschamp, Nicolai Ouroussoff is especially knowledgeable about recent architecture and goes further afield geographically than Muschamp, writing, for example, about architecture in Abu Dhabi ("A Vision in the Desert," February 1, 2007).

Chief theater critic since 1996, Ben Brantley is solid, responsible, and thoughtful without being dazzling or flamboyant. He has made a point of being skeptical about star worship. Writing with wit and verve, cultural critic Stephen Holden covers cabaret, popular music, and film. For example, on June 16, 2006, he had a nice piece on how singers in current musicals are better than the songs ("Grand Broadway Voices, Yours for a Song"). Holden also has been doing more film criticism, as in a December 4, 2009, review of *Everybody's Fine* entitled "De Niro Packs His Suitcase, Heading to Geezer Territory." Ben Sisario writes about pop music, while Nate Chinen does jazz with empathy and range, roaming from Dave Brubek, Lee Konitz, and Bucky Pizzarelli to more recent figures, although his taste is for the established figures.

The controversial Alessandra Stanley writes about TV, often with more fluff than flair, as in her April 29, 2008, page 1 article, "Not Speaking for Obama, Pastor Speaks for Himself, at Length": "Mr. [Jeremiah] Wright, Senator Barack Obama's former pastor, was cocky, defiant, declamatory, inflammatory and mischievous, but most of all, he was all over the place, performing a television triathlon of interview, lecture and live news conference that pushed Mr. Obama aside and placed himself front and center in the presidential election campaign." She sometimes is short on evidence and accuracy and long on sweeping generalizations. Stanley is a writer whose imagination often runs away from her facts. On July 18, 2009, she did a piece on Walter Cronkite that contained seven major errors.

In a June 16, 2004, piece, comparing David Letterman to Jay Leno, and faulting the former for fatigue and not putting forth "his best efforts on air," she herself seems to be guilty of the very thing she accuses Letterman of ("Leno vs. Letterman: A Battle of Wits With No Clear Winner"). Has Stanley become the Maureen Dowd of the *Times*'s cultural staff?

Under Keller, the *Times* has expanded its coverage of culture and perhaps continued a trend of being more elastic about what it considers culturally important. The *Times* now takes a strong interest in popular culture, in part because its editors realize that—like themselves—many of the same people who go to operas, classical concerts, and Broadway plays also watch *Madmen, Curb Your Enthusiasm, The Sopranos,* and *Sex and the City*—and perhaps have children who go to rock and hip-hop concerts. The *Times* has redefined "culture" to include every aspect of modern and postmodern popular culture—from visual arts and video arts (even porn) to ethnic music, including not only hip-hop but also Peruvian, Irish, and Turkish-Jewish folk music. It is trying to be more hip and striving to speak a younger urban and exurban audience.

VIII. The *Times* and Sexuality

In its role of daily magazine catering not just to serious readers of hard news but also to the kind of audiences the weekly news magazines reach, the *Times* seems to be trying to attract a younger audience by being hip and a tad risqué, even while giving its older readers a little libidinous excitement. Taking sex out of the closet is a welcome development and the *Times* should be applauded for helping to do so. But on occasion, the *Times*—under the guise of informing—is merely providing erotic titillation that plays to voyeuristic impulses that have many other outlets other than the daily newspaper. Some of the former executive editors and managing editors whom I interviewed between 2004 and 2007 wondered if the *Times* had lost its moorings and its taste.

The *Times* has extended its interest in popular culture to what I call "trash culture." Beginning in 2004, the *Times* tried to be hip and clearly was trying to get in tune with cutting-edge cultural trends, especially those of the younger segment of its audience (or at least the urban and exurban part). Or, as John Darnton, former cultural editor, said to me: "I think the culture report is now trying to consciously go down-market" (June 20, 2005). This trend to sexualize the *Times*, which began in summer and fall 2004 and peaked in 2005–2006, marked a departure from prior standards of *Times* taste and propriety.

Let me give some examples of *Timestrash,* by which I mean material presented in the guise of informing its readers, but also catering to the erotic interests of a segment of its audience. One of the most prominent pieces screaming the new direction the *Times* was taking toward sexuality is the lead story in the August 29, 2004, *SundayStyles* by Susan Dominus: "What Women Want to Watch" with the subheading "In Porn, the Acting is Hideous; the Décor, Worse. Can Playgirl TV Do Better?" The piece discusses a new video-on-demand service entitled Playgirl TV providing "sexually provocative material that women—and perhaps some gay men—would enjoy."

Robert Lanham's article in *SundayStyles* entitled "Wearing Nothing but Attitude" is about young adults in their twenties participating in a subindustry called "alt.porn" which "attempts to embellish pornography with a hip version by offering soft- to hard-core erotica" (May 1, 2005). The article was supposedly an investigation into the business of launching a porn site, but soon Lanham is writing about "XXX acts—often with multiple partners."

When the *Times* moved into areas of questionable taste and titillation for its own sake, one characteristic technique was the inclusion of quotes from supposed authorities. Thus Lanham quotes Gavin McInnes, the editor of *Vice*, "a trendsetting publication that has published pornography reviews." Typical of these sexually provocative feature articles, the material isn't organized particularly well and wanders around its subject at much greater length than necessary.

At times in the period from 2004 to 2008, it seemed that writing about sex in a provocative way helped a reporter get published, particularly in the *Arts* section. For example, a story in the *Arts* section on August 24, 2004, entitled "Sex, Sex, Sex: Up Front in Bookstores Near You" discusses forthcoming books featuring sex. By Edward Wyatt, this story of considerable length discusses the sexual memoir of a teenage girl (*100 Strokes of the Brush Before Bed*) who celebrates her sixteenth birthday by "having sex with five men at once" and another book entitled *The Surrender*, which is "a former ballet dancer's account of her spiritual awakening through anal sex." The article also discusses *How to Have a XXX Sex Life*, "by the Vivid girls, stars of pornographic films"; a novel by Pamela Anderson published with a nude pinup of her inside; *How to Make Love Like a Porn Star: A Cautionary Tale* by Jenna Jameson, described in Wyatt's words as "probably the most successful woman ever in the adult-film industry"; and *XXX: 30 Porn-Star Portraits*—the latter introduced by Gore Vidal. Also mentioned is the sensational 2002 memoir, *The Sexual Life of Catherine M.*—on the *Times* best-seller list for nine weeks—in which the French art critic Catherine Millet discussed her various orgies.

Jennifer Senior's article, "Everything a Happily Married Bible Belt Woman Always Wanted to Know About Sex and Was Afraid to Ask" (July 4, 2004), was about Linda Brewer, a woman who sells sex toys in the heartland. Given that Brewer, who did sales work for the direct-sales company, Passion Parties, had already received ample coverage in the daily *Times*, and that it was hardly news that women from every social class and cultural group are consumers of sex products, this redundant article seemed just another occasion for the *Times* to mention sex toys and wave its flag as sexually hip. If there was any point other than titillating the readers, I couldn't find it.

Like the networks and especially the cable stations, the *Times* clearly believes a little sex is good for readership and does not mind if younger readers are exposed. But although we are in an era of sexual frankness that I believe is much healthier than the 1950s attitude toward sex in which I grew up, and although far more explicit sex is accessible on cable networks such as *Showtime* and *HBO*, to say nothing of the *Playboy* channel, the *Times* stories often are more titillating and voyeuristic than they need be.

Nor is the *Arts* section immune from the borderline where *Timeslite* crosses into *Timestrash*. Take Charles McGrath's rather fawning article on Gloria Vanderbilt's new novel, *Obsession: An Erotic Tale*: "At 85, a Brahmin in Blue Jeans Writes of Sex, Masks and Veggies" (June 18, 2009). Another example of inflecting the rich and famous, his background piece is puff rather than a review for a volume that he says belongs on "the sex-book shelf": "Gloria Vanderbilt's new novel, *Obsession: An Erotic Tale*, which comes out next week, may be the steamiest book ever written by an octogenarian." Taking his cue from her text, which is "written in stylized literary prose that owes something to Pauline Reage's *Story of O*," he emphasizes sexual details that raise questions about his contention that "It's erotica, not porn": "But it nevertheless uses vocabulary and describes activities of a sort that readers of the *Times* are usually shielded from. There are scenes involving dildos, whips, silken cords and golden nipple clamps, not to mention an ebony, smooth-backed Mason Pearson hairbrush purchased at Harrods."

For another example of *Timestrash* posing as cultural criticism, take Manohla Dargis's "The Narcissist and His Lover," in the August 27, 2004, *Weekend*, discussing Vincent Gallo's film *The Brown Bunny*, in which Chloe Sevigny has oral sex on screen with Mr. Gallo. In the context of an arch view of the film, Dargis works in a fair amount of titillating and provocative prose. Dargis begins as if she were going to trash the movie, but by the third sentence, she is smarmily winking with us at the sheer audacity of the film: "Which isn't to say that this artful road movie from the director, narcissist nonpareil and most excellent huckster Vincent Gallo should be avoided, especially if you like your art-house exercises tarted up with some good old-fashioned, hotel-room smut." The review is in the genre of so-called writerly texts—the New Journalism taken to another, even more self-immersed level—where the reviewer's wit and playfulness are as much the subject as the work under review.

On August 20, 2006, a piece on wild parties entitled "Looking for a Way to Keep Rome Burning" was a flamboyant example of *Timestrash;* orgiastic "debauched"—to use the word of Melena Ryzik, the author—parties in which guests appear nude and perform oral sex on one another are the subject. Writing of Amanda Lepore, "the downtown [transsexual] promoter whose regular attire is none" and the reminiscences of Justine Delaney, who "fondly recalled" that "she would often witness people having oral sex—guy on guy, girl on girl, guy on girl, you know crazy stuff," Ryzik assures us that "frank nudity is no big deal" to the current generation of club goers.

Timestrash can even be foregrounded. The featured story on the nytimes.com home page at 11 p.m. on July 7, 2009, was Matt Richtel's "Pornographic Films without All That Plot," and contained a large clothed contemplative picture of Savannah Samson, who was described as "one of the industry's biggest stars." By 7 a.m., the story's title had been changed to "Lights, Camera, Lots of Action. Forget the Script," and the story had been taken off the home page and consigned to a still prominent place as the lead story in "Media and Advertising." But, under the subhead "Lights, Camera, Action. And You Want a Script, Too?" it was on the front page of both the New York and national print edition—and continued on page 3 with the same picture.

Perhaps the most disgusting *Timestrash* appeared on September 6, 2010, in the *Arts* section, when dance critic Alastair Macauley describes—albeit unfavorably—a performance by a "heavily pregnant" naked Ann Liv Young, a so-called performance artist who urinates and defecates onstage ("This Time the Trouble Isn't Wicked Stepsisters," September 6, 2010). On the very same day, *Arts* also discussed the S&M drama *Trust* (Eric Piepenburg, "Going to Extremes to Seek Dramatic Accuracy," September 6, 2010).

The *Times* understands that sex and shock sell. It is no secret that some *Times* readers watch porn. But does the *Times* need to target the Howard Stern audience and perhaps that tiny segment interested in the outer edges of the city's more bizarre subcultures? Don't *Times* senior editors realize that many of its readers feel insulted by such garbage and that foregrounding such articles undermines its stature? Or as Pulitzer-winning correspondent and former cultural editor John Darnton said to me: "You change the feel of the publication if you do all things for all people. So why not concentrate on your strength, which is being the critical disseminator of hard news with important feature stories in there, but [avoid] all this kind of silly pop culture things about metrosexuals? . . . Why should we try to be hip? . . . When the *Times* tries that it's like an elephant in a tutu. It's ridiculous and you look ridiculous" (June 21, 2005).

IX. Writing Lapses

Under Keller's editorship, a number of writing lapses have contin-ued, including the errors in the aforementioned Stanley article about Cronkite that were so serious as to merit an entire August 1, 2009, article by Hoyt, the public editor, "How did This Happen?" Although the need to use less newsprint especially impacted prolixity by 2009, editors still fail to insist on logical, forward-moving, succinct articles with a narrative thread.

For news stories, the *Times* needs to be sure that the essential facts are reported and should not assume its readers know those facts from TV news or the Internet. What happened to the thirty-five-word lead that answers the questions who, what, when, where, and why? Often stories—especially feature stories in *ThursdayStyles, SundayStyles, Dining, House and Home*, and Sunday's *Arts & Leisure*—wander about without argument or point.

An important related issue is the publishing of stories with mis-leading headlines. If the headline writer doesn't get the point, the story needs to be rewritten. The *Times* needs to avoid a disjunction between the headlines and stories that follow and needs to be sure that its headline writer understands the point of the story. The most egregious examples of oblique or misleading headlines occur in feature stories. But incongruous and misleading headlines can be found in important news stories, especially within the evolving news on the nytimes.com website.

By the time the newspaper comes out, especially in cases where a major story has evolved during the day on nytimes.com, one would expect the headline not only to be accurate but also to stress the major point. Yet the headline of Stephen Erlanger's January 6, 2007, story, "Day After Killings, A Hamas Leader calls for a Truce," obscured a story of virtual civil war between Hamas and the PLO. For weeks prior to Erlanger's piece, stories of violence between the two parties had been headlined with various ineffectual calls for peace by the Hamas leader, prime minister Ismail Haniya, and the PLO leader and Palestine president Mahmoud Abbas. Thus, isn't the real story either (a) how both leaders have either lost control of their constituents or (b) that both leaders are saying one thing for public consumption while pri-vately encouraging violence off camera or (c) a combination of both?

An interesting example of problems in online writing was the coverage of Caroline Kennedy's aborted quest—punctuated by her sudden withdrawal from consideration to be Governor David Paterson's appointee after Hillary Clinton was confirmed as secretary of state—to be named senator of New York. According to public editor Clark Hoyt in a February 14, 2009, piece entitled "A Balancing Act on the Web," "a hastily published article on the *Times*'s website highlighted a fear in newsrooms that the Internet, with its emphasis on minute-to-minute competition, is undermining the values of print journalism, which put a premium on accuracy, tone and context." He continued, "The offending article contained an anonymous political attack on Caroline Kennedy and broadcast vague allegations—highly exaggerated, it turned out—that she had nanny and tax problems."

The greater emphasis on the human dimension of news—the story of real individuals rather than abstract discussions of policy—can be a plus. We see this perhaps most emphatically in the *Metro* section in Peter Applebome's "Our Towns" columns. And under the then executive editor Howell Raines the *Times* did a magnificent job profiling 9/11 victims. Because it is impossible to replicate the entirety of an event and the way every participant is affected by it and to imagine the implications and aftershocks, it follows that at times focusing on the implications for an individual or family helps center a story. But at times the focus on the human drama—an opening anecdote about how a cataclysmic natural disaster or an international event touches a particular individual or family—is to the detriment of providing the essential story that first answers the traditional crucial news questions of who, what, when, where, and why.

Sometimes in Keller's *Times,* imaginative writing poses as reporting. Particularly when not covering hard news, the *Times*'s prose has become more subjective and more attitudinal. Let me give an example: Writing of Katie Couric on NBC's *Today,* which had recently changed producers, Alessandra Stanley in her "TV Watch" column writes, "[H]er image has grown downright scary: America's girl next door has morphed into the mercurial diva down the hall. At the very sound of her peremptory voice and clickety heels, people dart behind doors and douse the lights. Or at least change the channel. . . . Panic has set in at Rockefeller Center" ("Today's Seeks Yesterday's Glory," April 25, 2005). Stanley attributed some of this transformation to a recent change in producers, but she provides no real evidence to support her hyperbolic claims. Is this an example of the *Times* allowing its reporters to write as chic insiders, while exaggerating and distorting to amuse a hip segment of its audience?

Is the *Times* allowing its reporters to exaggerate and distort just to amuse its audience—and perhaps encouraging its writers to exhibit a flair for imaginative writing? To be sure creativity is part of journalism, particularly when writing features, but if a writer sacrifices accuracy and judgment for the sake of a self-satisfying posture, are we still in the world of newspaper journalism?

X. Corrections

The *Times*'s policy on errors is clear:

> As journalists we treat our readers, viewers, listeners and online users as fairly and openly as possible. Whatever the medium, we tell our audiences the complete, unvarnished truth as best we can learn it. We correct our errors explicitly as soon as we become aware of them. We do not wait for someone to request a correction. We publish corrections in a prominent and consistent location or broadcast time slot. ("Our Duty to Our Audience," *The New York Times Company Journalism Ethics Policy*, online)

To its credit, every day the *Times,* in section A under "Corrections: For the Record," prints corrections, large and small. If its columnists make errors they now are expected to correct them at the end of a subsequent column. As of August 2010, the corrections were listed by section rather than in descending order of importance. One might argue that minor corrections need to be separated from major ones. Thus, when former tennis player Martin Jaite was called a Chilean rather than an Argentine or a caption on vote-counting in Indiana for the 2008 democratic primary misidentifies a city in Lake County as Hammond rather than Crown Point, it is nice to have a "correction" (May 14, 2008). But when President Bush cited in egregiously mistranslated form remarks by Iranian officials speaking about their nuclear program in Farsi, we need a separate correction category, which needs to be highlighted, whether it be called "For the Record" or something else, and perhaps this needs to be in larger print.

The exacerbated race to get scoops about government incompetence and to discover the most sensational facts of a "discovery" or investigative story has caused serious problems. Reporters on occasion strain to find confirming facts as a way of making one's name as an investigative reporter; nor should we ignore the desire of competitive and ambitious reporters to outperform their colleagues at the *Times* and elsewhere as well as to please demanding editors and thus get promotions and better assignments. Furthermore, not only do senior editors want to outdo other news sources, but also *Times* journalists, editors, and publishers always cast a competitive eye on possible Pulitzers and other major awards.

The rush to provide instant analysis and background on unfolding stories—at times to be "politically correct"—also contributes to factual errors and distorted and hyperbolic perceptions. Overwrought stories such as that of rape and pillage in the aftermath of the August 2005 Hurricane Katrina in New Orleans or the unsubstantiated stories about Duke Lacrosse players raping a black exotic dancer required serious and embarrassing corrections. As Jonathan Landman said to me of the latter story "As a reader, I think our coverage was poor, very poor" (June 9, 2010).

Other sources of errors come from the desire to please and even manipulate officialdom as a means of getting further inside information, even as officialdom is doing the same thing to reporters to control the outflow of news in their favor. We know that this mutual process between reporter and government affected Judith Miller's reporting of WMDs. In *Game Change*, a gossipy book about the 2008 campaign, John Heilemann and Mark Halperin claim Maureen Dowd allowed David Geffen some editorial control over a column in exchange for an exclusive interview in which Geffen, a former Clinton supporter, said: "Everybody in politics lies, but they do it with such ease, it's troubling." Dowd denies the claim (Hoyt, "Secondhand Sources," Jan. 30, 2010).

Major errors can result from failure to check facts or overconfidence in star reporters or failure to examine the motives of sources. More editorial checking is required to avoid the kind of fiasco Calame described in his March 26, 2006, column in which he discusses a March 11, 2006, front-page *Times* article that profiled a man who was supposedly the hooded Abu Ghraib prisoner in a widely circulated picture, only for the *Times* to discover later the wrong man was the focus of the article (Calame, "The Wrong Man Deception, Mistaken Identity and Journalistic Lapses"). A peek at its own archives would have spared the *Times* this egregious error. Although the *Times* reported on the challenge to its story's accuracy on March 14, it was not until March 18, 2006, that it printed a retraction.

Major "lapses of fairness, balance, or perspective"—terms taken from the *Times* stylebook—are corrected by infrequent editor's notes, but at one point when I counted, I found that for every eighty or so "corrections," there has been one editor's note.

A front-page article on April 25, 2006, "One Day, That Economy Ticket May Buy You a Place to Stand," turned out to be fictional because the freelance reporter, Christopher Elliott, did not do his homework and the editors did not check up on him. The article was accompanied by an illustration of an airplane passenger leaning back against a vertical board instead of sitting. Although it is possible such an idea had been raised a few years ago, the claim that Airbus had pitched such an idea to Asian airlines was false, and Elliott had not done the digging and crosschecking required by a good reporter. His claim that the standing place would allow Airbus to fit 853 passengers was contradicted by an article four weeks earlier (edited by Phyllis Messenger, the same person who failed to edit Elliott's piece properly) that stated the plane actually had 853 seats. Certainly such a fiasco—which was not corrected for a week—raises questions about competence, authority, and gatekeeping. I might add that such a *Timeslite* story—in my opinion, one that had no place on page 1 even if it were true—belonged on the *Business* pages. Interestingly, associate managing editor Chuck Strum justified his lack of editorial intervention by saying, "The news desk treated this piece as a light feature. . . . It was a thin piece and seemed harmless enough" (Byron Calame, "Landing on Page 1 With Hardly a Wary Eye," May 21, 2006).

The article about standing airline passengers reveals that editors also sleep. And so do proofreaders. An example would be in the usually excellent Friday *Weekend Arts* where, on November 10, 2006, the caption under a large color picture of Velásquez's "Baltasar Carlos on Horseback (1634–1635)" was titled "Old Woman Cooking Eggs (1618)," the title of a color picture without caption that also was on the same page. Confusing the reader even further, the correction on November 11, 2006, did not include the fact that "Baltasar Carlos on Horseback" was not even mentioned in the article about Velásquez by Michael Kimmelman. On the prior day—November 9, 2006—there was a numerical error in the vote tally for a congressional election; both Iowa congressman Jim Leach and the man who defeated him had, according to the story, exactly the same number of votes. The *Times* could do better with typographical errors—and misuse of words—although it is impossible to eliminate them when printing one million words a week.

One expects accuracy from reporters, transparency about how stories are gathered, as little anonymous sourcing as possible—because anonymous sourcing leads to errors and distortions due to the source's self-interest and agenda—and simple fact checking from reporters and editors. But sometimes the *Times* corrects a story without telling its readers a prior story was false or woefully incomplete. Okrent raised the question of inadequate corrections in terms of a procedure journalists call a "rowback"—which he defines as "a story that attempts to correct a previous story without indicating that the prior story had been in error or without taking responsibility for the error"—and finds the *Times* wanting on a few occasions ("Setting the Record Straight—But Who Can Find the Record?" March 14, 2004). This was certainly the case in early 2008 when the *Times* simply dropped discussing McCain's implied affair with a lobbyist, after Keller and Abramson defended the controversial story in a "Talk to the Newsroom" piece on February 21, 2008.

XI. Conclusion: Evaluation of Keller

During his executive editorship, Keller has enjoyed the confidence and respect of his senior staff, who respect his honesty and intelligence. He is not a micro-manager and is by temperament a conflict-avoider. Yet, as I have been discussing and continue to discuss, he also has presided over some major errors in judgment as well as some dubious decisions in taste. Keller often tries to placate the staff and the *Times*'s critics. He is willing to acknowledge his mistakes but when he does so it is on narrow grounds. Often his explanations are balanced to the point of ambiguity and fuzziness. He responds with the minimum information necessary, whether it is explaining a reduction in the size of the paper and a cut in the news coverage or why photos can be misleading.

Throughout this book, I have been critiquing the contemporary *Times* and discussing Keller's problems and mistakes, but I do want to say here that Keller often has been a bold and courageous editor in an environment far more complex than that in which his predecessors worked. Far more than previous executive editors, he is under consistent scrutiny from outside and called on to make public statements and defend what he has decided. Keller operates in a universe far different from that of Rosenthal and Frankel. In the blogosphere and even on cable TV, the *Times* is put under a kind of scrutiny that earlier editors did not experience. Neither Rosenthal nor Frankel nor Lelyveld had a public editor or even a standards editor looking over their shoulders. They didn't need to go online and have a "Talk to the Newsroom" Q&A with readers.

The *Times* claims a complete separation between news and editorials and insists that the editorial page and news editors are not in regular consultation. The *Times* also claims a wall exists between the business management, on one side, and both news and editorials on the other. But as I mentioned, Arthur Sulzberger, Jr. meets weekly with the executive editor, the editorial page editor, and the current president and general manager, Scott H. Heekin-Canedy. Andrew Rosenthal, the current editorial page editor, was quite candid with me that Sulzberger has the authority to make editorial policy if he so wishes: "He reads the page. We talk about it. I report to him. He's my boss" (April 13, 2007).

Keller's laissez-faire approach to his editors allows great latitude in taste as well as excessively long feature articles that often lack substance. He has sent out a memo trying to curtail excessive length, but his and my—and some of his predecessors'—ideas of excessive are quite different. Landman observed to me, "Prolixity is an enemy that every executive editor since I've been here has attacked at one time or another. And I know, for myself, in the departments that I've run, that's a beast you want to slay. . . . [When I was editor of the *Metro* section] we worked pretty hard to make things shorter and cleaner and concise without losing the ability to be complete and thorough. And that's always the balance" (October 9, 2006). I think much of the *Times* could be leaner, tauter, and more directed to giving readers essential information about the news. At crucial times, I find the focus blurry and some of the investigative stories wordy, repetitious, and without discipline. As sometimes happens already, perhaps some of the backup evidence could be posted on the web page.

Reading Keller's *Times*, it is sometimes difficult to separate the forest from the trees and may lead the reader to wonder whether that is because the editors can't. For example, with all the articles devoted to the 2006 election, I felt, until the final two or three days, that the paper was missing articles that gave an overview of what was happening; I missed the kind of analyses I found in *The Economist* or, formerly, some of the late R. W. Apple's best synthesizing stories. The November 5, 2006, *Week in Review* before the election included some fine analyses, but on the whole I thought what the paper needed from September 1, 2006, on was one synthesizing column, perhaps entitled "The Election." Such a column appearing each day in the newspaper would have pulled together the often impressively focused coverage. Perhaps senior correspondents could have written the column three times a week. Certainly, Adam Nagourney, who filed some good campaign stories, could have been one, and maybe Carl Hulse could have been another. Where, as Raines would have said in one of his favorite metaphors, was the "theme in the pudding" of the election coverage? The coverage of the 2008 presidential campaign was better, although not without digressions and overkill; the primary campaign generated in print and online many trivial, prolix, space-filling articles, some of which were irrelevant the next day.

Even while acknowledging difficulties, Landman was eloquent in defending to me the current *Times* and seeing changed cultural and business conditions as an opportunity:

> Among the things that have changed is many more kinds of forms are possible: journalistic, literary, if you want to be grandiose. When you open things up, you loosen rules, and you stop making everything fit in the same box, then things are going to stick out. So, there's no question that sometimes, when you allow people to be more experimental, that experiments fail. And, if you don't allow a certain amount of failure in that way, nothing will change, you're not improving. So, I think, the forces that have loosened up in journalism are all to the good, that the writing is just infinitely better than it was a generation ago. The reporting is mostly better, it's more original, its tougher, more investigative. You know, not that there weren't tough, original investigative reporters, there always have been. But there's more. At the edges, people are trying stuff and it doesn't work sometimes. That's not the end of the world. . . . Within the limitations, you're willing to make mistakes up to a point. When you pass that point, and you get into Jayson Blair territory, that's unacceptable. (October 9, 2006)

Landman argues correctly that change is essential. But I argue that dumbing down the *Times*, stressing the lifestyles of the ultra rich, and letting the back-of-the-book sections include trash journalism have somewhat undermined the quality of the entire newspaper. Do Bill Keller and Arthur Sulzberger really want the Sunday *Book Review* to have a cover title with the awful pun "Hero and Heroin" for a review by the novelist Bret Easton Ellis (August 14, 2005)? Notwithstanding Keller's high-minded stance on the first amendment, the *Times*, in its necessary search for circulation and advertising revenue, may at times have strayed too far from its original mission as the best source of information in America.

Soma Golden Behr, retired assistant managing editor, would maintain the focus on gravitas without sacrificing the quest for a younger audience:

> I'm concerned about spending too much energy on . . . damn *Styles*; if I could've voted there would've been no *ThursdayStyles*. I don't think that was our option given our business situation. . . . And that bothers me because the average quality of the total goes down a tad if you produce something . . . on the edge [of quality]. I would rather produce the tough stuff; nobody's going to do it but us. In this society . . . there's so much we should be doing, and I'm concerned [about] that multi-purpose thing we're trying to be. . . . If we're doing it all and you used to expect all the time this serious stuff, and now it includes *Styles* and all those other things, then maybe it means we've diminished. (October 11, 2005)

Her comments to me are typical of those I heard during my interviews, mostly but not exclusively from older *Times* employees, and many readers of all generations would concur.

We need, finally, to ask a few pertinent (if not impertinent) questions about Keller's leadership. Has the ever-increasing focus on back of the book—and especially *Timestrash* and its cousin *Timeslite*—undermined the stature of the *Times*?

How can Keller justify the prissy decision of his senior editors (following archaic *Times* rules about so-called civil discourse) to omit the exact words that Jesse Jackson used in his anger at Obama in July 2008—"I want to cut his nuts off"—when his newspaper often has printed sexually suggestive if not salacious material? The *Times* missed reporting a crucial part of an important story. As Hoyt, disagreeing with that decision although more in agreement with *Times* absolutism about using salty language than I, observed: "Jackson is a major figure on the public stage. His comment accompanied by a vigorous slashing motion, spoke to a deep anger toward Obama and a fascinating generational schism among black leaders" ("When to Quote Those Potty Mouths," July 13, 2008).

Did Keller, with his hands-off style in direct contrast to the authoritarian Howell Raines, lose control of some of his section editors? Have business needs, as former managing editor Arthur Gelb and other former editors have suggested, undermined the *Times*'s ideals? Does skimming long, fluffy features take too much of the reader's finite reading time from the essential international, national, and cultural news? Is the *Times* undermining its coverage of the important issues of the day by presenting far too many diversionary words that dilute the product and its impact?

Keller's *Times* has produced major scoops. Most obvious is the story of domestic spying by the National Security Agency in late 2005. Perhaps more typical if not quite as important were the stories within a few days of each other in late November and early December 2006, stories that printed classified memos about Iraq strategies—one on November 8, 2006, by Stephen J. Hadley, national security advisor, for President Bush, the other from Donald Rumsfeld written November 6, 2006, two days before he resigned. These memos revealed that senior figures in the Bush administration were aware of the quagmire in Iraq (Michael R. Gordon, "Bush Adviser's Memo Cites Doubts about Iraqi Leaders," November 29, 2006; Gordon and David S. Cloud, "Rumsfeld Memo Proposed 'Major Adjustment in Iraq,'" December 3, 2006). Leaks of these memos may have come from administrative sources who wished to change policy by leaking news to the *Times*, or the leaks may have been a way that some administrative officials thought to assure the public that the administration had a grasp on reality.

My view of Keller's leadership balances strong unequivocal admiration, especially in his taking the reins from his predecessor, to a positive view with some serious reservations. When I interviewed Keller in 2004, relatively early in his days as editor, I found him a generous man who was less suspicious of the motives of other people than he might be and who wanted to run an open-door administration in which power and responsibility are delegated. In contrast to Raines, he ceded vast authority to his editors. As I spent some time these past six years—and especially in the period from 2005 to 2008—with former and current senior *Times* editors, I wondered on occasion whose hand was really at the tiller and whether Keller had the gumption to stand up to Sulzberger or to some of his own editors.

I think that historians of the *Times* will regard Keller well. Although in his early years he seemed a transitional figure, it becomes more clear now that he has successfully presided over a major change in which the website has become as much if not more the focus of attention than the daily newspaper. For all the missteps discussed in this book and for all the mistakes made in the accelerated news cycle of the Internet—including in early 2010 plagiarism by one of the business writers, Zachary Kouwe—and despite continuing criticisms directed at him that reflect the hum and buzz of the Internet's plethora of voices, Keller retains Arthur Sulzberger Jr.'s confidence. He has presided over significant staff cuts, but maintained the morale of the senior staff better than might be expected.

Perhaps aware that 2011 would be his last year, Keller began bold new initiatives. In August 2010, in the face of declining revenue in the *Sunday Magazine* and "*T*," Keller replaced Gerald Marzorati with a new *Sunday Magazine* editor, Hugo Lindgren, to oversee those sections. He has been giving new assignments to long time senior editors such as Jonathan Landman (cultural editor) and Richard Berke (national editor) and has reconfigured the masthead. According to Keller, "I've long subscribed to the principle, if it ain't broke, fix it anyway. . . . Sometimes the best way to keep people fresh and excited is to move them when they're at the top of their game" (cited in Richard Perez-Pena, February 19, 2010). Jonathan Landman and Richard Berke no longer hold the title of assistant managing editor. In early January 2010, Trish Hall joined the masthead as assistant managing editor and her specialty is features. She then became op-ed editor a year later. As of August 2011, prior to Jill Abramson's promotions to executive editor and Dean Baquet's to managing editor, Baquet, Tom Bodkin, Susan Edgerley, Glenn Kramon, Gerald Marzorati, Michael McNally, and Jim Roberts were assistant managing editors, while Abramson and Geddes were managing editors, and William E. Schmidt was deputy managing editor. On March 6, 2011, Lindgren introduced a reinvented *Sunday Magazine*. Marzorati has a somewhat vague portfolio, which might be called "special projects."

My guess was that the now sixty-two-year-old Keller would not be executive editor much beyond 2011, and the appointment of his successor has proven me correct. In the current rapidly evolving and cost-cutting environment, it is doubtful that any executive editor will serve more than a decade, to say nothing of the seventeen years served at the *Washington Post* by the retiring Leonard Downie Jr. or the *Times*'s own Turner Catledge (1951–1968). Indeed, a decade has been about the limit since Catledge, unless one includes Abe Rosenthal's years as managing editor (1970–1979), when he was often de facto executive editor, his official title from 1977 to 1988.

I regarded as a telling sign that Abramson was the leading contender when in 2010 she stepped down for six months from her managing editorship to focus on digital operations and strategy. The other managing editor, John Geddes, whose focus is news operations, has been less involved with the direct publication of the paper and more with production, budgeting, and staffing. His peers did not regard him as a serious candidate for executive editor. Nor was I surprised that Dean Baquet would succeed Abramson as managing editor.

After stints as managing editor and then editor-in-chief of the *Los Angeles Times*, Baquet returned to the *Times* in 2007 as chief of the Washington bureau and has been on the masthead as assistant managing editor. A former *New York Times* national editor, Baquet edited the largest American paper ever edited by an African American. He was interviewed for executive editor after Raines's banishment. Baquet, foreign editor Susan Chira, and business editor Lawrence Ingrassia each served in 2010 as acting managing editor for two months, and that probably meant that all three were possibilities for managing editor, depending on who became the next executive editor.

Editorial page editor Rosenthal, with his strong people skills and holding a position that both Frankel and Raines had held, must have been considered a possibilty for both positions. Landman, although he is no longer on the masthead, might have been a contender for managing editor and maybe a long shot for executive editor. Because he is approaching his mid-sixties, Schmidt, who for a short term edited the *International Herald Tribune* before it became the global edition of the *Times* under Martin Gottlieb, was probably not a candidate for the managing editor position.

Succeeding Keller, Abramson will be presiding over a newspaper and digital site that has been drastically reshaped in the last decade, especially from 2003 to 2011, the period of Keller's executive editorship.

8

Dramatic Changes in Sunday's Magazines

Competing for Attention Among Myriad Reading and Leisure Choices

As we seek out new readers across the country and around the globe (via the Web), I suspect we'll be doing a lot more things that haven't been done before.

—Gerald Marzorati, "Talk to the Newsroom,"
July 27, 2005

Our *Sunday Magazine* audience is basically people who are going to be okay with going to foreign movies or newfangled operas or experimental theatre. So I can edit for those people. I'm not going to do a Tom Cruise cover for these people.

—Gerald Marzorati, April 18, 2005

Traditionally, the *New York Times Book Review* and the *New York Times Sunday Magazine* have been among the centerpieces of the *Times* universe. Particularly high-income and well-educated readers used to spend a considerable amount of time on Sunday and subsequent days with these sections. In the 1950s and 1960s, articles in these sections, especially the *Magazine*, were influential and widely discussed.

I shall discuss developments in the Keller era in the Sunday magazines—the *Book Review*, the *Sunday Magazine*, and the various sections on sports, travel, fashion, education, and health that accompany the *Sunday Magazine*—and do so with an appreciation of their need to reach a larger audience, a younger audience, and one that has a wider range of interests and a different idea of what Sunday morning reading means. I focus on a handful of weekly issues of these sections, issues that I believe are representative of the magazines.

Gerald Marzorati has not only been one of the seven current assistant managing editors, but also the editor of the *Sunday Magazine* and the various Sunday supplement magazines now known as *"T"* sections. In summer 2010 he stepped down after seven years as the *Sunday Magazine* editor to oversee "new initiatives." He asserted to me that the primary function of the *Sunday Magazine* is to entertain and that the magazine needs to present itself in such a way that the reader will want to spend time with it: "I believe that magazines are pleasure vehicles, entertainment vehicles if anything else, which isn't to say that you don't do serious things, but you have to do them in a way that you can't just expect people to dutifully read them" (April 18, 2005). What he means is that like other feature sections—*Home, Sunday* and *ThursdayStyles, Dining,* and *Travel*—the *Sunday Magazine* is not essential reading to keep up with news, business, or sports; it not only competes with other *Times* sections for attention, but also with other magazines to which the reader might subscribe or pick up.

Marzorati is well aware that he is competing for readers' attention and that competition includes every other possible activity, from a Sunday outing with family to watching television news shows and football to getting information from and playing on the Internet. It also includes strong competition from other sections of the newspaper among an audience that spends less and less time reading the *Sunday Times*. For the magazines to survive, he needs to convince advertisers that they are still viable vehicles for selling products and to convince readers that it is worth spending their leisure time reading the magazines.

If my own informal survey is any indication, the *New York Times Book Review* and the *Sunday Magazine* are read far less than they used to be—and statistics bear out that the *Sunday Times*, like all Sunday papers, is read less than it once was—in part because potential readers have so many other reading and informational alternatives and in part because they have more appealing Sunday leisure choices. With the *Times* becoming more and more a daily magazine, it is not surprising to read on Marzorati's online Q&A with readers on July 25, 2006: "[I]t would not surprise me at all in the coming years if there are more *Times* magazines, with one or more of them distributed during the week."

I. The *Book Review* Under Sam Tanenhaus

The *New York Times Book Review* is far less important than it once was. Decades ago the *New York Review of Books* challenged the stature of the *New York Times Book Review* as the preeminent cultural arbitrator, and even though its circulation is a fraction of that of the *Times* (recently in the neighborhood of 131,000), it occupies a preeminent place among intellectuals. In subsequent decades, other newspapers and media—*Wall Street Journal, Washington Post, Los Angeles Times, Newsweek*—began to take book reviewing more seriously, and readers responded to their reviews. In recent years, the Internet, including Amazon's democratic site, where anyone can weigh in with an opinion, has added other voices to the jury that judges the importance of books. What has resulted is that the *Book Review*—notwithstanding efforts to reinvent itself—has become something of a lightweight journalistic publication that is read much more casually than it once was. Often the supposed review articles say more about the reviewer than the book.

Where the *Book Review* still excels is in bringing its readers' attention to more recent writers; although many of these are covered in the daily reviews, the *Book Review* has traditionally had a larger readership. Yet, although reviews in the current *Book Review* call attention to the existence of a book, they often fail to tell us enough of what that book is about. Subjective writing that reviews a work without telling the reader what the work is about and uses language as a self-dramatizing gesture often undermines the reader's confidence in the objectivity of the review.

Since 2004, when Sam Tanenhous took over the editorship of the *Book Review*, book reviews in the daily *Times* by Michito Kakutani, Janet Maslin, Will Grimes, and, on occasion, specialists, have often been more substantive, knowledgeable, and committed not only to discussing the book in depth, but in its historical and cultural contexts.

Like his predecessor Howell Raines, Keller felt that the book review needed a younger and less intellectual readership and that it should put more emphasis on middlebrow books. Keller wanted the *Book Review* to cover more nonfiction and more commercially successful books, including books by and about celebrities, whether they were well written or not. He believed that under Charles McGrath the *Book Review* had become predictable and dull and contained too many reviews of new fiction. " 'After all,' says Keller, 'somebody's got to tell you what book to choose at the airport' " (see Hammond and Heltzel, 2004).

Not surprisingly, Sam Tanenhaus's editorial practices take into account Keller's views. Tanenhaus, the editor since April 2004, was selected from a competition that included a diagnostic essay on how the section should change. Keller's charge to Tanenhaus included redesigning the *Book Review,* and that included jazzing up the graphics and visual presentation as part of the effort to give the book review wider appeal. He also was expected to put a greater emphasis on widely read middlebrow books.

Seeking a younger, larger, and less intellectual audience, Tanenhaus in his early years as editor selected reviewers whom he thought many of his readers would know. He seemed to encourage the kind of reviews that are really points of departure for the reviewers' occasional essays rather than serious engagement with the books under review. Perhaps because Tanenhaus publishes shorter pieces than the *Sunday Magazine* and generally accepts most of what he gets from those whom he asks to review, and because his choice of reviewers is often odd, the *Book Review* does not also produce the quality articles we might hope for, although, to be fair, it has been improving. Now, more often than in his earlier years, one finds more substantive reviews by qualified reviewers.

Imaginative coupling of reviewer and book subject may be justified when writing about popular culture, but shouldn't—for example— a specialist review a book about Indian culture in the Age of the Moguls? Tanenhaus seems more reluctant than his predecessors to invite academics who might be able to put works in their intellectual and cultural contexts, preferring instead a circle of journalists whose skills lie elsewhere. This stems from Tanenhaus's skepticism about specialized learning and intellectual authority and perhaps indicates the deep gulf between the academy and some of the journalists who write about literature. From my April 2005 interview, I got the impression that Tanenhaus seems to believe that most academics can't write or synthesize but rather burrow deeply, as if they were moles leaving piles of (erudite) dirt besides their holes.

For an example of problematic reviewing in Tanenhaus's early days, let us look at the April 17, 2005, *Book Review* that begins with David Gates's cover review of *The Outlaw Book of American Literature* edited by Neil Ortenberg, Barney Rosset, and Alan Kaufman. A *Newsweek* editor and—according to the editor's introduction—someone who writes novels thumbing his nose at "polite society," Gates drops lots of names in his review, but really doesn't have much of an argument or much of a sense of the American literary tradition. In the past, the *Times* would have turned to a major academic with impeccable credentials as an authority, or a New York public intellectual—or someone who combines both roles, like Morris Dickstein.

The same issue includes an essay entitled "Gonzo Nights," by Rich Cohen, identified as "a contributing editor for *Rolling Stone,*" whose account of a day with Hunter S. Thompson is a many times told and tedious tale of Thompson's behavior. The subheading "Guns, drugs and copious amounts of alcohol: A journalist looks at the chaotic end of Hunter S. Thompson" accurately describes the article's contents, but the piece evokes, I suspect, a giant yawn from most readers who are, like me, tired of hearing about Thompson's manic behavior.

Indeed, both the aforementioned articles reveal on the part of reviewers an underlying anger toward authority that I also felt when interviewing Tanenhaus, who seems to conceive of himself as an heir to this outlaw tradition, perhaps because he is a conservative in what he sees as the bastion of liberalism. He has written a sympathetic biography of Whittaker Chambers (1997) and *The Death of Conservatism* (2009). When in his twenties, he also wrote a now-out-of-print book entitled *Literature Unbound: A Guide for the Common Reader*, which showed that he then held conservative tastes in literature.

My first impression after Tanenahaus took over on April 12, 2004, was that the *Book Review* had on the whole been dumbed down; perhaps in its efforts to be *au courant* for a younger audience, he included soap operatic and self-indulgent books with a high gossip quotient and he sometimes chose reviewers who would take such narcissistic books seriously. In the ensuing years, I found tasteless reviews of sensationalistic books, which had the shelf life of a fruit fly. I read about acid trips with Hunter Thompson, Courtney Love's drug overdoses, Tom Sykes's and Charles Bukowski's alcoholism and resulting destructive behavior to others, Tennessee Williams's sexual high jinks and drug abuse, and Al Goldstein's self-loathing and destruction—all in one quite awful issue of November 19, 2006.

I often was puzzled by his choice of reviewers, as in the June 6, 2006, issue. Sarah Kerr's piece on Kazuo Ishiguro's new novel *Never Let Me Go* does little to place the book in the context of Ishiguro's literary achievement. Don't readers want to know about how this book resembles or departs from Ishiguro's prior work? Kerr never mentions what is distinctive about Ishiguro's work, especially his masterpiece, *The Remains of the Day*, and Kerr hardly explains how a scene in *Never Let Me Go* "calls to mind late Henry James." Is she the most qualified reviewer of this important author who, in *The Remains of the Day*, brilliantly draws on a tradition of unreliable and imperceptive narrators, while evoking the political tensions in England in the late 1930s, when England was reluctantly veering toward the world war? Barbara Ehrenreich, author of *Nickel and Dimed: On (Not) Getting By In America* (2001) is a writer whom I admire, but I would argue that the review of David Reynolds's historical and cultural study *John Brown, Abolitionist* should have been written by a well-published scholar steeped in nineteenth-century American history.

The November 19, 2006, *Book Review* provided a striking example of an issue with material of dubious value. Wearing the mantle of "The Outlaw Issue," it featured books about—as described by the graphic cover—"Bad Boys," "Mean Girls," "The Revolutionaries," "Beautiful Losers," and "Outlaws." Except for a review of Allen Ginsberg's *Collected Poetry*, by Walter Kirn, much of the issue was filled—in the guise of book reviews—with many times told tales about Bukowksi, Neal Cassidy, Courtney Love, Thompson, and other even lesser lights. Sexual gossip, alcoholism, and drug use seem to be the staples. Do *Times* readers want an essay by John Waters about his infatuation with Tennessee Williams's homosexual persona in the latter's autobiography, *Memoirs*? I found myself asking, "Where are the books and ideas?" and wondering how the *Times* could print an issue containing so much foolishness.

Let me cite another example of a book that was inadequately reviewed: Jan T. Gross's *Fear: Anti-Semitism in Poland After Auschwitz*, the lead review on July 23, 2005, should have been assigned to a Holocaust scholar—or, alternatively, to perhaps the author of a major Holocaust narrative, such as Elie Wiesel or Cynthia Ozick—rather than to David Margolick. A contributing editor at *Vanity Fair* and author of a book entitled *Beyond Glory: Joe Louis vs. Max Schmeling, and a World on the Brink*, Margolick is not an authority on the Holocaust and its aftershocks. That he misspells Jedwabne—the town in which Poles massacred 1,600 Jews in 1941—is perhaps an excusable error, but his review lacks an awareness of the history of Polish anti-Semitism or the various texts, fictional and historical, which discuss Polish complicity in the Holocaust.

Choosing which fiction books to review is not easy at a time when, beyond mass market stars like Danielle Steele, Ken Follett, and Alex Berenson, and living Nobel Prize winners like Toni Morrison and contenders like Philip Roth and the now deceased John Updike, it is not easy to decide what novels will interest readers or even what ones should be foregrounded. There is no question that publishing publicity generated by major houses as well as who knows whom among editors and reviewers play roles in who gets reviewed.

Byron Calame's December 18, 2005, column on the *Book Review* was notably generous in reporting Tanenhaus's party line about how the books to be reviewed and their reviewers are scrupulously selected. Tanenhaus claims he logs more than 6,000 books into his system and reviews 1,000. But how many books are published in the United States each year? Is his system covering all the important ones, including those by small university and specialized presses?

The *Book Review* offers—or should offer—an overview of books being published that the editors deem serious. Tanenhaus speaks about how all incoming books are first read by "previewers" who suggest four or five possible reviewers. But who are the previewers and what are their qualifications? Should they be anonymous? Are they authors themselves with prospective or current agents and prospective editors and publishers? Freelance writers? Young graduates of top English departments? Perhaps as the *Times* moves to greater transparency, the *Book Review* should let its readers know who the previewers are and how they are chosen.

Compiled from books it has reviewed, the *Book Review*'s December 4, 2005, review of the year's one hundred notable books did not include any university press books. The December 3, 2006, review of the one hundred notable books listed one university press book, Francis Fukuyama's *America at the Crossroads* (Yale), a political polemic by a neoconservative who expresses revisionist doubts about some of his former positions. For the most part, the *Book Review* ignored university press books in 2005 and 2006. Although sometimes publishing narrowly focused books (sometimes replete with complex if not arcane theoretical arguments), university presses nevertheless are an important part of intellectual life in America and the best of their books have an impact on intellectual issues, politics, history, and scientific progress.

In the aforementioned December 18, 2005, piece, Calame—the least critical and most gullible of the *Times*'s four public editors to date—gave the *Book Review* a free pass and did not test the assertions of Tanenhaus and his colleagues. I do not concur with his conclusion that "readers . . . are generally well served by the *Book Review's* screening process." Calame concludes, "My sense is that Mr. Tanenhaus and his editors genuinely care about general readers and the literary world" ("The Book Review: Who Critiques Whom—and Why," December 18, 2005).

Perhaps the senior *Book Review* people succeeded in blowing smoke in Calame's eyes. My sense from speaking to Tanenhaus—and reading the reviews over the years—is that too many of his reviewing choices often come from a circle of journalists known to him. What is clear to me is that he and his staff often miss important books, especially those by university presses, and often choose reviewers who are not particularly well-informed. Although it may seem benign to claim that, as Calame does when summarizing Tanenhaus's criteria for choosing a reviewer, "established authors have a right to be assessed by equally established reviewers," this can be an excuse for passing reviews around to a limited circle, often including people who know little about the subject.

One of the better pieces in late 2006 was staff member Rachael Donadio's December 10, 2006, discussion of Helen Vendler's role as an important critic of poetry ("The Closest Reader"), although even that piece could have been made more substantive by Donadio's discussing what is distinct about Vendler's work and how—by considering the New Critical tradition from which Vendler emerged—her formalism departs from current historical and political criticism.

On other occasions, seemingly unedited prose tends more to the narcissistic than to the kind of lucid discussion that reveals the contents of the book under review. For an example of a seemingly unedited review, take the following excerpt from a review essay about two books on competitive eating by Jay Jennings entitled "Gluttons for Reward" in the May 28, 2006, issue, which featured books about food: "Somewhere in the liminal static of my click lies the world of competitive-eating contests, which have in fact appeared on [ESPN and the Food Network] and which now have their own ruminant—in both senses of the word—Runyons, with surnames that sound like pasta (Jason Fagone) and Hungarian pastry (Ryan Nerz)." I have written a book on Damon Runyon and if I don't know what Jennings means, and cannot begin to follow the logic of a sentence—which ends with the tasteless kind of humor that makes fun of people's names—I wonder who can?

The occasional puffery of the *Times*'s own present and former editors and journalists hardly meets its own standards of objectivity. Should the lead review be of a book by a *Times* staff writer, as was the case September 17, 2006, when Frank Rich's *The Greatest Story Ever Sold: The Decline and Fall of Truth* was the subject of Ian Buruma's cover review entitled "Theatre of War"? Should retired Timesman John Darnton's *The Darwin Conspiracy*, a 2005 novel that received modest reviews and certainly was not a major popular or literary event, be mentioned in "Paperback Row"?

The December 4, 2005, list of one hundred books included, among the sixty-one notable nonfiction selections, six books by *New York Times* staff writers. Three others were by former and present members of the *Times*'s community of writers and editors, including one by a former executive editor—Joseph Lelyveld's *Omaha Blues*—and two by regular contributors to the *Sunday Magazine*. An admittedly tough question: Should such books, unless they have been valorized elsewhere by extraordinary recognition, be foregrounded by the book section?

II. *Timestrash* and *Timeslite* in the *Book Review*: Seeking Audience by Dumbing Down

Each of us will decide where the dotted line exists between *Timeslite*— frivolous material, often with no other point than to present social oddities and personal or group idiosyncrasies, the kind of material serious readers pick up only when they are having their hair cut—and *Timestrash*—that is, titillating material about sex or drugs or excessive drinking, gossip about celebrities, or unnecessarily gruesome details about violent crime. And each of us will decide whether the *Book Review* needs to accommodate *Timeslite*—which takes the form in the *Book Review* of autobiographies and biographies of celebrities—and/or *Timestrash*, which at times takes the form of soft porn.

An October 3, 2004, review of Toni Bentley's *The Surrender* by Zoe Heller appeared under the heading "The Beauty of Submission." Helen reports on how Bentley rhapsodizes about her spiritual awakening due to anal sex. Heller places the book in the context of other examples of "extreme female confession" ranging from "nymphomaniac picaresques" (Catherine M) and incest (Kathryn Harrison) to spanking fetishes (Daphne Merkin) and the obsessive cyber-stalking of ex-lovers (Katha Pollitt). Not only does Heller enable us to learn about "A-Man" introducing Bentley to "earth-moving sex," but also we learn that Bentley

> kept a tally of how many times she was anally penetrated and . . . the average number of anal episodes she was hav-ing, per year, week and day. She fetishized the accouter-ments of her sexual obsession—dedicating herself to finding the best and most economical lubricants, the most sex-friendly boudoir-wear. . . . [S]he also preserved her lover's used condoms, much as an acolyte might hoard religious relics.

Perhaps the review could have used a tad more distance and humor and been ironically aware of the craziness it describes. Was Bentley's book one of the important books published during the fall 2004 sea-son? And does it really require a two-page review? Isn't the review a tad obsessed with the book's author's obsessiveness?

Certainly, in 2004–2005, Tanenhaus had a bent toward *Timestrash,* as if he wanted to shock readers of that once most staid of *Times* sections, the *Book Review.* For example, is there any point in review-ing Elizabeth Hayt's *I'm No Saint: A Nasty Little Memoir of Love and Leaving,* which Amy Calhoun dismisses as combining "psychobabble and name-dropping" (December 25, 2005)? Do *Times* readers need to know that the author "performed oral sex on a bridesmaid just hours before her marriage"? When Calhoun archly observes that Hayt—and other authors of such narcissistic books—have "sex lives . . . as dar-ing as a tram ride through a nature park," we realize that Calhoun's review—presenting herself as savvy in the sexual ways of the world—itself is a kind of supposedly hip simulacrum of the books it purports to dismiss. In 2007, Tanenhaus ran an insipid review by Jane and Michael Stern entitled "Big," an autobiography by a porn star named Ron Jeremy, whose main attribute is a large penis and whom, we are told in the review, "performed in more than 1,700 porn films with over 4,000 partners" (February 18, 2007).

Although the voyeuristic and leering stress on sexuality somewhat abated by 2009, one can point to a more recent example of *Timestrash* in the *Book Review.* The aforementioned Toni Bentley's review entitled "Meet, Pay, Love" is featured on the cover page of the August 20, 2009, issue. Purportedly a review of "*Hos, Hookers, Call Girls, and*

Rent Boys: Professionals Writing on Life, Love, Money, and Sex," edited by David Henry Sterry and R. J. Martin Jr., the piece became the occasion for a good deal of uninformative sex talk on the part of Bentley.

I would suggest that if, as with the case of Calhoun's piece on Hayt—and perhaps Cohen's essay on Thomson, the Sterns on Jeremy, and Bentley's front-page review—a reviewer comes up with nothing substantive about a book or writes an insipid review, then the *Times* should negotiate a payment with the reviewer but not run the review.

III. The *Book Review* in 2008–2009

Let us turn to the 2008–2009 version of the *Book Review*. I noticed improvement in the direction of greater intellectual seriousness, better-qualified reviewers, especially for specialized subjects, and more university press books. As part of the integration of the online and published *Times*, the *Book Review* now has a substantial online component with weekly podcasts that include discussions of literary works, news about "the literary scene" and best-sellers, and a blog about books called "Paper Cuts," written by editors of the *Book Review*.

Tanenhaus certainly upgraded the graphics, making the *Book Review* more physically attractive, and he has improved the quality of reviews. But I am not sure he has made the *Book Review* more influential. The 2008–2009 version of the *New York Times Book Review* still lacks intellectual gravitas, although individual articles are notable exceptions. His reviewers, particularly those of nonfiction books, often are distinguished; however, they don't always seem to give the *Times* their best work.

By 2008–2009, Tanenhaus included more university and small press books as well as more literate and knowledgeable reviews of nonfiction works and better matches of reviewer and reviewed book. Examples in the same May 2008 issue are the choice of Douglas Brinkley, who edited Ronald Reagan's diaries, as reviewer of Sean Wilentz's *The Long Age of Reagan: A History, 1974–2008*, and of Jack Rosenthal, once a speechwriter for Robert Kennedy, to review Ted Sorenson's *Counselor: A Life at the Edge of History* (May 18, 2008). In the same issue, I also found David Shaftels end-page essay "Letter from Trinidad" about V. S. Naipaul somewhat more substantive than the customary closing essay, but would have appreciated a little more about Naipaul's body of work ("An Island Scorned," May 18, 2008). The books chosen for review included a larger range of books and publishers, including Ira Nadel's *David Mamet*, published by Palgrave Macmillan (February 24, 2008). Yet Tanenhaus still chooses magazine journalists when more qualified academics might be better suited to write an authoritative review.

A solid review was David Michaelis's March 2008 review of Todd DePastino's biography of Bill Maudlin entitled A *Life Up Front* ("He Drew Great Mud," March 2, 2008). Although Michaelis has written a biography of Charles Schulz and probably knows a good deal about the history of comics, he does not put Mauldin in the necessary context to help the reader who knows less about comics than he does. What we see here is a case where a more demanding editor could have gotten a fine piece by insisting on more context and background, but settled for a respectable piece.

Although I see improvement, I still question Tanenhaus's choice of reviewers. He still uses more generalists—often drawing from a recurring stable of journalists—than experts. If he must choose between recognizable names and those who have mastered a subject, he chooses the former—and some of the people he chooses are known to far fewer people than he realizes.

The ideal reviewer not only knows an author's prior work, but also, more importantly, is an expert on the subject before reviewing the book and can put the book in context. In his March 2, 2008, review of Jimmy Breslin's *The Good Rat: A True Story*, Marc Weingarten doesn't have much to add about Breslin or the Mafia. Why not select a reviewer familiar with the Mafia beat, such as the witty, savvy, and informed Sidney Zion, who at that point was still alive? If he refused, why not a *New York Daily News* or *New York Post* crime reporter or someone who has written one of the many books on the Mafia?

Clearly, in 2010 Tanenhaus was not getting the advertising to support a more ambitious publication. A major issue may be the format. Not enough space is available for serious sustained discussion. Many of his nonfiction reviewers are more comfortable with more spacious formats than the two thirds of a page left after the large graphic that frequently appears on same page. For example, one could imagine the distinguished historian Alan Brinkley writing quite a splendid review-essay on the failures of the Bush presidency when reviewing *Slate* editor Jacob Weisberg's *The Bush Tragedy*—a study of George W. Bush's psyche and his relationship with his father—rather than Brinkley's short workmanlike commentary "In Search of Bush" that appeared in March 2008. On the opposite page is another review of a book about George W. Bush by Jacob Heilbrun—a frequent contributor and author of a book about the "Neocons"—of Lou and Carl M. Cannon's *Reagan's Disciple* ("What would Reagan do?"). Heilbrun's review quotes a good deal from the Cannons but rarely makes a point of its own or has any real insights to share.

Considering these books cover overlapping terrain—and both reviews allude to Bush's search for a father figure—the *Times*'s readers would have been better served by one strong review of both books together. Indeed, would not the *Times* be better off with longer but fewer major reviews each week, even it meant that other books were reviewed briefly?

In 2010 there were still many reviews that were less about the books than the reviewers, where reviewers in the guise of doing New Journalism wrote about themselves rather than books, and where the book under review was not placed in the kind of literary and intellectual context that a well-informed reviewer would provide.

Although I found some notable exceptions—such as Lorraine Adams's May 18, 2008, review of Rabih Alameddine's *The Hakawati*—the fiction reviews often don't place the reviewed novels in the context of contemporary letters and fail to show much familiarity with the author's prior work and the culture from which it originates. Worse yet, some reviews do not give the reader enough of a sense of the book under review. On the whole I learn more about fiction from Michiko Kakutani. Yet I did like Tanenhaus's own somewhat hyperbolic August 29, 2010, review of Jonathan Franzen's *Freedom*, because it gave a sense of the novel's themes and formal narrative, while smartly placing it in the context of Franzen's prior novel, *The Corrections*. Interestingly, Tanenhaus, who is to my mind a much better writer than editor of the *Book Review*, gave himself the length that he very rarely gives other reviewers. In late 2007, he also took on the editorship of *Week in Review* (now in 2011 called the *Sunday Review*) as it evolved from a news summary with op-ed columns to an opinion and analysis section.

IV. Balancing Education and Entertainment
in the *Book Review*

My April 2005 interview with Tanenhaus made clear that he and I differ about what constitutes great book reviewing. For Tanenhaus, the review is an essay in itself where the reviewer can perform whatever tricks he wishes without too much concern for the book that is the nominal pretext for his review. A disciple of the New Journalism, where the persona of the essayist is as important as the subject, Tanenhaus gives his reviewers the opportunity to range afar and display whatever wit and verbal pyrotechnics they wish. Being smart is the goal of such reviewing, rather than being diligent. Put differently, if the *Times* reporting was as inaccurate and irresponsibly imaginative as the book reviewing, we would not expect accuracy or an effort to ferret out the truth in a complex world.

Good reviewing has an element of paraphrase. Distinguished fiction reviews give a sense of the book's plot, characters, setting, and style and a sense of how the novel fits into the author's evolving career and relates to other novels by similar writers; distinguished poetry reviews convey a feel for the art of poetry as well as for what else is being written by contemporaries and has been written by important predecessors. Thus, at some level, reviewing is a kind of sophisticated paraphrase based on the reviewer's contending with the author's language and a demonstration in brief of what that language has accomplished. Whether reviewing fiction or poetry, the informed reviewer is aware of influences and biographical data, even if influences and biographical material are not his primary focus. Distinguished nonfiction reviews should give some sense of the book's argument, the author's mastery of his or her subject, and the book's readability. The review should place the work in some relationship to other books on the subject. The reviewer should show that he or she has done considerable reading in the subject under review. She or he knows enough about the subject to understand new material and provide refreshing and important illuminating perspectives as well as notice limitations, distortions, and omissions.

An excellent book reviewer informs readers of what they will experience if they read the book and provides a sense of what distinguishes it from other books. Such a book reviewer is attentive to the process of a first reading and cognizant of the pleasures of rereading.

The reviewer has a responsibility and that responsibility is to mediate between book and audience.

Within the last year or so I have seen some fairly significant movement in the *Book Review* toward this educational model—informing readers about a book's contents and significance—and away from, as in some 2004 and 2005 book reviews, the book reviewer as a kind of entertainer—if not hipster and insider—who is playing an improvisational riff on his or her verbal instrument. But there is still a ways to go.

V. The *New York Times Sunday Magazine*

With a more relaxed time frame for editing, we should expect, compared with the rest of the paper, that the *Sunday Magazine* would have stronger articles—even distinguished and memorable pieces—as well as fewer errors and more stylistic polish, and this is generally true. In 2006, Gerald Marzorati, editor of the *Sunday Magazine* since 2003, was elevated to assistant managing editor—and a position on the masthead—in recognition of the growing empire over which he presided. This empire included not only the *"T"* magazine, but also the other supplements to the *Sunday Magazine*.

In the form of the *"T"* sections, the *Sunday Magazine* in 2008–2009 has a sequel varying in content from *Women's Fashion, Men's Fashion, Beauty, Women's Health, Men's Health,* and *Travel* in addition to supplements outside the *"T"* rubric addressing *Real Estate, Education,* and *Sports.* And within the weekly daily paper, we have magazine-like special sections dealing with *Sports* (Monday), *Science* (Tuesday), *Dining* (Wednesday), *Home and Style* (Thursday), and *Arts* (Friday). For a time, the *Times* published *Play,* a Sunday sports magazine, four times a year and *Key,* a Sunday real estate magazone, twice a year; but neither was part of *"T"* magazine.

During our April 18, 2005, interview, Marzorati said he sees his audience as those interested in middle- to highbrow culture and his role in part to foreground major cultural figures that may not have received the attention they deserve. He believes that "journalists in general . . . in the era of literary theory have grown increasingly hostile to intellectuals." Whereas Tanenhaus's attitude is an example of journalistic ambivalence toward intellectuals, Marzorati seems to view his own role as an enthusiastic but gentle teacher of "sophisticated urban readers or people who want to imagine themselves as sophisticated" rather than those on what he calls "the left/right continuum" (April 18, 2005).

Marzorati shares a tendency among *Times* people—not so different from other subgroups—to generalize from his own experience and to think that his hectic urban world is the world we all share:

> I wanted there to be a place in the magazine that was escap-ist. I count on attracting readers who want to be informed, of course, but I also count on attracting readers who want to be entertained—hence the crossword puzzle, the Ethicist column, and so on. We reach readers on Sunday morning, when a quiet break from the world, an escape, may be precisely what they have in mind. . . . Me, I want readers to find *something* to like in the magazine each week, and then take a bike ride or play with the kids. Hey, it's Sunday. ("Talk to the Newsroom," July 28, 2006)

But many of us don't think of Sunday as a mindless escape from daily life and in fact look forward to being challenged intellectually by our Sunday reading.

The 2003–2009 *Sunday Magazine* featured a cover story and, usually, a few shorter but substantial articles and two or three other shorter pieces on topical issues. Attractively packaged in comparison to the black-and-white version of prior generations, the *Sunday Magazine* has been part of the *Times's* movement to greater graphics within the newspaper and, even more, on nytimes.com

Something of a smorgasbord, the *Magazine* was organized for those who want to know what they are getting and who have limited reading time. What all *Times* section editors do is try to keep the attention of as many readers as possible on their section or subsection of the paper or on their material on the digital site. This was espe-cially true of the 2003–2010 *Sunday Magazine*, which included regular short features—"Questions," by Deborah Solomon (since 2003), "On Language" by William Safire (from 1979 until his death in 2009 and later biweekly by Ben Zimmer), and "The Ethicist," by Randy Cohen (since 1999), as well as diverse culturally and historically relevant articles such as Peter Landesman's July 11, 2004, piece on Saddam Hussein's then forthcoming trial ("Who v. Saddam?").

Marzorati claims that he edits the magazine for the pleasure of his readers and without worrying about the profit motive. But the magazine is so full of ads—and this even before turning to the "*T*" magazine—it might as well be a special supplement entitled "Lifestyles of the Rich." Thus it was not surprising that Marzorati's June 6, 2004, issue—one of his issues that from time to time focused all the longer articles and as many as possible of the recurring features on a single topic—focused on "money and the moral quandaries it presents." But the June 6, 2004, issue did so in a way that took it into the *Timeslite* realm.

Narrative journalism—journalism with an unfolding story to tell as opposed to journalism that immediately answers the questions who, what, where, why, and when—holds sway in the longer articles, but it is journalism with a topical focus, and that focus often is on the way we live. On April 18, 2005, Marzorati observed to me:

> [We] do a lot of long form journalism, which we call "The way we live now" stories that really try to get at the way people really go about their lives and reach decisions having to do with their families and their relationships. The story that we've gotten the most mail [on] was a story that was developed about this group of women that had gone to Princeton who ended up with these big jobs in corporations and then decided to leave their jobs in order to stay home with their kids. People went berserk.

Quite ambitiously, Marzorati in his early years wanted to establish a new hierarchy of what is culturally important or at least nudge readers to accept his judgments:

> I'm much more interested in spending a lot of time looking at what's out [there] in the culture and then deciding on . . . what we think is great. So in the last eight months, we did a huge cover story on Pedro Almodovar, the Spanish filmmaker that many of our readers would know a great deal about and would read. It was a 9,000-word piece. And the very first cover I did was to put Sofia Coppola on the cover of the magazine . . . .[A]t that time people looked at her as a rich, spoiled brat or someone who did a really bad job with *The Godfather, Part III*. I got into an early screening of *Lost in Translation*. I thought it was a remarkable movie. We decided to run the cover. . . . We

did a cover of Marilynne Robinson, who won the Pulitzer Prize for Fiction, we did a profile of John Patrick Shanley, who went off to win the Pulitzer Prize for Playwriting, we just did a profile of [the musician] Beck, who just put off a kind of remarkable mid-career album. I see us as [aimed at] mid-higher brow culture, if you will.

The *Sunday Magazine* occasionally has dazzling articles that combine reporting with value-added journalism. An example in the December 4, 2005, *Magazine* is regular contributor David Rieff's article about his mother, Susan Sontag. The article focuses on her unsuccessful battle with cancer and the medical and moral issues raised by her desire to stay alive at all costs, including paying for what she believed were the best treatments.

Rieff's eloquent, narrative-driven, but pointed article starkly contrasts with the plethora of *Timeslite* space-filling articles, to which even the *Sunday Magazine* is not immune. Thus, in the same issue, the cover article by Michael Lewis, "Coach Leach Goes Deep," is about a coach who is supposedly changing offensive football. This long article cries out for editing and should be on the sports pages in truncated form.

On occasion, the lead article has been just tasteless and foolish, a prime example of *Timeslite*. Such a case is Emily Gould's May 25, 2008, narcissistic and immature piece "Exposed: What I gained—and lost by writing about my intimate life online." Gould was once a major figure on a media blog called *Gawker* and then apparently became an object of ridicule in some parts of the blogosphere. Basically, she asks us to share her rambling self-therapy as she recovers from compulsive blogging and turns to compulsive magazine journalism in the form of the aforementioned article. If it is an example of the *Times Sunday Magazine*'s continuing quest to find a younger audience, its length and the quality of its prose are a deterrent.

In my interview, Marzorati expressed pride in introducing in fall 2005 "The Funny Pages," although those pages have disappeared and I found few people who read them. Marzorati likes to think of himself as a kind of cross between family man and urban hipster and is not above including hip language in his comments, as when he speaks of "scheming up the Funny Pages" and of "gigs" or of "old-timey" material ("Talk to the Newsroom," July 28, 2006).

Within the subsection entitled "The Funny Pages," Marzorati introduced into the *Sunday Magazine* a pure comic page, "The Strip." "The Funny Pages" also include "True-Life Tales" and "Sunday Serial," which each week contained a short chapter of a larger narrative. According to Marzorati:

> The other big thing [in addition to the escapist model] I had in mind was finding some way to evoke the funny pages of old-timey Sunday papers (though not of the *Times*, which never had them) in a contemporary way, and here, our popular culture presented a perfect opportunity. To me, the graphic novel—the book-length narrative told in comics-style by artists like Chris Ware and others—is one of the most vibrant young mediums we have. . . . ("Talk to the Newsroom," July 28, 2006)

"The Funny Pages" may have been a central part of Marzorati's escapist model, but they were a reason readers found the magazine more lightweight than in the past. In any case, they disappeared in the wake of the budget cuts demanded by the financial exigencies of recent years and possibly because Marzorati and his colleagues learned that they were not widely read.

Perhaps an article in the July 11, 2004, *Sunday Magazine* by former *Book Review* editor Charles McGrath, entitled "Not Funnies"—blurbed with the headline, "The most innovative novels being published now just may be those of some seriously strange cartoonists"—gives us an idea of what Marzorati had in mind. McGrath argued that just as the novel replaced poetry, so now comic books in the guise of graphic novels may replace novels: "Comic books are what novels used to be—an accessible, vernacular form with mass appeal—and if the highbrows are right, they're a form perfectly suited to our dumbed-down culture and collective attention deficit."

In the print edition and even more on its website, the *Times* from 1999 to 2009—and especially in the Keller years—made some movement in the direction of becoming "an accessible, vernacular form with mass appeal." The *Times*'s website has far more graphics than the newspaper—including Maira Kalman's monthly graphic opinion piece, "The Principles of Uncertainty," which appeared on the first Wednesday of every month for one year spanning 2006–2007. Kalman's pieces remind us that the comic page in the daily newspaper contains strips such as *Doonesbury, For Better or For Worse,* and *Dilbert* that are not so much funny as windows on contemporary life and often are really miniature essays in graphic form.

Marzorati likes little epiphanic stories that have the virtue of being brief and readable, such as the often successful feature "Lives" on the last page of each issue of the *Magazine.* The December 4, 2005, issue contained a nice if reductive piece, "Geese Flying," by Susan York, an artist influenced by Agnes Martin, who had died recently. Martin spoke in absolutes—"Never have children. Never do anything that will take away from your work"—but also encouraged York to be patient: "If I could tell you anything, I would tell you that you have time." The author eschewed Martin's advice about spending a year in the studio rather than going to graduate school, and found that graduate school did not prevent her from discovering who she wanted to be as an artist. If the reader knew something about the spare, disciplined minimalist art of Agnes Martin—not necessarily a household name—the piece made more sense.

The *Times* has, of course, been trying to expand its audience and to renew its audience with younger readers, and the *Sunday Magazine* is no exception. But in a world of journals devoted to pop music, like *Rolling Stone*—to say nothing of specialized websites—I wonder if the *Times*'s focus on developments in the kind of popular music favored by twenty- and thirty-somethings has the impact that some of its other cultural coverage now has. For example, its second featured piece in the *Sunday Magazine* of June 18, 2006, was an article clearly directed at a younger audience, "The D.J. Auteur" by Chuck Klosterman, which discussed a record producer named Brian Burton, who calls himself Danger Mouse. Supposedly, Danger Mouse is more creative than other producers, although no evidence is presented to support this contention. In the guise of trying to be hip and cool, this often impenetrable piece described the title figure as "a highly focused dude."

A good many band names are mentioned with little information for those not among the cognoscenti to tell us who they are (Nine Inch Nails, Tool, Beck, Gorillaz, OutKast) in the panoply of popular music and what distinguishes them. The article is in the mode of "inside baseball" directed at a subset of younger readers that rarely reads the *Sunday Magazine.* Some of my informal panel of younger readers knew who Danger Mouse was, but few of those who read the article learned anything they didn't already know. And those who did not already know about Danger Mouse or his supposed innovations did not learn much. This piece needed a broader historical context for those who might want to learn about contemporary music but for whom the Rolling Stones, the Eagles, and the Beach Boys were points of reference.

Often, the featured narrative articles go on far too long and need editing. On June 18, 2006, the issue in which the Danger Mouse article appeared, the cover story was a repetitious and wordy piece by Joseph Nocera—whose business page (and now op-ed) columns are often succinct and to the point—about the idea of a Phillip Morris executive that the government under the auspices of the FDA should regulate cigarettes ("If It's Good for Philip Morris, Can It Be Good for Public Health?"). Another article that went on far too long and was not deserving of its place as a cover article was Michael Lewis's September 24, 2006, piece, "The Ballad of Big Mike," about the discovery of a potential professional left tackle. Indeed, I was not convinced that this young man had the credentials to be admitted to a four-year college and thought the article was written with tunnel vision and somewhat inadvertently showed the corrupt side of college athletics.

Two definite improvements under Marzorati were the integration of the printed version and the website and the more attractive and less-crowded visual layout of the *Magazine*. "On the Web" was a small printed insert within the table of contents that pointed readers to prior installments of the *Magazine*'s "Sunday Serial" and graphic novel as well as to online pieces that complement the printed version of articles. On May 18, 2008, when one of the major print articles was Rob Walker's "Can A Dead Brand Live Again?" Walker also responded online to questions and comments about brands.

The 2008 version of "Departments" features "Puzzles"—the Sunday Crossword, which is still the main reason many readers open the *Sunday Magazine*, and the Cryptic Crossword—"Letters" (reader responses to prior articles), and "Lives" (a short personal essay on the last page). "Style" was another catchall *Sunday Magazine* rubric and one that mostly depended on photographs. On May 18, 2008, it included kitchen photographs from the Milan Furniture Fair; a short related piece on a new British contemporary furniture design company, Meta, which is an offspring of an old established company, Mallett; and—in keeping with the economic voyeurism of both pieces—a picture of a $700,000 wardrobe. The other May 18, 2008, "Style" article was a short piece about green garlic by chef Daniel Patterson, who has contributed a number of articles on food to the *Sunday Magazine*.

In the 2008 run-up to the election, as an obvious strategy to appeal to a wider audience than would an article on Danger Mouse, Marzorati chose topical articles that often highlighted politics. Buried on page 40—rather than foregrounded as the first story, as it should be, of the same May 18, 2008, issue—was a substantive if longish piece by Matt Bai on John McCain's foreign policy views entitled "The McCain Doctrine: Why Iraq is the Batttle He has Chosen to Fight." Covering national politics for the *Sunday Magazine*, Bai published a number of featured pieces on the 2008 election, including one on March 16, 2008, "What's The Real Racial Divide? What do Hillary Rodham Clinton's big-state victories say about race in America?"

That Marzorati knew his magazine section was competing for readers' attention against other sections of the *Sunday Times* as well as other activities dominates his decision making. He provided multiple paths for the reader to enter into the *Sunday Magazine*. Under the rubric "The Way We Live Now," we find "The Ethicist" by Randy Cohen and "On Language," established by William Safire and continued until 2011 by Ben Zimmer. Both features had strong followings, in part because each can be read in a few minutes, and also because the persona of each was lively and each was well written and often witty and smart.

Let's turn to a controversial but popular and often excellent section of Marzorati's *Sunday Magazine,* namely, Deborah Solomon's regular one-page interviews. Begun in 2003, they were remarkable in their succinctness and for the first few years seemed to get progressively better in terms of eliciting essential information. Certainly, it is impressive that each week Solomon was prepared to ask luminaries questions, and sometimes we learn a good deal of what most of us want to know about a subject in whom many readers may be at least somewhat interested. Both her September 3, 2006, interview with Gloria Steinem, who at age seventy-two was launching a new radio network for women with Jane Fonda, and her August 20, 2006, interview with Whoopi Goldberg, who was beginning a new radio show, were examples of the kind of middlebrow interrogations of established figures at which Solomon excels.

However, when interviewing heavyweights, at times her questions are more snippy than probing, and in response to such questions the answers at times seem like superficial sound bites. For example, her

November 20, 2005 interview of Jean Baudrillard, entitled "Continental Drift," does not go anywhere. Baudrillard's cynicism is an impenetrable shield—"All our values are simulated"—and someone who didn't know something about his theory of simulation could not possibly have learned anything substantive. The fault for such disasters may—as it seems in the Baudrillard interview—be divided among the interviewer, the interviewee, and the format, but it is difficult to assign exact proportions of blame. It would be nice if we could learn about this most complex French thinker in a few hundred words, but unfortunately without intellectual and historical context this is not possible. Nor do we know whether Baudrillard speaks, as the printed interview implies, in colloquial English or whether Ms. Solomon or someone else translated his words.

On October 3, 2007, in a piece entitled "Questioning the Questioner," *New York Press*'s Matt Elzweig, drawing on his interviews with NPR's Ira Glass and advice columnist Amy Dickinson, called attention to how Solomon makes up questions after the interview to match answers and changes the meaning of some answers. Tim Russert had made a similar complaint in a June 11, 2006, letter to the *Magazine* in which he spoke of Solomon's "deliberate mischaracterization of our conversation and her feeble attempt at humor." In his piece, Elzweig quotes New York Times Company Guidelines on Integrity (1999): "Readers should be able to assume that every word between quotation marks is what the speaker, or writer, said. The *Times* does not clean up quotations. . . . No one needs to be reminded that falsifying any part of a news report cannot be tolerated and will result automatically in disciplinary action up to and including termination."

The *Times* defended Solomon, but soon the *Sunday Magazine* added a caveat at the end of her column "Interview Conducted, Condensed, and Edited by Deborah Solomon." But I think that transcribing anything but the actual words of interviews is misleading, and I have transcribed actual words except for ellipses in my quoting *Times*'s editors, reporters, and business figures. In the face of the Jayson Blair scandal, I would think that the *Times*—namely Keller and Marzorati—would insist on reportorial accuracy.

Some of the interviews made the case that Solomon's column has outlived its best days and has become fey and repetitious, and that may be why she seems to have been dropped by Mazorati's successor. The May 18, 2008, piece, "Questions for Cynthia Nixon," was without any substantive meaning and seemed a leering and tasteless probe into Nixon's current relationship with a woman rather than a discussion of either the cultural significance of *Sex and the City* or what makes Nixon an effective and eclectic actress.

The *Sunday Magazine* has not lagged behind the rest of the paper in bringing sex into its pages with astonishing frankness. The lead article in the May 30, 2004, *Sunday Magazine* by Benoit Denizet-Lewis entitled "Whatever Happened to Teen Romance (And What is a Friend with Benefits)" is, yes, a titillating, voyeuristic, and exploitive piece in which we learn in detail how adolescents—including young adolescents—engage in experimental sex without commitment. In the article, we learn about "hooking up" by using the Internet, and what used to be called slutty behavior by teenage girls who perform oral sex on boys: "To a generation raised on MTV, AIDS, Britney Spears, Internet Porn, Monica Lewinsky and *Sex and the City*, oral sex is definitely not sex (it's just oral), and hooking up definitely not a big deal." The article almost stutters over the term *oral sex*, repeating it in three sentences in a row. The author includes online conversations between a senior high school girl and a guy with whom she has casual sex without even friendship. Giving contraception responsibility to his partner, he asks: "Do you have condom [*sic*]?" She answers: "Yes, dear." She tells him: "I'm gonna be boring tonite. . . . I'm not in the mood for nothing but str8-up sex [*sic*]." The article walks a fine line between being informational and titillating, but perhaps there are parents who have no idea what is going on among teenagers and some sensationalism is necessary to inform them. Denizet-Lewis also did a provocative but substantive story about gay black men living as straight men in the August 3, 2003, issue of the *Sunday Magazine*: "Double Lives On The Down Low," about AIDS and the black homosexual underground.

The *Sunday Magazine* has had some other tasteless moments. The end-page column, under the rubric "Lives," of the July 4, 2004, issue included a piece by Tony Hendra—the author of the best seller *Father Joe*—entitled "The Personal is Political," which was perhaps accepted and even in print before his daughter's charge that he molested her was fully investigated. The column was about Hendra's failed relationship with Diana Sand, a black actress who died at age thirty-nine. But in the *Arts* section three days earlier (on Thursday, July 1, 2004), in a piece probably published too late to kill the aforementioned end-page column, N. R. Kleinfeld took up the subject of Jessica Hendra's claim that she had been sexually molested by her father. Would the *Times* have printed Tony Hendra's article if it knew he molested his daughter? Such a lengthy article as Kleinfeld's (entitled "Daughter Says Father's Confessional Book Didn't Confess his Molestation of Her") with graphic descriptions of what Jessica Hendra said happened—along with confirming interviews—simply would not have been in the *Times* a decade ago, to say nothing of three decades ago. For me, the Kleinfeld piece was a necessary and disturbing complement to the Sunday column, but its excessive length undermined its impact and put it rather close to the borderline between, on the one hand, a solid feature and, on the other hand, *Timeslite* and perhaps *Timestrash*.

A final quibble: On occasion, the *Sunday Magazine* publishes long excerpts from books by its own reporters, columnists, and executive editors. Although perhaps this may be justifiable for a former *Times* employee—as in the case of excerpts from the aforementioned Lelyveld's memoir, *Omaha Blues*—I am still a bit uncomfortable with this practice. Because Lelyveld was executive editor, readers will suspect that he probably does not have to compete for space. I have even more qualms when the *Times* puts itself in a position of puffing its own current staff and helping them sell their own books. An example is present columnist Maureen Dowd's piece entitled "What's a Modern Girl to Do?" in the October 30, 2005, *Sunday Magazine*. Keyed to her recent book *Are Men Necessary?* the piece is a bland article announced provocatively on the cover as "Inner Sluts! Upstairs Maids! Are Modern Mores Killing Off What's Left of Feminism?" and iterating views from her columns.

VI. The *Sunday Magazine*, Part 2: "*T*"

Accompanying the *Times Sunday Magazine* is frequently a second magazine, and the primary purpose of that magazine is to raise advertising revenue. Edited by Stefano Tonchi, these sections—called in the Times building, depending on whom is speaking, variously "Part 2," "P2," and, more recently, "*T*"—took several different forms: *Women's Fashion, Men's Fashion, Beauty, Women's Health, Men's Health, Travel, Education*. Although Marzorati oversaw them, *Play* and *Key*—with their own special names and imprimaturs distinct from the rest of "*T*"—had their own editors and did not carry the "*T*" imprimatur.

Conceived by Marzorati as a "new style and luxury magazine," "*T*" is a subcategory of P2 and did not become the brand name for a number of rotating Part 2s in the *Sunday Magazine*. As Marzorati wrote in an email to me on October 2, 2006: "Under '*T*' there is Men's Fashion, Women's Fashion, Design, and Living (Food, essentially), and Travel." And in the July 28, 2006, "Talk to the Newsroom," he remarked: "I think '*T*' is interesting and beautiful, potentially, for everyone—even those who will never own a suitcase that cost a thousand bucks. I think fashion . . . is something you can learn more about and thus appreciate more." The justification for these glossy supplements is that the increased revenue supplements the news coverage, but the effect, because these "*T*" magazines often have only a modicum of content— and the thinnest of features—is to dilute the quality of the *Times* as a newspaper for the thoughtful and informed.

At a time when revenue is scarce and *Times* stock has been dropping precipitously, these magazines are a financial success. As current pubic editor Clark Hoyt wrote in December 2007:

> In an otherwise depressed newspaper world, where revenues are stagnant and layoffs and buyouts are frequent, "*T*," the fashion magazine of the *New York Times*, is a spectacular success. "*T*," published 15 times a year, is a glossy, unabashed tribute to the good life, as defined in its pages by Hästens mattress and box spring sets starting at $4,475, Swiss "coffee centers" topping $3,600, and a Roger Vivier satin clutch with silver sequins going for $15,000. The "*T*" magazines have been incredibly successful. . . . [T]he most recent edition, Holiday 2007, brought in between $4 million and $5 million in advertising revenue. ("A Semi-Nude Minor? In The *Times*?" December 16, 2007)

Cleary an advertising success, the glossy May 18, 2008, 170-page issue of "*T*" *Style* is subtitled *Summer Travel* and is a mélange of economic voyeurism and exotic information of use to the very few. To be sure, it does discover sites for the experienced and wealthy traveler and the wide-ranging ads do include pages taken by the states of New Jersey and Virginia pointing out summer travel opportunities. It has articles on where Canada's superrich vacation, as well as on Ischia, an island off Naples; Kangeroo Island, off southern Australia; and Namibia. The latter article features a beautiful model wearing designer clothes by such fashion goliaths as Versace and Diane Von Furstenberg. In fact, the issue is as much about fashion as travel, with a section entitled "The Get" featuring exotic products and boutique shops.

For the *Style* issues devoted to women's fashion, the "*T*" imprimatur is particularly successful in terms of advertising revenue. This section is clearly modeled on *Vogue,* to which it bears a strong resemblance. The October 22, 2006, fall issue of "*T*" on women's fashion was a whopping 302 pages, mostly advertisements. Typical of glossy women's magazines, we don't reach the table of contents until page 70 and then find five more pages of ads before finishing the contents on page 76. The percentage of actual article text is probably below 6 to 8 percent of this issue, and even the articles are likely to be puffs—as, for example, the final-page piece on the Cartier Love bracelet, a bracelet that is secured on the wrist by means of a tiny screwdriver and that recalls medieval chastity belts. The 240-page February 25, 2006, spring issue on women's fashion did not get to the contents of the issue until page 62, and the first article is on page 79. By contrast, the "*T*" fall 2006 *Style* issue devoted to beauty had only ninety-eight pages and still hadn't found its advertising base.

I am sure quite a few Jews other than my wife and myself found it amusing that one featured article in the spring 2006 issue of "*T*," Leslie Camhi's "Dangerous Beauty," is a version of "Is She Jewish?" The question is part of an informal colloquy, still taking place in Jewish homes, in which a positive answer—"Yes, so-and-so is Jewish"—expresses Jewish pride in Jewish celebrities. More importantly, this article reminds us of how the *Times* once played down its own Jewish identity and still on occasion tiptoes around the subject. Using the then-current Sarah Bernhardt exhibit in the Jewish Museum as a point of departure, Camhi nominally discusses the subject of "Jewish beauty," concluding—how surprising!—that "Though the stereotype—short, dark, curvy—lives on, Jews come in all shapes, colors, and sizes." Much of the article simply lists Jewish designers, mentions Jewish models (not so many), and speaks of Jewish actresses past and present, many of whom changed their names.

Those with a long memory will recall a time when such discussions did not take place in the *Times*. On occasion, *Timeslite* is simply foolish;

thus one of Camhi's characteristic rhetorical questions asks, "Was it Madonna's public embrace of the kabbalah that made the world suddenly safe for Jewish fashion icons?" The answer to such a stupid question is contained in her article, for Calvin Klein, Donna Karen, and Ralph Lauren, to say nothing of Bess Myerson and Lauren Bacall, paved the way. Lest we need forget the parlor game, the actress Rachel Weisz, the magazine's cover girl, is not only evoked in Camhi's last paragraph but is the subject of a laudatory if brief piece by Lynn Hirshberg, accompanied by stunningly beautiful photos by Raymond Meier, entitled the "The Rachel Papers," with the lead "The Thinking Man's Pinup or A Complex Cinematic Presence? The Fearless Beauty Rachel Weisz Says, Why Not Both?" I might add with a smile that a virtue of the "T" articles is that—albeit super-ficial—they are brief.

In a publication that is more of an advertising vehicle than reporting, the *Times* should also identify freelancers who contribute and tell us in a sentence what they do professionally so that we know if they have a special economic interest in puffing the products about which they are writing. In the aforementioned February 25, 2006, issue of "T" on spring fashion, the *Times* supplies an excessive biographical note to a handful of contributors—some of whom make rather abbreviated appearances (like Holly Brubach)—in stark contrast to their failure in other places to identify freelancers as more than "contributing writers." We do not know if the writers are under contract for a finite number of pieces a year or whether their real loyalty is to another publication or business or cause. In the women's fashion issue under discussion, does one assume that other contributors are regular *Times* staff if they are not on the magazine masthead?

Let us look at the February 24, 2008, "T" supplement, *Women's Fashion Spring 2008.* Clearly, with 286 pages, the issue is an advertising success of massive proportions. We don't reach the contents page until page 82 and the first of the thinnest of articles, "The Remix," begins on page 99.

This "T" issue contains the proliferation of articles that are almost devoid of meaningful content. This issue underlines that the "T" section has been on occasion sexually explicit and titillating. According to Jim Schachter, a deputy editor of the *Magazine,* " 'T' operates in several contexts . . . including 'the world of fashion magazines and fashion, where youth and unattainable beauty and charged sexuality are the currency of the day'" (Hoyt, "A Semi-Nude Minor? In The *Times*?" December 16, 2007).

That "*T*" magazine is on occasion sexually explicit and titillating is underlined by the February 24, 2008, issue. One featured article by Susan Campos, under the rubric "The Face," is about injecting human collagen into a woman's "G spot," and includes testimonies from women who get these shots—at a cost of $1,850 per shot—every four months to enhance their orgasms; according to one woman, "Instead of one orgasm, I now have two or three." In the same issue, Daphne Merkin—to whom the *Times* gives space generously for the purpose of putting her emotional life on display—writes with her usual frankness about her sex life, talks about the difference between male heels, male jerks, and male cads. Heels "resemble the actual footwear in the elevated proportions of their initial appeal, their suggestion of endless foreplay" ("Heel Girl").

Play, the sports supplement that appeared a few times a year, is more substantive than the "*T*" sections but, like the "*T*" sections, was based on the premise that another advertising vehicle will help pay the rent. Many of its ads were for such upscale products as Porsches and Movado watches. It folded in late 2008 because its was not attracting enough advertising.

Even with 126 pages, the introductory issue of *Play* on February 5, 2006, clearly had not yet found the desired number of advertising pages. The August 20, 2006, 92-page issue, I suspect, fell further short of meeting expectations. The section is another example of what Frankel called, in our April 16, 2005, interview, "the *Times* as shopping mall." The idea behind *Play* was that the *Times* believed it could convince advertisers to buy space in an occasional glossy product because there are enough inveterate upscale sports fans who will read a glossy section; the goal was to collect advertising for every conceivable product that might interest this targeted sports audience.

In the case of the first issue of *Play*, the articles revealed a section not only in search of a signature theme or style but a section with especially thin content. Retrospectively, the articles on the wonders of Bode Miller and the American ski team seem both poignant, given Miller's inept 2006 Olympic performance—no medals—and prophetic, given his 2010 Olympic successes. Michael Sokolove's piece on the Duke basketball coach, Mike Kryzewski, entitled "Follow Me," is far longer than necessary. Does Sunday's sports reader really want the inside scoop on his motivational talks—"release your inner women" according to the blurb underneath the title "Follow Me"—which earn him $50,000 a speech, a fee that will soon rise to $100,000?

At first glance the September 2006 issue of *Play* seemed to contain the same kind of articles that appear in the daily *Sports* sections. But a closer look does reveal a turn toward literacy that future issues tried to sustain, including often excellent writing. Writer-at-large and former *Book Review* editor Charles McGrath writes about the Cinderella story of a golfer unexpectedly succeeding on Golf's Senior or Champions Tour. Michael Kimmelman, the art critic, contributes a reasonably revealing but hardly earth-shaking one-page interview entitled "Return, Hingis."

David Foster Wallace wrote the stylistically brilliant if quirky cover article entitled—how is this for a pretentious title?—"Federer as a Religious Experience." Complete with footnotes in unreadable small print, it is a laudatory—if not hyperbolic—article with a subtitle that is more blurb than subtitle: "How One Player's Grace, Speed, Power, Precision, Kinesthetic Virtuosity, and Seriously Wicked Topspin are Transforming Men's Tennis." Written in the performative mode, and often more worshipful and hyperbolic than informative, Wallace's piece does include some memorable lines: "[T]he truth is that TV tennis is to live tennis pretty much as video porn is to the felt reality of human love." But Wallace's hyperventilating hagiography and convoluted analysis are disproportionate to the subject. What Wallace's article on Federer lacks are the wit, playful irony, and historical overview that make Roger Angell a great baseball writer.

On February 28, 2008, *Play*'s eighth issue only had eighty-four pages and clearly was not meeting advertising goals. Both Jonathan Mahler's "Oedipus Bronx," about the Steinbrenner sons succeeding their father as the dominant Yankee owners, and Chuck Klosterman's "What A Difference a Freakishly Long, Ungodly Talented, Defensive Wizard of a Man Makes," about Kevin Garnett's role in transforming the Celtics from losers back into winners, are the kind of pieces that contemporary sports fans enjoy. But I found a good deal of filler, too, as well as brief articles aimed at a narrow segment of the imagined full *Play* audience. A golf article entitled "Hey, Swinger" was more free advertising for golf products than an article about how to play golf.

If *Play* had appeared, say, every other week, and perhaps had more of the statistical analyses that sports fans love, it might have seriously competed with *Sports Illustrated* by quite overtly appealing to that magazine's core readers and advertisers. By trying to do something for everyone and reach every possible audience, *Play* didn't have a sharp focus. Conceived as a four-times-a-year publication, *Play* fired a warning shot across *Sports Illustrated*'s bow, but it turned out its ship didn't have the necessary artillery to make an attack.

VII. Final Thoughts on the *Sunday Magazine* and Its Supplements

In the face of the *Times*'s declining circulation numbers as a percentage of the population and of the *Times*'s declining advertising income as a percentage of gross national product, the *Sunday Magazine* has been—like the rest of the newspaper and the *Times* website—reinventing itself, often in exciting ways. The *Times* magazines are driven by the same forces that are driving the paper, namely the *Times*'s need to find a younger audience, to expand the geography of its audience, and to think about how the product (including the contents of the magazines) appeals to Internet users.

The *Times*'s problem is how to appeal to diverse audiences and give them reason to open the magazines without diluting the quality of its product or seeming to be trying to be all things to all people. In his July 28, 2006, online "Talk to the Newsroom" discussion, Marzorati addresses the issue of economic voyeurism:

> [W]hile I do not think the paper, in its news section, is biased toward liberals, or biased in favor of (or against!) Israel, I do think, in cultural matters—of which fashion and, more broadly, style, is one expression—we are biased (in terms of space devoted to coverage, photography, and so on) toward the rich. And the reason we are is that the *Times* . . . is an urbane, cosmopolitan paper edited from the world capital of urbanity and cosmopolitanism, Manhattan, which means we are biased in favor of change, possibility, mobility, individual liberty and going to bed late—oh, and the rich, who are rather concentrated among us.

Although strongly impressed with Marzorati's innovative spirit, I found this particular comment a tad glib; his defense of advertising many objects that only the very rich would purchase seemed more condescending and patronizing than I found him to be when I interviewed him on April 18, 2005. It reminded me of the tendency of the *Times* editors to take their own ad hominem experience and make that into editorial practice. That is, they have great confidence in their judgment and on occasion think their lives, values, needs, and desires are more representative than they in fact are, and they forget that we all do not live in metropolitan New York or Washington, D.C. area or comparable areas in major cities.

To equate richness with change, possibility, mobility, and individual liberty is a bathetic reduction of those terms. To be fair, Marzorati did somewhat reach out to the hoi polloi, or as he might put it, a large demographic audience: "I think style, more broadly, is being democraticized in America, reaching more kinds of stuff (why did my son want an ipod and not some other mp3 player?) and across all class lines . . . I think this represents an important change, and I think 'T' is the magazine of that change" ("Talk to the Newsroom," July 28, 2006).

The quintessence of economic voyeurism—the lifestyles of the rich and famous—may be the *"T"* sections and the other Part 2s where the ratio of substance to ads is very low. It is clear that the purpose of these special sections is to provide a segregated advertising platform for soliciting the wealthy.

Several of the retired senior *Times* people were particularly exercised about Marzorati's *"T"* sections. They object to these sections as being short on content and long on advertising. Indeed, in their view, these sections have hardly any substantive articles. Speaking of what she calls "the very thick *Sunday Magazine* supplements," Soma Golden Behr remarked in my June 11, 2005, interview with her, "Just look at them. They are one luxury ad. There are thousands of luxury ads. Very lucrative, I think, and I throw it in the pile, I'm not interested, but there are readers that are." In 2010, these *"T"* sections had not changed much since Behr's comment. Readers merely turn the pages for the ads, but the *"T"* section is rarely journalism.

In defense of Marzorati and the current *Times's* executive editor and publisher, one might ask why the *Times* should not have expanded its coverage of fashion and style and why its advertising shouldn't be—as newspaper advertising always has been—an inducement for shopping and a means of raising revenue. In the twentieth century, the daily newspaper became the source of information and, through its advertising, aroused the desires that consumer capitalism required. The *Times* has always lived off advertising targeted to an upscale audience.

If my informal survey is correct, the *Sunday Magazine* in 2010 was not the essential reading it once was and only part of this is due to readers spending less time with their *Sunday Times*. Marzorati flailed about in his effort to define the *Magazine*'s contents and audience and, on balance, had at best only limited success. The recurring features discussed here have worked best. Although some of the articles are to the point, many are longer than necessary and/or irrelevant to the lives we lead today. An example of an unnecessarily prolix article was the September 5, 2010, cover story, entitled "Tabloid Hack Attack" accompanied by a parody of a tabloid cover.

9

The Challenge to the First Amendment

The Judith Miller Saga and the
Story of Domestic Spying

The Bush administration is trampling on the First Amendment and well-established criminal law by trying to use a subpoena to force the American Civil Liberties Union to hand over a classified document in its possession. . . . The subpoena is also a prior restraint because the government is trying to stop the A.C.L.U. in advance from speaking about the document's contents. The Supreme Court has held that prior restraints are almost always unconstitutional. . . . The Supreme Court affirmed these vital principles in the Pentagon Papers case, when it rejected the Nixon administration's attempts to stop the *Times* and *The Washington Post* from publishing government documents that reflected badly on its prosecution of the Vietnam War. If the Nixon administration had been able to use the technique that the Bush administration is trying now, it could have blocked publication simply by ordering the newspapers to hand over every copy they had of the papers.

—"A Gag on Free Speech," *Times* editorial,
December 15, 2006

I've said on several occasions that I think that it was a mistake, a major mistake on my part, not to deal with the WMD business, which was largely a Judy Miller problem, immediately after I came in. I mean the reason I didn't was partly, it felt sort of soviet to come in and then immediately start bashing the previous regime. And I thought, and still think, that we published some bad stories to be sure, but that's grown into an urban myth that somehow

the NYT started the war in Iraq, as if George Bush felt he needed
our permission to do so.

                                        —Bill Keller, May 20, 2010

I. The *Times* and the First Amendment

In this chapter I discuss recurring issues that have contributed to
jeopardizing the *Times*'s stature, namely the *Times*'s responses to some
First Amendment issues and a number of dubious decisions the *Times*
has made in defining its responsibility to its readers.

The issues of when to rely on confidential sources and how much
constitutional protection reporters who use those sources should receive
are central to journalism in a democracy. In part because the *Times*
often breaks the most important stories that challenge the government's
secrecy, the *Times* is the number one target of those who wish to limit
the First Amendment.

Yet in recent years, the courts have held against the *Times* in crucial
cases where it tried to protect its sources. A notable libel case brought
by a government scientist, Stephen Hatfill, cited columnist Nicholas
Kristof's contention that Hatfill should be a suspect in the 2001 anthrax
letter attacks. A federal magistrate ruled against the *Times* for failing
to identify all of Kristof's sources, notably two FBI agents. In another
case, the Supreme Court refused to block a U.S. prosecutor's access to
reporters' phone records. In 2004, it looked as if a proposed federal
shield law that would help reporters protect their sources would be
passed by Congress, but the proposed law has not only been watered
down since then but remains still unpassed.

Notwithstanding that the *Times* egregiously erred in reporting
the accusations that Wen Ho Lee was a Chinese spy stealing nuclear
secrets before any formal charges were filed, one could argue that
the continuing erosion of freedom of the press accelerated when, as
the coda to the Wen Ho Lee fiasco, the *Times*, along with four other
news agencies, contributed $750,000 to a settlement of a civil suit
as a way of avoiding a contempt citation. Reporters from the *Times*
and other news agencies had been held in contempt for refusing to
disclose their confidential sources for their reporting about Lee. Lee
brought the case in 1999, the year he was accused by the government

of giving nuclear secrets to China. According to Adam Liptak's June 3, 2006, front-page article, "Specialists in media law said such a payment by news organizations to avoid a contempt sanction was almost certainly unprecedented" ("News Media Pay in Scientist Suit"). As a face-saving device, the *Times* claimed that it will never settle libel suits for money, and that this was completely different because it saved one of their reporters, James Risen, from the possibility of going to jail.

The *Times*'s benchmark for revealing secrets is the Pentagon Papers because those documents represent the historical fault line between a press that stands with the government in mutual trust and one that has an adversarial relationship based on standing up to the government. The Pentagon Papers showed that the government could lie to the public and manipulate the press, and the *Times*—notwithstanding occasionally being duped afterward—became from then on a more skeptical observer of government.

In 2005, the *Times* faced a First Amendment challenge from a hostile administration, and Keller—following the lead of Arthur Sulzberger Jr.—responded forcefully to an event of great moment to the *Times*. Judith Miller's 2005 jailing for refusing to name her sources when CIA agent Valerie Plame was outed (we now know) by Karl Rove, gave the *Times* a chance to reaffirm its position as the moral standard of the Fourth Estate. Miller's source was actually Cheney's chief of staff, I. Lewis "Scooter" Libby. The Bush administration had mean-spiritedly revealed Plame's position as a way of punishing her husband, former ambassador Joseph Wilson, for exposing the administration's false claims about the potential of Iraq's weapons of mass destruction (WMD). Specifically, Wilson took issue with the government's claim that Iraq was trying to buy uranium from Niger.

The *Times* was under perceived attack by special prosecutor Patrick Fitzgerald, who convinced the federal court that he needed to hear Miller's testimony. Earlier, when she refused and went to jail, the *Times* gathered in a circle like a herd of musk ox to defend her, even while privately wishing it were someone else or what its own editorial called "an ideal case" rather than one "so complicated and muddy" (July 7, 2005). Liptak's July 7, 2005, lead story quotes Keller: "The choice she made is a brave and principled choice, and it reflects a valuing of individual conscience that has been part of this country's tradition since its founding."

One problem that made this less than "an ideal case" is that Miller was something of an embarrassment to the *Times* because she played quite an important role in mustering support for the war with Iraq with her articles on WMDs. Because of Miller's checkered history as a reporter of Iraq's alleged weaponry, some liberal voices did not join inveterate civil libertarians in sharing the *Times's* outrage. It seemed more than possible that, in her refusal to name sources, Miller was trying to restore a reputation severely blemished by her claims that Iraq possessed WMDs, something *Times* reporter Lorne Manly alludes to without fully developing in "Women in the News: A Difficult Moment, Long Anticipated" (July 7, 2005). Yet Sulzberger and Keller supported Miller, whose stories about weapons of mass destruction turned out to embarrass the *Times,* because, as Okrent, the then public editor, wrote in an email to me on February 14, 2005, Sulzberger and Keller were "understandably committed to her [First Amendment] defense on the contempt citation, which does secure both her position and her prominence."

With all its resources and with the knowledge that it had been duped by the government during the Vietnam War and on many other occasions, the *Times* nevertheless believed in the existence of WMDs and, indeed, one of its reporters, namely Miller, a supposed expert in this area, gave credence to the government's position that the discovery of such weapons was imminent. Miller played a large role—along with Thomas Friedman's columns—in giving cover to Democrats who were ambivalent about supporting the war with Iraq, although Jonathan Landman, former deputy managing editor, demurred in an October 22, 2006, email to me:

> Neither Judy nor the *Times* played anything like a uniquely decisive role in making the Bush administration's case for war, which was set in its course a year before the invasion (as our stories at the time showed). Clinton-era national security experts like Kenneth Pollack were also making the case for war. The *Washington Post* editorial page (among many others) was doing the same. Bill Keller, as a *Times* columnist, was doing so, even as *Times* editorials were in opposition. And it's easy to forget that even in anti-war precincts like the UN, French and German intelligence . . . there was general agreement that Saddam possessed chemical and biological weapons.

Looking back, Alexander Cockburn's August 18, 2003, column in *CounterPunch*, "Judy Miller's War," has much merit, even if we concede that Miller was probably not deliberately lying:

> We do know for certain that all the sensational disclosures in Miller's major stories between late 2001 and early summer 2003 promoted disingenuous lies. There were no secret biolabs under Saddam's palaces; no nuclear factories across Iraq secretly working at full tilt. A huge percentage of what Miller wrote was garbage, garbage that powered the Bush administration's propaganda drive towards invasion. What does that make Miller? She was a witting cheerleader for war. She knew what she was doing.

Miller's articles and media interviews about bio-terror helped arouse public alarm and simultaneously puff her 2001 book *Germs,* co-authored with *Times* reporters Steven Engelberg and William Broad. Retrospectively, Cockburn's questioning the integrity and judgment of the *Times* seems even more apt: "Didn't any senior editors at the *New York Times* or even the boss, A. O. Sulzberger, ask themselves whether it was appropriate to have a trio of *Times* reporters touting their book, *Germs,* on TV and radio, while simultaneously running stories in the *New York Times* headlining the risks of biowarfare and thus creating just the sort of public alarm beneficial to the sales of their book?" Cockburn even wonders if Miller's finding an envelope of white powder on her desk—soon revealed as harmless—during the anthrax frenzy in October 2001 might have been a publicity stunt to sell her book.

The *Times* is basically a conservative institution deeply committed to seeing itself as a preserver of crucial values, most notably those encompassed by the First Amendment. When defending these values, it is uncompromising in its defense of what it believes are the prerogatives of a free press and unwilling to bend to other views of the Constitution. Thus, in 2005, the *Times*—perhaps making a mistake in judgment—convinced itself that there seemed to be little if any distinction between the publishing of the Pentagon Papers and Miller's defiant refusal to report what she knew about the revelation that Plame was a spy.

In a divided country that is obsessed with national security in the wake of 9/11, it is difficult to find issues that are pure and simple. The *Times* defended Miller's unwillingness to testify to a grand jury about her sources as a First Amendment issue as well as a continuation of its courageous stand when publishing the Pentagon Papers. But other significant members of the media took a different view. Rather than have its reporter jailed with Miller, *Time* magazine—a Time Warner subsidiary—elected to turn over its reporter's notes. At about the same time the *Cleveland Plain Dealer* announced it would not publish the results of two investigative reports because it feared that their sources might be jailed, although later it did run one of the reports after *Scene* magazine wrote about suspected corruption of a former mayor of Cleveland. But the *Times* remains in word if not always in deed unyielding in its defense of First Amendment rights.

The *Times* devotes its entire editorial page to one subject only on what it regards as an extraordinary occasion. The single July 7, 2005, editorial—entitled "Judy Miller Goes to Jail"—has something of an apocalyptic tone: "She is surrendering her liberty in defense of a greater liberty, granted to the press by the founding fathers so journalists can work on behalf of the public without fear of regulation or retaliation from any such government." In the July 7 editorial, the *Times* cites a tradition dating to 1857, when its journalist J. W. Simonton was held in contempt by the House of Representatives for writing about bribery in Congress and refusing to reveal his sources; ultimately the corrupt congressman resigned. (We might recall that the 1857 *Times*, while a respectable four-page paper with a circulation of 40,000, was the same paper in name only, since Ochs had not yet bought and transformed the *Times* into the influential and important paper that it was to become.)

In the July 7, 2005, editorial, the *Times* invokes Reston's citing of Madison in defense of the *Times*'s defying the Nixon administration by printing the Pentagon Papers and fighting a court order to cease publication. The *Times* did what it could to place Miller in the context of martyrs to a free press. In the left column next to the July 7, 2005, article about Miller's going to jail, the *Times*—under the heading "Journalists Who Served Time"—ran a list in chronological order of those who went to jail for refusing to provide the courts with evidence. The most recent example was Myron Farber, a *Times* reporter who refused to turn over notes of an investigation of a doctor accused of murdering his patients. The list was accompanied by pictures of many of them, including Farber, as if this was a hagiography of those who defended freedom of the press. The next day, the *Times* even went so far as describing the minimum-security prison in which Miller was incarcerated.

II. Judith Miller's Release

On September 29, 2005, Miller's release from incarceration and her agreement to testify only after receiving a waiver from her source, Scooter Libby, was at first considered a triumph. Arthur Sulzberger insisted that it foregrounded the *Times* as a defender of the Fourth Estate's absolute right to protect its sources. The left lead article, "Times Reporter Free From Jail; She Will Testify"—by David Johnston and Douglas Jehl—was accompanied on the continuing page by a picture of Miller flanked by her lawyers (September 30, 2005). The article includes quotations by Sulzberger and Keller approving of Miller's prior refusal to testify in the federal inquiry about who leaked Plame's identity as a CIA employee.

While Sulzberger was apologetic for the WMD stories, he was defiant about the *Times's* behavior in protecting Miller's sources. He blamed her plight on our living in a "highly politicized time in our society" (November 10, 2005; interview with Charlie Rose). But in the same interview, he was unwavering in his defense of the *Times's* support of Miller:

> I am absolutely clear that she was protecting a core value of the *New York Times* and of journalism. . . . Judy went to jail for a cause we believe in. She got out when she got the appropriate waivers and the appropriate limits.

Sulzberger thinks his support of Miller is a defense of democracy. A skeptic might note that he is also defending disinformation policies by the government that were a threat to democracy and undermined the public's right to know. These policies were furthered by Miller's complicity, even if she were cynically being manipulated by government sources. Others within and outside the *Times* think Miller was protecting her friends within the administration—including those who spread disinformation undermining the public's right to know—and that Sulzberger made a major misjudgment in an effort to regain high ground in the post Blair–Raines period.

In many ways, Miller's behavior in both instances—her WMD claims and her refusal to reveal her source for what she knew about Plame to the grand jury—is certainly far more reaching in its consequences than the Jayson Blair case. Who shot whom in a spate of serial killings in a Washington suburb—the subject of many of Blair's errors in fall 2002—has all but faded from memory.

What the Blair and Miller cases have in common is that they both stem from a similar lack of editorial control on Raines's watch. Certainly a combination of editorial gullibility and a reporter's pathological zeal to outdo his or her peers contributed to the Blair fiasco as well as the Miller situation. Paradoxically, while Raines was perceived as an autocrat, he allowed a handful of employees to operate without editorial control. Miller is the prime example because senior editors were not aware of her sources.

The media was not as universally sympathetic to Miller's plight as one might have expected. The *Times* cannot evoke an "us versus them" mentality in a world where who is "us" is very much up for grabs. For one thing, in the post-9/11 world of 2005, there was greater ambivalence about the balance between a free press and the exigencies of national security. Moreover, support for the Fourth Estate as institutionally objective and above the fray—much of which is continually under attack as leftist in its leanings by right-wing broadcast media such a Fox and Rush Limbaugh and his ilk and the right-wing blogosphere—has eroded.

III. Issues Raised by the Judith Miller Case

Well before she was fired, earlier editors and longtime reporters had a mixed view of Miller, saying that her zeal needed to be tempered by editorial judgment. Former *Times* executive editor Joseph Lelyveld believes that she was a good investigative reporter when paired with a less zealous and more balanced colleague or when working as part of a team. Yet on June 22, 2005, he concluded to me: "She just lacks one thing, and that's judgment. She is the victim of the last person she had lunch with. The last thing she heard is what she believes. . . . You've got to question [her] sourcing; you've got to ask all the hard questions that might knock it down." Or as Frankel put it in my interview with him on April 16, 2005:

> She's very aggressive, very ambitious and very smart and very political. And she was a favorite of Abe Rosenthal's because they shared certain sympathies, particularly about Israel. I made her deputy editor in Washington and it was a total failure because of the nature of her personality; she didn't mix with the staff. We moved her away and put her in the media department, away from politics. And then she left to write a book and I was told she would never be back, that the project would take her years, and I was delighted. After I left, suddenly there she was again. And there she was again on Middle East issues and so on and I thought it was very careless for the paper to allow it.

During my June 22, 2005, interview with assistant managing editor Glenn Kramon, he said there was "more division [within the *Times*'s senior editors] on the Miller situation" than on anything else.

In my October 11, 2005, interview with Byron Calame, he reminded me of the legal and financial implications of confidentiality for the *Times*:

> You have to remember there's a clear high court decision that says that if a reporter commits a newspaper to confidentiality, the newspaper is held responsible. And they have to pay the fine, damages. . . . [E]ditors have to be more careful about when their individual reporters are making really strong confidentiality agreements. . . . [W]hatever Judy commits to, [the *Times*] is committed to, until [the *Times*] finds some reason to abrogate [the agreement].

Many thoughtful observers, among them the *Times*'s first public editor Dan Okrent and its third public editor Clark Hoyt, believe that reporters should identify their sources. In its July 7, 2005, editorial, the *Times* assured readers that it "has gone to great lengths lately to make sure that the use of anonymous sources is limited." Ironically, Miller's defense for her Iraq errors was that her "sources were wrong," which is exactly the problem with unidentified sources. In the case for which she went to jail, it seemed at first strange that Miller was protecting sources for an article she didn't write, but, later, after she testified, it became apparent that she had not only relied on Scooter Libby before but, as we have seen, been complicit with the administration in providing justification if not propaganda in the period leading up to the war. While she may have been protecting someone who had been her source on more significant issues, she was perhaps protecting herself from the accusation that she had been used and manipulated by an administration zealot within Dick Cheney's orbit.

One way the news media has supposedly changed is that it has become more skeptical of talkative government sources who give them privileged information. But more often than not, newspapers and broadcast media provide space and airtime for officials to press their agendas and make their points; often the various media outlets allow disinformation to pass as information because they do not take the time to examine what is being said. Although this is more prevalent in broadcast journalism, especially with live interviews, it does happen in the press more than it should and that includes the *New York Times*. What I mentioned in chapter 1 bears repeating: Two factors contribute to this tacit complicity in providing less than accurate information:

1. Reporters and government officials, especially in Washington, still send their children to the same schools, eat at the same restaurants, live in the same neighborhoods, and go to the same dinner parties.

2. Reporters and government officials still rely on one another to do their jobs, in some cases trading information back and forth like baseball cards.

Miller became a mirror image of the administration in her desire to control and manipulate the news, in this case not about the war but about her incarceration for upholding free speech. In fact, she also is a party to stifling dissent and supporting the discrediting of Joseph Wilson, a critic of the administration's claim that Saddam Hussein sought material in Niger for developing his nuclear program. Her real—but unwritten—story could have shone new light on how the administration manipulated the news. Her position in July 2003 on the war was not substantially different from that of Libby's and Libby would have known this from reading her articles. When she describes Libby's main theme, she might as well be describing her own: "[T]he administration had ample reason to be concerned about Iraq's nuclear capabilities based on the regime's history of weapons development, its use of unconventional weapons and fresh intelligence reports" ("My Personal Account: My Four Hours Testifying in the Federal Court Room," October 16, 2005).

Like Libby, Miller was looking for justification for her position. Perhaps she thought there was a conspiracy within the *Times* to undermine her stature. Her paranoia echoed that of Cheney and Libby; a close friend, Claudia Payne, claimed that Miller was afraid to enter the Times building alone ("The Miller Case: A Notebook, a Cause, a Jail Cell, and a Deal," October 24, 2005). Miller shared with Libby, who seems her confidant if not her consigliore, her "frustration" that she "was not permitted to discuss with editors some of the more sensitive information about Iraq." Like Libby, she was involved in a hedging strategy. To deflect attention from having been manipulated by the administration to promulgate WMD mania—even while she was attempting to manipulate the administration to give her unique access—she insisted on going to jail despite the fact that Libby seems a year before to have offered to waive his privilege to remain unidentified.

Miller did further damage to her reputation at the Libby trial. As Frankel observed: "Miller's role in the case served no one very well. On cross-examination, she was rattled into multiple confessions of uncertainty, poor memory and wobbly note-taking. She had suffered nearly three months in jail to serve the principle that reporters had a duty to keep their promises of confidentiality to sources—but finally accepted Libby's longstanding offer to waive his protection as well as Fitzgerald's agreement . . . [that he would] avoid asking her about other sources" ("The Washington Back Channel," *New York Times Sunday Magazine*, March 25, 2007).

From an historical perspective, we now see that the *Times* overlooked the following:

1. The possibility that Miller compromised her integrity and allowed herself—either willingly or unwillingly—to be manipulated by the administration in her Iraq coverage before and after the war began.

2. The reality that the *Times* protected a source, namely Libby, who was involved in deliberately spreading gossip or disinformation.

3. The reality that the *Times* put protecting its own reporter—and one many senior editors had come to consider unreliable and possibly unstable—ahead of reporting the news and its obligations to its readers.

According to Don Van Natta, Adam Liptak, and Clifford J. Levy, the *Times* "limited its own ability to cover aspects of one of the biggest scandals of the day"—although the *Times* does not indicate whether the "scandal" was (a) the claims by Miller and Michael Gordon of WMDs to justify the war; (b) the administration's revelation of Valerie Plame's identity as a way of discrediting her husband; or (c) the administration's manipulation of the press, especially the *Times* itself through manipulation of a senior reporter—or, as I believe, all three (Van Natta, Liptak, and Levy, "The Miller Case: A Notebook, a Cause, a Jail Cell, and a Deal," October 16, 2005).

Miller's personal account and the aforementioned accompanying article by *Times* reporters Van Natta, Liptak, and Levy reveal a shocking lack of integrity on her part. She is willing to identify Libby as a "former Hill staffer" rather than as a "senior administration official." She is Libby's puppet, "recommending to editors that we pursue a story" about Plame on the grounds that the *Times* "had an obligation to explore any allegation that undercut Wilson's credibility," as if his wife's CIA connections (or her sex life or how she spent her money) would have anything to do with *his* credibility—unless one was alleging she was a mole planted by the Iraq government! Reading between the lines, we see that Miller not only is a gossipmonger of the worst sort, but that at times she is disorganized, gullible, unreliable, and unprofessional.

Many states have shield laws but the federal government does not, and in 1972 the Supreme Court ruled 5-4 that the First Amendment does not protect a reporter from having to testify before a grand jury. The *Times* took the matter to court but could not get legal relief for Miller. As Nicholas Lemann said in his November 7, 2005, *New Yorker* article:

The result has damaged not just the Administration, which last week saw one of its highest-ranking members indicted, but also the press. Here was a case where talking to the press was precisely the crime being investigated; where the anonymous sources were not whistle-blowers taking on an Administration but an Administration taking on whistle-blowers; where the reporters were not lonely crusaders but members of the journalistic establishment; and where the law seemed to be on the side of the prosecution. ("Telling Secrets," 52)

Although Lemann thought that the *Times* had given us "too much information," I thought it hadn't given us enough. It needed to further open the doors and windows to the relationship between government and sources. Nor did I agree with Lemann that the system works or that "attention will shift quickly away from the press and towards the many troubles of the Bush White House" (56). Lemann did not seem to quite get the lesson, namely that the press and particularly the *Times* have been exposed—by its decision to defend a reporter who didn't deserve defense in the guise of serving a principle—as less interested in serving the public than its own interests.

Although leaks often have social value in producing a version of events different from the official version, I think what Lemann calls the "valuable" and "continuous traffic between reporters and their sources" needs to be defined to a much greater degree by identification of sources (56). Certainly, the Miller case does not show value to society but misplaced loyalty, paranoia, and failure of the *Times* to fulfill its institutional responsibility to readers. Miller finally testified after jail chipped away at her resistance and she felt that martyrdom had perhaps resurrected her reputation. But for a year, the *Times* could not tell the full story of how the Plame story was planted and how both Miller and Libby behaved in the traffic between reporter and source.

IV. The *Times* Coverage of Miller's Case as a News Story and Its Responsibility to Its Readers

When on October 11, 2005, I asked the blunt Jill Abramson what she regrets about how the *Times* handled the Miller case, she responded, "The entire thing." Important stories about Libby's role in the leak case were killed, according to the October 16, 2005, article, and millions of dollars in legal fees were incurred that could have gone to pay the salaries of dismissed employees as a result of budget cutbacks or could have been used to hire enough reporters to ensure adequate foreign coverage in Zimbabwe, Haiti, and Lebanon. Basically, to protect Miller, the *Times* audience was for a time deprived of essential information and the integrity of the *Times* was compromised because what it printed was all the news that fit its own purposes.

It looks as if the *Times* willfully turned an embarrassment—the quality of Miller's reporting and her manipulation by the government—into a principle about shielding reporters' notes. Questions abound: Was Miller protecting her source because, if she revealed it, she might be asked what her sources were for the WMD stories? In his aforementioned November 7, 2005, *New Yorker* article, Lemann persuasively remarks:

> Meanwhile, in Washington, the old journalistic way of doing business had not, it turned out, actually vanished from the scene along with the Alsop brothers and Walter Lippmann. . . . Especially in the small world of foreign policy and national security, the reporters and columnists for the leading news organizations tend to be assigned to their beats semi-permanently, and to have close, confidential relationships with officials. (50)

Was the *Times* being manipulated by the administration? Did Miller have a stake in discrediting those who believe, unlike her and the administration, that the existence of WMDs was a sham? Is it possible Miller herself has CIA ties or back channel ties to the CIA or direct ties to the Bush administration? In her October 15, 2005, personal account, she acknowledges, "During the Iraq war, the Pentagon had given me clearance to see secret information as part of my assignment 'embedded' with a special military unit hunting for unconventional weapons." But, then again, Miller seems to have a hyperbolic imagination and continually exaggerates her importance.

In an October 23, 2005, email to me, Jonathan Landman said he believes that Miller never had security clearance:

> The security clearance business is a red herring. There was no security clearance. Nobody at the Pentagon has ever heard

of such a thing. Present and former top editors have never heard of such a thing. Her colleagues have never heard of such a thing. What she had was a slightly beefier version of the agreement that all embedded reporters in Iraq had— beefier because she was with an intelligence unit. Perhaps Judy in her self-aggrandizing way wanted people to believe she was in some special rarefied class. But it's just nonsense.

Judith operated under her own rules because Howell Raines and Gerald Boyd wanted it that way. Previously, she was under very tight supervision by Steve Engelberg. She produced excellent journalism, including remarkable pieces from central Asia on the soviet biological weapons program and of course her contribution to the Pulitzer-winning stuff on Al Qaeda.

In his May 26, 2004, Editor's Note, when Keller criticized some of the *Times* coverage before the war and cited six articles, he did not mention that five were either written by or co-written by Miller; his silence was puzzling, especially because one of his first acts after taking over as editor July 30, 2003, was to remove Miller from covering Iraq and weapons issues. Why did the *Times* write more than fifteen editorials in support of Miller—one jointly written by Sulzberger himself and Russell T. Lewis, the then chief executive officer of the *New York Times*—urging a federal shield law for reporters, although Miller had, more than any reporter other than Blair, embarrassed the *Times*? The Sulzberger and Lewis editorial took up the cudgels for Miller after the special prosecutor held her in contempt. In that piece they called for the long-debated federal shield law for journalists so that the press can perform its First Amendment duties of helping "to hold government accountable to its citizens": "[The shield law] is an essential tool that the press must have if it is to perform its job [which] is the ability to gather and receive information in confidence from those that would face reprisals for bringing important information about our government into the light of day for all of us to examine" ("The Promise of the First Amendment," October 10, 2004).

Why was Miller able, even after the Blair scandal, to behave as she did? How could the *Times* tolerate someone who, in the Raines era, superciliously self-defined her position as "Miss Run Amok" to the former investigative editor Douglas Frantz and asserted that she could do "whatever I want"? In an October 22, 2005, column entitled "Woman of Mass Destruction," Maureen Dowd called for the *Times* to fire Miller, and wrote: "Sorely in need of a tight editorial leash, she was kept on no leash at all, and that has hurt this paper and its trust with readers. She has more than earned her sobriquet 'Miss Run Amok.'" In response to Miller's claim that she was wrong about WMD because her sources were wrong, Dowd reminds us "investigative reporting is not stenography."

In her dissing of Miller, Dowd speaks not only of her "operatic" style but also of "her tropism toward powerful men." According to what Raines told me, "There is no question that Judy had a very active social life." Did Miller's place in Manhattan society as the wife of the powerful publishing figure Jason Epstein give her some protection from being called out on her wrongheaded Iraq stories? Was her erratic and unprofessional behavior tolerated because of her and her husband's friendship with publisher Arthur Sulzberger Jr.—and the knowledge of senior editors who knew of that friendship? As Raines said in my December 13, 2005, interview, "It was widely perceived that Judy got away with whatever went on there because she was a part of [Arthur's] circle."

Dowd basically called for the *Times* to fire Miller because Miller had done major damage to the paper's reputation. Commenting on her desire to return to the *Times* and to cover, in Miller's words, "the same thing I've always covered—threats to our country," Dowd writes in an explosive final sentence: "If that were to happen, the institution most in danger would be the newspaper in your hands." (Interestingly Dowd thinks of the *Times*—as do most senior *Times* people—not as a mere newspaper but as an institution.)

On the day following Dowd's October 23, 2005, column, public editor Byron Calame took up the case, concluding that "whatever the limits put on her, the problems facing her inside and outside the newsroom will make it difficult for [Miller] to return to the paper as a reporter" ("The Miller Mess: Lingering Issues Among the Answers"). Calame was puzzled about whether Miller had a security clearance that restricted her ability to share information with editors. Under a nondisclosure form that she had signed, Miller claimed that she had been allowed, as Calame put it, "to discuss her most secret reporting only with Mr. Raines and Mr. Boyd." Calame called for addressing the "apparent deference to Ms. Miller by Arthur Sulzberger Jr. and top editors and why this occurred."

Neither Sulzberger nor Keller reviewed her notes or inquired as to whether Miller had proposed a story about the Plame leak, something she claims she did but that her then Washington editor, Jill Abramson—who, if my one-to-one interview is any criterion, seems straightforward and blunt if at times a tad abrasive and impatient—says she didn't. Because Miller didn't write the story, Calame noted that readers "were deprived of a potentially exclusive look at an apparent administration effort to undercut Mr. Wilson and other critics of the Iraq war."

In the wake of her departure, it became clear that Miller was much resented and even hated at the *Times* because of her special relation to Sulzberger and her (arrogantly) operating outside editorial constraints during the Raines era and apparently beyond. But why, at an earlier time, didn't Miller's colleagues more forcefully insist that the *Times* address Miller's behavior? It seems to me, as in the Jayson Blair matter, that there was a conspiracy of silence with an undertone of whining. I would have expected a full investigation on the order of the Blair matter because this has done far more damage to the *Times* than the revelations of Blair's fakery. Although an investigation began under the leadership of Landman and resulted in the October 16, 2005, article, it never—as it should have—reached back into the past to see how Miller came to her power and prominence at the *Times*.

Some observers mistakenly thought the Miller fiasco might bring Keller down or at least that it would begin a concatenation of events that would lead to a gracious early retirement. In 2005, I doubted that because within the *Times* there has been a strong effort to assign blame for Miller's behavior to Raines and his managing editor, Gerald Boyd. In Landman's October 23, 2005, email to me, he recalls: "Raines and Boyd ran Engelberg [Miller's editor when she was doing investigative journalism] off the paper, [and] then did the same to his extremely capable successor, Doug Frantz. That's when Miller —not working alone, please remember—wrote the bad WMD stuff with Raines's enthusiastic encouragement." Is it possible that Miller lost her moorings and began to invent stories? More likely, as we learned later, she was being deliberately used by the Bush administration—with the purpose of winning support for its war policy—to funnel supposed leaks to the public. Were not the *Times* and Sulzberger and Keller manipulated by Miller?

The Miller story is one about how not to run a newspaper and the need for editorial control and intervention. As David Ignatius, former executive editor of the *International Herald Tribune* wrote in an October

5, 2005, piece, "Lessons of the Miller Affair," in the *Washington Post*, "Reporters shouldn't be able to decide unilaterally to whom they will attach their newspaper's reputation. Editors should agree to absolute confidentiality only in the most rare cases." Even allowing for some gloating on the part of its media rivals, it was clear that the *Times* had blemished its reputation. In its continuing knee-jerk support of Miller, it did not understand what was at stake. Indicting the news media and, specifically, the *New York Times*, Robert Scheer wrote: "The First Amendment protection is not a license for mischief on the part of journalists eager to do the government's bidding. To the contrary, it was conceived by the Founders to prevent government from subverting the free press in an effort to misinform the public" ("A Free Press Subverted—by the Press," *The San Francisco Chronicle*, November 2, 2005). What Miller should have done is confront Libby for trying to spread gossip and rumors or, as Scheer suggests, write a story about how "a White House official was planting information to disparage a critic of its war policy." Were Libby not a fellow insider who supported the war, would she have willingly acceded to Libby's demand that she identify him as a former Capitol Hill staffer? Frankel calls Libby's demand a "devious dodge even by Washington's rules of engagement" and "one that should have lead Miller to realize that the remedy for bad leaks is more leaks" ("The Washington Back Channel," *New York Times Sunday Magazine*, March 25, 2007). Or perhaps her support of the war blinded her to how she was being used, but, given what I know of her, I find this doubtful. (Because my efforts to interview her were unsuccessful, I am using her personal statement, published in the *Times* on October 16, 2005, as a source.)

Had Miller been properly vetted by *Times* editors, knowing of her reputation for unreliability, perhaps they would have seen what Libby was trying to do, namely to undermine the source—Joseph Wilson—who had categorically discredited George W. Bush's claim in his January 2003 State of the Union address that Saddam Hussein was seeking material for a nuclear program in Niger. Had Miller and other reporters testified a year earlier, perhaps John Kerry would have been president.

Miller seems to have gone to jail as an act of martyrdom for the purposes of resurrecting her career. She desperately tried to change the conversation from her being a pawn of the administration's run-up to the war to her being a major figure in the defense of the First Amendment. It certainly seems as if Libby waived confidentiality before Miller went to jail, and the *Times* let her stand on principle according to the best construction—or perhaps let her stand on a technical nuance. When Miller did testify to the grand jury, it was unclear what changed after Miller went to jail to protect her source. Did she just get tired of standing for her principle or did the *Times* learn something new about the case and then tell her it was pulling the plug on defending her?

In the case of Miller, Arthur Sulzberger Jr. jeopardized the reputation of the *Times* by abdicating his responsibility to his readers. His metaphor for ceding control to her is fey and feckless: "This car had her hand on the wheel because she was the one at risk" (Van Natta, Liptak, and Levy, October 16, 2005). Sulzberger's seemingly ingenuous explanation may hearken back to a policy that not only was part of the underpinnings of the glory days of the Pentagon Papers but a policy that went back to his great-grandfather, Adolph Ochs. As Harrison Salisbury observed about Neil Sheehan's role in obtaining the Pentagon Papers: "It was an unwritten rule on the *Times* that if a man did not feel it appropriate to reveal the sources of a story, he was not pressed for it. The Ochs rule held: If you hire a man, trust him; if you don't trust him, don't hire him" (Salisbury, *Without Fear or Favor*, 16). Of course the *Times* had ample reason not to trust Miller after her wrong-headed WMD stories.

In an October 21, 2005, email to the *Times* staff, Keller concluded that even if he knew what he knew now "we would have to fight this case in court." But he acknowledges that he should have known more about Miller's "entanglement with Libby," and, if he had this knowledge, he might have been more willing to "support efforts exploring compromises." According to Keller, "we were facing an insidious new menace in these blanket waivers [of confidentiality], ostensibly voluntary, that Administration officials had been compelled to sign." Keller is referring to a George W. Bush administration policy that its own officials waive confidentiality. The purpose of the policy was that the administration could then turn around and question its officials about leaks.

In his characteristic defense of the *Times*—which does on occasion teeter on "the *Times*, right or wrong"—Landman observed in an October 22, 2006, email to me:

> And of course there is a first amendment issue here. . . . One
> can make tactical decisions about which cases to pursue,
> and criticism of the *Times* in this context is fair. But people
> who don't like Miller and root against her shouldn't pretend
> that there aren't real principles at stake, and real risks to
> free expression in Fitzgerald's inquiry.

Yet it is clear, due to the murky context that we have been discussing, that the *Times* is on the defensive when arguing that in this case they were defending sacred constitutional principles.

V. The Denoument: Miller's Resignation

On November 9, 2005, the final chapter of Miller's relationship with the *Times* occurred when the *Times* announced her retirement in an online story that day by Katherine Q. Seelye. But Miller continued to defend herself in print and to make public appearances; indeed, the same day that she posted her farewell letter, her self-rehabilitation campaign began.

Both Seelye's slightly different story and Miller's letter appeared in the print edition the next day. Miller's letter was not on the op-ed page but among the *Letters to the Editors*. In her newspaper piece, Seelye reported that "Ms. Miller originally demanded that she be able to write an essay for the paper's op-ed page challenging criticisms made of her by some on the staff" but that the *Times* refused ("Times Reporter Agrees To Leave the Paper," November 10, 2005). Seelye's article also summarized a Keller letter that was on the web, in which he expressed regret that he had used the word "entanglement"—which for some had sexual nuances—to describe her relationship with Libby.

The *Times* has not denied that Miller operated without full editorial control and supervision. On November 10, 2005, Arthur Jr. appeared as a guest on the *Charlie Rose Show*; while insisting that the *Times* was defending the First Amendment, he acknowledged that Miller was no longer a tenable reporter: "We didn't bring the degree of editorial skepticism that we should have brought to that story of Weapons of Mass Destruction. . . . I think it's fair to say that those stories would not have run in the *New York Times* today. We have learned so many lessons between that overheated period that followed 9/11 and today" (transcript of interview provided by the *New York Times*).

In the Rose interview, Sulzberger was rather nervous and fidgety, although in his characteristically aggressive and assertive mode he tried to project his confident self. He spoke as if the Miller case were a minor bump in the road, assuring his audience that the Blair matter was much more serious and that under current editorial controls the WMD fiasco couldn't happen again. Sulzberger's strong suit is not self-awareness, and when he asserted that he was not sure there was damage to the *Times*, he was either not being honest with his audience or with himself.

Sulzberger tried to put the Miller case in a long tradition of the *Times's* refusal to be intimidated by government. He also assured viewers that his family—which controls the board of directors of the New York Times Company and to whom he is finally responsible—was fully supportive of his decisions in this matter. Rose certainly did not make too many inroads in Sulzberger's defenses or penetrate his shield.

Sulzberger is a canny performer, as I learned from my own interview with him, and behind his poise and geniality is, at times, a strong belief in his own judgment if not presumptive privilege. Answering only questions he wishes to answer, interrupting or ignoring your comments, and often changing the subject to one he wishes to discuss, Sulzberger tries to control the agenda. He does not entirely avoid giving the impression that questioning him is an imposition and that he would rather be elsewhere, enjoying the company of others rather than submitting to uncomfortable questions. He identifies with the *New York Times* so closely that he takes a criticism of the *Times* as a criticism of him.

The *Times* and Miller engaged in a catfight. The *Times's* editors made a decision to cut its losses and, as with Raines, once they did so they turned on their own. Keller ordered an investigation and assigned a top team of reporters. Keller originally thought of David Barstow and Adam Liptak, both of whom worked together on the 14,000-word Blair report under the leadership of deputy managing editor Landman, but Barstow demurred because he was close to Miller. Instead, Don Van Natta along with Jamie Scott and Clifford J. Levy were chosen to work with Liptak. According to Seth Mnookin, "The *Times* reporters working on the story found that the editorial board and many of the paper's top executives either refused to speak to them or were prohibited from doing so" (Mnookin, "Unreliable Sources," *Vanity Fair*, January 2006, 135). Sulzberger wouldn't let Russ Lewis, former president and CEO of the New York Times Company, speak to them. On October

16, 2005, the investigative story appeared, along with Miller's account of her grand jury testimony; the story stressed that the *Times* regarded Miller as what Mnookin calls a "renegade reporter" who misled editors.

In her defense, Miller turned upon those very people who supported her: "If [Bill Keller] failed to listen to these briefings about my sources and plans, that is not my fault" ("Other Voices: Judith Miller Responds to the Public Editior," November 13, 2005). Her November 10, 2005, letter claimed that she had "chosen to resign," although Seelye cited Catherine Mathis, the senior spokesperson who "said it had been made clear to Ms. Miller that she would not be able to continue as reporter of any kind, not just one covering national security" ("Times Reporter Agrees To Leave the Paper," November 10, 2005). Miller claimed that had she not testified she was in danger of being charged with "obstruction of justice, a felony," but no reporter has ever been charged with obstruction of justice for failing to reveal sources. Nor is it likely that special prosecutor Patrick J. Fitzgerald would have called another grand jury.

Curiously, Miller responded to criticism that she should have stayed in jail more than to criticism that going to jail was itself an error because a waiver that would have satisfied her and the *Times* might have been negotiated much earlier: "For me to have stayed in jail would have seemed self-aggrandizing martyrdom or worse, a deliberate effort to obstruct the prosecutor's inquiry into serious crimes" (October 16, 2005). But for her to go to jail at all may have been that very martyrdom. What she did was obstruct the American public's right to know. She doesn't seem to realize that the real story was the administration's disinformation campaign and her complicity in that campaign.

Undoubtedly, the legal agreement that was reached with Miller includes some clauses about what the *Times* and Miller may and may not divulge.

VI. The Damage to the *Times*

After Libby's indictment for perjury and obstruction of justice, we read in the *Times* about the need for the Bush administration to clean house and reevaluate whom they can rely on. But didn't the *Times* need to revisit its behavior, and decide whether, knowing what it knew after the indictment, its defense of Miller's refusal to testify was justified? The *Times* might have gone the extra mile in ensuring that it was not guilty of even a partial coverup as well as of letting damage control deflect it from what had gone wrong.

The *Times*, like the Bush administration itself, did some hunkering down. For example, the lead editorial of October 29, 2005, the day after the Libby indictment, asserted: "We have no reservations about the obligation . . . to stand behind our reporter while she was in jail. We also think Ms. Miller was right on the central point that the original blanket waiver was coerced."

Had Miller testified a year before, Libby would have been exposed much sooner and the kind of disinformation campaign he conducted— no doubt orchestrated by Cheney—might have stopped sooner. Had Keller and Sulzberger insisted on all the facts from Miller, perhaps they would have chosen a different path. As Keller retrospectively remarked during my May 20, 2010, interview with him:

> I think it's important to stand by the principle that you need to protect your sources but . . . we probably could have found a way to cut bait on that issue earlier and spared her from going to jail. . . . Walter Pincus at the *Washington Post* was in a similar situation [and] . . . found a way to testify without, in his view, violating any corporate rules of journalism. And I think if we worked harder we might have been able to find a way to do that too.

The more that came out about what Libby was up to—and his indictment and conviction for obstruction of justice, perjury, and making false statements to federal investigators speak volumes—the more the *Times*'s reputation was tarnished. By allowing Miller to shape the *Times*'s reporting of an egregious campaign of slander and falsification—including outing Valerie Plame as a CIA agent when it might endanger her—the *Times* undermined its readers' confidence in its commitment to truth.

Looking back from our present vantage point, we can see that the *Times* suffered major damage from the Miller fiasco. It undermined public confidence in the judgment and competence of the publisher and executive editor. The *Times* blindly defended a reporter whose behavior didn't justify that defense. I have no reason to doubt the integrity of Sulzberger and Keller, but the *Times* looked noticeably smaller because of their decisions. It was their responsibility to know the facts and their implications and to put their readers' interests first. In his 2005 apologies to his staff, Keller came across as a decent man, but one—still in the early years of his editorship—somewhat cowed by both Sulzberger and Miller. As Keller observed to me on May 20, 2010, "I think she had always had supporters/sponsors in high places in part because she often got dramatic stories; . . . [Arthur, Jr. protected] her because he thought that she would break stories that would be good for the paper."

It is all very well to talk about laws "shielding" sources, but the country is at risk when the most important newspaper in the world shields its readers from the facts and the interests of one reporter are put ahead of our need to know. Keller, if not Sulzberger himself, owed the *Times*'s readers an explanation and an apology for how it handled the Miller case. Keller—and ultimately Sulzberger—is to blame for failing to supervise Miller and for allowing her interests to take precedence over the interest of the *Times*'s readers.

Indeed, perhaps even public editors Calame and Okrent, who represent the public and especially the *Times*'s readers, could have pressed more vigorously. To be sure, news reporting took precedence over very ambiguous principles. Rereading the WMD articles, it is clear how little factual information was really being passed on and how much Miller relied on gossip. Any article—to say nothing about one on the front page that appeared after the invasion of Iraq—with the headline "Illicit Arms Kept Till Eve of War, An Iraqi Scientist is Said to Assert" should be ipso facto considered an embarrassment if it depends, as it did, on an "an American military team" quoting an "unnamed scientist" (April 21, 2003).

VII. The Use of Confidential Sources

Most of us would like freedom of the press and the use of confidential sources to be invoked only when reporters can tell us what we need to know, as in the case of Watergate, where Deep Throat helped Woodward and Bernstein unravel the far-reaching misuse of power. We do not have the same tolerance when anonymous sources are serving their own interests, as when Miller was told about WMDs or when Libby tried to use her as part of an unscrupulous campaign to discredit Joseph Wilson who, on the side of the truth, was trying to expose a scandal of disinformation abut purported Iraqi WMDs. We need reporters who can make this distinction and who are not the tools of government policy or the funnels for administration propaganda.

The very practice of confidential sources has come under scrutiny. In his November 20, 2005, public editor's column, "Anonymity: Who Deserves It?" Calame raises some important issues about anonymous sources, but still has a more latitudinarian view than I do. After the Blair fiasco, it became the *Times*'s policy that at least one editor had to know the name of a confidential source. In June 2005, Keller tightened the guidelines: "Readers are to be told why the *Times* believes a source is entitled to anonymity—a switch from the previous practice of stating why the sources asked for it" (Calame, "Anonymity: Who Deserves It," November 20, 2005). But given the cozy relationship between political figures and news reporters, particularly in Washington but often even in foreign capitals, this can become a distinction without a difference.

Writing in the *Sunday Magazine* about the Libby trial after Libby was convicted of four counts of perjury and obstruction of justice, Max Frankel observed:

> Libby peddled secrets . . . to defend misjudgments and mis-representations on the path to war in Iraq. . . . The messy relations [of reporters] with officialdom were uncomfortably on display. We heard about celebrated correspondents routinely granting anonymity—better called irresponsibility—to government sources just to hear whispered propaganda and other self-serving falsehoods. We learned how our patriotic guardians of wartime secrets wantonly leak them to manipulate public opinion, protect their backsides or smear an adversary. And we learned again how clumsy are the criminal laws with which high-minded prosecutors try to discipline the politics of Washington. ("The Washington Back Channel," March 25, 2007)

In principle, the *Times* tightened source control in 2004 by requiring that at least one editor be told the identity of any confidential source. The then standards editor, Allan Siegal, outlined to Calame some of the questions he asked when randomly checking three stories each day:

"Why was the material permitted to be used anonymously? What was the rationale behind granting anonymity? What attempts were made to get his source on the record?" (Calame, "A Conversation with the Standards Editor," August 28, 2005). But instances of the *Times*'s over-use of anonymous sources recurs regularly and has been the subject of several columns by Clark Hoyt, Calame's successor.

Like their media brethren, the *Times*'s reporters are still using confidential sources when they might be doing further spadework to ascertain facts. The *Times*'s editors need to be pushing their reporters to get their sources to reveal their identities. Anonymous cheerleading by senior officials for their own policies still occurs quite frequently. As Calame noted: "Puffery with the protection of anonymity can be used in pursuit of ends as devious as those sought through unattributed negative comments" (November 20, 2005).

In answering questions online the week of April 10, 2006, Keller gave the company line:

> I'd much rather have a single source with first-hand knowl-edge of the information than several sources who heard about it third-hand. Sourcing is mainly a qualitative problem. Our aim is not to curtail the use of anonymous sources for the sake of meeting a quota. Our aim is to make sure that when we do use anonymous sources, it is justified by the value of the information, and that we have given the readers critical information about the sources. . . . One reason we require that an editor know the identity of every unnamed source is to make sure someone in addition to the reporter is asking about the sources' reliability and motives. That, to me, is the most important test. And there I would say we are doing markedly better than in the past. ("Talk to the Newsroom")

To a different online query, about how the Bush administration used anonymous sources in self-serving ways, Keller responded:

> The larger import of your question is that anonymous quotes can be a tool for manipulating reporters. That is certainly true, which is why we have tried—with some success, but not perfect success—to fight the casual use of anonymous sources, and, when we need them, to do all we can to

inform the readers about the reliability and motives of the unnamed source.

But I would argue that the *Times* needs to be explicit not only about why the teller wants to be anonymous, but why a story needs anonymous sources at all. One way to achieve transparency is to allow readers to know more about how a story is put together and what would be missing without those sources. Quoting administration sources justifying their own policy decisions and then quoting the same source for attribution as if it were a second supportive opinion is hardly ever justifiable.

On occasion, confidential sources are essential to breaking a major story, but the *Times*'s senior editors need to insist that their reporters and editors be much more vigilant about not only analyzing the motives of sources who wish to remain anonymous but also providing those analyses within the story. It may be too much to ask reporters (especially investigative reporters) to do away with anonymous sources, but it is worth noting *USA Today*—to be sure, a far different kind of publication than the *Times*—has been doing this for some years.

An official who is acting as a source can inflate his own self-importance and pretend to know more than he does or can have his or her own agenda. The term *senior administration official* can be used loosely by a reporter—and even agreed upon as a descriptive tag by both source and reporter prior to the source's speaking—in what has been described as "source inflation." Often, anonymous sources add nothing to the essential story, and there is no reason at all to use them. For example, in an October 29, 2005, article after the grand jury refused to indict Karl Rove for obfuscating his role in revealing the identity of Valerie Plame, one irrelevant quote at the end of the article is attributed to "A Republican close to the White House" (Anne E. Kornbluth, "At Milestone in Inquiry Rove and the GOP Breathe a Bit Easier"); this was at a time when—in the temporary euphoria of Rove's being spared by the special prosecutor—virtually every Republican figure was willing to talk. In an October 28, 2005, piece following the withdrawal of Harriet Miers's nomination to Supreme Court Justice, why—when it adds nothing to the story—summarize the views of "A Republican sympathetic to Mr. Rove" (Robin Toner, David D. Kirkpatrick, and Anne Kornbluth, "Steady Erosion in Support Undercuts Nomination")?

Certainly those chronic press offenders who, like Karl Rove—and most of his entire staff—are known to be manipulators should never receive the cover of anonymity. Attributing administrative gossip to "an official who works closely with Karl Rove," a man known for his disinformation, should have become off limits.

To be sure, the *Times* has been—at least on occasion—questioning the use of anonymous sources. It not only has criticized the *Washington Post* for not revealing its sources for its article about CIA prisons in Eastern bloc countries where torture is condoned, but it rather gleefully reported in its lead November 17, 2005, story that Bob Woodward of the *Washington Post* knew that Valerie Plame was a CIA agent earlier than anyone else and didn't tell anyone of that knowledge or his source (reported by Todd S. Purdum, David Johnston, and Douglas Jehl, with Purdum the writer: "New disclosure could prolong Inquiry on Leak/ A Surprise in CIA Case/ Testimony by a Reporter Complicates the Task of the Prosecutor"). Without quite saying so, one implication of the story about Woodward on the heels of Miller's resignation is that the *Washington Post* was in no position to gloat about the *Times*'s handling of Miller's behavior. After all, the hero of Watergate has also been engaging in the wrong-headed protection of unsavory sources.

It may be that the entire way that the news is gathered needs to be fine-tuned. Newspapers and the news media need to regain the public's confidence, and that includes the *Times,* whose deserved reputation for integrity has been compromised. Once it may have been accepted procedure for the media and the government to manipulate one another—say, during the two world wars. But it is no longer accept-able to a diverse America where each institution—president, Congress, and press—views each other with suspicion bordering on paranoia. We need to know who is saying what so we can judge their motives.

However, reporting information gathered from anonymous sources in totalitarian countries does raise different issues. Let us consider an article in this same time period when the Miller controversy was foregrounded, namely Michael Slackman's "In the Fief of the Assads, Friends Melt Away" (November 2, 2005). Although one might under-stand that quoting a Syrian official making negative comments about Assad might leave that official exposed to jail or worse, the *Times* should ask if the information provided is absolutely vital or merely supple-mentary. Thus, identifying the source of a provocative statement—"The regime is crippled at the highest, closest, smallest circle"—as "a Syrian political analyst who has worked closely with the people in power" leaves us wondering about the Syrian political analyst's own history and motives. We are not sure how much of the foregoing Slackman article depends on this anonymous speaker's presentation of debates within the inner circle and how much on Slackman's own knowledge of Syrian politics. These source issues are symptomatic of congenital problems in reporting on totalitarian countries, but we need to be wary of such information, and the reporter needs to do everything possible to confirm what he or she is being told and to indicate to readers what cannot be confirmed.

The standard for citing sources on domestic issues, particularly when what is quoted approaches gossip, should be even more rigorous than citing sources in totalitarian countries. Frankel defends a "sloppy" system that "breeds confusion," but one that produces valuable leaks as well as self-serving ones. Frankel has in mind the Pentagon Papers, but what about, as the 2007 Libby trial showed, the large role that false leaks played in the run-up to the Iraq war and in the subsequent spin cycle? Those false leaks proved a major embarrassment to the *New York Times*.

Frankel's concern that the press may be less vigorous if a prosecutor can excavate its anonymous sources by prodding the sources with threats is a legitimate one, but should we be satisfied with a system of complicity—and, on occasion, duplicity—that has enabled government to dupe its constituencies? Isn't there something tautologically absurd in Frankel's bemoaning damage to a system that has not been working and concluding "that tolerating abusive leaks by government is the price that society has to pay for the benefit of receiving essential leaks about government" ("The Washington Back Channel")?

Calame's December 3, 2006, column, "Scoops, Impact, or Glory: What Motivates Reporters," seemed to once again give the *Times* a pass on sources. Why did Calame in preparing his own article give half-dozen editors and half-dozen reporters "confidentiality"? "I talked to a half-dozen *Times* reporters and a half-dozen editors. . . . In an effort to avoid righteous platitudes about newspapering, I promised confidentiality to these journalists." Shouldn't he have pointed out that *all* sources—even reporters and editors—could be manipulative and have motives of their own? Indeed, weren't the *Times* editors and reporters, given their more stringent policy about sources, hypocritical in asking for—or even accepting—anonymity?

In my research for this book, I taped the editors and some reporters and did not find that they needed promises of confidentiality, except once in a great while when they asked that something be off the record. From my taped interviews, I felt that reporters and editors were motivated by a desire to inform, pride in finding out what they felt the public needed to know, and zeal to present important news first. No doubt other motives play a role such as the desire to impress those making decisions about their competence in terms of both future internal promotion and of outside recognition in the form of awards and prizes. But while aware of the complexities of motives and the desire that I write approvingly about those I interviewed, I was nevertheless impressed by the idealism of those reporters and editors with whom I spoke. Once my interviewees got going they became increasingly open and often went beyond their original intent in sharing information, at times including unsubstantiated gossip that I have not included in my book. My sense from writing this book and from other life experiences is that people have trouble holding back when they begin speaking. Were the *Times*'s (and other media's) reporters and editors to insist adamantly on identified sources, I believe a vastly increased number of sources would agree to be disclosed, with the result that full disclosure would evolve into a more standard practice.

VIII. Domestic Spying by the Government in the Guise of Anti-Terrorism, and the *Times*'s Response

The *Times* saw itself as defending civil liberties and the freedom of the press against a bullying government that used the excuse of the events of September 11, 2001, to create a climate of fear and then used that climate to infringe on civil liberties. Thus the *Times* cast itself as an adversary to the administration. By burrowing within the George W. Bush administration, and finding knowledgeable sources who were uncomfortable with administration policies, the *Times* believed it was doing an essential public service by informing American citizens of unprecedented attacks on their civil liberties As Keller put it in his June 25, 2006, online letter to readers after publishing a story about how the government watches bank accounts as a way of tracking possible terrorist funds:

> Since September 11, 2001, our government has launched broad and secret anti-terror monitoring programs without seeking authorizing legislation and without fully briefing the

Congress. Most Americans seem to support extraordinary measures in defense against this extraordinary threat, but some officials who have been involved in these programs have spoken to the *Times* about their discomfort over the legality of the government's actions and over the adequacy of oversight. We believe the *Times* and others in the press have served the public interest by accurately reporting on these programs so that the public can have an informed view of them.

The *Times* was criticized for radically different reasons both by an angry President Bush and by those who felt that Bush was subverting the Constitution—and the latter group included mainstream politicians as well as civil libertarians. Although Bush thought publication jeopardized the war on terror, his opponents thought that withholding the story about the government monitoring bank accounts reflected terrible judgment on the part of the *Times*. When the nation is in imminent danger, presidents may compromise constitutional liberties, but we expect the *Times* to hold the bar for imminent danger extremely high, especially when dealing with an administration that often cried "wolf" when there was no wolf.

The *Times* withheld for a year its knowledge of domestic spying before publishing the story by James Risen and Eric Lichtblau on December 16, 2005, a date that closely coincided with the publication of Risen's *State of War: The Secret History of the CIA and the Bush Administration*. Although the article provides a plug for the Risen's book, it also ensured that the *Times* could not be scooped by its own reporter and raised once again the question of the multiple roles its reporters are playing.

By postponing the story about domestic spying, the *Times* continued to be the news rather than merely report the news, and its credibility continued to be challenged. Calame's "Behind the Eavesdropping Story, a Loud Silence" (January 1, 2006) speaks to his frustration at being unable to discover the reason why the *Times* didn't publish the story earlier or exactly why it published the story when it did so. In an April 10, 2006, talk at Cornell University entitled "Individual Rights Versus National Security: What do we need to know in the Post 9/11 Age," Pulitzer Prize–winner Eric Lichtblau was no more helpful about why the *Times* withheld publication, hiding behind the explanation that the decision was made above his head and claiming that he is glad the story was published at all. If the *Times* could reveal the story without compromising national security in December 2005, why couldn't it have done so much earlier and why can't the *Times* explain the reasons for the delay to their readers, whose trust is essential to the *Times*'s mission?

In his 2006 talk, Lichtblau was extremely critical of the administration's "crackdown on public information" and its presumption—anathema to a democracy—after 9/11 that only the most innocuous and banal information should be released. He spoke of the adversarial relationship between government and the press and the chilling effect of a tendency to make the receipt of classified information a crime.

Calame was clearly miffed that, "for the first time since [he] became public editor," neither Keller nor Sulzberger responded to his questions. But he also gave the *Times* credit for publishing the piece "in the face of strong White House pressure to kill it" (January 1, 2006). The aforementioned Risen and Lichtblau's December 16, 2005, article recalled that "some information that administration officials argued could be useful to terrorists has been omitted" (quoted in Calame's piece). Given the Bush administration's record for duplicity, lack of respect for the law, and virtual obsession with manipulating the media, one needs far more explanation than Calame's wishy-washy article provided for the delay.

What seems to be at play in part is protection of sources. But, we need to ask again, by keeping secrets, did the *Times* once again put its commitment to protecting the government's illegal behavior ahead of the need to tell its readers the full story of a frontal attack on the constitutional rights of American citizens? Moreover, the *Times* knew about the eavesdropping before the November 2, 2004, election. Thus, the *Times*'s failure to report it and give the electorate the fullest information about the Bush administration—its tacit complicity with the administration—affected Kerry's challenge to the White House and perhaps helped Bush be re-elected.

Shouldn't the *Times* have given a precise explanation of why it became a secret sharer of this heinous program? The *Times* was the gatekeeper that decided that it would keep the Bush administration's secrets during a period when the administration had demonstrated time and again that it didn't deserve to be trusted.

The failure to publish the domestic spying story for a year is an issue about which both the *Times*'s columnists and readers radically disagreed. One set of *Times* critics felt that the *Times* was, like the administration, stonewalling its readers (and its public editor) and acting like the administration. Rather than help bring to light the reasons for its behavior, it shrouded them in darkness. The other group of pundits and readers felt that the *Times* is wrong in publishing classified information at any time and, as one put it in a letter to the public editor, believed the paper should be "severely punished" (Steve Cochron, Letters to the Public Editor, January 8, 2005).

Let us now turn to the *Times*'s journalistic response to the government's secretly monitoring bank accounts. Lichtblau and Risen's June 22, 2006, story about how the government was secretly monitoring international bank transactions as a way of tracking terrorists brought forth outraged comments from the president and right-wing journalists ("Bank Data Secretly Reviewed by U.S. to Fight Terrorism"). Some zealots accused the *Times* of treasonous behavior. The *Times* defended its decision, notably in a June 25, 2006, online letter to readers from Keller and a July 1, 2006, op-ed article written jointly by Keller and Dean Baquet, then editor of the *Los Angeles Times* ("When Do We Publish a Secret?").

Within the *Times* house there was some division about the decision to reveal the bank account monitoring. In his July 4, 2006, article Nicholas Kristof acknowledges that he might have decided differently, but—and this is a big but—he strongly asserts that "the press-bashers" do not have much "credibility" and that "journalists regularly hold back information for national security reasons" ("Don't Turn Us Into Poodles"). Frank Rich, characteristically the most aggressive of the *Times* columnists in calling the Bush administration to account, concluded: "The assault on a free press during our own wartime should be recognized for what it is: another desperate ploy by officials to hide their own lethal mistakes in the shadows" (Can't Win the War? Bomb the Press!" July 2, 2006). Recalling the assault on the *Times* and the *Washington Post* over the Pentagon Papers—as noted, a linchpin of *Times* mythology—he recalled the hyperbole used by the Nixon White House about the consequences to military security and relationships with other countries, none of which occurred. What did happen, as Abe Rosenthal reminisced, "was that Americans learned how 'secrecy had become a way of life' for the American government from Kennedy through Nixon" (Rich, "Can't Win the War? Bomb the Press!" July 2, 2006).

Keller and Baquet invoked Justice Hugo Black's response to the efforts of the government to suppress the Pentagon Papers: "The government's power to censor the press was abolished so that the press would remain forever free to censure the government. The press was protected so that it could bare the secrets of the government and inform the people." What the *Times* was doing, Keller and Baquet argued, was bringing information to its readers that the administration does not want the public to know, specifically "classified secrets about the questionable intelligence that led the country into war" or, put another way, classified information that shows the public had been duped (July 1, 2006).

In their July 1, 2006, op-ed piece, Keller and Baquet carefully explained how they withheld information at the government's request and how they always gave the administration a chance to comment and, if it chose to argue against publication: "often, we agree to participate in off-the-record conversations with officials, so that they can make their case, without fear of spilling more secrets onto our front page." Indeed, as Keller and Baquet point out and we have discussed, the *Times* withheld the story about domestic spying by means of wiretapping for over a year, and that, I suspect, was far more constraint than Justice Black had in mind when he spoke about a press "forever free to censure the government" and "bare the secrets of the government" to the people.

In his June 25, 2006, online letter to readers, Keller eloquently defined the opposing interests of the press and the government:

> The press and the government generally start out from opposite corners in such cases. The government would like us to publish only the official line, and some of our elected leaders tend to view anything else as harmful to the national interest. . . . Editors start from the premise that citizens can be entrusted with unpleasant and complicated news, and that the more they know the better they will be able to make their views known to their elected officials. Our default position—our job—is to publish information if we are convinced it is fair and accurate, and our biggest failures have generally been when we failed to dig deep enough or to report fully enough. After the *Times* played down its advance knowledge of the Bay of Pigs invasion, President Kennedy reportedly said he wished we had published what we knew and perhaps prevented a fiasco. . . . The question we start with as journalists is not "why publish?" but "why

would we withhold information of significance?" We have sometimes done so, holding stories or editing out details that could serve those hostile to the U.S. But we need a compelling reason to do so.

Both the Keller letter and the Keller and Baquet column contain somewhat self-serving references to the fact that journalists live in cities marked for terror, as if that were sufficient justification for the original decision not to publish: "We [journalists] live in and work in cities that have been tragically marked as terrorist targets" (Keller and Baquet, "When Do We Publish a Secret?"). But raising the possibility of future terrorism somewhat reiterates the Bush administration's reasons for suspending civil liberties; to the extent that the *Times* followed the lead of an administration that uses scare tactics and plays fast and loose with facts, we lose a free press.

What is at stake here is an independent press, an informed citizenry, and liberties guaranteed by the U.S. Constitution. As Paul K. McMasters, ombudsman at the First Amendment Center, puts it: "While the First Amendment protects the press from overt government censorship, it can't fully protect the press from full-time government hostility or part-time citizen apathy" ("Reasons to Worry about Media Meltdown," *Ithaca Journal*, December 7, 2006).

10

Struggling with Its Ethnic Heritage

Has the *Times* Waged War Against the Jews?

The *Times* did a very poor job on the Holocaust, as we all agree. And then they opposed the state of Israel.

—Max Frankel, April 16, 2005

[Arthur Hays Sulzberger's] son was totally different. Punch Sulzberger was an avid supporter of Israel. In fact one of the biggest disagreements we ever had was when I opposed, at the time, the bombing of Iraq by Israel.

—Max Frankel, April 16, 2005

It's a major headache for anybody trying to operate the *Times* in New York and being besieged by the professional Jewish lobby. . . . the only friends that I felt I had through a lot of those periods were Israelis, who were vigorous at criticizing their own government.

—Max Frankel, April 16, 2005

I. Historical Perspective

In this chapter, I discuss how and why the *Times*, owned by Jews, downplayed the Holocaust and opposed the creation of Israel, and how even now it bends over backward to be fair to the Palestinians. Many Jews have never forgiven the *Times* for its past and, even now, look unkindly on its efforts to take a balanced position toward the longstanding Israeli–Palestinian conflict as well as the more recent wars with Hezbollah and Hamas and other aspects of its relations with its Middle Eastern neighbors. Within the 1999–2009 period, the continuing issue of how the *Times* addressed the Holocaust and Israel and how it now addresses the Israeli–Palestinian conflict has affected the *Times*'s stature with a significant segment of its readership and potential readership.

Adolph Ochs, a German Jew from Chattanooga, bought the *Times* in 1896, when it had a circulation of 9,000, and built the circulation to 465,000 by the time he died in 1935. His credo, "To Give the News Impartially, Without Fear or Favor," is still a respected ideal of the *Times*. Ochs was opposed to the Zionist dream of a Jewish state in Palestine. Like many German Jews whose families arrived mid-century—his father Julius Ochs came to the United States in 1845 and prospered—Adolph Ochs, and especially his brother George, who was mayor of Chattanooga, were assimilationists. They patronized recent immigrants who spoke Yiddish and retained European Jewish customs (Talese, 111).

The Ochs family moved East—George to manage a newspaper that Adolph had bought in Philadelphia, Adolph to New York. In the East, they learned—even more emphatically than in the South—that no matter how assimilated they thought they were, to some they would always be Jews. At various times the Ochs and Sulzbergers were made conscious of the fact that they were Jews. When they were admitted to private secondary schools—as George's son, John Oakes, was to Lawrenceville—it was as part of a minute Jewish quota. But they tried to separate this awareness from their roles as publishers of the *New York Times* and from their interactions with the Gentile world.

Ochs married the daughter of Isaac Wise, a giant in the American Jewish Reform movement and an anti-Zionist who saw Judaism as a religion and did not think of Jews as a special race. Ochs's views had a strong affinity with those of Wise; according to Ochs, "Religion is all I stand for as a Jew" (Leff, *Buried in the Times*, 26). Ochs was succeeded by his son-in-law Arthur Hays Sulzberger, who remained publisher for 26 years (1935–1961), during which time Iphigene Sulzberger—his wife, Ochs's daughter, and Wise's granddaughter—was reputed to have considerable influence on the *Times*. According to Harrison Salisbury she was more liberal than her husband and she was a great admirer of Adlai Stevenson (Salisbury, *Without Fear or Favor,* 90). While her views on Holocaust coverage did not differ from her husband's, she was more committed to Israel.

An extremely assimilated Jew who traced ancestors back to before the Revolutionary War, Arthur Hays Sulzberger, Ochs's son-in-law and successor, didn't like such phrases as "the Jewish people," preferring that editors use "people of the Jewish faith" or, simply, "Jews." Sulzberger believed Jews should be thought of as a religious group rather than a race or nationality, and disliked newspapers that emphasized the Jewish identity of people in the news. He did not believe Jews needed their own state or political and social institutions.

By today's standards, Sulzberger was something of a radical assimilationist, but such views were not uncharacteristic of German Jews whose families emigrated in the mid-nineteenth century. Sulzberger's most egregious public assimilationist position occurred in 1939, when he, along with other prominent Jews, advised President Roosevelt not to appoint Felix Frankfurter to the Supreme Court because they feared the appointment would increase anti-Semitism in America (Talese, 111–112). In 1946, the *Times* refused to publish an ad submitted by the American League for a Free Palestine (Talese, 112).

Until the later years of the twentieth century, the *Times* went to objectionable extremes not to favor Jews. As Guy Talese notes, the Jewish leadership of the *Times* historically would "bend over backwards to prove" that it was not a Jewish newspaper, but rather "a good citizens' newspaper, law-abiding and loyal, solidly in support of the best interests of the nation in peace and war" (113). The *Times* was conscious in those years of not having too Jewish a face. Talese writes of Amory Howe Bradford, who had risen quickly with the *Times* hierarchy in the 1950s and became general manager in 1960: "[Bradford] was also a kind of house Protestant in *The Times'* hierarchy, one who could represent the paper very well in those tight social circles where Jewish executives might not feel entirely welcome" (344).

For decades the *Times* required that Jews named "Abe" sign their names with initials—A. H. Raskin, A. H. Weiler, A. M. Rosenthal—and those with Jewish-sounding names, unless their name was Sulzberger, were less likely to get foreign assignments. As Salisbury and Gelb note in their memoirs, "The *Times* didn't like Jewish-sounding bylines" (Gelb, 229; Salisbury, 403). The exception was Meyer Berger—called Mike by everyone on the paper—who did get a byline for his "About New York" column, but perhaps that was acceptable because his very name,

"Meyer Berger," was ostentatiously identified with the ethnic diversity of New York City. At one point Rosenthal's name was removed from a banner story on Israel, and the article appeared without a byline. When he succeeded James Reston, who had the title of executive editor, Rosenthal was given the title managing editor and waited eight years— after Reston's brief and unsuccessful stay as executive editor—before being given the appellation executive editor. But, to his credit, Arthur Hays Sulzberger's son, Arthur Ochs "Punch" Sulzberger, appointed Rosenthal and, later, Frankel to the executive editorship. Punch was CEO and chairman of the board of the New York Times Company when his son Arthur Jr. appointed the Jewish Joseph Lelyveld. The son of a Jewish father and a Christian mother, Arthur Jr., as Tifft and Jones write, "could define himself as one or the other, depending upon the occasion," although a trip to Israel as an adolescent sharpened his sense of his Jewish heritage (*The Trust*, 652).

What Arthur Hays Sulzberger did not want was for the *Times* to be seen as a Jewish newspaper that was specially pleading for Jews. This dovetailed with the administration's view that Americans would not fight a war on behalf of Jews and that it needed—in the years leading up to World War II—to downplay atrocities to Jews as a reason to fight the war. Finally, as a Reform Jew who wished to think of himself as as American as Christian Caucasians and as a member of the establishment, Arthur Hays Sulzberger had a strong aversion for thinking of the Jews as a special ethnic group. As Laurel Leff puts it, "Philosophically, he considered singling out Jews to be a concession to Hitler's racial views and a contravention of his Reform Jewish convictions that the Jews were not a race but a people. . . . Sulzberger maintained that the only hope for European Jews was if their plight could be linked to that of other groups because . . . .a minority could not save itself" (Leff, 346–347). Thus, Sulzberger did not support lifting immigration quotas to allow Jews fleeing Germany to enter the United States. Leff quotes a July 22, 1939, editorial that is the quintessence of Sulzberger's position about German refugees, most of whom were Jewish: "It is not a Jewish problem or a Gentile problem. It does not belong to Europe or America. It is the problem of mankind" (33).

By reporting less than it knew about the Holocaust and the effects on Jews of Hitler's rise in the 1930s, the *Times* failed morally to fulfill its gatekeeping function. Sulzberger's strong belief that Jews "are neither a race nor a people" shaped the *Times*'s response to the

Holocaust and put him at an oblique angle to Hitler who regarded the Jews as a race and acted upon that belief (Leff). An October 1943 editorial about the Warsaw Ghetto uprising, which spoke about 500,000 "persons . . . herded into less than 7 percent of Warsaw's buildings" and the deportation of "400,000 persons," never mentioned that the persons were Jews. Sulzberger responded to criticism: "It is perfectly true that in our editorial we chose to think of Jews as human beings instead of a particular religious group, and apparently Zionists don't like that" (Leff, 221). Sulzberger completely missed the point that he had a responsibility not merely to Jews but to all Americans and to the world. Put blatantly, his responsibility was to highlight one of the worst atrocities in recorded human history: the extermination of an entire people. Like many assimilated Jews whose families had prospered in America and saw themselves first as Americans rather than as Jews, Sulzberger did not want to see the Jews as a race or people and did not understand that, given Hitler's ideology, he as a major American Jewish publisher had *no choice* other than stressing the consequences of Hitler's views. Building on a tradition of European anti-Semitism, Hitler created a world in which Jews were the victims of genocide; the only way to report it and to raise the world's consciousness was to accept Hitler's premise that Jews are a race because the alternative was to be a bystander. But Sulzberger chose to be an ostrich and ignore the essential fact that Hitler was eradicating European Jews.

What this episode in the *Times*'s history points up is how the misjudgments of one powerful member of the Fourth Estate can have a profound effect on history. The *Times*'s failure to report the obliteration of the Jewish presence in Europe gave cover in the media to those whose concern for Jews was limited or who felt that if the *Times* didn't focus on Jews, maybe the story was not all it was rumored to be.

Another major source of continuing Jewish displeasure with the *Times* is that Arthur Hays Sulzberger did not support the Zionist dream of establishing a Jewish state. He published an editorial on January 22, 1942, that denounced Jewish nationalism and all exclusively Jewish fighting units opposing Hitler. In the aforementioned *Times* October 1943 editorial on the Warsaw Ghetto uprising, the ghetto victims and fighters were not identified as Jews. By contrast, a December 31, 1943, editorial originating in the *Jewish Times* and also appearing, according to Leff, in nine other publications, argued: "Is it not a tragedy, a moral tragedy, another instance of Jewish self-hate, when a great paper like the *Times*, founded and published by Jews, tried to extirpate from its columns everything Jewish, even the things in which Jews must justly take pride?" (cited in Leff, 221).[1]

Nourished by the *Times*'s original failures in covering the Holocaust and its anti-Zionist position and continually fed by other real and imagined slights, many Jews today perceive the *Times* as (a) less than even-handed in its coverage of the Arab–Israeli conflict; (b) condescending and patronizing to Orthodox—and particularly Hasidic—Judaism; and (c) failing to chronicle anti-Semitism here and abroad and to highlight such insults and dangers as the Iranian president in 2006 calling the Holocaust a Western fiction and threatening to obliterate Israel.

During the McCarthy era, Sulzberger was slow to see that the witchhunt for Communists within the media and especially the film industry had a strong stench of anti-Semitism. In December 1955 and January 1958, thirty-seven past or present *Times* employees were subpoenaed by a Senate Internal Security subcommittee (headed by James Eastland) that was investigating Communism in the press. Indeed, perhaps because of its Jewish ownership as well as its influence and supposedly liberal bent, the *Times* seemed the major target because the lion's share of all subpoenas—thirty-seven of fifty-three—were directed at it. At first Sulzberger fired those who took the Fifth Amendment, but soon the *Times* adopted a feistier position, even though it did not forthrightly embrace the right of its employees to take the Fifth Amendment.

Resentment continues today in some parts of the Jewish community about how the *Times* reported the Holocaust. Although for several decades, the *Times* has been reasonably supportive if often critical of Israel, some observant Jews and fervent Zionists still deeply resent the Ochs-Sulzberger family as "self-hating Jews" and bitterly criticize the *New York Times* not only for past sins but also for current policies. In 1969, Talese wrote that the *Times* hierarchy was still embarrassed by "American Jews who dwelled on their Jewishness" (113). Even today, a sensitive reader is aware of how the *Times* bends over backward not to be known as a Jewish newspaper and treats ultra-Orthodox Jewry (the *haredi*) as curiosities who follow bizarre rituals.

---

[1] I am much indebted to her *Buried by the Times*, Cambridge: Cambridge University Press, 2005.

Thus, although secular and assimilated Jews have been among the most enthusiastic readers and advocates of the *Times*, it is fair to say that the perspectives shared by many Zionist and religious Jews about the shortcomings of the *Times* have deep roots. Between 2002 and 2008, when it closed, these perspectives found their voice daily on the pages of the *New York Sun*, under former editor of the *Forward*, Seth Lipsky, who was also the paper's president. Editorially, the paper announced from the outset that it would be unabashedly pro-Israel and philo-Semitic. As Eric Boehlert wrote in April 2002 in the online journal *Slate*:

> The *Sun*'s worldview was summed up on launch day in an unsigned editorial, "The War Against the Jews." Decrying anti-Semitism, "a virus that has claimed millions of lives over the centuries," the editorial drew a parallel between the Holocaust and recent pro-Palestinian demonstrations held in America, because they "are by and large rallies that support an anti-Semitism that is unthinkable to those who know the history." . . . [Another] editorial's anti-Palestinian rhetoric was extreme by the standards of the mainstream press: "Years from now, students of history are going to look back on the American funding of the Palestinian Authority the way they look back now on, say, the collaboration of the Swiss banks with the enemy in World War II." ("*The New York Sun*'s Not-so-bright Debut," April 25, 2002)

The now defunct *Sun* was on the watch for any pro-Palestinian behavior on the part of the administration and covered any violence against Israel or Jews. Extremely sensitive to slights to Jews, the *Sun* was on the look out for journalists, public figures, and even professors who were critical of Israel; an example is an April 18, 2006, piece by Eliana Johnson and Mitch Weber entitled "Yale's Next Tenured Radical?" which calls attention to the hiring of a professor whose scholarship, in the *Sun*'s view, is virulently anti-Israel and who speaks of "a Zionist cabal" influencing American foreign policy. Interestingly, readers of the *Sun* whom I know personally—all educated Jews—read it as a corrective to the *Times*'s coverage of Jewish issues and especially the Middle East, which they perceive as strongly tilted against Israel.

Many Jewish readers felt that the *New York Sun* not only reported more fairly and with more balance about Israel but that it more accurately reflected a Jewish perspective. The *New York Sun* claimed that the *Times* had wrongly accepted a report clearing some Columbia professors of alleged anti-Semitism in exchange for—as the *Times* put it in a lengthy and apologetic April 6, 2010, editor's note—not "seek[ing] reaction from other interested parties" (Okrent, "EXTRA! EXTRA! Read Not Quite Everything About It," April 10, 2005). Notwithstanding the apology, the damage had been done.

II. (Mis)Reporting the Holocaust

Let us look more closely at the *Times*'s Holocaust coverage. Had the *Times* done more to expose the Holocaust, maybe more could have been done to save victims. Furthermore, as the nation's most influential paper, the *Times* shaped the way other newspapers and media reported the news. Moreover, because it was known that Jews owned the *Times*, the indifference by the newspaper enabled others to overlook Hitler's policy of mass extermination of an entire people. Indeed, I think that the failure to foreground the enormity of the Holocaust and to put its editorial muscle behind attempts to save Jews may be the *Times*'s greatest failure.

What is clear from reading the *Times* during the war years is that Sulzberger did not want to focus on the suffering and victimization of Jews. During the war, this was not atypical of some parts of the Jewish community, many of whom were embarrassed by depictions of Jews as helpless victims and guilty that they weren't able to do more to help.

We need to remember that *survivor* is a later term. In the United States during the post–World War II decade and beyond, survivors were called "refugees" or "displaced persons" in private conversation and public schools; even in the suburban Hebrew school I attended for a few hours twice a week and on Sunday morning, the term used was *refugees*.

Why was the Holocaust a suppressed subject? Did American Jews feel they had something to be ashamed of because they did not prevent the destruction of their European counterparts? Did they fear provoking American anti-Semitism by special pleading? Was it that Jewish parents thought that children's sensibilities could not deal with the horrors of genocide?

On November 14, 2001, Max Frankel wrote an important piece for the *Times* 150th anniversary edition entitled "Turning Away from the

Holocaust." Some would argue that Frankel is more forgiving than he should be and finds more excuses for the *Times*'s myopic and aberrant behavior than he should. He acknowledges that "Like most—though not all—American media, and most of official Washington, the *Times* drowned its reports about the fate of Jews in the flood of wartime news. The *Times* generally took the view that atrocities inflicted on Jews, although horrific, were not significantly different or more noteworthy than those visited on tens of millions of other war victims." He wants to put the *Times*'s reporting in the context of "the century's bitterest journalistic failure." In doing so, he acknowledges—and in retrospect I see this as a chilling indictment of the *Times*'s behavior—that "Only six times in nearly six years did the *Times*'s front page mention Jews as Hitler's unique target for total annihilation."

As Frankel admits, newspapers like *PM*—a New York daily—and the *New York Post* and magazines like *The Nation* and *The New Republic* were more attentive. During the period of Hitler's rise *The New Republic*, *The Nation*, and *PM* "ardently advocated rescue measures" and foregrounded coverage of the plight of the Jews. For example, on November 15, 1939, after the publication of a White Paper, *The New Republic*—then a weekly—indicted England for sitting down with Hitler at Munich when it knew how the Nazis were treating Jews: "London knew all about those dreadful stories when Chamberlain sat down with Hitler at Munich. . . . The White Paper is published now only because the two countries are at war and it makes good propaganda. Diplomats have strong stomachs" (Leff, 349). By contrast Sulzberger, the anglophile, usually gave the British a free pass.

What we do need to remember is that the *Times*—and its editorial stance—embraced the government's wartime policies and rarely questioned its judgment. Even in its one lead editorial on the Holocaust on December 2, 1942, following the State Department's unofficial confirmation that two million Jews had been slain, the *Times* shamefully refused to focus on the Jews as the major victims. Rather the editorial, "The First to Suffer," stressed that "people of other faiths and races" would soon be victims. It is not too much to say that throughout World War II, the *Times* did not highlight the Jews as victims of Hitler's atrocities or focus on his ethnic cleansing or realize how what Lucy Dawidowicz has called "The War Against the Jews" took precedence over the other battles Hitler was conducting, especially once the Germans realized that defeat was inevitable.

The *Times* prided itself on its focus on all victims of the Nazis rather than the genocide being committed against Jews. Arthur Hays Sulzberger was very much aware that in five polls taken between March 1938 and April 1940, 60 percent of Americans thought Jews had "objectionable" qualities and another poll showed the same percentage thought persecution in Europe was at least partly the Jews' own fault. As Frankel put it, rather too gently, "Papers owned by Jewish families, like the *Times*, were plainly afraid to have a still anti-Semitic society misread their passionate opposition to Hitler as a merely parochial cause." Rereading the *Times*, we ask what could its publisher and senior editors have been thinking? Where was its moral compass? Wasn't anyone willing to stand up and be counted at its editorial meetings?

Only during one forty-eight-hour period in March 1943, as Frankel and others have noted, did the *Times* somewhat rise to the occasion. The *Times* foreign columnist, Anne O'Hare McCormick, wrote on March 3, 1943, about the Madison Square Garden rally calling for the rescue of Jews. On that day, the *last* of seven editorials in the *Times* suggested that free nations might lift their immigration restrictions. The preceding day the *Times*'s front page had carried a headline "SAVE DOOMED JEWS/HUGE RALLY PLEADS" but it was the smallest of eleven front-page headlines that day. When the editorial page returned to the subject a year later, "it urged," according to Frankel, "saving 'innocent people' without ever using the word Jew" (November 14, 2001).

Frankel notes that on the inside pages. "The *Times* was much less hesitant about offering persuasive and gruesome details of the systematic murder of Jews." But reading the wartime *Times*, one sees that, as Frankel puts it, "No article about the Jews' plight ever qualified as the *Times*'s leading story." On December 18, 1942, the smallest of the twelve headlines on page 1 reported "ALLIES CONDEMN NAZI WAR ON JEWS" and a brief editorial observed that the Allies were responding to "officially established facts" (cited in Frankel, November 14, 2001). Missing, as always in the *Times*'s editorial coverage, is the tone of high moral outrage that one would have expected about genocide that had already claimed two million victims.

On July 2, 1944, a story appeared on page 12 limited to four column inches reporting "authoritative information" that 400,000 Hungarian Jews were "deported to their deaths and an additional 350,000 were to be killed in the next three weeks." On the same day, when these horrors occurred, a story about July 4 celebrations appeared on page 1. In 1945, at the end of World War II, a story entitled "1,000,000 Jews slain by Nazis" was relegated to page 7; another reported that nearly 400,000 "Europeans" had been killed by Hitler and waited until the seventh paragraph before using the word "Jew." Another source of resentment is that the front-page story of the liberation of Dachau never mentioned the word "Jew." A week later, a column by Cyrus Sulzberger, Arthur's nephew and chief foreign correspondent during the war, about Russian estimates of the death toll at Auschwitz never indicated that the victims were Jews.

Indeed, the one reporter who might have been able to insist on front-page coverage of the Holocaust was the aforementioned Cyrus Sulzberger, but he, like his assimilated uncle, did not focus on the plight of Jews. On January 4, 1945, he recommended to managing editor Edwin L. ("Jimmy") James that a Jew not be assigned to cover Palestine: "Because the Palestine question is bound to boil up. I think the *New York Times* would be in a better position having a non-Jewish reporter covering it no matter how objective a Jewish reporter might be" (quoted in Leff, 322).

Frankel quotes Laurel Leff, who in 2005 published an invaluable book entitled *Buried in the Times* about the *Times*'s failures in reporting the Holocaust: "You could have read the front page of the *New York Times* in 1939 and 1940 without knowing that millions of Jews were being sent to Poland, imprisoned in ghettoes and dying of disease and starvation by the tens of thousands. . . . In 1944, you would have learned from the front page of the existence of horrible places such as Maidenek and Auschwitz, but only inside the paper could you find that the victims were Jews. In 1945, [liberated] Dachau and Buchenwald were on the front page, but the Jews were buried inside" (Frankel, November 14, 2001, quoted from Leff's article in the March 2000 *Harvard International Journal of Press/Politics*). Anticipated by the aforementioned article, Leff's 2005 book is a scathing indictment of the *Times*'s selection and arrangement of news and its outright omissions. She makes a compelling argument that the *Times*'s narrative of the Holocaust was hopelessly inadequate and inept.

During the years of Hitler's reign, the *Times* published not six stories on the front page, as it does now, but twelve to fifteen stories, and yet only 44 of 24,000 stories specifically concerned Jews (Leff, 341). From September 1939 to May 1945 the *Times* published 1,186 stories about what was happening to Jews in Europe—about 17 a month, but these stories about the "discrimination, deportation, and destruction of Jews" made the front page only twenty-six times and "only in six of those stories were Jews identified as the primary victims" (Leff, 2–3). The Holocaust story was never the lead story that appears in the right-hand columns: "When the Holocaust made the *Times* front page, the stories obscured the fact that most of the victims were Jews, referring to them instead as refugees or persecuted minorities" (3).

Newspapers decide how to organize the narrative of the news. Their selection and arrangements shape what we know. During wartime, readers conferred their trust on both political leaders and newspapers. After World War II, there was a desire—even a fervent hope in the aftermath of a national trauma—to believe in both political leaders and newspapers as vessels of truth, but gradually that faith has eroded due to a series of events beginning with the Cuban Missile Crisis and including the Vietnam War, the Pentagon Papers, Watergate, and the run-up to and reporting on the Iraqi war. We now know about government prevarication, journalistic complicity, and journalistic failures. As a nation we are skeptical if not cynical about almost anything we are told, and we suspect and impugn the motives of the tellers.

It is absolutely clear that earlier readers of the *Times* had greater faith in the paper's gatekeeping role than they do now. As former editor of *The Nation*, Oswald Garrison Villard wrote in 1944: "No important journalist can possibly do without [the *Times*], and it has literally made itself indispensable to anyone who desires to be thoroughly informed as to what is happening on this globe. To miss even an issue is a detriment to all who deal with foreign affairs" (quoted in Leff, 12; from Villard, *The Disappearing Daily*, 78).

Just as nations set policies that affect and control the life of their citizens—and in wartime that control increases dramatically even in democratic countries—so newspapers have editorial policies for managing information. The *Times*'s management of information during wartime played a role in insulating the Holocaust from its audience. Newspapers can imprison information or can, to use Leff's grim term evoking Hitler's Final Solution, bury it. Basically, the *Times*'s coverage of the Final Solution—as well as the rising tide of German and European anti-Semitism, the concentration camps, the death camps—was marked by neglect and understatement. Looking back, we can see that the *Times* rarely expressed editorial outrage and did not shape its news coverage to arouse its readers.

Leff's argument depends on four major interrelated points: The *Times*'s failure to foreground on its front pages and lead articles the information at its disposal, namely that the Germans were committing genocide against a particular people; the downplaying even in its back pages that victims were Jews; the moral failure of the Jewish ownership of the *Times* to take the lead in informing the world of what was going on and in editorials to give the subject the focus it deserved; and, finally, the failure of the *Times* to fulfill its responsibilities as the unique and powerful newspaper of influence and record that was read by governments and influential people outside government. She makes a compelling case that information about extermination camps was available in 1942 and 1943, albeit from secondary sources such as "exile governments, Jewish groups, German and local newspapers and, to a lesser extent, allied governments" (Leff, 332).

Had the *Times*, with its great influence, used its front page to expose and foreground the horrors of Hitler's policies beginning in 1933, perhaps the world's consciousness would have been raised. But the Berlin bureau chief Guido Enderis was sympathetic to the Nazi regime and "blunt[ed] coverage of the Nazis' most extreme anti-Semitic actions" (343). Even though its chief foreign correspondent, Fredrick Birchall, a former acting managing editor, won a Pulitzer for reporting from Germany, from our 2006 vantage point—aided by Leff's research—we know that the *Times* could have been more zealous in documenting the systematic attack on the basic human rights of Jews from 1933. Enderis's cozy relationship with the regime kept the Berlin bureau open long after other American news media were expelled, but this was done at the expense of the *Times*'s integrity. By the time the war began, the Berlin bureau was staffed by Enderis and two inexperienced reporters.

Under the managing editor, the aforementioned "Jimmy" James, the *Times* was willing to make compromises to keep the Berlin bureau open. James, whose management style was to assign responsibilities to others and not meddle, was willing to cede authority about what was on the front page to the night editors—known as the bullpen—under the direction of managing editor Raymond McCaw. Assistant manager Neil MacNeil actually made the decisions about what appeared on the front page. Commenting on the Catholic orientation of a "bullpen" insensitive to Jews, Leff recalls a bromide that I heard on occasion in the 1940s, 1950s, and even 1960s, namely that the *Times* was "owned by Jews and edited by Catholics for Protestants." But much of the fault also lay with the journalists themselves; as Leff explains, reporting of the Final Solution was marred not only by ineptitude in the *Times* Berlin bureau but elsewhere as well: "Riven by distrust of each other's abilities and motives, hobbled by their own limitations as journalists, members of the *Times* Stockholm and Berne bureaus did not pursue the story of what was happening to Europe's Jews, nor did they receive directions from New York to do so" (149).

Had the *Times* editorially supported more liberal immigration policies, had it supported emigration to Palestine in the early Hitler years, had it supported military actions (such as bombing the concentration and especially the extermination camps and/or the railroad transportation system that fed the camps), Jewish lives could have been saved. As the war turned toward the Allies' advantage, had the *Times* editors vigorously urged dropping troops behind the lines to liberate the camps, perhaps the public and the government would have paid attention. Had the *Times* editors, instead of putting on page 6 Bernard Valery's unusually explicit June 16, 1942 story, of the murder of 60,000 Vilna Jews by the "German controlled Lithuania police," foregrounded it as the lead story, maybe America's conscience would have been stirred. But even that crucial Valery story was eviscerated by a second-paragraph demurral claiming that "The Polish refugee's story of the Vilna massacre of which he said he was an eye-witness, is impossible to confirm" (quoted in Leff, 137). One would have thought the news in a United Press report of a World Jewish Congress report that one million Jews had been massacred was also worth more than a *Times* page 7 report. By contrast, the *New Republic* on December 21, 1942, carried an eloquent article by Varian Fry, "The Massacre of Jews," which foregrounded the horror of two million Jews being slain with another five million as potential victims and the United States for not relaxing visa procedures and faulted the news media for not being more attentive and strident (816–819).

Fry graphically highlights some of the worst Nazi excesses in the 1930s leading to Kristallnacht. Although originally a writer and editor, Fry, working under the auspices of a private organization called the Emergency Rescue Committee, saved a few thousand Jews from Vichy and has been called the American Schindler. Fry wrote about the evidence he had accumulated from various sources, including the New York Office of the General Jewish Workers Union of Poland and the World Jewish Conference in Geneva, as well as letters and reports he had received from various sources in occupied Europe: "Letters, reports, cables all fit together. They add up to the most appalling picture of mass murder in all human history. Nor is it only the Jews who are threatened" (818). Interestingly he, too, adds a codicil about the suffering of others, but throughout the article the focus is on what he calls in the lead paragraph "the systematic extermination of Jews" (816). And his article is eloquent, angry, and even bitter when he speaks of how the remaining five million "are scheduled to be destroyed as soon as Hitler's blond butchers can get around to them" (816).

Never once did the *Times* speak in these terms, either in its editorials, or its op-ed pages, or in its news columns, and rarely in citing quotes of others within its news stories. True, horrific headlines appeared on inside pages such as a page two headline on April 2, 1943, "French Jews sent to a Nazi Oblivion." But identifying the source as the World Jewish Conference, which in turn learned it from "a prominent French Jew who had escaped to a neutral country," gave skeptics a chance to think it must be an exaggeration. Of course, it was difficult in 1943 to have reporters embedded behind the lines. It is poignantly ironic that the *Times* was so insistent on verifying sources in the face of overwhelming evidence of mass Jewish deaths in Europe and of the incredible difficulty of finding death camp escapees and yet it has been so slack on other occasions in its more recent history, occasions—including claims of WMDs in Iraq—that we have discussed in prior chapters.

Often one source for horrific stories was the Germans themselves. In one case, the World Jewish Conference reported, according to the *Times*, "the Germans had informed several foreign consulates that by tonight all Jews of foreign citizenship, including neutrals like the Swiss and Turks, must be out of France" (April 2, 1943). That the article is based on secondhand information—and from the World Jewish

Conference passing on what the Germans told foreign consulates—and has no byline (but rather was identified as "wireless to the *New York Times*") undermines some of its authority. By contrast, the December 21, 1942, Varian Fry *New Republic* piece depends on Fry's establishing within his article his credentials as an empathetic observer who, it was later learned, was also a participant in rescuing Jews.

The aforementioned former editor of *The Nation,* Oswald Garrison Villard, took the *Times* to task in his 1944 book *The Disappearing Daily* for not vigorously defending "the horribly ill-treated Jewish people. . . . For never were human beings more entitled to be defended and championed by a great organ of public opinion; certainly never have men and women anywhere been tortured and slaughtered in such numbers with less reason" (quoted in Leff, 281).

But most of the mainstream press focused on the war and did not stress the plight of the Jews. It would be as if Hurricane Katrina were covered as a story about weather rather than a story about victims or as if 9/11 were more about terrorists using aircraft as weapons rather than about the victims and their families. Even first-person stories by *Times* reporters about the liberation of camps focused on "political prisoners"—as if Jews fell within that category—and stressed that the prison inhabitants challenged the Nazi regime. Thus, genocide was submerged. The *Times* wrote five stories about the liberation of Belson and yet these stories mentioned Jews only once, although as Leff points out, 40,000 of 55,000 survivors were Jews. And the *Times* did not make clear why so relatively few Jews were in many camps, namely, because they had been killed or starved to death.

From our vantage point, we see that the Holocaust story was underplayed and, indeed, at the 1996 centenary celebration exhibit of Ochs's taking control of the *Times* at the New York Public Library, Arthur Gelb acknowledged the validity of the criticism. To some extent Frankel's and Gelb's explanations illustrate the folk wisdom (which I have heard called Callaghan's Law) that when you have dug yourself a deep enough hole, you need to stop digging. The *Times* cannot really talk itself out of the hole that it dug for itself. Nevertheless, the *Times*'s public expiation of its editorial sins has its internal and external purposes. Not only does it make the newspaper's staff feel better able—by means of profuse apologies—to claim moral high ground, but also it wins public esteem by showing itself willing to participate in self-examination and self-criticism.

III. The *Times* and Israel

Arthur Hays Sulzberger helped found, with a group of Reform Jewish rabbis, the American Council on Judaism in 1942, a group that opposed a Jewish state because it wanted to define Jewishness in religious rather than nationalistic terms. In the face of Jewish outrage, Sulzberger hired Bernard Richards, who was on the staff of the Jewish Information Bureau in 1943, to advise him on Jewish matters and perhaps mend fences with Jewish readers and Jewish critics. Without disclosing he was on the *Times* payroll, Richards wrote letters to various publications defending Sulzberger. But in January 1944, Sulzberger opposed Jewish rescue efforts of Jews facing extermination. After the war, Sulzberger's continued opposition to Israel as a separate state earned him the opprobrium of most American Jews.

As we have noted, Arthur Hays Sulzberger's basic tenet—and the underpinning of his anti-Zionism—was that Jews were a religious group not a race or a people. Even after World War II, and after touring concentration camps and, on a second tour, displaced persons camps, Sulzberger had not changed his mind about "downplay[ing] the extermination of Jews" (Leff, 319) or about his opposition to a Jewish state. In a July 18, 1945, editorial, the *Times* argued for "solv[ing] the problem of religious discrimination" in Europe even while acknowledging that most of the 1.25 million Jews who remained in Europe did not want to return to "living in communities where they were so frightfully abused" (Leff, 323). But by 1946, the tide among American Jews was turning and more and more of Sulzberger's anti-Zionist allies were now supportive of a Jewish state.

The *Times* supported the partition of Palestine in 1947 as a way of supporting and of bolstering the prestige of the fledgling United Nations. But it did not endorse Israel's Declaration of Independence in May 1948. A few months later, Sulzberger wrote in a letter to a fellow anti-Zionist: "I feel no closer to the state of Israel than I do to Britain or China" (Leff, 328). He never visited Israel and gradually disassociated himself from formal ties to Reform Judaism, although he always considered himself a Jew (Leff, 328–329).

Aware of his Jewish readership, Sulzberger did assign a reporter, Irving "Pat" Spiegal, to cover "Jewish News" and write about Jewish committees and congresses, including Zionist ones. But this was considered even by his senior staff a kind of bone he was throwing to an enclave with which he had an ambiguous relationship. Under the influence of his wife, Iphigene Ochs Sulzberger, who, according to what Max Frankel told me, "was always for the creation of [the state of Israel]," Arthur Hays Sulzberger eventually accepted Israel (April 16, 2005). Gradually, under his son, Arthur Ochs "Punch" Sulzberger, the *Times* took a more enlightened view of its Jewish roots and let Jewish editors lead the paper.

In his "Turning Away from the Holocaust" piece, Frankel unconvincingly claims that the media's sensitivity to "ethnic barbarities in far-off places like Uganda, Rwanda, Bosnia, and Kosovo" now derives from its failures to "fasten upon Hitler's mad atrocities" (November 14, 2001). With a combination of ingenuousness and idealism—but lacking empirical evidence—Frankel concludes that the *Times*'s prior failure "leaves [reporters and editors] obviously resolved that in the face of genocide, journalism should not have failed in vain."

In fact, traditional print journalism—and even digital journalism—usually is too late to save the first wave of victims. One could cite as examples the killing fields in Cambodia; atrocities in Rwanda and Uganda; the fate of South Vietnamese who opposed Ho Chi Minh after the Americans left; those—mostly Kurds and Shiites—slaughtered by Hussein in Iraq; victims of tribal and ethnic rivalries in Africa, including Darfur, as well as in the Balkans—indeed, all those worldwide who have opposed autocrats or racial and ethnic hegemony, and are thus for political reasons the objects of violence. But although journalism is not always effective in stopping genocide, the ensuing victims—often a much larger number than the first wave—have at least a chance if the light is shone on political massacres.

IV. Return of the Repressed

The *Times*'s comparative silence about the Holocaust mirrors the much more striking silence of the American community that, despite the Nuremberg trials and the gruesome pictures in *Life* magazine, chose to repress their guilt not only for assuming the role of helpless onlookers but even for their tacit complicity. We now know how much the American political leadership knew and how little they did about it. Thus, a conspiracy of silence obscured the ineffectuality and complicity of the American political establishment.

With the atrocities and deprivation of constitutional rights experienced by African Americans, particularly in the South, the *Times* and other media rightfully focused attention in the later 1950s and 1960s on the civil rights movement in the U.S. But there was surprisingly little linkage in the media, including the *Times*, to the relatively recent wartime persecution of Jews and especially the attack on the civil rights of Jews in Germany in the 1930s, an attack that preceded the worst atrocities. Nor did the *Times* stress the prominence of Jews—perhaps responding in part to their own realization that the world stood in silence when they were victims in Europe—in the civil rights movement.

That the *Times*'s editorials downplayed the effect of Hitler on European Jews, usually didn't identify Jews as the victims, and pushed the Final Solution to back pages affected the way America—including Jews who read the *Times* daily and thought it was the received word on the world—understood the Holocaust. One cannot blame the *Times* for the reticence on the part of some assimilated Jews to discuss the Holocaust, but one can say that their views and their discourse were shaped and enabled by the *Times*. In contrast, American Jews living in areas where the Jewish population was dense, especially those first- and second-generation Jews from Poland, Lithuania, and Russia, were outraged at the *Times*'s indifference and the indifference of their fellow Jews; that resentment lives in some of their offspring.

Relating the reasons for revisiting the Holocaust trauma in France to the larger pattern throughout the world, Roger Cohen perspicaciously wrote in the *Times* on October 19, 1997:

> As a bloody century wanes, repentance is in vogue, a sort of global purging of the soul before the millennium. A world relatively becalmed, perhaps moderately bored, is confronting the upheavals of the past hundred years as a form of atonement. British colonialism, Nazism, Communist totalitarianism, apartheid: the candidates for expiatory examination are rich and varied. But nowhere, perhaps, is the process more fraught or obsessive than in France's contemplation of its treatment of the Jews during World War II.
>
> The forces pushing France toward an orgy of retrospection are similar to those at work elsewhere: the passing from power of the generation that lived the war years; the end of

the Cold War with its bending of truth to strategic impera-
tives; the odd moral magnetism of the number 2000, so
evocative of a circle completed as to be an invitation to what
Pope John Paul II has called "the purification of memory."

Here, as in other countries, there appears to be an
almost physical realization of the sheer weight of the century's
slaughter, and the triumph of the ideology of human rights
in a post-ideological age leads naturally to the examination
of past brutality.

If we substitute "the *Times*" for France in the aforementioned
quote and acknowledge that the *Times*'s errors were more those of
omission rather commission, aren't Cohen's terms also appropriate to
explain the *Times*'s attempt at expiation? Isn't Leff's book *Buried by the
Times: The Holocaust and America's Most Important Newspaper* part of
the reexamination of past brutality?

Cohen's comments are all-more telling and pointed when we
remember that the received version of France's role in World War II
was created by the *Times* as much as by any Western media. In part
it is because of the rather gentle way that the Vichy government was
presented in the *Times* that the French were given a pass on their wartime behavior. Leff demonstrates that "*Times* correspondents wrote story
after story rationalizing the French government's anti-Semitic legislation
and excusing the deplorable conditions in the French camps" (Leff, 78).
The *Times* overlooked Vichy anti-Semitism while blaming the bulk of
anti-Semitism on the Germans (Leff, 101). Vichy controlled the southern third of France, and the two *Times* reporters who covered Vichy,
Gaston H. Archambault and Lansing Warren, were less than zealous
in reporting the French treatment of Jews during the occupation; in
fact, as Leff notes, they "almost never reported the news of the French
government's mounting anti-Semitic decrees without interpreting the
moves to cast the Vichy government in the most positive light" (82).

Each country, including the United States, wrote its own version
of postwar history, often to suit the needs both of rebuilding its self-
esteem and of its contemporary political situation. Those needs included
the geopolitics of the Cold War. The government and the media told
us that the United States, England, and France won the war, when in
fact France was a defeated country complicit in the Holocaust. Little

mention during the Cold War period was made of the Soviet's role and their terrible human losses. In the last few years, we also have seen the image of neutral Switzerland tarnished as we have learned about Switzerland's role in expropriating Jewish money after the war as well as laundering expropriated German money and harboring and protecting Nazi assets during the war.

Decades passed before France began as a nation to reexamine its role and realize that only a comparatively few partisans resisted the Vichy government, while the vast majority cooperated with a government that rounded up and deported Jews beyond the Nazi demands. Finally, fifty years later, French war criminals such as Maurice Papon were brought to trial. Even in 2010, new revelations from the repressed French political past came to light. In France after the Allied victory, 300,000 French collaborators were arrested and 7,037 were put to death. But then followed twenty-five years of silence after the war before a period of reexamination. Now after another silence, a new generation in France—and, indeed, in other European countries—is seeing the past far differently from the way their parents or grandparents did. What Craig R. Whitney said about France in the October 6, 1997, *New York Times* applies to many other nations:

> France did not come easily to willingness to go through with [Papon's] trial, which examines a subject that was long taboo—crimes committed in the name of France not just by egregious collaborators and disgraced Vichy leaders convicted of treason like Marshal Henry Philippe Pétain, who died in prison, and Prime Minister Pierre Laval, who was executed, but by anonymous civil servants and other French functionaries who stayed at their jobs. . . . Many did terrible things that were later enfolded by a collective loss of memory in a nation all too eager to forget. ("France Amasses Bitter Evidence 5 Decades After Holocaust")

The *New York Times* played a large role in defining how Americans saw the French role in World War II and allowing Americans to join the French in the belief, "encouraged," as Whitney puts it, "by the Resistance leader, Gen. Charles de Gaulle, President of France from 1958 to 1969, and other postwar leaders . . . that the ultimate responsibility of the Nazi occupiers and the illegitimacy of the Vichy regime absolved France from complicity in the crimes of the Holocaust."

Of course, the contemporary obsession with writing (righting) historic wrongs in which the *Times* has been participating is a necessary and salutary return of the repressed. Apologizing for the past may make members of institutions that either turned their heads from atrocities, or were compliant, feel better, but it does little for the survivors and their relatives and less for the victims. How else do we account for the burgeoning interest in Holocaust studies? What is it about our time that has brought the Shoah to the fore? Is it in part what we might call the CNNing of the world, so that now the Jewish global village can look into its past together, while forming an elaborate support group? Have the Europeans become a related codependent support group, responding to and reflecting on the Jewish angst, often by denying, sublimating, editing, reconfiguring, evading, and sometimes by sorting a little dirty laundry in public—for example, the 1997 Maurice Papon trial in France—so as to avoid our seeing the graves in the basement? What Michael André Bernstein writes is relevant to the *Times*'s self-examination and self-critique:

> If anything can be concluded from the ceaseless outpouring of works in every genre and medium about the Nazi genocide, it is how central that cataclysm has become to the self-interrogation of the culture we inhabit today. Although among non-Jews the consensus evolved only very gradually, by now there is a surprisingly widespread sense that the Shoah constitutes the defining event of the Second World War, that the extermination of European Jewry was not merely one among many competing projects of the Third Reich, but rather the very essence of Nazism, and that the universe of the death camps created a decisive breach in the fabric of the modern world. ("Lasting Injury," *TLS*, March 7, 1997)

What Lucy Dawidowicz has called "The War Against the Jews" was the defining event of World War II and the steps leading up to it. The *Times*'s reporting of "The War Against the Jews" did a disservice to its readers—including national and world leaders—and the rest of the world's free press that depended upon it for leadership.

V. Covering Israel's 2006 Confrontation with Hezbollah and Hamas

Many Jews objected to the *Times*'s supposed even-handedness in cover-ing Israel's July–August 2006 war with Hezbollah and the 2008–2009 Gaza war with Hamas. In the first conflict, should more attention also have been paid to the presence in the Hezbollah arsenal of Iranian weapons and the possibility of Iranian military advisors? Certainly, far more than the *Times*, the *New York Sun* emphasized the Iranian threat to Israel and focused on the statements of the Iranian president, who denies the Holocaust, wants to obliterate Israel, and sponsored a large exhibit of anti-Semitic art in Tehran.

Fair coverage is a difficult concept and I have no simple formula. Was it fair to have more photographs and accounts of Lebanese dead than Israeli dead because far more Lebanese died? Was it fair to show more pictures of suffering Lebanese civilians rather than of Israeli civilian casualties because the Israelis have bomb shelters and seem to have made partial provision for their civilians to withstand rocket attacks? By taking refuge among civilians, did Hezbollah cynically disregard the very civilians they should be protecting? Should daily articles remind readers of the long- and short-range historical context and who provoked the violence? On the other hand, need every article about Lebanese victims stress how Hezbollah fighters fired their rockets from civilian areas and took refuge among the civilians?

Perhaps each day's coverage of international conflicts should include a brief factual overview based on prior reporting. In this case, such a factual overview would remind readers that the Lebanese government ceded the area near the Israel border to Hezbollah—a group trying to destroy Israel—and allowed them to practice terror-ism against Israel and to control supply lines throughout the country. It might remind readers that for years Israel has had to contend with suicide bombers attacking civilians.

Although the *Times* was supportive of Israel's aggressive attacks on Hamas and Hezbollah in July 2006, it characteristically worried about excessive and disproportionate force on the part of Israel. In one of its early editorials after Israel first began to respond militar-ily to a kidnapping by Hamas and rockets from Gaza and to take an even more vigorous military approach to Hezbollah rockets and the Hezbollah's kidnapping of two soldiers, the *Times* called for restraint. Not only American Jews but also others of Israel's friends wondered if the *Times*'s continued call for restraint and its editorial warnings to Israel about "disproportionate" force would have occurred if it were the United States rather than Israel that had been attacked by its neighbors.

The succinct, lucid, and informed articles by Stephen Erlanger—supplemented by the reporting of colleagues and analyses from Washington by such writers as Helene Cooper—were as good as any media coverage in putting the war into context. For example, on July 15, 2006, Erlanger's lead story "Israel Vows to Rout Hezbollah as Violence Escalates" was accompanied by a trenchant first-page article by Cooper entitled "U.S. Needing Options, Finds its Hands Tied." Under the sub-heading "Turmoil in the Middle East," the *Times* reporters—reporting from Beirut, Baghdad, the Gaza strip, and St. Petersburg, where Bush was conferring at the annual summit meeting of the world's economic powers (known as the G8)—provided a panoramic overview of the international ramifications as well as detailed war coverage supplemented online with poignant pictures.

As events unfolded in July 2006, the *Times*'s editorials first offered tempered support for Israel's aggressive response and the Bush administration's deliberately glacially slow diplomatic response so as to give Israel time for its military response. But, although supporting the release of soldiers held hostage, the *Times*'s editorial support for Israel's war effort soon eroded and the news stories became less sympathetic. In a July 25, 2006, editorial entitled "No More Foot Dragging," urging a diplomatic solution, the *Times* contended: "Ms. Rice needs to make clear to Israel that more civilian deaths in Lebanon won't make Israelis safer." In a July 29, 2006, article entitled "A Right Way To Help Israel," the *Times*—even while acknowledging the legitimacy of Israel's response—seemed to take a strong stand against continued U.S. support for the Israeli military campaign.

After Israel's bombing of Qana led to substantial civilian losses—"many of them children" according to the *Times*'s August 1, 2006, editorial—the *Times* became more strident in calling for a cease-fire. This editorial did not mention either the kidnapping of Israeli soldiers or Hezbollah's rocket barrages on Haifa, although it did mention the necessity at some point—but not linked to a cease-fire and, indeed, after Beirut's airport and seaport were opened—"of making sure that Syria and Iran do not resupply Hezbollah with long-range rockets capable of hitting Israel." One need not be a Zionist zealot but merely a fair-minded observer to ask what guarantees would Israel have once Israel agreed to a cease-fire before an international force and monitoring system was in place?

Following the Qana tragedy, which may have been exaggerated and perhaps partially staged, the *Times* increasingly focused on the Lebanese as victims without explaining how Hezbollah fighters and their rockets were embedded in the population and in fact using civilians as human shields, in part as a cynical Hezbollah ploy to create the image of the Israelis as heartless murderers. In its August 7, 2006, editorial, "A Truce for Lebanon," the *Times*, accepting the possibly inflated Lebanese casualty count, concluded: "This ugly war has already killed about 700 Lebanese and more than 90 Israelis. Close to one out of every four people in Lebanon have been routed from their homes. With the human price of combat so high, this settlement must be built to last." The first sentence doesn't allot blame or recall historical contexts—such as the kidnapping of Israeli soldiers or years of Hezbollah rocket fire on the Israelis—but treats the war as if it were a natural disaster like an earthquake or a hurricane: "It is now 26 days since Hezbollah and Israel began their latest combat—a very long time for the world to allow such a deadly conflict to rage in the Middle East powder keg. Yet the fighting still continues. Diplomats still dither over cease-fire details. Innocent people still keep dying."

Some of the *Times*'s reporters in Lebanon were extremely sympathetic to the Lebanese point of view and oblivious to Israeli suffering or the war's context. Throughout the war and in its aftermath, Hassan M. Fatah and Sabrina Tavernise's articles from Lebanon not only continued to represent Hezbollah's claim that Lebanon was a victim, but also became increasingly strident in playing advocate. Fatah's July 21, 2006, article on Lebanese fleeing Tyre—"In Scramble to Evade Israeli Bombs, the Living Leave the Dead Behind"—emphasized unburied dead as civilians fled. The story stressed the horrible effects of Israeli action without mentioning the context—Tyre was the Hezbollah center—or comparable effects in Northern Israel, which had been under rocket attacks for days, or the rockets fired regularly from Gaza since Israel's withdrawal: "Officials at the Tyre Government Hospital inside a local Palestinian refugee camp said they counted the bodies of 50 children among the 115 in the refrigerated truck in the morgue, though their count could not be independently confirmed." Underneath the headline is a photograph captioned "Residents of Tyre, Lebanon, headed north

Thursday after being warned by the Israeli military to leave," but the photograph of people on a bus could have been taken anywhere in the Middle East—or, indeed, wherever Arabs live. And how do readers know that some of these faces are not Hezbollah terrorists? And should the *Times* have included photos of Israelis fleeing Haifa?

On August 16, 2006, the *Times* carried a typical bylined story by Fatah under the headline—headlines were presumably provided by the *Times* headline editors in New York—"Destruction: As Cease-Fire Holds, Lebanese Dig for the War's Victims in the Rubble of Many Towns." The story was accompanied by a Lynsey Addario photograph captioned "Lebanese emergency workers lined up coffins for a mass burial in Tyre yesterday. The dead had been brought from around southern Lebanon." Fatah begins:

> SREIFA, Lebanon, August 15—The reality of the war came out of the rubble in bits and pieces on Tuesday—an army boot in one town, a gold wedding ring in another, a pair of jeans elsewhere—all the pieces of lives lost in the destruction wrought by the monthlong conflict that came to a halt on Monday in a tenuous cease-fire.
>
> On Tuesday, secrets buried in southern Lebanon's ruins began to emerge as Lebanese Red Cross workers, health workers and Hezbollah members set upon the heaps of stone and concrete in towns along the Israeli border, digging out bodies of men, women and children trapped there for weeks. The work will last for weeks in towns with names that have become synonymous with tragedy.

Many readers had a problem with Fatah's never mentioning the context for the destruction or that Hezbollah was embedded in the civilian population of villages in Southern Lebanon. Nor did he mention the damage that Hezbollah inflicted on Israel's civilians or that Israel separates its civilians from its military to avoid civilian casualties.

On August 15, 2005, the day after the ceasefire, the *Times* ran Sabrina Tavernise's article depicting Hezbollah fighters as victors and heroes: "Hezbollah Fighters Limp Out Into the Light, Yet Manage a Bit of a Swagger" with the subheading "The fighters emerged from shrapnel-spattered buildings in Khiam, Lebanon, with the confidence of men who felt they had won." The article is far more laudatory than the headline and is accompanied by a picture by João Silva with the caption "The ceasefire in Lebanon allowed fighters in Khiam, a mountain village less than a mile from Israel, to evacuate the wounded Monday and plan for what comes next."

Tavernise was consistent in her favoritism and apparently unchecked by her editors. For example—as if to emphasize the Israelis' heartless cruelty—on August 8, 2006, Tavernise's left lead article "After Bombs Kill Loved Ones, Life Turns Ghostly in Lebanon" with the sub-heading "Through Grief and Regret, A Father Stumbles on"—the only front-page war article that day—stresses the Lebanese as victims and indicts Israel's choice of targets. To be sure, there is a cursory reminder that "across Lebanon and Israel, missiles, rockets, and bombs punched holes into families," but perhaps there should have been a balancing first-page story about Israeli victims.

Tavernise's pro-Hezbollah and anti-Israel sentiments dominate her stories. Take her August 18, 2006, story, "Civilians: A Girl's Life Bound Close to Hezbollah," under which is a picture by João Silva of a Muslim woman—who could be any Muslim woman—dressed in black with only her face exposed, with a picture of a benign smiling Hassan Nasrallah, the Hezbollah leader, overlooking her as if to bless the martyrdom of her family. The caption reads: "Raja Fadlallah's mother and sister stayed in the south to feed Hezbollah fighters; they died in an air strike, and a brother died in Bint Jbail." Another picture by Silva accompanies the long page 11 story with the following caption: "Workers searched for bodies in the rubble of a building where at least five people, including 17-year-old Zahra Fadlallah, were killed in an air strike." Although we know that captions can be arbitrary, here we have a historically important picture with nothing in the picture to indicate that the caption is accurate.

Located and dated "Ainata, August 17," Tavernise's piece depicted Hezbollah as both a civilian group providing essential services—within a loosely defined state in Southern Lebanon—and a political group with a socially beneficent agenda rather than a military organization: "It has a vast social services network that pays for health care and education, performs weddings and reduces electric bills—important considerations for Shiites in the south, who are some of the country's poorest citizens."

John Kifner's lead story on August 16, 2006, stressed how Hezbollah was in the forefront of rebuilding efforts and reported without irony on the "victory speech [of] Hezbollah's leader, Sheik Hassan Nasrallah" ("Hezbollah Leads Work to Rebuild, Gaining Stature/Filling Void in Lebanon/Militia Moves Fast With Bulldozers and Pledge of Cash from Iran"). Where is the mention of how the Israelis in the north are aiding its citizens or making efforts, after a constant barrage of rocket fires for weeks, to resume their lives? To be sure, on August 16, 2006, there was—at the bottom of an inside page—a much smaller piece, Dina Kraft's "Putting A Value on Rebuilding A Major Target of Hezbollah" about the war's financial cost and compensation provided by the Israel government. Her focus was on Kiryat Shmona—a small city very close to the Lebanese border—but was there balance in the coverage or, to restate a point I have been making, at least an allusion to a historical perspective explaining why this war took place? Another Kraft piece on Kiryat Shmona in the August 20, 2006, paper entitled "After the War, an Israeli City Starts Over." focused on damage done to one family's house, accompanied by a photograph of a family member sitting in her front yard with "her foot on a Katyusha rocket that crashed through her roof." But this Kraft article lacked the graphic intensity of the aforementioned pictures of Lebanese death and devastation.

The blog *Aish.Com* showed in an August 10, 2006, film how some of the *Times* photographs of the war's devastation in Lebanon had been staged by demonstrating that the same people appear in different costumes. Kathleen Parker, a Gannett columnist, wrote about a variety of staged images of the war in her August 15, 2006, column, "A Digital War of Images Attacking Israel": "The blogosphere has been buzzing the past several days about doctored photographs, faked footage and even the possibility that Qana was manipulated, if not orchestrated, by Hezbollah." She cites the reputable blog *Power Line* and another blogger, Dr. Richard North, of *EU Referendum,* who has raised legitimate questions about the way that the Qana tragedy was exaggerated and perhaps partially staged.

Lorne Manly's August 14, 2006, piece, "In Wars, Quest for Media Balance Is Also a Battlefield," was a somewhat belated and rather disappointing effort on the part of the *Times* to acknowledge that how the war was covered is itself a major story. The article, although a featured story in the *Business* section, should have been a front-page story in the "A" section. On the same day, Maria Aspan's article in the *Business* section, "Ease of Alteration Creates Woes for Picture Editors," complemented Manly's article.

These articles followed by many days the revelation that Adnan Hajj, a Lebanese freelance photographer, had doctored pictures of the war—published by Reuters—to make the damage appear worse than it was. Although the technology to manipulate photography digitally has existed for two decades, and Hajj's were particularly sloppy, it took a blogger—rather than the *Times*'s staff—to recognize the manipulation. The *Times* stories address neither Aish's claims that pictures were staged with some of the same people appearing in different roles nor the possible manipulation of the Qana tragedy. On the whole, I would say the *Times* struck out on what seemed to be a major story.

Many factors went into the *Times*'s war coverage. According to Keller, the aim is "to portray [over time] the full range of the war's consequences" (quoted in Lorne Manly, August 14, 2006). Although the *Times* may have tried to show civilian victims on both sides, the coverage of devastation stressed the plight of Lebanese civilians. Again, not enough mention was made that Hezbollah is embedded within the civilian population and, in effect, uses civilians as human shields.

The cynicism of Hezbollah's using civilian casualties for propaganda purposes and the justice of Israel's position should have pushed the *Times* to stress more often and more emphatically the reasons for the horrific pictures emanating from Lebanon. If Israel's casualties were fewer, it was because Israel had put in place shelters to protect its civilians from the rocket barrage that Hezbollah launched and because Hezbollah couldn't control the accuracy of these rockets. As Max Boot, a senior fellow at the Council of Foreign Relations, put it: "Hezbollah is winning the war of images because it's not being pinned with immoral and unconscionable war tactics, not to mention the genocidal war aim to wipe Israel off the map." It is worth noting that this quote about Hezbollah's "genocidal war" against Israel appeared in the fifth to last paragraph of Manly's long article (August 14, 2006).

I found disappointing Byron Calame's September 10, 2006, public editor column, "Picturing the Conflict: Perspective Versus 'Balance.'" He did not address the issue of doctored photos. As the gentle and uncritical Calame did a bit too often, he accepted what the *Times*'s editors told him and gave the newspaper a free pass.

Calame did not address the issues of how Hezbollah used innocent civilians as shields and were rebuilding homes in areas in which its forces often sought refuge as a guerilla army. He mentioned that "photographers were actively discouraged" from taking pictures of Hezbollah fighters, but does not stress how they were actively encouraged to take pictures of dead children and destroyed homes. He disregarded the argument that the morality of Hezbollah's behavior in triggering the war needed to be part of the coverage and continually foregrounded. Instead, he attributed the view "that Hezbollah wants to destroy" Israel to the contention of "some supporters of Israel" and "the goals and motives they attribute to Hezbollah," as if we should have some doubt about what Hezbollah is about (September 10, 2006).

The *Times*'s coverage of the Israeli invasion of Gaza in January 2009—in response to rocket attacks on Israel civilians—raised some of the same issues. I found the *Times*'s coverage even-handed, including its reporting of some outrageous behavior on both sides. Yet coverage of the Gaza War probably should have put emphasis on fatal rocket attacks in Haifa and the barrage of rockets fired from Gaza.

A 2010 controversy, discussed by Clark Hoyt in his February 6, 2010, public editor column, focused on whether Jerusalem bureau chief Ethan Bronner should be reporting on Israel after his twenty-year-old son enlisted in the Israeli Defense Forces. Hoyt's conclusion is that Bronner should not be reporting from Israel "for the duration of his son's service," although there has been no indication that his reporting has been skewed ("Too Close to Home"). But would he be reassigned if his son were fighting for the United States in Iraq and Afghanistan? We might remember, too, that for a long time, the *Times* wouldn't send Jewish reporters to the Middle East.

VI. Conclusion: Today's *Times* and the Jews

Daniel Okrent, the first public editor, who received many complaints from Jews about the *Times*'s coverage of the ongoing Israeli–Palestinian conflict, remarked to me on October 11, 2004, before the 2006 outbreak:

> Observant Jews despise the *Times* and they say it is in league with Arafat. When there are articles on the Mid-East conflict, the next day we receive letters from these Zionists calling the *Times* anti-Semitic. . . . Observant Jews really despise Thomas Friedman. . . . During the high holy days there are rabbis in New York who get together and launch a boycott on the *Times* (and we are talking about tens of thousands of

copies). This isn't even in places in Brooklyn only, but also in places like Larchmont! Their complaint letters accuse the *Times* of being anti-Israel, and often unreasonably complain that the *Times* is anti-Semitic. The *Times* is not anti-Zionist or anti-Semitic!

In an April 25, 2005, public editor column, "The Hottest Button: How the *Times* Covers Israel and Palestine," Okrent took up this issue: "An article about the Israeli–Palestinian conflict cannot appear in the *Times* without eliciting instant and intense response." He concluded that the *Times* is neither anti-Palestinian nor anti-Israeli and its reporting does not take sides in the Israeli–Palestinian conflict: "The *Times* today is the gold standard as far as setting out in precise language the perspectives of the parties, the contents of resolutions, the terms of international conventions."

But, as I have been arguing here, the *Times* has not always been as even-handed as Okrent suggested. My discussion of the 2006 war between Israel and Hezbollah shows that even with the intent of balanced coverage, articles and pictures can give a distorted view, especially if they are not presented within a historical perspective that iterates basic facts. Far more frequently than it does, the *Times* needs to give background and context to reports of the cycle of violence and retaliation in the Middle East and to explain why Israel—with admittedly superior weaponry—is striking back at those who seek to destroy their country and encourage suicide bombers who attack innocent civilians going about their daily activities. Individual stories often need a paragraph or two of explanation, and I would suggest for this—and other hot spots—a monthly update that provides a long view of where we are in the ongoing narrative. This might help partisans on both sides to have a broader understanding of the underlying issues and to help all of us readers understand what is going on. How many readers understand the difference between Hamas and Hezbollah? Do we need to be reminded about why the Shiites and Sunnis are fierce enemies and how that itself—as well as other and various sectarian divisions—is a factor not only in Iraq but also in Lebanon?

The *Times* continues to have something of a bipolar attitude toward Jews and Jewish issues. Orthodox and especially Hasidic Jews still feel that the *Times* is condescending to them. Even now the *Times* seems embarrassed by the behavior of ultra-Orthodox Jews or Haredi—as do many American Jews visiting Jerusalem and seeing their increasing presence and control—and at times writes about their customs and behavior as if they were a recently discovered Stone Age tribe living in the Amazon. An instance is a piece by Fernanda Santos, "Reverberations of a Baby Boom," which discusses the growth of the Satmar community in Kiryas Joel in Orange County. Santos writes of the community's unwillingness to practice birth control as an aberration. He stresses that its members speak Yiddish, as if speaking Yiddish—as well as not having radios, televisions, or computers—were a social offense. Santos seems to regard the desire of its members to live together as a curiosity (August 27, 2006).

The current *Times* may, in its gatekeeping function, make choices that do not please Jews or the friends of Israel, but the *Times* is neither anti-Semitic nor anti-Israel. For many Jews, the *Times* still bears the weight of its Holocaust coverage and its anti-Zionism. In one of my epigraphs to this chapter, Frankel's comment about the "professional Jewish lobby" indicates a wary sense that nothing can please some Jews, and I have heard this expressed in different ways by others in the *Times*'s offices. Because of past insensitivities, the *Times* does carry a historical burden to be aware of Jewish sensibilities whether addressing how Jews live in the United States or the politics of the Middle East. Thus, not only Orthodox Jews in outer borough enclaves, but assimilated urban and suburban Jews, with some justification, feel that the *Times* is more likely to depict victims of Israeli retaliation than to depict victims of the Intifadas, Hezbollah, or Hamas.

The *Times* carries a similar burden to be aware of the sensibilities of ethnic or other groups that it may have slighted in the past and to be as sensitive as possible to the feelings of diverse segments of America. Awareness of ethnic, gender, and sexual orientation is part of the *Times*'s current understanding that it does not write for a hypothetical ideal reader but rather for many different communities of readers in America and, indeed, the world. But the *Times* also must be sure not to sacrifice the accuracy, judgment, objectivity, and fairness that are major parts of great journalism.

11

Conclusion

Where Is the *Times* Going?

News is what somebody, somewhere is trying to suppress; the rest is advertising.

—Lord Northcliffe, British newspaper baron

We want to be swift and fresh on the web but we also want deep added-value coverage. . . . But the bottom line is this: We can never lose what makes *The New York Times* special. We cannot stop pursuing stories that go deep, putting the news in context and uncovering information that you can't find anywhere else.

—Richard Berke, "Talk to the Newsroom; Assistant Managing Editor for News," March 17, 2009, nytimes.com

[T]he quality of public discourse, I think, has gotten rougher and rougher and less and less civil, and the degree of suspicion of institutions like the *New York Times* is higher than I can recall.

—Clark Hoyt, May 19, 2010

I don't think it's a given that the print *New York Times* will be gone in twenty years. . . . [Given the loyalty of our print readers] I think it's entirely possible that it will be there, but I don't think it will be the central or our main product in twenty years. . . . Our job . . . is to inform and educate and provoke the people who care, who are engaged, who are by and large well educated.

—Bill Keller, May 20, 2010

We will stop printing the *New York Times* sometime in the future, date TBD [To Be Determined].

—Arthur Sulzberger Jr., addressing a London media conference
September 8, 2010; *Huffington Post*, September 10, 2010

I. The Challenge to Remain a
Cultural Bellwether and a Viable Business

In 1971, former *Times* managing editor Turner Catledge wrote, "[A] great newspaper is to some extent a political institution; to maintain its power it must sometimes use its power sparingly. It must set priorities and decide on which issues it will push ahead and on which it will bide its time" (Catledge, 268). Although the power of the *Times* has diminished and Catledge's comment seems a bit overwrought in retrospect, he gives us an important clue to the position the *Times* saw itself occupying. The *Times* will continue to have influence in the national and international community, but it will never be as dominant as it once was. Simply put, newspapers—even the *Times*—are only one source of knowledge for informed people. Readers give newspapers less time and the *Sunday Times*, in particular, has lost its place as a centerpiece of its readers' Sundays.

To call the current period in the history of newspapers a transition is to understate what is occurring. As if he were a ship captain without a chart, Keller has been presiding over a voyage without knowing the destination. As Jonathan Landman put it to me, the cargo remains the same: "It's understanding, comprehension. It's the ability to be an engaged citizen. . . . I think the *Times* knows very well what its values are and what it chooses to offer to society and culture. The form of that is very much up in the air because of the changes we're all familiar with" (June 9, 2010).

Yet, as Landman observed to me four years earlier, "If the *Times* was now what it was in the fifties, it would not exist. Nobody would read it, not anybody. A lot of things have changed; expectations have changed" (October 9, 2006). But in the world of the Internet, it is not clear what these new expectations are or what readers of the future will want. Will readers want succinct analytic news articles on the model of *The Economist*? Do they really want long and thorough investigatory articles about water problems in India, like the three-part series by Somini Sengupta (September 29–October 1, 2006), which even some *Times* editors thought was far too lengthy? More recently, articles on the effects of the recession on a California neighborhood called Beth Court—a block of eight homes in Moreno Valley, California, about sixty miles from Los Angeles—needed to be more succinct and more tightly presented.

In explanation of what he calls "the great newspaper blight . . . [that has] reduced print journalism . . . to the verge of ruin," Russell Baker includes, "the industry-wide failure of entrepreneurial imagination" ("Decline But Not Fall," *NYR*, September 20, 2010, 30–34). Expressing agreement with the *Washington Post's* Walter Pincus, Baker wrote: "Newspapers had lost audience through self-indulgence; they wrote stories for themselves instead of readers and produced blockbuster stories designed to win journalism prizes but destined to be unread by masses of people uninterested in the subject matter."

Although some of its audience still read the *Times* for literary pleasure, most of today's time-conscious readers want information efficiently delivered. What the *Times* still does well is international news and middle- to highbrow cultural news, investigative reporting, and, at times, serious metropolitan news. But at times, the *Times* has become prolix beyond belief. On many days, it devotes almost as much space to the four sections under the auspices of *Style—Home, Dining, ThursdayStyles,* and *SundayStyles*—as it does to national news. And cultural news, which has been very much in the ascendancy since 2005 because most readers come to this news without having had a cable news or Internet update already, outpaces international news in the amount of coverage. Much of the cultural news is popular culture and some of it is on the borderline between culture and gossip (i.e., the *Times's* coverage of the fuss in April 2006 about the *New York Post's* "Page Six"). As former cultural editor John Darnton remarked to me: "I think if you now look at the culture section every day of the week and measure the column inches, it will outrank foreign news by far, not even counting the *Weekend* section or *Arts & Leisure*" (June 21, 2005).

Advertising, which grew explosively in the 1920s, enabled publishers to keep the cost of purchasing the paper low. Newspapers other than the *Times* generally favored local news over political and diplomatic news, for local news, along with local and brand name advertising, was what readers wanted. Readers were interested in local sports events, local crime reporting, what was going on in theaters on Saturday night, and what job openings were to be found on Monday morning. Examining the city's spectacles, sensational crimes, and sporting events became a part of the very essence of city life. Even while choosing a different path with a stress on international and national news, the *Times* rarely forgot that its New York audience enjoyed reading about the growth and excitement of the city in which that audience lived and the culture that made it the most important city in the United States.

Implicit and explicit in our discussion has been the decline of the newspaper as a central factor in the American culture. Although our focus has been on the *New York Times*, we have only to look to the *Washington Post*, its most prestigious rival, to see a similar narrative. As Richard Perez-Pena wrote on June 24, 2008, upon the resignation of Leonard Downie, the *Washington Post*'s executive editor, after seventeen years: "The *Post* is struggling with declining circulation and ad revenue, even as it draws record numbers of readers online" ("Washington Post Editor to Step Aside"). In fact, the *Post*'s nine-million monthly Internet readers are third after that of the *New York Times* and *USA Today*. But the *Post* cut its news staff by more than four hundred, in part by drastically reducing its overseas staff, and by the end of 2009 had lost more than 136,000 subscribers. What Hal Espen says about the *Post* could be said in even stronger terms about the *Times*: "The Post remains a great newspaper. It once was a great business" (Hal Espen, "Beyond the Paper," review of Dave Kindred, *Morning Miracle: Inside the Washington Post: A Great Newspaper Fights for its Life*, *New York Times Book Review*, August 22, 2010).

When we look to other major American newspapers, we learn that between 1998 and 2008, the news staff of the *Los Angeles Times* shrank from 1,300 to 720. Other newspapers, such as the *Rocky Mountain News*, perished, whereas others survived in drastically reduced form. Detroit's daily newspapers are delivered three days a week; the *Seattle Post Intelligencer* is a web-only publication with a tiny staff (Michael Sokolove, "What's a Big City Without a Newspaper," *New York Times Magazine*, August 6, 2009).

In 2008, Downie's replacement at the *Post*, Marcus W. Brauchli, was charged with integrating the print and online news editions, something the *Times* and the *Wall Street Journal* have already done (Richard Perez-Pena, "Washington Post Signals Shift with A New Editor," July

8, 2008). By then this integration was not only the shape of the *Post*'s future, but also the shape of the present and perhaps should have been the shape of the recent past. In the second half of 2008, the *Times* finally integrated its website with that of its other most prestigious newspaper product, the *International Herald Tribune*.

II. The Public Trust

Given the current suspicion of the media in the United States, the *Times* cannot depend on the public trust. In 2005, Richard A. Posner cited figures from National Opinion Research Center indicating that (a) public confidence in the press declined from 85 percent in 1971, with "most of the decline occurring since 1991"; and (b) if anything public confidence further declined since 1991 ("Bad News," *New York Times Book Review*, July 31, 2005). Posner cited an Annenberg Public Policy Center poll that found 65 percent of respondents believe that most newspapers either ignore or cover up a mistake that they find and 79 percent believe that media companies hesitate to cover negative stories about substantial advertisers.

The *Times* is besieged by critics from the left and right of the political spectrum. Whereas Howard Friel and Richard Falk in *The Record of the Paper: How the New York Times Misreports US Foreign Policy* (2005) take the *Times* to task for being too conservative on foreign policy and for ignoring the standards of international law when evaluating U.S. foreign policy in the cases of the Vietnam and Iraqi wars, Bob Kohn in *Journalistic Fraud* (2003) argues that the news is presented to support the liberal bias of the editorial pages.

One need not subscribe to Friel and Falk's left-leaning political perspective to agree that the two authors quite convincingly advocate an editorial policy of what they call a "strict scrutiny standard . . . that evaluate[s] the legality of actions taken in response to reported facts" (254). Specifically, "strict scrutiny" "would have permitted the *Times* to confirm that a US invasion of Iraq would violate international law without Security Council authorization, even if Iraqi WMD possession were to be confirmed, which it never was" (255). Notwithstanding the *Times*'s penitence expressed to readers for relying on administration sources to raise the alarm about Saddam Hussein, the *Times* has historically had difficulty adhering to "strict scrutiny." Such difficulty derived not only from the *Times*'s scrupulous concern about national security considerations, but also from its inherent trust in successive administrations until the recent George W. Bush administration. Fear of unpatriotically betraying national security interests has been a bogeyman within the highest circles of the *Times*. Even various administrations in whose judgment the *Times* had some confidence have been able to manipulate that fear.

The *Times* is also under siege from the right. Mention the *Times* to some conservative Republicans, and they respond with a disdainful sneer. In *Journalistic Fraud: How the New York Times Distorts the News and Why it Can No Longer Be Trusted*, and in television appearances, Bob Kohn has charged the *Times* with distorting the news in the interests of a political agenda. The aim of his 2003 book, he claims, "is to convince the publisher of the *Times* to reverse the ideologically tainted news reporting practices that are destroying the integrity of the newspaper." Arguing that it is journalistic fraud for the *Times* to pass off its opinions as news, his book is repetitious and draws heavily on such pundits as the outspoken conservative Ann Coulter to support his view that impartiality has been abandoned and news is distorted to support liberal political views.

The *Times* not only needs to be willing to make changes, it needs to take seriously some aspects of the animosity it evokes even if only to acknowledge its awareness of its place in a deeply divided culture. Certainly, the public editor's response to complaints helps. More than his predecessors, Bill Keller has tried to understand the *Times*'s opponents, whose views are often far more partisan than those of its own conservative columnists.

Part of the *Times*'s crisis is that public trust in all media reporting continues to slip; fewer than one in five believe what they read in print (Alterman, *The New Yorker*, March 31, 2008, 49). Yet, for many people, newspapers do provide necessary information and reading paper-and-ink is a different, more reflective, and more contemplative experience than using the Internet. We do participate with our fellow readers in a community activity and, yet, with the diminishment of the *Times*'s stature, the nature of that community becomes fragmented and each community has its own sets of "truths" and "facts" (Alterman 58). Because we have less and less a process of verification, it is all the more important that the *Times* knows what it is talking about, whether it is weapons of mass destruction in Iraq, Wen Ho Lee's loyalty, accusations of rape by the Duke Lacrosse team, or John McCain's propriety in spending time with an attractive young lobbyist.

Recently there have been claims that all news is distorted by economic and political considerations. In this vein, Robert Darnton argued,

> [N]ews has always been an artifact and . . . it has never corresponded to what actually happened. . . . We take today's front page as a mirror of yesterday's events, but it was made up yesterday evening—literally, by "make-up" editors, who designed page one according to arbitrary conventions: lead story on the far right column, off-lead on the left, soft news inside or below the fold, features set off by special kinds of headlines. Typographical design orients the reader and shapes the meaning of the news. News itself takes the form of narratives composed by professionals according to conventions that they picked up in the course of their training—the "inverted pyramid" mode of exposition, the "color" lead, the code for "high" and "the highest" sources, and so on. News is not what happened but a story about what happened.
>
> Of course, many reporters do their best to be accurate, but they must conform to the conventions of their craft, and there is always slippage between their choice of words and the nature of an event as experienced or perceived by others. ("The Library in the New Age," *The New York Review of Books*, June 12, 2008, 72)

Although not disagreeing with Darnton, I would argue that the angle of distortion varies greatly and that for the most part the *Times* is consistently among the most reliable, in part because its ethos encourages accuracy and its editors will assign choice stories to those who meet its criteria of truthful reporting of facts and probing analyses. If nothing else, the competition among reporters and editors for external recognition in terms of prizes fosters the search for truth.

Indeed, because of its fundamentally democratic history, the United States has had more tolerance for the chaotic diversity of opinion than most other nations. For example, Putin is part of a history where first the tsars and then the Bolsheviks insisted on a unified ideology to further their goals. (see Frank, "Idealists on the Run," *The New York Review of Books*, June 12, 2008, 50–52.) We need to understand the October 2006 assassination of prominent Russian journalist and Putin critic Anna Politkovskaya in this context.

Yet, one major problem is that now the *Times* is often anticipated in presenting the facts and is consequently stressing its value-added analysis in an ever rising tide of interpretive articles. Readers hear voices with points of view rather than a presentation of facts. In its online "Reader's Guide," the *Times* distinguishes among such categories as "Man in the News," "Reporter's Notebook," "Journal," "News Analyses," and "News-Page Column," but few readers are aware of these fine distinctions. Yet many if not most readers bridle at the very idea of reading opinion pieces intermingled with supposed news. As public editor Arthur Brisbane wrote in his very first column on September 5, 2010, "In an Age of Voices, Moving Beyond the Facts": "Call it commentary or call it opinion, but call it something that people can understand. That, or abandon the sacred cloak of impartiality."

III. Opening the Doors and Windows:
Process and Transparency

In the 1999–2009 decade under discussion, the *Times* moved to greater transparency, especially under Keller. The online "Talk to the Newsroom" series—which by 2010 had virtually lapsed except for a summer 2010 discussion of the publication of the WikiLeaks documents on the Afghanistan War—has been an excellent step toward transparency. In my May 19, 2010, interview with Clark Hoyt, weeks before he retired from his three years as public editor, he observed, "[T]he overwhelming majority of people here have been candid, professional, open, willing to talk to me; you know that no one is required to talk to me except the publisher, the executive editor, and the editor of the editorial page."

In my October 11, 2005, interview with Hoyt's predecessor, Byron Calame, Calame told me that he was not always happy with the cooperation he got from the staff. When I asked, "Are you getting the cooperation you want from the *Times* staff?" he responded: "Not truly, but I wouldn't necessarily expect them to answer all of my questions. One example that's already been mentioned in my column is I'm very concerned about the use of freelancers at the *New York Times* and at other quality newspapers. I asked for how much in dollar terms the *New York Times* was spending on freelancers compared to ten years ago, twenty years ago, and they declined to tell me." Yet we need, as

Calame stressed, to be concerned with what happens when the behavior of the *Times* becomes a story in itself—that is, the misreporting of the existence of WMDs, the misjudgments in the Wen Ho Lee case, the Judith Miller–Libby situation, or the Jayson Blair scandal. Calame praised the *Times* generously for its "valuable and extensive explanations" of the aforementioned, although I would argue that the *Times* was a long way from full disclosure on the Miller case. I would hardly call this, to quote Calame's words in his December 4, 2005, column, "When the Newspaper is the News," an "outstanding [example] of no holds-barred journalism."

Ferreting out business information about the New York Times Company and the *Times* itself still can be difficult, notwithstanding the reports they are required to release by the SEC. The coverage of the *Times* as a business enterprise needs to go well beyond *Times* staff reporters who are paid by that very business. In the contemporary skeptical period, when the *Times* has embarrassed itself a number of times and has come under great scrutiny, the *Times* should be more proactive about allowing other views of itself to appear as long as they are not written by cranks.

Perhaps a senior writer other than the public editor should have the *Times* as his or her beat when necessary, and that writer perhaps should be edited by the public editor—the public ombudsman—if by anyone. Rather than, as Calame proposed, the *Times*'s arranging with other respected papers to provide online links to articles about developments involving the *Times*, I propose that the *Times* actually allow the public editor to select those stories and have them appear under his auspices. The public editor even might print in hard copy reputable and responsible comment from the blogosphere. Yes, this would extend his mandate. But for many readers, the *Times* is both the print newspaper and the digital site, and for some the *Times* is still the print version.

IV. Taking Stock

As we have seen, the newspaper industry—including the *Times*—is in crisis. As Eric Alterman has written: "[T]rends in circulation and advertising—the rise of the Internet, which has made the daily newspaper look slow and unresponsive; the advent of Craigslist, which is wiping out classified advertising—have created a palpable sense of doom" (*New Yorker*, March 31, 2008, 48).

Since 1990, one-fourth of newspaper jobs have ceased to exist, because readership has declined. Less than 20 percent of those aged nineteen to thirty-four look at a daily newspaper, and those who do read it spend less than fifteen hours a month (Alterman, 49).

In the face of declining newsroom budgets, even coverage of Iraq drastically diminished from 18 percent of news coverage in the first nine months of 2008 to 3 percent in the early months 2008 ("The War Endures, But Where's The Media?" March 24, 2008). One explanation is that interest in the war was flagging, but perhaps decreased coverage by the national media was a contributing reason that interest was declining.

For many months an explanation was that resources were shifted to the 2008 presidential candidates, but after the campaign, news from the Iraq war zone did not return to its former level and, except for the *Times*, has remained relatively skimpy and relied strongly on brief Associated Press updates. Indeed, fewer newspapers could even afford to cover the candidates in detail. For example, only a few dozen journalists of the 650 on the premises for a Cleveland debate paid the more than $2,000 to be on an Obama charter flight. According to the *Times*'s Jacques Steinberg, "In the weeks leading up to the 22 Democratic nominating contests on February 5, and in the weeks since, few newspapers beyond *The Washington Post, The Los Angeles Times, The Chicago Tribune, The Wall Street Journal,* and *The New York Times* have sought to shadow the candidates on a near-daily basis" ("Buzz on the Bus: Pinched, Press Steps Off," March 26, 2008).

The *Times* still has loyal readers who are passionate about their paper, and I am one of them, although I now also read the website many times a day. It is safe to say that the average *Times* reader spends more time reading the paper than readers of other newspapers. Although I have seen varying statistics, it seems fair to say that a *Times* reader spends in the neighborhood of forty-five to forty-eight minutes with the daily paper and about sixty-eight to seventy-two minutes with the *Sunday Times,* but it also is fair to say that the numbers have been declining and accurate figures would need to take account of the fact that many print readers also spend time on the digital site.

A major part of the threat to the *Times*'s position has been a loss in confidence on the part of some readers and potential readers in the

Sulzberger-Keller *Times* and the perception that, as Michael Wolff put it in a devastating, sarcastic, and rather hyperbolic May 2008 *Vanity Fair* article, "[Arthur] Sulzberger Jr. is a weak link" ("The War on the Times," 131). Wolff contends that Keller "has never seemed to quite have his heart in it—his has been a soft, hesitant, often odd, seldom necessary *New York Times*" (131). Nor does Wolff have much respect for Janet L. Robinson, president and chief executive officer, who reports to Arthur Jr. rather than the board.

Notwithstanding Wolff's various fantasies of how the *Times* could be taken over by the highest bidder—perhaps Warren Buffett, Michael Bloomberg, the Washington Post Company, or a hedgefund pushing the family to take the company private and thus setting the stage for a lucrative offer from another buyer—I am quite doubtful that this will occur in the foreseeable future and certainly not while Punch Sulzberger, Arthur's father, is alive. Of course, paradoxically, the importance of the *Times* is also confirmed by what I call "Timesology"—that is, discussion by outsiders of its political and financial problems in conspiratorial terms that recall the CIA's efforts to penetrate the mysteries of the Chinese Politburo's Standing Committee.

The contemporary *Times* is trying to respond to essential changes in the concept of a daily newspaper. In his April 10, 2006, online response to questions about how the front page is selected, Keller alluded to the necessity of finding an alternative to the "factual outline" in the form of analysis, photographs, profiles, or focus on colorful features that might have been overlooked:

> We think it's okay to include in our front-page portfolio something that is fun, human, or just wonderfully written. . . .
>
> The notion of a Page 1 story, in fact, has evolved over the years, partly in response to the influence of other media. When a news event has been on the Internet and TV and news radio all day long, do we want to put that news on our front page the next morning? Maybe we do, if we feel our reporting and telling of it goes deeper than what has been available elsewhere. But if the factual outline—the raw information—is widely available, sometimes we choose to offer something else that plays to our journalistic advantages: a smart analysis of the events, a vivid piece of color from the

scene, a profile of one of the central figures, or a gripping
photograph that captures the impact of an event, instead of
a just-the-facts news story.

As Arthur Gelb, former managing editor, told me in 2005, the
Times for a long time set the standard in presenting news: "[The *Times*]
was still developing news. That gave the paper a feeling of currency
and a strong significance on national, international, and sometimes
cultural news" (June 21, 2005). Well after the rise of television, Gelb
claimed, "We gave the definition to news. No anchorman on TV (in
my era) would go on TV without knowing what the *Times* put on
page one." Even now the *Times* is the source of much print, digital,
radio, and television news across America. The *Times* provides the
factual underpinning of much of the pundits'—liberal and conservative—commentary, but it is rarely given attribution. On its website, the
Times often breaks stories, but to protect its reputation, it does tend
to be more cautious than some of its media competitors. On occasion,
while gathering confirming or modifying facts, the *Times* misses the
first faint heartbeat of a story's life.

In Gelb's view, what characterized the Abe Rosenthal era was
focus on sharing the excitement of the developing story with readers
(June 21, 2005). A developing story is the earliest version of history,
but instant history needs constant amendment. The *Times*, with its large
staff of experienced reporters, still does developing stories well—for
example, 9/11; Hurricane Katrina, which hit New Orleans August 29,
2005; the Mumbai attacks of November 26, 2008; the 2009 Iranian
election and its consequences. But the *Times* must compete with CNN,
which covers such stories continuously, and with various websites,
including independent bloggers. My view is that what the *Times* can
do better than anyone—and what its readers expect and want—is
ongoing analyses and investigative stories reflecting the experience,
judgment, and contextual knowledge of its journalists. An important
example in the foreign news area was a July 14, 2008, piece on the
spreading influence of the Taliban in Pakistan by Pir Zubair Shah
and Jane Perlez ("Pakistan Marble Helps Taliban Stay in Business"), a
piece that depended on the *Times* having the resources to visit remote
areas of Pakistan. But at home, too, such articles as "Medical Papers
by Ghostwriters Pushed Therapy" by Natasha Singer, August 4, 2009,

demonstrated how a probing study of court documents reveals strikingly important information.

Relying more and more on the so-called New Journalism—which is now four decades old—and foregrounding personal anecdotes and stylistic experimentation for its own sake, the *Times* sometimes forgets that people read the *Times* mostly to be informed and still want to know from the first paragraph the basics: Who? What? When? Where? How? Countless articles begin with an anecdote focusing on a particular person (and all too often the writer's interaction with that person). In the ensuing paragraphs the piece wanders in and out of a subject. What results is reader impatience for being asked by the *Times* to invest time in an article without much argument, insight, resolution, or closure. Were it not for the headlines of some articles, one would not know what one is reading—and sometimes the headlines do not help because they are in an incongruous relationship to the article, perhaps because the headline writer was as puzzled as the reader about the article's central premise.

Is it possible that the sheer bulk of the *Times* actually undermines circulation? I have often heard potential readers say that they didn't buy the daily paper—or, even more often, the Sunday paper—because they didn't have time to read it or that it has become bulky, unwieldy, and unmanageable. Is it possible that a disaggregated two-section newspaper with a "B" section including a few pages each for culture, business, and sports would sell to a significant body of readers, especially if it were priced lower than the daily $2 and $5 for Sunday ($6 outside the metropolitan New York area)?

To give a sense of how Sulzberger was thinking in 2005, let us look back again at the November 11, 2005, interview with Charlie Rose. That Sulzberger was conscious of the *Times* not only as a newspaper, an American institution, and a publicly traded company, but also as a family business in which he had a major stake, reveals the complicated role he plays as publisher and CEO of the New York Times Company: "[W]hen the time comes for the next generation of leaders to take over the *New York Times* newspaper and company, [I want to see that] they are handed as strong and as powerful an institution as I was handed in my time."

Wasn't Sulzberger not only speaking to readers, but also to Wall Street and perhaps to himself, as if he knew at some level that the gathering storm clouds threatened the very existence of *his* print newspaper? He was speaking as the chairman of the New York Times Company more than as the publisher of the printed newspaper or digital site. He was assuring current and potential investors that the *Times* was in good hands. His opening words were to speak about the "extraordinary year . . . a year of remarkable invigorations" when of course what Rose and his listeners were interested in was why Judith Miller was fired that day, why the *Times* failed to report accurately the WMD story, and why it withheld information about the government's effort to discredit Joe Wilson, Valerie Plame's husband.

In 2005, Sulzberger had a way of presenting facts when he hadn't been asked about them that bordered on bragging. He was like a little leaguer who if asked the score tells you how many hits he had. Thus when Rose asked him about the economic future of the paper, he responded with an advertisement for the now defunct *TimesSelect*, the online service for which—following the example of the *Wall Street Journal*—the *Times* had begun to charge: "Less than two months ago we launched this new product called *TimesSelect*. We, for the first time, took [a] significant amount of our reporting, actually our columnists, and we put it behind a wall and said, I'm sorry, if you don't subscribe to the *Times*, you're going to have to pay for this. And we have 270,000 people in less than two months who are now getting *TimesSelect*. Half of them, roughly half of them because they subscribe to the paper and therefore they're getting it free, and the other half are paying." At about $50 for access, the 135,000 who were paying brought in $775,000—a significant sum, but hardly enough to have turned the *Times*'s business problems around or to balance the lost advertising revenue from those who wanted to reach the entire *Times* Internet audience rather than the segment represented by *TimesSelect*. Thus, *TimesSelect* was abandoned as a failure because advertisers didn't like the pay wall and consumers were not accustomed to paying for what many competitors were providing for free.

V. The *Times*'s Own *International Herald Tribune* as a Model of Succinctness

For international news, the *Times* might look to *The Economist* or its own publication the *International Herald Tribune* for succinct and well-argued analytic presentations of important issues.

The *International Herald Tribune,* whose primary office is in Paris with a second major office in Hong Kong, is published six days a week—but not on Sunday—in several major cities and is sometimes supplemented by an English-language version of a local newspaper. It is edited in Paris and Hong Kong, and Sulzberger's cousin Michael Golden is the publisher. Until May 15, 2008, Michael Oreskes was executive editor.

In June 2008 the *Times* announced a restructuring with a stress on integrating the websites of the two papers. Martin Gottlieb was given the title of editor, global editions, a title he still holds in 2011.

The 2005–2010 *International Herald Tribune* ran about twenty-six pages—with six columns, like the *Times*—and devoted a good deal of its space to business news, clearly targeting as a principle audience a cosmopolitan American business audience with interests in Europe and Asia. The perspective is less the United States than the world. Even much of its international coverage—like reporting on the World Trade Organization—stresses economic issues.

Although the *International Herald Tribune'*s article selection is understandably more Eurocentric than the *Times* would wish to be, its succinctness, clarity, and efficiency could provide a model for the *Times.* The *International Herald Tribune* better answers the who, what, where, when, and how questions because its space limitations require that it do so. Shorter and more pointed versions of prolix *New York Times* articles appear to advantage in the *International Herald Tribune.*

Typically, about seven international news pages are followed by a page or so of national news and then followed by two pages of "Views," beginning with the editorials and including letters. On a given day, the *International Herald Tribune* might reprint one or two other *Times* columnists and, along with its own editorials, one from the *Times* or another publication owned by the *Times.* The *International Herald Tribune'*s international articles are likely to include either news follow-up stories or enterprise stories or synthesizing overviews. The *International Herald Tribune'*s manageable one-section length makes it more readable and is one of the reasons, I believe, for its appeal. Whether it be cultural news in Europe or Asia, sports, or travelers' updates about strikes and weather that might cause delays, the *International Herald Tribune'*s stress is on what the reader needs to learn in a finite amount of reading time.

VI. The Shape of the *Times*'s Future:
Suggestions and Speculations

What will the *Times* of the future look like, whether in print or on the Internet?

Without doubt, the integrated *Times*—newspaper and website—will continue to evolve into a daily magazine, focusing less on news as its commodity and more on analyses, investigatory journalism, and the value-added aspect that provides practical information about finance, health, food, travel, and home for its readers. As the Pew Research Center for the People and the Press reported on July 30, 2006, "More than three-quarters of newspaper readers (77%) say they spend a lot or some time reading articles about health and medicine, while 63% spend time with articles on technology; neither subject was asked about in 1985. Since that time, news about business, food and diet, and religion has grown more popular with readers" ("Online Papers Modestly Boost Newspaper Readership"). Since 2006, in response to what the *Times* believes from its audience surveys are the desires of its audience, that trend has accelerated in the *Times*.

The *Times* still has the resources to do investigatory reporting that neither the net or cable can do. What Landman said to me on January 21, 2005, is still true today: "Fox News is talk radio with a camera. . . . You get a tsunami and CNN is there, good for CNN but only up to a point." If at various times oil or gold are commodities that reach record values because of a perceived shortage, news as a commodity is shrinking in value because there is a surplus and much of it is trivial. Before the *Times* morning editions are read, the factual news available has been on cable television and all-news radio; indeed instant—often superficial—analyses may have already taken place not only on politically charged talk radio but also among talking heads on television and Internet blogs. Thus, the *Times* needs to rely on analysts like Linda Greenhouse and Adam Liptak on the Supreme Court who know more about their subject than almost anyone else.

The value-added aspect will focus more and more on investigatory stories—what is often called at the *Times* "enterprise reporting," namely, what longtime former sports reporter Murray Chass defined to me as "going out and digging up stories that wouldn't cross your eyes on a daily basis" (June 22, 2005). Value-added reporting increasingly will stress how to live better—and indeed this kind of material (how to be healthy, how to invest, how to care for the aged) is increasingly dominating television news. The *Times's* challenge will be to provide better reporting in these areas in terms of depth, context, and accuracy. As Lawrence Ingrassia, the business editor, convincingly insisted to me: "What's going to sell newspapers is what is going to make you feel that you need to read the newspaper" (April 18, 2005).

More and more, the website has become the driver of the *Times's* product. The *Times* updates its website continuously. Now that it is charging non-subscribers, one can guess that at some point in the future, the *Times* may even charge its subscribers. Of course, the *Times* will need a dramatic increase in its Internet advertising revenue. To further integrate the Internet experience with the published newspaper experience and to create the premier media website, the *Times* will continue to develop not only audio podcasts, videos, slide shows, supplementary historic material, archives, and graphic components, but also its blogs.

Not only do readers—and especially younger readers—go online for information, they also make transactional decisions based on Internet information. In the category of help wanted ads alone, the Internet—with free or cheap advertising—cost newspapers $1.9 billion in revenue between 1996 and 2004 (Fine, "MediaCentric," July 4, 2005, 24). By selling Internet classified advertising at reduced rates to compete with the mostly free advertising offered by Craigslist and others, some newspapers, including the *Times*, have been exchanging higher-margin for lower-margin business.

Realizing, as the major editors already do, that many of its columnists begin to repeat themselves and virtually stutter in paragraphs, the *Times* needs to give its regular op-ed columnists a time-limited appointment rather than a virtual lifetime appointment. In the mode of Frank Rich's former Sunday column and the public editor's bi-weekly column, the *Times* also should have some regular op-ed columnists who appear on a less frequent basis, possibly as infrequently as once a month.

In summer 2008, I bought a copy of the *Times* national edition printed in Lakeland, Florida, with Florida weather on the top of page 1. But little else was customized. Even the extended weather discussion in section "C" highlighted Northeast weather and a national forecast. Surely the paper would have a wider appeal if the "New York Report," which follows the "National Report" in the "A" section, was instead a regional report, in this case on Florida developments. Indeed, the sports news was dominated by New York team talk rather than by the then recent success of the Tampa Bay baseball team.

Going forward with more and more discrete editions tailored to particular areas and building on the Chicago, Bay Area, and Texas editions already in place, the *Times* will undoubtedly customize sports, business, and the arts. To be sure, several of the articles in the New York arts section have national implications, but Florida readers—including transplanted New Yorkers living in Florida—might enjoy a few stories about arts in Florida. The "D" section, Tuesday's *Science Times*, would still serve a national audience, but why couldn't there be room on an inside page for some area-specific pieces on recurring regional weather patterns—hurricanes, drought, fires, earthquakes, volcanoes—and how they impact physical and mental health?

Wouldn't the *Times* be much more of a national paper with a regional focus if it had advertising as well as *Real Estate* and *Job* sections for several major geographical areas? Would not such a policy increase revenue? For years, I have thought that the *Times* should develop several different and customized versions, includ-ing metropolitan news focusing on New York, Washington, Boston, Chicago, Atlanta, San Francisco, and Los Angeles and maybe such other important cites as Miami, Houston, Dallas, and Detroit. Indeed, on September 4, 2009, the *Times* announced a San Francisco edition. According to Perez-Pena: "Both the *Wall Street Journal* and the *New York Times* are planning to introduce San Francisco Bay Area edi-tions, hoping to win new readers and advertisers there by offering more local news, in what could be the first glimpse at a new strategy by national newspapers to capitalize on the contraction of regional papers" ("*The Wall Street Journal* and *The New York Times* Plan San Francisco Editions," September 4, 2009). Since then the *Times* has been rethinking how to publish a national edition with regional appeal and has introduced customized editions for the Bay Area, Chicago, and Texas, and that trend will continue.

The *Times* needs to balance between being a national print and digital news source and being a resource for transplanted New Yorkers. In my February 17, 2006, interview with the then new national editor, Suzanne Daley, she told me that she had won the job by proposing more of a focus on national issues: "I felt that the national desk had somehow disappeared, that the national report was a Washington report and that we were not tapping into . . . life in America anymore, that . . . we wrote a lot [about] court rulings, but we had abandoned the big issues; we didn't have a poverty writer, we . . . never covered unemployment, we didn't cover the homeless anymore."

Giving more coverage to national issues, as Daley suggested, increases the *Times*'s appeal beyond New York. Perhaps more importantly, adding a local dimension to different national areas and major cities—in the order of the recently reinvented Sunday *Metropolitan* section for the New York edition—is an even more effective way of reaching a larger audience.

In his online comments during the week of April 10, 2006, Keller wrote about the *Times*'s aim to be at once a New York newspaper and to find metropolitan stories that have a national impact and national stories that have a New York impact:

> There's a limit to how local any paper can be in a sprawling region. . . . [T]he New York region still accounts for roughly half of our readership, and the city itself—as a cultural and financial capital, as an American gateway, as an urban laboratory and showplace—is part of our identity, not to mention a story of great consequence beyond this region. The big institutions and industries that touch many lives, we cover intensively: City Hall, Albany, the Metropolitan Transit Authority, the police, the school system, the universities, Wall Street, Broadway, the fashion industry, and so on.

Is it possible to be a New York metropolitan area newspaper and a national paper? With its Chicago and Bay Area editions, the 2010 *Times* began moving in the direction of publishing several different national editions, with each edition targeting particular regions. The *Times* has recognized the need to customize the national edition—as the *International Herald Tribune* customizes its product not only for Europe and Asia but for major countries—so as to produce more focused metro sections with regional political news as well as regional sports and cultural news, including discussions of museums and plays in a particular city or region. Now the New England edition and the Washington edition do very little of this—less than was once intended—and not a fraction as much as is necessary to compete for attention with the *Washington Post*. In the case of the *Boston Globe*, this may be deliberate because the *Times* owns the *Boston Globe*.

In 2011, the national edition has less New York news but, except for the Chicago, Texas, and Bay Area editions, does not replace the omission with a focus on the region. Were the *Times* to produce different editions for ten or so major cities and regions so as to include local news, targeted major metropolitan news, and sports, the *Times* would be far more appealing to readers in those areas. This could take the form of the kind of a special regional major city section similar to the special national section that in some countries accompanies the *International Herald Tribune* or the special Mexico supplement of the *Miami Herald*.

Each city could have its own metro diary and columns about its towns. For example, readers in Atlanta would enjoy reading about their city's sports teams, cultural events, and local politics from the perspective of a national paper. This wouldn't replace the local paper for many readers, but would supplement it. For visitors and transplanted New Yorkers, the paper might be slightly less appealing than the New York edition but popular features such as the New York metro diary could be retained online, and perhaps even in print.

Many people to whom I spoke over the past seven years while I have been writing this book, and especially young people, are intimidated by the length of the *Times*. They would prefer a more concise paper. They mention that they don't buy the paper—don't even pick it up on campus where it is free—because they don't have time to do it justice. The *Times* should not expect younger readers—attuned to getting their news from websites, including nytimes.com—to pay $5 or $6 for a Sunday paper that they read for an hour or less or $2 for a paper they read for perhaps thirty minutes at most.

One can imagine a future printed *Times* that decouples its daily magazine sections from its news and sells as an option—even while maintaining its current print format for those who still prefer it—a shorter national newspaper with only international and national news resembling the current *International Herald Tribune*. In the Times building this is called "disaggregation" but it is not taken seriously. Indeed, I believe the *International Herald Tribune* could be a model for the kind of disaggregation that would enable *Times* newspaper readers to purchase a two section newspaper, the "A" section devoted to foreign and national news with a strong focus on analysis in the mode of the *Economist,* the "B" section composed of selections from the current *Business, Sports, Arts,* and, on the appropriate day, *Science, Dining,* or *Style.* Such an edition, recalling what the *Times* once was before Rosenthal invented the multisection newspaper, might be in the twenty-four to thirty-two page range or perhaps a little longer, but no more than forty pages. Those who wanted the magazine-like sections would pay more than those purchasing the basic print two-section newspaper; perhaps readers also could buy the magazine sections separately. The *Times* already sells its Sunday *Book Review* separately for $1.75 per issue.

The more succinct print *Times* of the future will, I hope, expand international news, which occupies a smaller and smaller percentage of the total newspaper. At times, even in its "World Briefing," the *Times* does not sustain its coverage of major stories, but rather intermittently touches on them. Indeed, I would argue that "World Briefing" should be far longer and comment on the major crisis areas even when they begin to fall slightly beneath the War on Terror benchmark (in summer 2011: Lebanon, Zimbabwe, Chechnya, Darfur, Haiti) a few times each week and virtually every major nation at least once a week.

I think the *Times* could sell a reduced paper edition—without the fluff I have called *Timeslite* and *Timestrash*—with a focus on opinions, investigatory journalism, cultural coverage, and analytic foreign news. I believe that there would still be a market for a Sunday edition, with reduced fluff and an expanded *Book Review.* The *Times*'s strength is the knowledge and professionalism of its reporters, columnists, and editors. As Michael Hirschorn remarks, "[F]or now, at least, there's no online substitute for institutions that can marshal years of well-developed sourcing and reporting experience—not to mention the resources to, say, send journalists leapfrogging between Mumbai and Islamabad to decode the complexities of the India-Pakistan conflict" ("Endtimes," *Atlantic,* January/February, 2009). Were the Times Company to publish only a Sunday paper edition and perhaps even a daily newspaper the size of the *International Herald Tribune* or a twenty-four- to thirty-page daily two-section newspaper with *Sports* and *Business* in the second section and a strong component of cultural news, both the production and delivery costs would drop precipitously. Were costs shared with other media entities, as the *Times* has been doing on a limited basis with NBC, newsgathering costs would be much reduced.

It is just possible that a compact and succinct *Times* strong on international news and analyses—both of which the *Times* alone has the resources to provide—and inflected with a few pages of science and health news on Tuesday and its exceptional cultural coverage on Friday might enable the *Times* to remain in print, at least in the foreseeable future, although as Sulzberger himself now realizes, a day may come when the print edition does not exist. It may well be that the putative compact and succinct *Times* I am suggesting will be the *Times*'s only print product for an interim period before the death of the print *Times*. But the time will almost certainly come when the only newsgathering product available for readers will be the digital nytimes.com.

Whether in a shorter or current version of the print edition or on its digital site, I think *Times* writing could be more succinct and tighter. Reading the *International Herald Tribune* makes me even more aware of this. Most people I know who read the *Times*—and read it loyally, intensely, and thoughtfully—do not read it for the same kind of pleasure and experience that they read the *New Yorker*. But they still admire elegant, stylish, and witty writing and take pleasure when they find it in the *Times,* whether in op-ed columns, news analyses, features on New York City, the Sunday magazines, or various back of the book sections.

Clearly, the metamorphosis—and makeover—of the *Times* is a continuous process and one fraught with difficulties. As Tancredi puts it in Tomasi di Lampedusa's Sicilian masterpiece, *The Leopard,* "If you want things to stay as they are, they have to change." To sustain its circulation and its advertising base, the *Times* will always need to speak to its readership. In reinventing itself in this period of crises and turmoil, the *Times* is still searching to find its core readership in a world in which the Internet has become increasingly the information centerpiece. By discovering and circulating information—about the world and our nation, about New York City and New York State, about science and health, about culture and sports, about business and style—through its published newspaper and website, the *Times* is innovating even as it is doing a version of what it has always done. Embracing this paradox, the *Times* seeks to be a *Times* for our time: flexible, relevant, timely, less cumbersome, and more aware of a diverse national audience with wide-ranging informational needs and interests.

VII. Can the *Times*—and the Newspaper Industry—Recover From Its Current Malaise?

Let us think of the *Times*—and, indeed the printed news media—as a patient and, now that we have offered a diagnosis, think about its chances of short- and middle-term recovery as well as long-term recovery. Those short- and middle-term chances depend in large part on the answers to the following questions:

1. **Can the *Times* continue to charge for Internet content or will its readers seek other free sources?** It is incumbent on the newspaper industry that it charges for content. As David Carr has remarked, "Setting the price point at free—the newspaper analyst Alan D. Mutter called it the original sin—has brought the industry millions of eyeballs and a return that doesn't cover the coffee budget of some newsrooms" ("United, Newspapers May Stand," March 8, 2009). The *Wall Street Journal* and *Consumer Reports* have been charging for access to their online sites. They have convinced readers that they offer something special affecting their pocketbooks—most notably, analytic financial articles—although almost everything of importance can be found elsewhere online, often in the *Times*.

2. **Can the *Times* charge news aggregators like Google and the *Huffington Post* for its content, content that often is harvested for the purposes of the aggregator?** If they don't charge, or charge only nominally through its news bureau, the *Times* is giving their product away to rivals for free.

3. **Can the *Times* refuse to take generic ads—often sold at fire sale prices—that generate little revenue potential while filling up the website?** Carr's view of the dilemma: "Newspapers once thrived by selling scarce ad positions. The downside is turning down ads, and who can afford that right now?"

4. **Can the U.S. government be convinced to amend the Newspaper Preservation Act, which makes consolidation difficult?** Rather than combine, newspapers are forced to enter into joint operating agreements that are more costly. Thus, the *San Francisco Chronicle* and the *San Francisco Examiner* have been sharing expenses and losing $1 million a week, and the *Chronicle*—with its great tradition—will either sell or close unless it lays off half its decimated newsroom. *The Seattle Post-Intelligencer* has already joined those newspapers reduced to online publication with a skeleton staff.

   Carr notes: "The Justice Department still holds that combining local dailies is anticompetitive, but if that antiquated logic continues to prevail, there won't be much left to regulate. . . . Regulatory reform will allow the industry to consolidate to an economically feasible model and preserve newsgathering. Does Seattle need two newspapers? Did Denver? Sure, it's preferable for all kinds of reasons. But one is better than none."

5. **Have the *Times*'s various failures damaged its prestige to the point where fewer people trust it?** I am thinking most notably about Judith Miller's articles about WMDs, which stoked the fires for the Iraq war, but also about the *Times*'s failure to report how the Bush administration was using the excuse of national security to set aside the Constitution by wiretapping citizens and monitoring bank accounts. Additionally, the *Times* had to back down from the accusation that Wen Ho Lee was a spy and from the inane article about John McCain and the lobbyist Vicki Iseman. Despite a "settlement," the *Times* refused to retract the article, claiming that the focus was on McCain's staff's concern about the appearance of a romantic relationship rather than on a romantic relationship. (Dean Baquet, the *Times* Washington bureau chief, in a memo to his staff, said, "We paid no money. We did not apologize" [*Washington Post*, February 20, 2009].)

   Despite the errors and misjudgments, I believe that the *Times* still retains considerable stature. As I have stressed, it is the worst newspaper in the world except for all the others.

6. **Can newspapers become nonprofits on the model of universities and live on endowments?** David Swenson and Michael Schmidt have argued for making newspapers into endowed nonprofits:

> Endowments would enhance newspapers' autonomy while shielding them from the economic forces that are now tearing them down. . . . By endowing our most valued sources of news we would free them from the strictures of an obsolete business model and offer them a permanent place in society, like that of America's colleges and universities. Endowments would transform newspapers into unshakable fixtures of American life, with greater stability and enhanced independence that would allow them to serve the public good more effectively. As educational and literary organizations devoted to the "promotion of social welfare," endowed newspapers would benefit from Section 501(c)(3) of the I.R.S. code, which provides exemption from taxes on income and allows tax deductions for people who make contributions to eligible organizations. . . . Aside from providing stability, an endowment would promote journalistic independence. The best-run news organizations insulate reporters from pressures to produce profits or to placate advertisers. But endowed news organizations would be in an ideal situation—with no pressure from stockholders or advertisers at all. ("News You Can Endow," January 27, 2009)

While, according to the same law cited by Swenson and Schmidt, the *Times* as an endowed newspaper could not endorse candidates, Swenson and Schmidt correctly argue that the *Times* could still discuss political issues. NPR and PBS as well as the BBC are publicly funded and prone to intervention but for the most part have risen above public pressure. But "for the most part" is not "always," especially in the case of PBS, where under pressure, conservative pundits proliferated on such political panel shows as *Washington Week*. Nevertheless, endowed newspapers would be under enormous political pressure from various interest groups, most notably from those contributing to the endowment. And if public funds were used in the endowment mix, there would be even more complaints from some public officials about fairness when addressing controversial issues, even to the point of arguing for creationism as a legitimate point of view.

One can point to examples of nonprofit support of print in America. The Christian Science Church supported the well-regarded *Christian Science Monitor*, which no longer has a daily print edition but now has an online edition Monday through Friday and a weekly printed edition. The investigative magazine (and digital site) *Mother Jones* is a nonprofit.

But who would endow the *Times* so that it would generate the hundreds of millions necessary to maintain it? Joan Kroc left NPR $200 million and NPR has not been insulated against significant layoffs. Where could the *Times* find the $5 billion Swenson and Schmidt propose as necessary? Would the *Times* have fundraising campaigns like NPR and public television? Would the *Times* seek corporate sponsorship that certainly would raise questions about its independence? Would the *Times*, like universities, have a fundraising staff? To be sure, although a board of directors could help ensure independence, how many *legacy newspapers*—a current term for the major papers like the *Times*, the *Washington Post*, and the *Los Angeles Times*—could be supported by endowment, particularly in the current economic climate?

7. **Do enough people want a newspaper that strives for objectivity, tries to get accurate information, and maintains a huge staff for those purposes?** In a March 18, 2009, column entitled "The Daily Me," Nicholas

Kristof writes: "When we go online, each of us is our own editor, our own gatekeeper. We select the kind of news and opinions that we care most about." Citing what he calls an often replicated "classic study," he regretfully observes, "there's pretty good evidence that we generally don't truly want good information—but rather information that confirms our prejudices. We may believe intellectually in the clash of opinions, but in practice we like to embed ourselves in the reassuring womb of an echo chamber. . . . The decline of traditional news media will accelerate the rise of The Daily Me, and we'll be irritated less by what we read and find our wisdom confirmed more often." According to Richard Perez-Pena's discussion of a July 2009 Pew survey, not only has trust fallen to a new low but also that what trust remains depends to an extent on party affiliation: that is, Democrats trust CNN and Republicans—if they trust any media source—trust Fox News:

> Trust in news media has reached a new low, with record numbers of Americans saying reporting is inaccurate, biased and shaped by special interests. . . . On crucial measures of credibility, faith in news media eroded from the 1980s to the '90s, then held fairly steady for several years, according to Pew surveys that have asked some of the same questions for more than two decades. But in the two years since the last survey, those views became markedly more negative. ("Trust in News Media Falls to New Low in Pew Survey," September 13, 2009)

Nevertheless, the *Times* does have a devoted readership as well as over 17 million users per month of nytimes.com, and these readers are among the most influential people in America and the world.

8. **What about a different size newspaper with even smaller pages than the somewhat shrunken pages the *Times***

now presents? That is difficult, because as Richard Berke observed in March 2009: "The *Times* is printed at 24 plants around the country. Each one would have to be reconfigured for the new format, at huge cost. . . . We seriously considered using a smaller format for our international edition, the *International Herald Tribune*, which will introduce an elegant new broadsheet design on March 30, 2009" ("Talk to the Newsroom," March 16–29, 2009).

9. **How will the *Times* renew its newspaper readership by interesting younger readers?** Are younger readers even interested in anything but local news on the Internet? David Carr has noticed at a conference of young people he attended in Austin, Texas, that young readers often ignore complimentary newspapers. "They stare into cell phones and PDAs—ignoring, or perhaps not even seeing, news they stepped over that was physically packaged and shipped many hours before. . . . They were riveted by news on the small screen, most of it up-to-the-minute and highly personal—a recommendation from a friend about a band or film to see, a blog post about a missed conference panel, or a feed of festival updates. Twitter . . . was far and away the dominant news platform for the conference" ("In Austin, a Thriving Weekly with a Mission," March 22, 2009).

I have seen the same thing when watching students ignore free copies of the *New York Times* at Cornell and various other universities I have visited. But they will pick up the *Cornell Sun* or whatever university newspaper is being distributed. Carr points out that the weekly free *Austin Chronicle* thrives "with a relentlessly local news agenda—state government, the school board and the City Council, along with deep coverage of the arts—and a willingness to lead, as opposed to simply criticize, in artistic matters." But this does not mean the *Times* cannot get younger readers if the *Times* were to follow some of my suggestions above.

VIII. Coda: Epitaph or a Strong Glimmer of Hope?

The *Times* continues to exude optimism and to believe it has almost a divine right to survive. In his most recent online "Talk to the Newsroom" Q&A session, on February 2, 2009, executive editor Bill Keller wrote:

> First, there is a diminishing supply of quality journalism, and a growing demand. By quality journalism I mean the kind that involves experienced reporters going places, bearing witness, digging into records, developing sources, checking and double-checking, backed by editors who try to enforce high standards. I mean journalism that, however imperfect, labors hard to be trustworthy, to supply you with the information you need to be an engaged citizen. The supply of this kind of journalism is declining because it is hard, expensive, sometimes dangerous work. The traditional practitioners of this craft—mainly newspapers—have been downsizing or declaring bankruptcy. . . . The *Times* has some advantages that buy us time to make the transition successfully. Like everyone in the news business, we have been buffeted by forces, some of them cyclical (namely a global economic crisis that is a great story to cover but a depressing experience to live through) and some structural (the migration of audiences and advertising revenue to the Web). But we've fared better than our competitors. We remain profitable. (The printed newspaper makes money all by itself. The website adds another increment of profit.) The cash flow necessary to pay our bills—despite some of the nonsense you may have read elsewhere—is not about to run dry any time soon.

Did Keller's February 2009 optimism take account of all the facts? On September 22, 2010, the New York Times Company released a relatively gloomy update for its third-quarter 2010, which shows that, compared to third-quarter 2009 (hardly a boom quarter), the company, except for a one-time gain, basically had a $.05 to $.07 loss and that print advertising, revenue, and circulation are all down, while digital advertising (which still does not compensate for lost print advertising) is up 14 percent.

Is the only hope of survival a complete shift to digital? Faced with falling advertising revenue and rising costs, the *Times* is looking for every possible means to supplement its revenue stream, from selling framed pages from former issues to charging a fee to hear its staff talk about issues. Whether the *Times* acknowledges it or not, decisions about its product are driven by economics, and the traditional separation between the *Times* as a news organization devoted to creating, forming, and reflecting the values of the community and the *Times* as business is a luxury that cannot be sustained. Traditionally, the *Times*, like most of the best newspapers, acts "at once as [the] public's guide and its follower, its critic and its servant, its creator and its voice" (Edward Rothstein, "When the News Was New," January 23, 2009). If the *Times* were to abandon or severely reduce its print edition and create a financially viable product, it would, sadly and of necessity, be a follower in responding to cultural changes in technology and consumer needs as well as to business advertising patterns. But by continuing to make major adjustments in response to the digital generation, the *Times* has preserved much of its role as a newsgathering voice and given itself a long-term chance to survive in digital form and perhaps as a printed paper.

Were the *Times* to cease publication, what would an Internet only *Times* look like? Probably very much what nytimes.com looks like today but with a much smaller staff that focuses on newsgathering rather than on news distribution. Michael Hirschorn speculates: "Forced to make a Web-based strategy profitable, a reconstructed website could start mixing original reportage with *Times*-endorsed reporting from other outlets with straight-up aggregation. . . . *Times* readers might actually end up getting more exposure than they currently do to reporting resources scattered around the globe, and to areas and issues that are difficult to cover in a general-interest publication" ("End Times: Can America's Paper of Record Survive the Death of Newsprint? Can Journalism?" *Atlantic*, January/February 2009). In fact, the *Times* did try this for a little while with its expanded nytimes.com "Extra Home Page."

If the *Times* were reduced to a website, the *Times* would continue to be the leader in international news. But even in that category—an expensive category, as I have discussed—there would be cutbacks because the digital advertising model and paid digital circulation would probably not support the current newsgathering operation. The *Times* would probably need to ask all the American television networks and cable stations like CNN—which now maintain skeleton foreign staffs—to share in some of the costs of sustaining twenty-six foreign bureaus; perhaps for its international coverage the *Times* might partner with such entities as Reuters, the BBC, and—even more than it does now—AP.

The question that must be asked and that I have been asking is whether the *Times* can create a business model to support a readership increasingly turning for its news and analysis to the Internet and twenty-four-hour cable TV (with some stations specializing in finance and sports). The answer, I believe, will be, "No, not as the daily newspaper as we knew it," and various changes have already proven that answer right.

To be sure, many have prophesied that we are witnessing the demise of the *Times*. As Hirschorn puts it in the January/February 2009 *Atlantic*, "With more than $1 billion in debt already on the books, only $46 million in cash reserves as of October [2008], and no clear way to tap into the capital markets (the company's debt was recently reduced to junk status), the paper's future doesn't look good." The *Times*'s tepid response to Hirschorn's article in the form of a letter by Catherine Mathis, senior vice president for Corporate Communications, scolded Hirschorn for not consulting the *Times* before printing the article and included its usual bromides when discussing its financial situation: "This is a challenging time in our industry and for the U.S. economy. Employees are concerned about their jobs. People in the media industry are working extraordinarily hard to find creative solutions to the issues they face. It is a time for clear thinking and analysis, not uninformed speculation" (online, *Atlantic*, January 12, 2009).

What will the future bring? In the immediate future, the *Times* has begun, as of March 2011, to try again to charge for the Internet, perhaps in terms of usage. Further down the road the Sulzbergers, reliant on dividends for income when there are no dividends and may not be in the foreseeable future, may have to sell to a wealthy investor like Bloomberg. Although it is hard to imagine the *Times* as nonprofit foundation along the models of NPR, PBS, or even the BBC, it is not impossible.

The *Times* is the last media source standing for foreign news in American newspapers, radio, and television and, indeed, for much domestic news. With its twenty-six foreign bureaus (including one for the UN), over 1,100 newsroom staff, and with its ability to probe deeply in investigatory stories and offer value-added stories on every aspect of life, with its expert coverage of the arts as well as health and science, the *Times* is unique and irreplaceable. If any news source had sent a cub reporter to interview Fred Thompson in Iowa during the 2008 primary campaign, the paper would have probably gotten an acceptably chatty if soon dated story. But to run, as the *Times* does better than any other American news source, a full bureau in Afghanistan or Iraq or Pakistan requires translators, armored vehicles, local sources who need to conceal their identity, and, most important, experienced world-class reporters and staff.

In the second half of 2004, I began planning a book tentatively entitled *The Metamorphosis of the Times*, with the subtitle *The Transformation of the Old Gray Lady*. As I progressed in my research and interviews with *Times* luminaries, I began to realize the *Times* was in deep trouble and retitled my book *Crisis and Turmoil at the New York Times: 1999–2009*. Now, as I write in March 2011, it has been clear for at least four years that the *Times* is facing a financial crisis that threatens its very existence. While at times I thought a more suitable title might be *Obit: The New York Times as Newspaper (1895–2009)*, I am now reasonably confident that the printed *Times* will survive in some form for the foreseeable future, and the digital *Times*—possibly, as I have suggested, under different ownership and even ownership concepts—will gradually take its place. There is, I believe, still ample evidence that a cadre of loyal readers not only understands the central role of quality journalism in a democracy but want a daily printed newsgathering operation that produces quality journalism.

Selected Bibliography

When not otherwise specified, all articles and interviews refer to the *New York Times*.

Aish.com. "Photo Fraud in Lebanon," http://www.aish.com/v/is/91361839.html.

Alterman, Eric. "Out of Print," *New Yorker*, March 31, 2008, 48–59.

Associated Press. "N.Y. Times to Reduce Page Size, Cut Jobs," July 18, 2006, online.

Auletta, Ken. "Opening up the Times," *New Yorker*, June 28, 1993, pp. 55ff.

———. "The Howell Doctrine," *New Yorker*, June 10, 2002. pp. 48ff.

———. "The Inheritance," *New Yorker*, December 19, 2005. pp. 66.

Baker, Russell. "Decline But Not Fall," *NYR*, 57:14, September 20, 2010, 30–34.

———. "Goodbye to Newspapers," *NYR* 54:13, August 16, 2007; online p. 9.

———. "A Bad Morning at the *New York Times*," *NYR* 57:7, April 29, 2010, 6–8.

Bakhtin, Mikhail. *Rabelais and His World*. Trans. Helene Iswolsky. Cambridge, Mass.: MIT Press, 1965.

Bass, Gary. "Word Problem," *New Yorker*, May 24, 2004.

Bender, Thomas. *New York Intellect: A History of Intellectual Life in New York City, from 1750 to the Beginnings of Our Own Time*. New York: Alfred A. Knopf, 1987.

Berger, Meyer. *The Story of The New York Times 1851–1951*. New York: Simon and Schuster, 1951.

Bernhardt, Debra. *Ordinary People, Extraordinary Lives*. New York: New York University Press, 2000.

Bernstein, Michael Andre. "Lasting Injury: Competing Interpretations of the Nazi Genocide and the Passionate Insistence on its Uniqueness," *TLS*, March 7, 1997, #4901, 3.

Blodget, Henry. "New York Times (NYT): Here's How Much Cash We Need To Survive," *Silicon Alley Insider*, December 9, 2008.

Bowden, Mark. "The Inheritance," *Vanity Fair*, May 2009.

Burrows, Edwin G. and Wallace, Mike. *Gotham: A History of New York City to the 1890s*. New York: Oxford University Press, 1999.

Catledge, Turner. *My Life and the Times*. New York: Harper & Row, 1971.

Cockburn, Alexander. "Judy Miller's War," *CounterPunch Diary*, August 18, 2003.

Darnton, Robert. "The Library in the New Age," *NYR* 45:10, June 12, 2008, 72–80.

Diamond, Edwin. *Behind the Times: Inside the New York Times*. New York: Villard Books, 1994.

Douglas, Ann. *Terrible Honesty: Mongrel Manhattan in the 1920s*. New York: Farrar, Straus and Giroux, 1996.

Douglas, Susan. *Listening In*. New York: Random House, 1999.

Ellison, Sarah. "How a Money Manager Battled the New York Times," *The Wall Street Journal*, March 21, 2007, 1, 16.

Fine, Jon. "MediaCentric: Media, Market and Advertising in the 21st Century: Net to Newspapers: Drop Dead," *Business Week*, July 4, 2005, 24.

Frank, Joseph. "Idealists on the Run," *The New York Review of Books*, 45:10, June 12, 2008, 50–52.

Frankel, Max. *The Times of My Life and My Life with the Times*. New York: Dell, 1999.

Friel, Howard, and Falk, Richard. *The Record of the Paper: How the New York Times Misreports US Foreign Policy*. London and New York: Verso, 2005.

Fritzsche, Peter. *Reading Berlin 1900*. Cambridge, Mass.: Harvard University Press, 1996.

Fry, Varian. "The Massacre of Jews," *New Republic*, December 21, 1942, 816–819.

Gelb, Arthur. *City Room*. New York: Putnam, 2003.

Ignatius, David, "Lessons of the Miller Affair," *Washington Post*, October 5, 2005.

Halberstam, David. *The Powers That Be*. New York: Alfred A. Knopf, 1979.

Halperin, Susan. "Making a Conspiracy of Silence," *NYR* 56-18, November 19, 2009, 33–37.

Hamilton, James T. *All the News That's Fit to Sell: How the Market Transforms Information Into News*. Princeton, NJ: Princeton University Press, 2005.

Hammond, Margo, and Hetzel, Ellen. "The Plot Thickens at the *New York Times Book Review*," January 20, 2004, Poynter online.

Hirschorn, Michael. "End Times: Can America's Paper of Record Survive the Death of Newsprint? Can Journalism?" *Atlantic*, January/February 2009. See Mathis, Catherine, online response, *Atlantic*, January 12, 2009.

Jackson, Kenneth. *New York Encyclopedia*. New Haven: Yale University Press, 1995.

Jameson, Fredric. *PostModernism or, The Cultural Logic of Late Capitalism*. Durham: Duke University Press, 1993.

Kahn, Bonnie Menes. *Cosmopolitan Culture*. New York: Athenaeum, 1987.

Keen, Andrew. *The Cult of the Amateur: How Today's Internet is Killing Culture.* New York: Doubleday, 2007.

Kennedy, David M. *Freedom from Fear: The American People in Depression and War 1929–1945.* New York: Oxford University Press, 1999.

Kern, Stephen. *The Culture of Time and Space, 1880–1919.* Cambridge: Harvard University Press, 1983.

Kohn, Bob. *Journalistic Fraud: How the New York Times Distorts the News and Why it Can No Longer Be Trusted.* WNB Books: Nashville: WNB Books, 2003,

Kuypers, Jim A. *Press Bias and Politics: How the Media Frame Controversial Issues.* New York: Praeger, 2005.

Leff, Laurel. *Buried by the Times.* Cambridge: Cambridge University Press, 2005.

Lemann, Nicholas. "Fear and Favor," *New Yorker,* February 14 and 21, 2009, 168–176.

———. "Telling Secrets," *New Yorker,* November 7, 2005, 48–56.

Lipstadt, Deborah. *Beyond Belief: The American Press and the Coming of the Holocaust 1933–1945.* New York: The Free Press, 1986.

Lopate, Phillip. *Writing New York: A Literary Anthology.* New York: The Library of America, 1998.

Massing, Michael. "Now They Tell Us," *NYR* 51:3, February 26, 2004, 43–44.

McMasters, Paul K. "Reasons to Worry about Media Meltdown," *Ithaca Journal,* Dececember 7, 2006.

Mnookin, Seth. *Hard News: The Scandals at the New York Times and Their Meaning for American Media.* New York: Random House, 2004.

———. "Unreliable Sources," *Vanity Fair,* January 2006, 134ff.

Mumford, Lewis. *The Culture of Cities.* New York: Harcourt, Brace, and Company, 1938.

New York Times Staff, The. *The Newspaper: Its Making and its Meaning.* Intro. by John E. Wade. Charles Scribner's Sons, 1945.

Okrent, Daniel. *Public Editor #1: The Collected Columns (With Reflections, Reconsideration, and Even a Few Retractions) of the First Ombudsman of the New York Times.* New York: Public Affairs, 2006.

Parker, Kathleen. "A Digital War of Images Attacking Israel," *Ithaca Journal,* August 15, 2006.

Posner, Richard. "Bad News," *NYT Book Review,* July 31, 2005, 1, 8–11.

Project for Excellence in Journalism. "2006 Report on the News Media," 2006, http://www.stateofthemedia.org/2006/index.asp.

———. "2009 Report on the News Media," 2009, http://www.stateofthemedia.org/2009/narrative_newspapers_audience.php?cat=2&media=4.

Raines, Howard. "My Times," *Atlantic,* May 2004, 49–81; quotes taken from online http://www.theatlantic.com/magazine/archive/ 2004/05/my-times/2952/.

Raines, Howell. *The One That Got Away: A Memoir*. New York: Scribener, 2006.

Rasmussen Report, "30% Read Local Print Newspaper Regularly, Just 8% Read It Online That Way," March 4, 2009. http://www.rasmussenreports.com/public_content/lifestyle/general_lifestyle/march_2009/30_read_local_print_newspaper_regularly_just_8_read_it_online_that_way.

Reston, James. *Deadline: A Memoir*. New York: Times Books, 1991.

Rice, Andrew. "Murmurs of a Reckoning," *Slate*, September 9, 2007, http://www.slate.com/id/2173641/.

Robertson, Nan. *The Girls in the Balcony: Women, Men, and The New York Times*. New York: Random House, 1992.

Rykwert, Joseph. *The Seduction of Place*. New York: Pantheon, 2000.

Salisbury, Harrison. *Without Fear or Favor*. New York: Times Books, 1980.

Scheer, Robert. "A Free Press Subverted—by the Press," *The San Francisco Chronicle*, November 2, 2005, B9.

Shafer, Jack. "Reassessing Miller: U.S. Intelligence on Iraq's WMD Deserves a Second Look. So Does the Reporting of the New York Times's Judith Miller," *Slate*, May 29, 2003.

———. "The Public Editor as Duffer," *Slate*, May 9, 2006.

Shepard, Richard F. *The Paper's Paper: A Reporter's Journey Through the Archives of the New York Times*. New York: Times Books, 1996.

Talese, Gay. *The Kingdom and the Power*. New York: Bantam, 1970.

Taylor, William R. *Inventing Times Square: Commerce and Culture at the Crossroads of the World*. New York: Russell Sage: Foundation, 1991.

———. *In Pursuit of Gotham*. New York: Oxford University Press, 1992.

Tifft, Susan E., and Jones, Alex S. *The Trust: The Private and Powerful Family Behind the New York Times*. New York: Little Brown, 1999.

Villard, Oswald Garrison. *The Disappearing Daily: Chapters in American Newspaper Evolution*. New York: Alfred A. Knopf, 1944.

Wolff, Michael. "The War on the *Times*," *Vanity Fair*, May, 2008 (#573), 126–32.

Index